W9-ACN-469

ROWAN UNIVERSITY
CAMPBELL LIBRARY
201 MULLICA HILL RD.
GLASSBORO, NJ 08028-1701

650
Essential
Nonprofit
Law Questions
Answered

650
Essential Nonprofit Law Questions Answered

BRUCE R. HOPKINS

WILEY

John Wiley & Sons, Inc.

This book is printed on acid-free paper. ∞

Copyright © 2005 by John Wiley & Sons, Inc. All rights reserved.

Published by John Wiley & Sons, Inc., Hoboken, New Jersey
Published simultaneously in Canada

No part of this publication may be reproduced, stored in a retrieval system, or transmitted in any form or by any means, electronic, mechanical, photocopying, recording, scanning, or otherwise, except as permitted under Section 107 or 108 of the 1976 United States Copyright Act, without either the prior written permission of the Publisher, or authorization through payment of the appropriate per-copy fee to the Copyright Clearance Center, Inc., 222 Rosewood Drive, Danvers, MA 01923, 978-750-8400, fax 978-646-8600, or on the web at www.copyright.com. Requests to the Publisher for permission should be addressed to the Permissions Department, John Wiley & Sons, Inc., 111 River Street, Hoboken, NJ 07030, 201-748-6011, fax 201-748-6008.

Limit of Liability/Disclaimer of Warranty: While the publisher and author have used their best efforts in preparing this book, they make no representations or warranties with respect to the accuracy or completeness of the contents of this book and specifically disclaim any implied warranties of merchantability or fitness for a particular purpose. No warranty may be created or extended by sales representatives or written sales materials. The advice and strategies contained herein may not be suitable for your situation. You should consult with a professional where appropriate. Neither the publisher nor author shall be liable for any loss of profit or any other commercial damages, including but not limited to special, incidental, consequential, or other damages.

For general information on our other products and services, or technical support, please contact our Customer Care Department within the United States at 800-762-2974, outside the United States at 317-572-3993 or fax 317-572-4002.

Wiley also publishes its books in a variety of electronic formats. Some content that appears in print may not be available in electronic books.

KF
1388
.29
H667
2005

Printed in the United States of America

ISBN 0471-71524-7

10 9 8 7 6 5 4 3 2 1

3 3001 00913 057 5

Preface

Nonprofit law is rich, vibrant, and expanding; no end to the proliferation of this fecundity is in sight: much new law is being concocted and is swiftly emerging. A challenge for a chronicler of developments in the nonprofit field is to make a summary of all of this existing and unfolding law, in some instances complex and foreboding, interesting and useable.

Part of the solution of this dilemma lies in the writing (as in style), which often amounts to translation, and part lies in the presentation (format). As to the latter, for this book, the question-and-answer format was selected.

The intent here as to the matter of usefulness is to resolve it by means of the format. The law in the nonprofit sector is separated into 19 parts (chapters). The questions answered in each part are numbered and listed at the beginning of the book. The reader thus need only correlate the question in mind with one of the 19 categories, then sift through the listed questions until the one is found that best matches the particular question to be answered. If that does not work (although there are 650 questions and answers), the index may be consulted.

The approach of this book is to capture the basics of this law and point the reader to the areas where expansion of present law and emergence of new law is occurring. As of late 2004, it appears that much new nonprofit law is in the offing. References to these portents are sprinkled throughout the book.

The book is envisioned as a quick reference guide and a springboard to more detailed material (if needed). It stands alone, for lawyer and nonlawyer alike, as a source for a speedy answer to the pressing or nagging question. For those who want more detail, these Wiley books (the first three supplemented annually) are available:

- *The Law of Tax-Exempt Organizations* (8th edition)
- *The Tax Law of Charitable Giving* (3rd edition)
- *The Law of Fundraising* (3rd edition)
- *Planning Guide for The Law of Tax-Exempt Organizations*

For information on a more current basis, readers are invited to consider *Bruce R. Hopkins' Nonprofit Counsel*, a Wiley monthly newsletter.

The law affecting and regulating nonprofit organizations continues to be a source of amazement for this writer. It just keeps growing; issues continue to multiply; the

Department of the Treasury, the Internal Revenue Service, other federal agencies, and state governments inexorably crank out statutes, regulations, rules, forms, and instructions. Courts amply do their part in stirring this pot. (Where all this is leading is anyone's guess.)

This book endeavors to provide a quick-access understanding as to where we are in the realm of nonprofit law (as of the close of 2004) and some peeks into a future where the only certainty is more law.

December, 2004   Bruce R. Hopkins

List of Questions

Self-Dealing and Conflicts of Interest

Special Considerations

CHAPTER 11   Private Foundation Rules   184

Disqualified Persons

Private Foundation Rules

Q 14:1 A tax-exempt organization often needs more money than it can generate through gifts, grants, and dues. Management of the organization is thinking about raising money by charging fees for

Exceptions

Colleges and Universities

650

Essential
Nonprofit
Law Questions
Answered

CHAPTER 1

General Operations of a Nonprofit Organization

A lawyer representing nonprofit organizations faces, on a daily basis, a barrage of questions about the rules governing the organizations' formation, administration, operation, and management. Some of these questions may be answered using state law rules, some with federal law rules. More frequently than nonlawyers might suspect, there is no law on the particular point.

These questions may require answers from an accountant, a fundraiser, an appraiser, or a management consultant, rather than a lawyer. For example, a lawyer is not professionally competent to answer these questions: "How much can I be paid?" or "How much is this gift property worth?" Even regarding matters that are within the lawyer's province, however—legal standards—the law is often very vague. Much of the applicable law is at the state level, so there can be varied answers to questions. Yet federal law on the subject is building.

Here are the questions most frequently asked about general operations of a nonprofit organization—and the answers to them.

Q 1:1   What is a *nonprofit organization*?

The term *nonprofit organization* is a misleading term; regrettably, the English language lacks a better one. It does *not* mean that the organization cannot earn a profit. Many nonprofit organizations are enjoying profits. An entity of any type cannot long exist without revenues that at least equal expenses.

The easiest way to define a nonprofit organization is to first define its counterpart, the *for-profit organization*. A for-profit organization exists to operate a business and to generate profits (revenue in excess of costs) from that business for those who own the enterprise. As an example, the owners of a for-profit corporation are stockholders, who take their profits in the form of dividends. Thus, when the term *for-profit* is used, it refers to profits acquired by the owners of the business, not by the business itself. The law, therefore, differentiates between profits at the *entity level* and profits at the *ownership level*.

Both for-profit and nonprofit organizations are allowed by the law to earn profits at the entity level. But only for-profit organizations are permitted profits at the ownership level. Nonprofit organizations rarely have owners; these organizations are not permitted to pass along profits (net earnings) to those who control them.

Profits permitted to for-profit entities but not nonprofit entities are forms of *private inurement* (see Chapter 6). That is, private inurement refers to ways of transferring an organization's net earnings to persons in their private capacity. The purpose of a for-profit organization is to engage in private inurement. By contrast, nonprofit organizations may not engage in acts of private inurement. (Economists call this fundamental standard the *nondistribution constraint*.) Nonprofit organizations are required to use their profits for their program activities. In the case of tax-exempt nonprofit organizations, these activities are termed their *exempt functions*.

NOTE: The prohibition on private inurement does not mean that a nonprofit organization cannot pay compensation to its employees and others. The law requires, however, that these payments be reasonable.

Consequently, the doctrine of private inurement is the essential dividing line, in the law, between nonprofit and for-profit organizations.

Q 1:2 Who owns a nonprofit organization?

For the most part, a nonprofit organization does not have owners who would be comparable to stockholders of a for-profit corporation or general partners in a partnership. There are some exceptions: a few states allow nonprofit corporations to be established with the authority to issue stock.

NOTE: This type of stock does not pay dividends, because that would contravene the prohibition on private inurement (see Q 1:1). The stock can be transferred to others, however, by sale, gift, or otherwise.

Stock in a nonprofit organization is used solely for purposes of ownership. Any *person* (an individual, a business entity, or another nonprofit organization) can be a shareholder under this arrangement.

TIP: When a nonprofit organization is being established and those forming it want to ensure their control of it, irrespective of the composition of the board of directors, setting up a stock-based nonprofit organization often is the answer (see Q 1:23).

Q 1:3 **Who controls a nonprofit organization?**

It depends on the nature of the organization. Usually, control of a nonprofit organization is vested in its governing body, frequently termed a board of directors or board of trustees. Actual control may lie elsewhere—with the officers or key employees, for example. It is unlikely that control of a large-membership organization would be with the membership, because that element of power is too dissipated. In a small-membership entity, such as a coalition, control may well be with the membership.

Q 1:4 **Sometimes the term *not-for-profit organization* is used instead of *nonprofit organization*. Are the terms synonymous?**

As a matter of law, no. People use the two terms interchangeably in good faith, but the proper legal term is *nonprofit organization*.

The law uses the term *not-for-profit* to apply to an activity rather than to an entity. For example, the federal tax law denies business expense deductions for expenditures that are for a not-for-profit activity. Basically, this type of activity is not engaged in with a business or commercial motive; a not-for-profit activity is essentially a hobby.

The term *not-for-profit* is often applied in the nonprofit context by those who do not understand or appreciate the difference between profit at the entity level and profit at the ownership level (Q 1:1).

Q 1:5 **How is a nonprofit organization started?**

Nearly every nonprofit organization is a creature of state law (or District of Columbia law). (A few nonprofit organizations are chartered under a federal statute.) Thus, a nonprofit organization is started by creating it under the law of a state.

There are only four types of nonprofit organizations: corporations, unincorporated associations, trusts and limited liability companies. The document by which a nonprofit organization is formed is generally known as its *articles of organization*. For a corporation, the articles are called articles of incorporation. For an unincorporated association, the articles are in the form of a constitution. The articles of a trust are called a trust agreement or a declaration of trust.

Most nonprofit organizations also have a set of *bylaws*—the rules by which they are operated. Some organizations have additional rules: codes of ethics, manuals of operation, employee handbooks, and the like.

A nonprofit organization formed as a corporation commences its existence by filing articles of incorporation with the appropriate state. Some states require the filing of trust documents. It is rare for a state to require the filing of a constitution or a set of bylaws as part of the process of forming the organization. (Bylaws and similar documents may have to be filed under other state laws, however.)

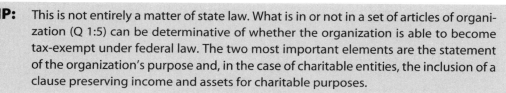

NOTE: These observations pertain to the filing of the document as part of the process of creating the nonprofit organization. An entity that is soliciting contributions is likely to have to file its articles of organization and bylaws in every state in which it is fundraising, as part of the solicitation registration requirements (Chapter 13).

Following the creation (and, if necessary, the filing) of the articles of organization, the newly formed entity should have an organizational meeting of the initial board of directors. At that meeting, the directors will adopt a set of bylaws, elect the officers, pass a resolution to open a bank account, and attend to whatever other initial business there may be.

Q 1:6 How does a nonprofit organization incorporate?

The state usually has a form set of articles of incorporation. A lawyer who knows something about nonprofit organizations can prepare this document or the incorporators can do it themselves. They need to agree on the organization's name, state the corporate purposes, list the names and addresses of the directors, name a registered agent, and include the names and addresses of the incorporators. The incorporators are the individuals who sign the articles.

TIP: This is not entirely a matter of state law. What is in or not in a set of articles of organization (Q 1:5) can be determinative of whether the organization is able to become tax-exempt under federal law. The two most important elements are the statement of the organization's purpose and, in the case of charitable entities, the inclusion of a clause preserving income and assets for charitable purposes.

Q 1:7 Who are the incorporators?

Under the typical legal requirement around the country, anyone who is 18 years of age and a U.S. citizen can incorporate a nonprofit corporation. Each state's law should be confirmed on the point, however. The initial board members can be the incorporators. Many states require three incorporators.

Some groups are very sensitive to the matter of who is listed as an incorporator. They see the articles of organization as being of great significance to the organization—a document to be preserved and treasured for posterity. Others prefer to let the lawyers working on the case be the incorporators. No particular legal significance is attached to service as an incorporator.

Q 1:8 Can the same individuals be the directors, officers, and incorporators?

Generally, yes. Again, the law of the appropriate state should be reviewed.

Q 1:9   What about the registered agent?

Typically, the registered agent must be either an individual who is a resident of the state or a company that is licensed by the state to be a commercial registered agent.

Q 1:10   What does the registered agent do?

The registered agent functions as the corporation's point of communication to the outside world. Any formal communication for the corporation as a whole is sent to the registered agent. Thus, if the state authorities want to communicate with the corporation, they do so by contacting the agent. If someone wants to sue the corporation, the agent is served with the papers.

Q 1:11   Does the registered agent have any liability for the corporation's affairs?

No. The registered agent, as such, is not a director or officer of the corporation. Thus, the agent has no exposure to liability for the corporation's activities. The agent would be held liable for his or her own offenses, such as breach of contract.

Q 1:12   Can the same individual be a director, officer, incorporator, and registered agent?

Yes, unless state law expressly forbids such a multirole status, which is unlikely. The registered agent—if an individual—must be a resident of the state in which the entity is functioning (Q 1:9), but the requirement of residency is not applicable to the other roles.

Q 1:13   How does a nonprofit organization decide the state in which to be formed?

Generally, a nonprofit organization is formed in the state in which it is to be headquartered. Most frequently, this is the state in which those who are forming the entity and who will be operating it are residents and/or maintain their offices. An organization can be formed in only one state at a time.

Occasionally, however, another state's law contains attributes that are desirable for those who are forming a nonprofit organization. For example, only a few states permit the creation of a nonprofit corporation that can issue stock. An organization seeking this feature can be formed in one of those states and then qualified to conduct its activities in the state where its principal operations will be (Q 1:23).

 **TIP:** A nonprofit organization (particularly a nonprofit corporation) must be qualified to *do business* in every state in which it has an operational presence. In some states, for purposes of this qualification, the solicitation of gifts (irrespective of the means) is considered doing business.

An entity that is formed in one state (the domestic state) and is doing business in another state (the foreign state) is regarded, by the latter state, as a *foreign* organization.

Q 1:14 **How does a nonprofit organization qualify to do business in another state?**

A nonprofit organization qualifies to do business in another state by filing for a *certificate of authority* to do business in the state. The process of obtaining this certificate is much like incorporating in a state. Also, the entity is required to have a *registered agent* in each state in which it is certified to do business (as well as in the domestic state).

 **TIP:** The law of each state should be checked to see what persons qualify to be registered agents (Q 1:9). An organization that is doing business in several states may find it more efficient to retain the services of a commercial firm licensed to function as a registered agent in all of the states.

Q 1:15 **What is the legal standard by which a nonprofit organization should be operated?**

It depends on the type of organization. If the nonprofit organization is not tax-exempt, the standard is nearly the same as that for a for-profit entity. If the nonprofit organization is tax-exempt, but is not a charitable organization, the standard is higher. The legal standard is highest for a tax-exempt charitable organization. In general, the standard is easy to articulate, but often difficult to implement.

Q 1:16 **What is the standard for an organization that is tax-exempt and charitable?**

The legal standard by which all aspects of operations of the organization should be tested requires *reasonableness* and *prudence*. Everything the organization does should be undertaken in a reasonable manner and to a reasonable end. Also, those working for or otherwise serving the charitable organization should act in a way that is *prudent*.

The federal tax exemption granted to charitable and certain other forms of tax-exempt organizations can be revoked if the organization makes an expenditure or engages in some other activity that is deemed to be not reasonable. The same is likely true at the state level: unreasonable behavior may cause the attorney general to investigate the organization.

Q 1:17 **What is the rationale for this standard for charities?**

The principles underlying the laws concerning charitable organizations, both federal and state, are taken from English common law, principally those portions pertaining to trusts and property. The standards formulated by English law hundreds of years ago for the administration of charitable trusts were very sound and very effective, and they underpin the laws today. The heart of these standards is the *fiduciary* relationship.

Q 1:18 What does the term *fiduciary* mean?

A *fiduciary* is a person who has special responsibilities in connection with the administration, investment, and distribution of property, where the property belongs to someone else. This range of duties is termed *fiduciary responsibility*. For example, guardians, executors, receivers, and the like are fiduciaries. Trustees of charitable trusts are fiduciaries. Today, a director or officer of a charitable organization is a fiduciary.

Indeed, the law can make anyone a fiduciary. As an illustration of the broad reach of this term, in a few states, professional fundraisers are deemed, by statute, fiduciaries of the charitable gifts raised during the campaigns in which they are involved.

Q 1:19 What is the standard underlying fiduciary responsibility?

In a word, *prudence*; a fiduciary is expected to act, with respect to the income and assets involved, in a way that is *prudent*. This standard of behavior is known as the *prudent person rule*. This rule means that fiduciaries are charged with acting with the same degree of judgment—prudence—in administering the affairs of the organization as they would in their personal affairs. Originally devised to apply in the context of investments, this rule today applies to all categories of behavior—both commissions and omissions—undertaken in relation to the organization being served.

Q 1:20 What is the meaning of the term *reasonable*?

The word *reasonable* is much more difficult to define than *prudence*. A judge, attorney general, IRS agent, and the like will say that the word is applied on a case-by-case basis. In other words, the term describes one of those things that one "knows when one sees it," much like obscenity.

The term *reasonable* is basically synonymous with *rational*. A faculty of the mind enables individuals to distinguish truth from falsehood and good from evil by deducing inferences from facts. Other words that can often be substituted for reasonable are *appropriate, proper, suitable, equitable,* and *moderate*. Whatever term is used, an individual in this setting is expected to use this faculty and act in an appropriate and rational manner.

Q 1:21 Who are the fiduciaries of a charitable organization?

The principal fiduciaries of a charitable organization are the directors. The officers are also fiduciaries. Other fiduciaries may include an employee who has responsibilities similar to those of an officer, such as a chief executive officer or a chief financial officer who is not officially a director or officer. Outsiders, such as people who are hired to administer an endowment fund or pension plan, are fiduciaries with respect to the organization. Each of these individuals has what is known as *fiduciary responsibility* (Q 1:19).

Q 1:22 **What happens as the nonprofit organization grows, achieves a higher profile, and needs to add individuals to the board? How do those who created the entity retain control of the organization? After all their hard work, they definitely don't want some other group to run off with the organization.**

That is certainly true. This is a very common problem. An illustration is an organization that provides scholarships. Over time, the gift support and scholarships increase, as does the number of benefited students and grateful family members. More people will take interest in the organization. Some donors may ask whether they can join the board. Others will encourage the original board members to add individuals to the board who are professional educators and can bring expertise to the organization. Some private foundations interested in making grants may want the organization's board to be more reflective of the community.

Suppose, for example, that there are four educators in the community who are very suitable for inclusion on the board—and they are willing to serve. The three founders freely acknowledge they could use the help. But, with a board of seven, the original three would probably lose control. The educators could vote the three out of their directors' seats and out of their offices. After all of their hard work and success, the founders of the organization could be completely excluded from its operations.

The three existing board members have understandable worries.

Q 1:23 **Can the founding board have it both ways? Can it retain control of the organization and, at the same time, have an expanded and more professional governing board?**

Yes. There are four ways to do this.

1. Be certain that the other board members are friends and other colleagues who will not subsequently attempt to wrest control of the organization away from the founders. This approach works only to the extent the loyalty remains.
2. Have two classes of members, with the founders in one class and all other board members in the other. The governing documents then provide that certain decisions can be made only after a majority vote of both classes.
3. Use the membership feature. The founding individuals become members of the organization. The governing documents then provide that certain decisions can be made only by the members and/or that all board members can be removed by the members.
4. Issue stock, if permitted. In a few states, nonprofit organizations can be created with the authority to issue stock. The controlling individuals become stockholders. The governing documents then provide that certain decisions

are reserved to the stockholders and/or that all board members can be removed by the stockholders.

 **TIP:** Before any of these approaches is utilized in a particular case, the law of the appropriate state(s) should be examined to be certain it is permissible.

Q 1:24 What are the rules regarding the development of chapters?

There is very little law on this topic. A nonprofit organization that wants to have chapters is free to do so. The principal legal question for an organization with chapters is whether the chapters are separate legal entities or are part of the "parent" organization.

Thus, the rules as to chapters are likely to be confined to those the principal organization devises. A good practice for the main organization is to develop criteria for the chapters and then "charter" them according to the criteria. Some parent organizations execute a contract with their chapters, to be in a position to enforce the criteria. To some extent, then, the proper process for the creation and maintenance of a chapter program is akin to franchising in the for-profit setting.

There are no rules—other than those that an organization devises for itself—regarding the jurisdiction of chapters. A chapter can encompass a state, a segment of a state, or several states. There is no legal need for uniformity on this point; chapters can be allocated on the basis of population.

Q 1:25 Do chapters have to be incorporated?

No, there is no legal requirement that chapters be incorporated. (Basically, there is little law mandating that any nonprofit organization be incorporated.) It is a good practice to cause the chapters to be corporations, however, so as to minimize the likelihood of liability for the parent organization and the boards of directors of the chapters.

Again, this pertains to the question of whether the chapters are separate legal entities (Q 1:24). A chapter can be a separate legal entity without being incorporated; for example, a chapter can be an unincorporated association. (It is not likely that the chapter would be in trust form (Q 1:5).) In most instances, chapters are separate legal entities. This means, among other elements, that they must have their own identification number (they should not use the parent organization's number) and pursue their own tax exemption determination letter (unless they are going to rely on the group exemption).

Q 1:26 What is the role of a lawyer who represents one or more nonprofit organizations?

Overall, the role of a lawyer for a nonprofit organization—sometimes termed a *nonprofit lawyer*—is no different from that of a lawyer for any other type of client. The tasks are: to know the law (and avoid malpractice), represent the client in legal matters to the fullest extent of one's capabilities and energy, and otherwise zealously perform legal services without violating the law or breaching professional ethics.

The typical lawyer today is a specialist, and the nonprofit lawyer is no exception. Nonprofit law is unique and complex; the lawyer who dabbles in it does so at peril. A lawyer may be the best of experts on labor or securities law, and know nothing about nonprofit law. The reverse is, of course, also true: the nonprofit lawyer is likely to know nothing about admiralty or domestic relations law.

The first task listed above is "to know the law." That is literally impossible: no lawyer can know all of the law. The nonprofit lawyer, like any other lawyer, needs to be just as aware of what he or she does *not* know as to what is known. The nonprofit lawyer may be called in as a specialist to assist another lawyer, or, occasionally, a nonprofit lawyer may turn to a specialist in other fields that can pertain to nonprofit entities, such as environmental or bankruptcy law.

Some lawyers represent nonprofit organizations that have a significant involvement in a field that entails a considerable amount of federal and/or state regulation. This is particularly the case with trade, business, and professional organizations. These lawyers may know much about the regulatory law in a particular field, yet know little about the law pertaining to nonprofit organizations as such.

Q 1:27   How should the lawyer representing a nonprofit organization be compensated?

There is nothing unique about the compensation arrangements for lawyers representing nonprofit organizations (other than the fact that the compensation may be comparatively lower). Most lawyers representing nonprofit organizations will determine their fee solely on a hourly rate for the time expended. In these circumstances, the client is entitled to a statement (usually monthly) that clearly reflects the time expended, how it was expended, who expended it (including paralegals), and the hourly rates. These statements usually itemize expenses to be reimbursed.

It is good practice to provide the nonprofit organization client, at the outset of the relationship, with a letter that spells out the billing practices.

Some lawyer–client relationships in the nonprofit realm are based on a retainer fee arrangement. The client pays the lawyer a fixed fee for a stated period, irrespective of the volume of services provided. The retainer arrangement gives the nonprofit organization a budgeting advantage: it knows what its legal fee exposure will be for the period. The lawyer gains an advantage of cash flow. Both parties should monitor the arrangement on an ongoing basis—the lawyer to ward off undercompensation and the nonprofit organization to avoid overcompensation.

The fee arrangement may blend a retainer with additional hourly rate fees for specified services.

Other fee relationships include bonuses and contingencies. A nonprofit organization should always be mindful of the private inurement constraint—the rule that compensation, including legal fees, must always be reasonable (Q 1:16).

CHAPTER 2

Boards of Directors and Conflicts and Liability

For a nonprofit organization, the board of directors is (or should be) the critical body that determines the entity's programs and investments and provides management guidance. The role of the officers and employees is important, but the board of directors has the responsibility to frame the organization's overall policy directions and objectives. The governing board is also the locus of ultimate responsibility for the organization's activities—and can be a prime target when matters of liability arise.

The board is particularly significant for charitable organizations. In this context, the members of the board are fiduciaries; they are charged with treating the organization's assets and other resources with the same degree of care and sustenance that they would their own. When there is wrongdoing or misguided practices are revealed, the abuse is all too frequently traceable to an inattentive or passive—or captive—board of directors. More frequently than before, government regulators are placing greater duties and responsibilities on the board of directors, in the hope of averting misdeeds.

Here are the questions most frequently asked about the role of the board of directors and officers, the rules as to proper expenditures of funds, self-dealing and conflicts of interest, and board members' liability—and the answers to them.

Q 2:1 What is the origin of a board of directors of a nonprofit organization?

There are many ways for the board of directors of a nonprofit organization to originate. Often these individuals are elected by a membership. In some instances, they are appointed by another body, such as the board of directors of a related nonprofit or for-profit organization. They may be *ex officio* directors—on the board because of a position they hold with another entity.

TIP: The term *ex officio* means "by reason of the office." The phrase has nothing to do with the individual's ability to vote. All too frequently, it is assumed that *ex officio* board members, for that reason, cannot vote; many sets of bylaws have been written on that premise. The assumption is wrong, however. It is, therefore, a good practice to state in the bylaws whether any *ex officio* board members may vote.

It is common to have a self-perpetuating board—one whose members periodically elect themselves and/or others to the board position. The origin of the board of directors of a nonprofit organization may be a blend of these options.

NOTE: This is largely a state law matter. The law of the appropriate state should be checked before any option in this regard is selected.

In many states, the names and addresses of the members of the board of a nonprofit corporation must be stated in the articles of incorporation. It is usually appropriate to provide in the same document how the board of directors is derived.

NOTE: Sometimes the terminology of this topic is confusing. The governing board of a nonprofit organization may be termed a board of directors, board of trustees, board of governors, or some other title. The name itself rarely has any legal significance. The use of *trustees* is normally associated with charitable organizations. When a charitable organization is closely affiliated with another organization (whether or not tax-exempt), misunderstanding can be eliminated by calling the board of the charitable entity a board of trustees; the other board can then be the board of directors or given another title.

Q 2:2 What are the rules concerning the composition of the board of directors?

For the most part, the law does not contain rules of this nature (Q 2:3). Most frequently, the rules governing the composition of the board of directors of a nonprofit organization are those imposed by the organization itself. Some of these outcomes, of course, are attributable to the type of organization involved. For example, a broad-based membership organization is likely to have a different governing structure than a private foundation with two or three trustees. Likewise, where one nonprofit organization controls another nonprofit organization, the relationship usually is structured by means of interlocking directorates; the governing instruments of the controlled entity will spell out how the controlling entity selects the board of the controlled entity.

There may be some federal tax implications in this area. In a few situations, the tax law imposes rules concerning board composition. For example, in the law concerning supporting organizations (see Chapter 10), there are rules that mandate certain forms of overlapping board and limitations on the extent to which disqualified persons can control the organization. The rules of the facts and circumstances test (see Q 2:5, Q 10:7) address board composition. The Internal Revenue Service (IRS) is becoming more aggressive in requiring certain board compositions. As illustrations, the IRS will not allow a tax-exempt hospital's board of directors to be dominated by the medical staff physicians, and the participation of a public charity in a limited partnership may be conditioned on the requirement that representatives of other partners are not on the board of the charitable organization. Moreover, the IRS did not hesitate to, in a closing agreement with a nonprofit hospital, observe that the board of directors of the institution failed to adequately be aware of, review, and assert control over certain of the hospital's actions. A by-product of intermediate sanctions (Chapter 7) may be the expansion of boards of directors of some charitable and social welfare organizations. But, for the most part, the federal tax law is silent on the composition of the board of directors of a nonprofit organization.

Q 2:3   How does a charitable organization know whether its board of directors is lawfully constituted?

The subject of board composition is essentially a matter of state law. Most states' laws contain the criteria for members of the board of nonprofit organizations, particularly nonprofit corporations. For example, the law in most jurisdictions requires at least three directors and specifies that each of them must be at least 18 years of age. There usually are no other limitations. Some states require only one director.

There may be some federal tax requirements that bear on this point (Q 2:2).

Q 2:4   What is the function of the board of directors?

There is considerable disagreement on this point. The ideal standard is: setting of policy, objectives, and general direction for the nonprofit organization. The board is there to *direct* but only in an overarching, big-picture sense. That body should not micromanage the entity.

In practice, a board's degree of involvement has every sort of gradation. The size of the board and the frequency of its meetings can be determining factors. Many boards of directors retain ongoing management authority between board meetings by means of executive committees. These committees, however, tend to be composed of individuals who are also officers, so the role of that group also shares in the role of the officers (Q 2:11).

Particularly in the case of charitable organizations, the members of the board are *fiduciaries* (Q 1:18). Because of this standard, these individuals are required to act with the same degree of judgment—prudence—in administering the affairs of the organization as they would in their personal affairs (Q 1:19).

The officers and key employees should administer the nonprofit organization on a day-to-day basis, not the board of directors. But, in actuality, board members often inject themselves into the details of administration. The law basically is powerless to draw lines here; the degree of management involvement by an individual board member usually is a function of the tolerance of the other board members, the energy and personality of the board member, and the amount of time he or she has available for the pursuit.

Q 2:5 Must the board of directors of a charitable organization be representative of the community?

For the most part, no. Neither federal nor state law dictates the characteristics of a nonprofit board to that extent. There are a few exceptions (Q 2:2) but, to date at least, they are minor. Nearly all charitable organizations are free to have on the governing board anyone the board wants.

The principal exception on this topic is a rule in the facts and circumstances test (see Q 10:7). This test looks to whether the organization has a governing body that represents the "broad interests of the public," rather than the personal or private interests of a few individuals. Qualifying boards are those that are composed of (1) community leaders, such as elected or appointed officials, members of the clergy, educators, civic leaders, or other such individuals representing a broad cross-section of the views and interests of the community; (2) individuals having special knowledge or expertise in the particular field or discipline in which the organization is operating; (3) public officials acting in their capacities as such; (4) individuals selected by public officials acting in their capacities as such; and (5) in the case of a membership organization, individuals elected pursuant to the organization's governing instrument or bylaws by a broadly based membership.

Also, the rules concerning supporting organizations can determine the composition of the board of directors of a supporting organization (Q 10:23).

Q 2:6 Can the organization's board be only family members?

Yes. It is common for a nonprofit organization—charitable or otherwise—to be founded by one or two individuals. In the beginning, these individuals may comprise or dominate the board of directors and also be the officers of the organization. This type of organization is the nonprofit equivalent of what is known in the for-profit sector as a *closely held corporation*. Close governance in the nonprofit sector is completely in conformity with the law.

TIP: Despite the fact that a close board is wholly legal, it likely will subject the organization to a greater degree of scrutiny by government officials, particularly when they are concerned about private inurement or private benefit (see Chapter 6). The IRS occasionally will balk at a close board when considering recognition of tax-exempt status, although technically the IRS has no general authority to preclude one.

It is common, for example, for a private foundation to be structured in this fashion; it is the principal reason these entities are considered *private* charities (Q 10:2).

In most jurisdictions, as few as three directors are required for a nonprofit corporation. (The minimum number of directors for a nonprofit corporation varies from state to state. Some states require only one.) If an entity is to be a corporation and it has the requisite number of directors, this approach is fully lawful.

Q 2:7 Can the family-member directors also be the officers of the nonprofit organization?

Yes. The law in most states requires a president, a treasurer, and a secretary. Board members can also be officers. One individual can hold two officer positions, except that the same individual cannot be both president and secretary. (Frequently, an organization's documents must be signed by the president and attested to by the secretary. The law does not recognize as effective an attestation of one's own signature (Q 2:10).)

Q 2:8 In any instance, can the same individual be both a director and an officer?

Yes. There is no legal prohibition against the dual role. In fact, in both nonprofit and for-profit organizations, some or all of the officers are quite commonly members of the board as well.

Q 2:9 What is the function of the officers?

The law is rather vague on this point. An officer usually is expected to provide more "hands-on" management than a director but not as much as a key employee. These distinctions often become muddled, particularly when the same individual plays two or more of these roles (Q 2:4, Q 2:10). Further, the degree of involvement by an officer is likely to be determined by whether he or she is a volunteer or is an employee.

Specifically, the function of the *president* is to serve as the chief executive officer of the organization. It is common to state in the entity's bylaws that, subject to the overall supervision of the board of directors, the president shall perform all duties customary to that office.

The function of the *treasurer* is to have custody of and be responsible for all funds and assets of the organization. He or she keeps or causes to be kept complete and accurate accounts of receipts and disbursements of the organization. The treasurer is responsible for the deposit of moneys in such banks or other depositories as the board of directors may designate. He or she is to periodically render a statement of accounts to the board. It is common to state in the entity's bylaws that, subject to the overall supervision of the board of directors, the treasurer shall perform all duties customary to that office.

NOTE: Proper management practice is to obtain a security bond to protect the organization should the treasurer abuse that position for personal gain.

The functions of the *secretary* are to keep an accurate record of the proceedings of all meetings of the board of directors, and to give notice of meetings and other events as the law or the bylaws may require. It is common to state in the entity's bylaws that, subject to the overall supervision of the board of directors, the secretary shall perform all duties customary to that office.

Q 2:10 Can the same individual hold more than one officer position?

It depends on the positions. For example, it is common for the same individual to be the secretary and treasurer. By contrast, it is not a good idea to have the same individual be the president and secretary. The law often requires the signatures of both of these officers on legal documents and contemplates two individuals. The laws of some states prohibit an individual from being both president and secretary of a non-profit corporation.

Q 2:11 What are the methods by which a board of directors of a nonprofit organization can vote?

The methods by which a board of directors of a nonprofit organization can vote is a subject of state law; nearly every state's nonprofit corporation act addresses the subject. Obviously, the board members can meet and cast votes while they are together (assuming a quorum is present). Most states allow these boards to act by written consent in lieu of a meeting, although the members must be unanimous on any decision so made. If state law approves (and, in some instances, if provided for in the bylaws), the members can hold a meeting by conference call, as long as all of them can hear each other. Thus, for example, unless state law expressly permits the practice, members of the board of directors of a nonprofit organization cannot vote by mail ballot.

CAUTION: That observation does not apply to members of the organization itself. Most state laws allow them to vote by mail.

Q 2:12 Can members of the board of directors of a nonprofit organization vote by proxy?

No, unless state law expressly provides for voting in this manner (and this is highly unlikely). This is a form of voting that is fairly common in the nonprofit sector, yet technically is not proper. (This means that board decisions made by proxy voting may, if challenged, be void and unenforceable.)

The reason for this is that the concepts underlying the functioning of a nonprofit organization's board of directors are derived from common law precepts pertaining to charitable trusts. The law contemplates that trustees of these trusts will meet and debate in formulating policies for the organization. Since they can have a meaningful dialog only if they are interacting in person (in the days before the telephone and video conferencing), the law discourages decision making other than that following in-person deliberations. The dictates of fiduciary responsibility require personal attendance on occasions when the organization's course for the future is being shaped. Thus, only those statutory exceptions to this common law principle can render lawful means of voting without assembly of the board. But even contemporary statutory law frowns on voting forms that are least likely to draw the board together: proxies and mail ballots.

Q 2:13 **What material should be in the minutes of meetings of boards of directors of nonprofit organizations?**

There is no particular rule of law that applies to the contents of minutes of directors' meetings. These minutes should be complete, in that they reflect all material subjects discussed at the meeting, and accurate. Statements that are defamatory, willful misrepresentations of fact, or incriminating should be avoided.

These minutes should tell the substantive story of what transpired at the meeting; they should not be verbatim transcripts of the dialog or otherwise be in exhaustive detail. They should enable someone looking at them years later to glean the essence of the meeting and the decisions made at it. Those looking at the minutes may not be confined to subsequent boards; other readers can be representatives of government or the media. Thus, how matters are stated can be as important as what is said. In one instance, a public charity described a series of apparent private inurement transactions in a set of board minutes, which the IRS reviewed on audit; the contents of the minutes were cited by the IRS as a factor in revoking the organization's tax-exempt status. Ultimately, it is a question of judgment as to what goes in and what stays out of corporate minutes; there is no bright line of distinction as to what is suitable for inclusion in the document. This is a judgment that can easily be questioned with the benefit of hindsight.

Q 2:14 **Is it a concern as a matter of law whether directors are termed trustees?**

No. Nearly all state laws use the term *directors*. The words *director* and *trustee*, however, are essentially synonymous. If an organization wants to be certain of avoiding adverse technicalities, it need only reference the word *director* once in its bylaws and then note that the term to be used thereafter is *trustee*.

The word *trustee* is usually utilized where the entity is a charitable one (although the word is often also used to describe an individual who oversees a pension or similar fund). *Trustee* carries with it a higher degree of panache and dignity than does *director*; sometimes it is preferred for that purpose alone. On a more practical level, the terms can be functionally used in the case of related organizations, to avoid confusion. For example, in the case of a business association and its related foundation, the board members of the association can be labeled *directors* and those of the foundation's governing body *trustees*.

EXPENDITURES OF FUNDS

Q 2:15   How do these rules apply to the expenditures of funds?

The board of directors of a nonprofit organization, as part of its overall role in setting policy and direction (Q 2:4), should establish a budget, which governs the basic parameters of the expenditures of the organization's funds. This pertains to outlays for program, management, and fundraising.

Q 2:16   What is expected in terms of program expenditures?

The primary purpose of a nonprofit organization is to carry out its program function—termed the *exempt function* in the case of tax-exempt organizations. Thus, the law expects that the primary expenditures of a nonprofit organization will be for its program activities.

There are, however, no mechanical tests for measuring what is *primary* or, as is often the term, *substantial*. A tax-exempt organization can have some unrelated business activity but there is no precise standard as to how much; unrelated business obviously cannot dominate the organization's affairs (see Chapter 14, particularly Q 14:2). The states cannot regulate charitable fund raising on the basis of the amount of the charity's fund raising costs (see Chapter 13, particularly Q 13:4). The blend of the three types of outlays will vary according to the type of organization and the particular circumstances it is in.

TIP: From time to time, the IRS will apply what it terms the *commensurate test* to the activities of a charitable organization. This involves an analysis as to whether the organization is engaging in adequate exempt functions, in relation to the resources that it has. For example, an application of this test (which the IRS subsequently abandoned) was to assert that an organization that allegedly devoted too much of its income to fund raising should lose its tax exemption because of transgression of the commensurate test.

Q 2:17   What are the rules pertaining to employee compensation?

The subject of key employee compensation is under intense scrutiny at the IRS, at the Department of the Treasury, and on Capitol Hill. This interest in employee compensation by tax-exempt organizations was a major force in enactment of the *intermediate sanctions* rules (Chapter 7). These rules impose excise taxes on amounts of excess compensation paid to insiders and require the employee to repay the employer organization the amount of compensation that is considered unreasonable. The rules are termed *intermediate* because, in most instances, they are applied instead of revocation of the organization's tax-exempt status.

The rules as to employee compensation are vague. They are built on the concept of *reasonableness* (Q 1:20). A charitable organization's ongoing tax-exempt status (federal and state) is predicated on the assumption that the compensation of all employees is reasonable. The current focus is primarily on executive compensation. For an employee who is an *insider* with respect to the organization, excessive compensation is a form of *private inurement* and can be a basis for revocation of exempt status (Chapter 6). If the employee is not an insider and the amount of excess compensation is more than incidental, the result is *private benefit*, which also is a ground for loss of tax-exempt status.

Whether an individual's compensation is reasonable is a question of fact, not law. Lawyers usually cannot credibly opine on that subject. There are, however, compensation experts who can legitimately advise on the appropriateness of amounts of compensation. In many instances, prudence can lead an organization to procure a formal opinion from one of these experts as to the reasonableness of the compensation of one or more employees.

What lawyers can do is evaluate an individual's compensation using the various criteria that the law has devised for assessing reasonableness. (These tests are summarized at Q 6:8.)

The lawyer's lot in these situations can be illustrated by the following example. A client charitable organization was hiring a new executive director, and the lawyer was asked to review the proposed contract and advise the organization accordingly. Nothing in the contract was separately inappropriate, but it was the lawyer's judgment that the overall package of salary and benefits was much too generous, to the point of being excessive. This was completely a judgment call, the use of intuition. Three aspects of the proposed arrangement were particularly troubling:

1. The incoming executive's compensation package was twice that of the outgoing executive director.
2. The salary alone was one-eighth of the organization's annual budget.
3. The individual being hired was a member of the board of directors of the organization.

To further worsen the situation, the new executive director was given express authority to consult (for fees) and to earn other forms of outside income.

The lawyer was obligated to advise the client that there was a substantial likelihood that the compensation package would be considered excessive by federal or state government authorities, and that the organization's tax exemption may be endangered. The lawyer could not point to anything specific; the client was provided with a judgment, based on an understanding of the case law. The client (specifically, the chairman of the board of directors) was very unhappy with the lawyer's position. The board went ahead and hired the individual as planned; the lawyer's days of representing that particular organization are over.

Q 2:18 **The management of a charitable organization wants to redecorate the offices of the organization and purchase new furniture. How much money can it spend and how "fancy" can it be?**

A precise monetary amount cannot be provided for this sort of thing. There is no mechanical standard for determining the extent of these types of expenditures. Those involved, as *fiduciaries*, can lawfully use the organization's income and assets for office decoration, furniture, and so forth, as long as they stay within the bounds of what is *reasonable* and *prudent* (Q 1:18–Q 1:20, Q 2:5–Q 2:6). To use other words that are easy to articulate, but often difficult to apply, they should avoid outlays that are *lavish* or *extravagant*.

An example may help clarify this matter. In 1994, the State of New York concluded an examination of a charitable organization, which culminated in a settlement. This three-year investigation led to a document concerning what the attorney general referred to as the "financial administration and spending practices" of the organization. The state concluded that the board of trustees of this organization "failed to exercise appropriate cost controls in its management" of the entity. This finding specifically referred to the construction and furnishing of the entity's headquarters.

The New York attorney general found that the organization incurred "excessive" costs in furnishing the offices. The settlement required the trustees of this charity to, in the future, "exercise cost consciousness at all times" when making spending decisions. An expense policy document observed that, "[a]s it is not always possible to apply hard-and-fast rules to every situation, all trustees and employees are expected to use common sense in the disbursement of" the organization's funds. This "standard" is nothing more than another iteration of the doctrines of *reasonableness* and *prudence*. The standard used in the settlement was that of *cost consciousness*.

NOTE: This settlement with the attorney general in New York required each of the organization's 14 trustees to pay $10,000 to the organization as restitution for the excessive costs incurred in constructing and furnishing the headquarters.

These guidelines are useful in testing the wisdom of decisions by the leadership of charitable organizations.

TIP: This settlement agreement is not *law*. It only applies to the parties and only involves the State of New York. (The document specifically states that there was no admission of any wrongdoing.) It is being emphasized only because of the pertinence of its provisions and the lack of such specific guidance elsewhere.

Equally useful is the *front-page-of-the-newspaper test*. Envision how a director of a charity would feel if a story about the organization's fiscal practices appeared on the front page of the community's newspaper. A classic example of the disasters that can be created when the front-page test is failed is the series of experiences suffered by the United Way of America because of the doings of its then president.

Q 2:19 Does this standard of fiduciary responsibility apply to every expense incurred by a charitable organization?

Yes. For example, the settlement in New York (Q 2:18) also pertained to travel, hotel accommodations, location of board meetings, and use of consultants.

Q 2:20 **What are the rules for charitable organizations concerning travel by board members, officers, and employees?**

The New York settlement agreement (Q 2:18) is useful as a guideline. The standard to be used is *cost consciousness*. When the directors of the organization are prudent, they authorize spending of the organization's money as if it were their own. For example, if a director travels via a commercial airline at his or her own personal expense, does he or she fly first class? If not, it is hard to justify first-class travel at the expense of the organization.

NOTE: First-class air travel while pursuing a charity's affairs is not illegal or otherwise inherently impermissible. Only justification of the practice is involved.

Thus, the attorney general, in the New York settlement, required the charitable organization to use the "most economic available" air-fares. The organization was largely prohibited from paying or reimbursing for first-class airfares and using chartered airplanes. Generally, the use of limousines was also prohibited unless "international officials or other dignitaries" are involved.

Q 2:21 **What about spousal travel?**

This is a very difficult and sensitive subject. The settlement in New York generally prohibited the organization from paying or reimbursing travel expenses for spouses or other close family members. The only exception is when the individual provides a "specific contribution for the program for which the travel is incurred through an active participation in a scheduled program." Moreover, where the spouse or family member is that of an employee, prior approval of the chief executive officer is required; where a trustee is involved, prior approval of the chairman of the audit committee is required.

Also, federal tax law relates to this subject. There is no income tax deduction for amounts paid or incurred with respect to a spouse (or dependent or other individual) accompanying an individual (or an officer or employee of the business) on business travel, unless the accompanying individual is an employee of the taxpayer, the travel of the accompanying individual is for a bona fide business purpose, and the travel expenses would otherwise be deductible by the accompanying individual. The business expense deduction, however, is available where the payment is treated as compensation to the employee. A tax-exempt organization is not concerned with these rules as to tax deductions. Where an exempt organization pays for the travel expenses of a spouse, that payment is additional income to the employee of the organization, unless the purpose of the presence of the spouse is the performance of programmatic, administrative, or other services that further the organization's exempt purposes.

Q 2:22 **What about the use of hotels?**

A tax-exempt organization can pay for the use of hotels for conferences, board meetings, and so forth. As always, the standard to follow is (Q 2:18) *reasonableness*. The

New York settlement guidelines, with their emphasis on *cost consciousness*, generally require the use of "available corporate and discount rates," and prohibit the payment of "deluxe or luxury" hotel rates and the use of hotel suites. These guidelines pertain only to the use of hotels by trustees and employees; they do not specifically apply to the use of hotels for conferences and other programmatic purposes. The only exception is when a suite is used for business purposes; even then, the use requires the prior approval of the chief executive officer. The guidelines expect avoidance of locations where a sports competition or other special event is taking place, or where a particular hotel is hosting a major convention or similar event.

Q 2:23   What about the expenses of meals?

As a general proposition, a charitable organization can pay for meals for the board, employees, and the like, where done in a business context. The standards are *reasonableness* and *cost consciousness*. There should not be payment or reimbursement for meals that are lavish or extravagant. There should be appropriate documentation of the amounts incurred and the business purpose for them.

Q 2:24   Can a board member borrow money from a charitable organization?

In general, the answer is yes. There are, however, several aspects to keep in mind. One is the matter of perception. A form of behavior may be legally permissible, yet still look bad. Remember the *front-page-of-the-newspaper test* (Q 2:18). This type of transaction also has the negative connotation of *self-dealing*. Nearly all charitable organizations can lawfully engage in forms of self-dealing, but they must be prepared to withstand charges of potential wrongdoing.

Once again, the standard of *reasonableness* applies. There will not be private inurement in a loan to a board member if the features of the transaction are reasonable. The factors governing reasonableness in this situation are the reason for the loan, the likelihood of repayment, the amount of the loan, whether it is memorialized in a note, the rate of interest, the extent and amount of security, the arrangements for repayment, and the length of the borrowing term. From the standpoint of the organization, the borrowing is an investment, but those same dollars could be invested in a more conventional and secure manner. The state attorney general is likely to look closely at this type of borrowing, particularly where the loan is not being paid according to the terms of the note.

NOTE: Special rules in this regard pertain to private foundations (see Chapter 11).

Q 2:25   Can a charitable organization purchase or rent property from a board member?

Again, the simple answer is yes. These circumstances have to be tested against the same considerations as those involving a loan to a board member (Q 2:24). The standard is one of reasonableness and the transaction would be a form of self-dealing.

The factors governing reasonableness in these situations are the specific reasons for rental of that particular property, the amount of the rent, whether the arrangement is memorialized in a lease, and the length of the lease term.

NOTE: Special rules in this regard pertain to private foundations (see Chapter 11).

Q 2:26 Besides expenses, what else should a charitable organization be concerned about?

The tests of what is *reasonable* and *prudent* are overarching; they apply to all expenditures, including legal and fundraising fees.

There are two other areas of some sensitivity: (1) the location of board meetings and (2) competitive bidding.

Expenses for board meetings are the subject of the New York settlement (Q 2:18). The guidelines there are quite useful in setting general parameters. The settlement document states that the primary factors to be considered in selecting locations for board meetings (including meetings of committees) are the programs, purposes, and costs of the meetings. The charitable organization is to take into account the programmatic benefits of the location, whether it has existing facilities already available, the cost of travel and hotel accommodations, seasonal factors, the feasibility of having only a delegation of the board attending the meeting instead of the full board, the feasibility of paying for program participants to travel to the organization rather than having the board travel to their location, and the scheduling of committee or board meetings on consecutive days. The board must approve in advance the location of all of its meetings.

NOTE: This matter of the full board attending meetings or educational functions can be problematic, particularly where the surroundings are luxurious. On one occasion, all seven members of the board of a charitable organization attended a seminar held at a fine resort. All of them were having lunch at the same table, as part of a group luncheon, when they were joined by one of the morning's speakers, an assistant attorney general of the state. Early into the meal, this government official realized that the seven were attending the seminar at the behest of the same charity (some were members of the same family). There was palpable unpleasantness during the balance of the meal.

Where a committee meeting is held at a time other than a full meeting of the board, the committee must approve the site and date of the meeting in advance. The meeting minutes must specify the purpose of any meeting held and the reason for the site selected, if the meeting is not held at a facility of the organization.

Concerning competitive bidding, there are no legal requirements other than the very general one of *prudent behavior*. The New York settlement documents require that all contracts, including leases and contracts for professional services, be procured via competitive procedures to the maximum extent feasible. Moreover, the awards are to go to firms whose "experience and capabilities are most advantageous" to the organization.

The New York settlement requires that these contracts be in writing and state the fees or rates to be charged, the time for completion, and the estimated total cost. All contracts in excess of $50,000 must be the subject of written proposals or competitive bids. When the organization evaluates proposals from qualified vendors, the primary consideration is to be cost. Other factors to be taken into account are prior experience, reputation, location, and minority participation.

The organization's vice president for finance must prepare an analysis of the basis on which a vendor was chosen, irrespective of whether the contract was awarded following competitive bidding or on a single-source basis. This analysis must be reported to the organization's audit committee.

SELF-DEALING AND CONFLICTS OF INTEREST

Q 2:27 What is *self-dealing*?

Self-dealing occurs when a person is engaged in a transaction with a nonprofit organization while at the same time having a significant relationship with the organization. The person is on both sides of the deal, hence the term. For example, self-dealing occurs where a nonprofit organization purchases an item of property from a business that is controlled by an individual who is on the board of directors of the nonprofit organization.

The term *self-dealing* is used particularly in the private foundation rules (see Chapter 11). There, the person self-dealing with a foundation is termed a *disqualified person*. In the realm of public charities, such a person is known as an *insider* (Q 6:2). For charities, an insider is likely to be about the same as a fiduciary (Q 1:18).

In the private foundation setting, a disqualified person includes each member of the board of directors or trustees, each of the officers, key employees who have duties and responsibilities similar to those of officers, substantial contributors, members of the family of the foregoing, and corporations, trusts, and estates that are controlled by disqualified persons.

Q 2:28 Is self-dealing the same as a conflict of interest?

No. The concept of a conflict of interest is broader than the concept of self-dealing. One common characteristic that these terms have, however, is that both are derogatory. Neither practice is necessarily illegal. (If a disqualified person with respect to a private foundation engages in an act of self-dealing, he or she will likely become subject to one or more federal excise taxes imposed as penalties (Q 11:6).)

A conflict of interest presents itself when a person who has a significant relationship with a nonprofit organization also is deriving, or may be in a position to potentially derive, a benefit from something the nonprofit organization is doing or may be doing. The person may be able to obtain some personal benefit from these circumstances; because of the duality of interests, the person is conflicted. An act of self-dealing between a nonprofit organization and an insider with respect to it also is an instance of a conflict of interest. A conflict of interest can be present, however, without a specific transaction or arrangement having yet arisen. Also, insiders are not always directly involved in a conflict-of-interest situation. For example, a charitable organization may be contemplating making a research grant to a scientific institution; a board member of the grantor entity has a conflict of interest if his or her brother or sister is a researcher at the grantee institution.

A conflict-of-interest transaction is a transaction with the nonprofit organization, or any of its affiliates, in which an individual connected with the organization (usually its directors and officers) has a direct or indirect interest.

 **NOTE:** A conflict of interest can often be resolved by disclosure of the conflict to the board of directors of the nonprofit organization. Indeed, some nonprofit organizations have formal policies to this end (Q 2:27). Problems associated with self-dealing, however, usually cannot be remedied merely by disclosure.

Q 2:29 What is the source for a requirement that board members disclose (in writing) any possible conflict of interest they might have with the nonprofit organization they serve?

This requirement generally is not in the law; at most, it may appear in the law of a particular state. Thus, in nearly all instances, the source of this obligation will be in a conflict-of-interest policy developed by the nonprofit organization. The most common form of this policy is a written statement of the policy adopted by the board of directors of the nonprofit organization.

NOTE: Some of the watchdog agencies (such as the Council of Better Business Bureaus) require the adoption of a conflict-of-interest policy as a condition of their approval of a charitable organization. (See Q 3:1.)

Q 2:30 What language should be contained in a conflict-of-interest statement?

A conflict-of-interest policy should annually elicit from each individual covered by it the disclosure of any organization that does business with or is in competition with the organization, where the individual (and/or any of his or her immediate family members) serves as a director or officer of that other entity. Similar disclosure should be made with respect to an individual's participations in partnerships, consulting arrangements, and other circumstances where the individual has significant influence over management decisions.

Moreover, the same type of disclosure should be made where the individuals receive compensation from another entity over a certain threshold (such as $10,000) or where there is an equity or debt relationship over a certain threshold (such as 10 percent).

The conflict-of-interest statement should obligate the director, officer, or any other individual to disclose a conflict of interest to the board of directors of the organization. It should require that the disclosure be reflected in the minutes of the board meeting, along with the potential adverse consequences to the organization.

The board of directors of the organization should be required to determine whether the disclosure was made adequately and forthrightly (which may require some questioning and other discussion at the board meeting), and whether the organization should proceed with the transaction involving the conflict (if that is the case). A conflict-of-interest transaction should be subject to approval by the board by a process more stringent than would otherwise be the case (such as by a two-thirds vote when normally only a majority vote would be required). The interested director or officer should not be counted in ascertaining the presence of a quorum for the meeting or in the vote itself. It is preferable that this individual not be present at the time of the voting.

Q 2:31 Is a conflict-of-interest policy legally binding on the individuals covered by it and/or the nonprofit organization?

It should be. If the policy is adopted by the organization's board of directors in conformance with the requirements of state law and the organization's bylaws, usually pursuant to board resolution, the policy is legally binding. It is in the nature of a contract between the directors and officers of the organization and the organization itself, and between and among these individuals.

Q 2:32 How does an individual know when a conflict of interest is present?

For the most part, the conflict-of-interest policy—most likely stated on the conflict-of-interest disclosure form that is annually prepared by the covered individuals—will spell out what the conflicts are. Still, some judgment may be required in determining whether there is a conflict. For example, it may not be clear whether an individual has a "significant influence over management decisions" (Q 2:30). The initial determination may rest with the covered individual. The most prudent practice is: when in doubt, disclose the matter to the board of directors.

Q 2:33 What are the obligations of a board member or officer when a conflict of interest is disclosed?

The principal obligation is met when the disclosure is made. The other obligations should be to be subject to questions by the board as to the conflict (actual, potential, or perceived), to answer those questions, to disclose to the organization any adverse consequences resulting from the conflict of which the individual is aware, and to refrain from voting on the transaction involved (if any), from being included in the quorum for the meeting, and from being present during that voting (even if the policy may not specifically require absence (Q 2:30)).

Q 2:34 How should a nonprofit organization respond to disclosure of a conflict of interest?

The disclosure should be made only to the board of directors (Q 2:30). As soon as is reasonably possible following the disclosure, the board of directors should discuss the matter at a board meeting. If a particular transaction is involved, the board should vote on the conflict before considering the transaction. It is the responsibility of a board of directors to determine whether there is a conflict of interest and, if so, whether to proceed with the transaction or to use other means to reconcile the conflict.

Q 2:35 What are the penalties when a conflict of interest is breached?

The penalties, whatever they may be, would be levied by the board of directors on the individual who breached the conflict of interest policy. The range of these penalties is likely to be determined by state law and the organization's bylaws. The options include a gentle rebuke, a serious rebuke, a censure, and/or removal from office.

NOTE: Some organizations state in their conflict-of-interest policy that a transaction may be void or voidable if not approved by the board of directors in accordance with the conflict of interest policy. This practice is quite suitable when the only parties to the transaction are the nonprofit organization and one or more individuals covered by the policy (for example, a lease between the organization and a company wholly owned by a board member). Where the transaction involves other parties who are not covered by the conflict-of-interest policy, however, a voiding of the transaction pursuant to the policy could be an illegal breach of contract that would subject the organization (and perhaps one or more board members) to a lawsuit.

Q 2:36 Can a nonprofit organization receive contributions from a corporation or foundation where a board member has a conflict of interest?

In general, yes. It is unlikely that these contributions would be inappropriate as a matter of law. For the most part, gifts from this source would not contravene the conflict-of-interest policy of the organization because money is flowing to it, rather than from it. There is always a possibility, however, that the recipient organization could find itself in an awkward or embarrassing position as a consequence of these gifts (remember the front-page-of-the-newspaper test (Q 2:18)). Prudence is always in order in this context.

Q 2:37 **Can a nonprofit organization negotiate for discounted prices for goods or services to be purchased from a source where a board member or officer has disclosed a conflict of interest?**

Absolutely. The essence of the requirements in this area is disclosure, not a prohibition. The transaction may proceed if the conflict of interest is fully disclosed and considered by the board of directors, and the board decides that (1) the transaction would be reasonable with respect to the organization and (2) the presence of the conflict did not significantly influence the action of the board with respect to the conflict. These determinations should be reflected in the minutes of the relevant board meeting (Q 2:13).

TIP: A conflict of interest does not automatically mean that private inurement or private benefit has occurred (Chapter 6). The potential for difficulties of that nature is greater, however, and the parties should act with caution. If the nonprofit organization is a private foundation and the transaction is with one or more disqualified persons with respect to the organization, the application of the private foundation rules (particularly those pertaining to self-dealing) should be carefully checked (Chapter 11).

Q 2:38 **Are there guidelines on or limitations to the extent or nature of the discount value or percent of purchased goods or services?**

No. The emphasis in this area is on disclosure and on whether to proceed with the transaction. The greater the discount or the smaller the percentage of purchased goods and services, the more likely the transaction will be deemed fair and reasonable to the nonprofit organization.

EXPOSURE OF THE BOARD TO LIABILITY

Q 2:39 **What happens if the board of directors of a nonprofit organization makes a mistake?**

The answer depends on the nature of the "mistake."

1. Was the mistake an "honest" one, or did it involve the kind of behavior that the board knew or should have known was inappropriate or insufficient? The action or decision should be tested against the principles of *fiduciary responsibility* (Q 1:19). Whose interests were being pursued, the organization's or those of one or more individuals? Did the mistake entail a violation of a law? Is it a civil or criminal violation? Did the board seek the advice of a lawyer or other appropriate professional before undertaking the transaction? In essence, the question always is: Did the board members act *reasonably*? In this context, that means: Did they act in *good faith*?
2. Did the mistake damage the organization or any other person?
3. How easily can the mistake be undone?

4. What protections were in place to shield the organization and the directors from liability?

For example, the board of the organization involved in the New York settlement (see Q 2:18) was charged with the mistake of condoning lavish and extravagant expenditures. Their "mistake" damaged the organization, but corrective action could be and was taken: the New York attorney general mandated that each member of the board was to pay the organization $10,000 as restitution for his or her misconduct. A few other states will surcharge the directors for similar behavior.

When an action by a board of directors of a nonprofit organization causes damage, either to the organization or to someone else, most consequences do not include personal liability on the part of the directors. Instead, the offensive activity is considered by the law to be a responsibility of the organization itself. Thus, the likelihood that the members of the board of directors of a nonprofit organization will be punished in some way because they did something they should not have done (a commission) or they failed to do something they should have done (an omission) is remote.

But suppose that (1) a board approves a significant investment that was speculative, (2) the organization incurs a substantial economic loss as a result, and (3) it is subsequently shown that the board should have known that the investment was inappropriate. In these circumstances, there could be adverse consequences. An attorney general may pursue a surcharge of the board and/or proceedings to remove and replace one or more board members.

Still, it is unusual for members of the board of a nonprofit organization to be found personally liable for something done or not done involving the organization. This is particularly true where the transaction or other behavior is outside the realm of investment decisions. Yet it can happen. In one case, some members of the board of a charitable organization were found to have conspired to discharge an employee on the basis of racial discrimination. Their acts violated civil rights laws and the individuals were found personally liable. Personal liability can also arise in the areas of defamation, antitrust, and fundraising regulation. (For the latter, see Chapter 13.)

Q 2:40 How likely is it that a member of the board of directors of a nonprofit organization will be found personally liable for something done or not done while serving the organization?

The likelihood is not great because the law first regards the action or nonaction as that of the organization. Even if there is liability, the liability almost always is that of the organization. This is particularly true where the organization is a corporation (Q 2:41).

Still, a member of the board of directors (or an officer) who is held personally liable will not find solace in knowing that he or she stands with a select few. Personal liability may attach where the conduct is wrongful and willful, continuous, and not due to reasonable cause. (See Q 2:42.)

Q 2:41   How can a nonprofit organization provide some protection for its board against the likelihood of personal liability for the result of something they did or did not do while serving the organization?

Basically, there are four means of protection. One of them is to *incorporate* the organization. The law recognizes corporations as separate legal entities, and the corporate form usually serves as a shield against personal liability. For corporations, liability is generally confined to the organization and does not extend to those who manage it. In those extreme cases that are the exception to this rule, the jargon is that the corporate shield has been pierced.

Today, when a nonprofit organization is formed, the resulting entity is usually a corporation. Most lawyers advise their individual clients not to sit on the board of directors of a nonprofit organization that is not incorporated.

The second form of protection is *indemnification*. A nonprofit organization should provide in its articles or bylaws that it will pay the judgments and related expenses (including legal fees) incurred by the directors and officers (and perhaps others), when those expenses are the result of a commission or omission by those persons while acting in the service of the organization. The indemnification cannot extend to criminal acts and may not cover certain willful acts that violate a civil law.

NOTE: Because the resources of the organization are involved, the true value of an indemnification depends on the economic viability of the organization. In times of financial difficulties for a nonprofit organization, an indemnification of its directors and officers can be a classic "hollow promise."

Indemnification is often confused with *insurance*, the third form of protection. Instead of shifting the risk of liability from individuals to the organization, however, insurance shifts the risk of liability to an independent third party—an insurance company. The resources of the insurer, rather than those of the insured, are then used to resolve the dispute. Some risks, such as those arising from violation of a criminal law, cannot be shifted to an insurer.

There is one caution here: an officers' and directors' liability insurance contract is likely to contain an extensive list of civil law transgressions that are *excluded* from coverage. These may include offenses such as libel and slander, employee discrimination, and antitrust activities—the most prevalent types of liability in the nonprofit context. Thus, when reviewing a prospective insurance contract that seems to offer the necessary coverage, the "exclusions" paragraphs should be carefully reviewed.

This type of insurance can be costly. Premiums can easily be thousands of dollars annually, even with a sizable deductible. Although the costs of these premiums have dropped in recent years, many nonprofit organizations still cannot afford them.

NOTE: Because of the inadequate coverage and high cost of currently available insurance, in some states, nonprofit organizations are being created for the purpose of facilitating smaller nonprofit organizations' access to various types of insurance. These organizations—because they have this insurance-related function—cannot qualify for tax-exempt status.

Unfortunately, due to rampant litigiousness in our society, the risks of liability usually are too great for any organization that functions without this protection. The premium for this type of insurance simply must be regarded as a "cost of doing business."

It is critical that the organization purchase officers' and directors' liability insurance. A lawyer will likely recommend to any individual that he or she not serve on the board of a nonprofit organization that does not have adequate insurance of this nature.

The fourth of these protections is the newest of them: *immunity*. This form of protection is available when the applicable state law provides that a class of individuals, under certain circumstances, is not liable for a particular act or set of acts or for failure to undertake a particular act or set of acts. Several states have enacted immunity laws for officers and directors of nonprofit organizations, protecting them in case of asserted civil law violations, particularly where these individuals are serving as volunteers.

Q 2:42   Does a nonprofit organization really have to indemnify its officers and directors and purchase liability insurance? Can't they just be certain their acts are always in good faith?

Unfortunately, reliance on assumptions of good faith can prove traumatic and expensive. A lawyer will recommend both an indemnification clause and officers' and directors' liability insurance.

There is no question, however, that the most important protection against legal liability is to act in ways that ward off liability. There are several ways to avoid personal liability while fulfilling the spirit and the rules of fiduciary responsibility. They are:

1. Learn about the legal form of the organization and its structure. For example, if the organization is a corporation, obtain copies of its articles of incorporation and bylaws—and read them. Compare the organization's operating methods with the structure and procedures that are reflected in these documents.

2. Learn how and why the organization operates—the purposes of its programs, their number, possible overlap of efforts, and the nature of its membership and/or other support.

3. Committees, subsidiaries, directors' "pet projects," members' personal interests or contacts, or community needs may have introduced activities (and

corresponding budget outlays) that were not authorized in the normal way. Some may deserve more recognition and support, while others may be (albeit innocently) endangering the organization's tax-exempt status. Find out exactly what the organization is *doing*.

4. Directors should never be afraid to ask about any arrangements or information that is unclear to them. Individuals with fiduciary responsibilities (Q 1:19) should not fret about asking what may seem to them to be "dumb questions" in the presence of the other directors; many of them are likely to have the same questions on their minds.

5. Magazine articles and books describing the proper role for directors and officers of nonprofit organizations will help to update the individual's knowledge as to permissible and innovative practices. Officers and directors should periodically attend a seminar or conference to further their understanding of and effectiveness in their roles.

6. This is both the easiest and hardest rule to follow: the director or officer should, at all times, engage in behavior that prevents (or at least significantly minimizes) the possibility of personal liability even if the organization itself is found liable. The individual, being a fiduciary, has a duty to act in a prudent manner (Q 1:19). Constant awareness of that duty offers no small measure of self-protection.

CHAPTER 3

Corporate Governance Principles

The newest issue of the day, in the law, for nonprofit organizations is application of corporate governance principles to these entities. Some of the evolving concepts are new. Scandals embroiling for-profit corporations and accounting firms—involving fraud, tax avoidance, conflicts of interests, and questionable accounting practices—led to enactment of the Sarbanes-Oxley Act in 2002. The principles embodied in that legislation are quickly being imported into the nonprofit sector, as manifested by a range of initiatives at the federal and state levels.

The questions being asked in this context concern the basics of corporate governance principles, the evolving governance precepts, the interrelationship of these principles with board member responsibilities and liability (Chapter 2), and the role of the watchdog agencies' guidelines.

Here are the questions most frequently asked about corporate governance principles—and the answers to them.

Q 3:1 What is the meaning of the phrase *corporate governance principles*?

Traditionally, the law as to governance of a nonprofit organization—corporation or otherwise—has been largely confined to state rules. These principles, however, are now quickly becoming part of the federal tax law. In late 2004, it is apparent that much new federal law on the subject is imminent: legislation, regulations, and IRS forms and instructions, for example.

The essence of the emerging corporate governance principles is that a charitable organization (and perhaps other types of tax-exempt entities) must be *managed* by its board of directors or board of trustees. It is becoming unacceptable for a board to meet infrequently and be merely the recipient of reports from an organization's officers and staff. The developing law is requiring the board of the nonprofit organization to become directly involved, be knowledgeable about the organization's

| **33**

programs and finances, understand the climate in which the entity operates, avoid conflicts of interest, place the objectives of the organization above personal desires—and *govern*.

These emerging principles are also forcing structural changes in the operations of nonprofit organizations. No longer are the operative documents only articles of organization and bylaws. The law is beginning to demand organizational and management policies and procedures, conflict-of-interest policies, codes of ethics for senior officers, investment policies, and written program objectives and performance measures. Independent audit committees are becoming common. Lawyers, accountants, and other consultants must be hired directly by the board, not the executive staff. Compensation arrangements for top positions have to be approved at the board level. Independent auditors may have to be rotated periodically, such as every five years. Corporate executives may have to certify financial statements and perhaps annual information returns.

Federal tax or other law may contain rules on topics that previously have been the sole province of state law, such as the composition of the board, the compensation of the board, a requirement of some independent board members, and prohibition of board service by certain individuals. The IRS may be accorded the authority to require the removal of board members, officers, or employees in instances of law violations. The agency may also be given the ability to prohibit certain types of individuals from sitting on the boards of nonprofit organizations, particularly charitable ones.

Q 3:2   What are these emerging concepts?

The basics as to corporate governance principles are beginning to yield specific requirements. Much of what is inventoried next is not law, yet law (federal and state) on these points seems to be in the immediate offing. Here are the concepts that appear to be emerging:

- The governing board must establish basic organizational and management policies and procedures for the nonprofit organization, and review any proposed deviations.
- The board must establish, review, and approve program objectives and performance measures.
- The board must review and approve the organization's budget and financial objectives.
- The board must review and approve significant transactions, investments, and joint ventures.
- The board must oversee the conduct of the organization's programs and evaluate whether the programs are being properly managed.
- The board must review and approve the auditing and accounting principles and practices used in preparing the organization's financial statements (and, as noted, must retain and replace the organization's independent auditor).
- The board must establish and oversee a compliance program to address regulatory and liability concerns.

- The board must establish procedures to address complaints and prevent retaliation against whistleblowers.
- The board may be required to adopt a policy forbidding loans by nonprofit organizations to their directors and/or officers.
- The board may be required to adopt a policy pursuant to which a nonprofit organization's lawyers are required to report breaches of fiduciary responsibility to the chief executive.

Many of these precepts will be reflected in the annual information return, in the form of questions as to whether the organization has prepared certain documents and developed certain policies and procedures. That is, the foregoing and/or other requirements may have to be confirmed on the organization's annual return. Penalties for breach of board member duties (see Q 3:4–Q 3:6) may be introduced into federal law.

Congress, the IRS, or other entities may establish *best practices* for nonprofit organizations. In determining the nonprofit organization recipients of federal grants and contracts, the government agency involved may be required to give favorable consideration to organizations that are accredited by IRS-designated entities that establish best practices for tax-exempt organizations. The IRS and the Office of Personnel Management may establish best practices for charitable organizations participating in the Combined Federal Campaign. There may be a federal law prudent investor standard.

Q 3:3 What is the law as to board management responsibilities?

One of the principles that has been in the law for centuries is that trustees of charitable trusts are deemed to have the same obligation (duty of care) toward the assets of the trusts as they do toward their personal resources. Their responsibility is to act *prudently* in their handling of the nonprofit organization's income and assets. The trustees are *fiduciaries*; the law (for now, largely state law (see above)) imposes on them standards of conduct and management that, together, comprise principles of *fiduciary responsibility*. Most state law, whether statute or court opinions, imposes the standards of fiduciary responsibility on directors of nonprofit organizations, whether or not the organizations are trusts and whether or not they are charitable.

The contemporaneous general standard is that a member of the board of a nonprofit organization is required to perform his or her duties in good faith, with the care an ordinarily prudent person in a like position would exercise under similar circumstances, and in a manner the director reasonably believes to be in the best interests of the mission, goals, and purposes of the organization.

Thus, one of the main responsibilities of nonprofit board members is to maintain financial accountability and effective oversight of the organization they serve. Fiduciary duty requires board members to remain objective, unselfish, responsible, honest, trustworthy, and efficient in relation to the organization. Board members are stewards of the entity, and are expected to act for the good of the organization rather than for their personal aggrandizement. They need to exercise reasonable care in all decision making, without placing the nonprofit organization at unnecessary risk.

The duties of board members of nonprofit organizations can be encapsulated in the *three Ds*: duty of care, duty of loyalty, and duty of obedience. These are the legal standards against which all actions taken by directors are tested. They are collective duties adhering to the entire board and require the active participation of all board members. Accountability can be demonstrated by a showing of the effective discharge of these duties.

Q 3:4   What is the *duty of care*?

The duty of care requires that directors of a nonprofit organization be reasonably informed about the organization's activities, participate in the making of decisions, and do so in good faith and with the care of an ordinarily prudent person in similar circumstances. This duty, therefore, requires the individual board members to pay attention to the entity's activities and operations.

This duty is carried out by these acts:

- Attendance at meetings of the board and committees to which assigned
- Preparation for board meetings, such as by reviewing the agenda and reports
- Obtaining information, before voting, to make appropriate decisions
- Use of independent judgment
- Periodic examination of the credentials and performance of those who serve the organization
- Frequent review of the organization's finances and financial policies
- Oversight of compliance with important filing requirements, such as annual information returns (see Chapter 5)

Q 3:5   What is the *duty of loyalty*?

The duty of loyalty requires board members to exercise their power in the interest of the organization and not in their own interest or the interest of another entity, particularly one in which they have a formal relationship. When acting on behalf of the organization, board members must place the interests of the entity before their personal and professional interests.

This duty is carried out by these acts:

- Disclosure of any conflicts of interest
- Adherence to the organization's conflict-of-interest policy
- Avoidance of the use of corporate opportunities for the individual's personal gain or benefit
- Nondisclosure of confidential information about the organization

Although conflicts of interest are not inherently illegal—in fact, they can be common because board members are often affiliated with different entities in their communities—how the board reviews and evaluates them is important. Conflict-of-interest policies can help protect the organization and board members by establishing a process for disclosure and voting when situations arise in which board members may actually or potentially derive personal or professional benefit from the organization's activities (Q 2:29).

Q 3:6 What is the *duty of obedience*?

The duty of obedience requires that directors of a nonprofit organization comply with applicable federal, state, and local laws, adhere to the entity's articles of organization and bylaws, and remain guardians of the mission.

The duty of obedience is carried out by these acts:

- Compliance with all regulatory and reporting requirements, such as overseeing filing of annual information returns (see Q 3:5) and payment of employment taxes
- Examination and understanding of all documents governing the organization and its operation, such as the bylaws
- Making decisions that fall within the scope of the organization's mission and governing documents

Q 3:7 Can an organization owe a fiduciary duty to another organization?

Yes, in limited circumstances. There can be a *formal* fiduciary relationship in this setting, such as a financial institution serving as trustee of an entity, an organization serving as a or the general partner in a limited partnership, an arrangement between a principal and agent, and entities in a joint venture. An *informal* fiduciary relationship can arise from a moral or personal relationship of trust and confidence; this relationship can be established by a long relationship of working together toward a mutual goal, such as a joint acquisition and development of property. Informal fiduciary relationships are, however, infrequently recognized, because a fiduciary duty is an extraordinary one and is not lightly created.

Q 3:8 How does all of this relate to board member personal liability?

Generally, if a director carries out his or her duties faithfully, and in adherence to the three Ds, the director will not be found personally liable for a commission or omission. Personal liability (Chapter 2) can result when a trustee or director—and an officer or key employee—of a nonprofit organization breaches standards of fiduciary responsibility.

Q 3:9 How do these principles relate to watchdog agencies' principles?

From a compliance perspective, nonprofit organizations are principally concerned with operating in conformity with the law or rules of the accounting profession. There is, however, another consideration with which some organizations must also cope: the role and influence of the *watchdog agencies* that monitor and publicize the endeavors of nonprofit entities, principally those that solicit contributions from the public. These agencies have and enforce rules that sometimes are inconsistent with or attempt to supersede law requirements. For example, these standards may include requirements about board composition and frequency of board meetings.

A charity watchdog agency basically has three functions:

1. It writes standards to which charitable organizations are expected to adhere.
2. It enforces the standards, in part by rating organizations in relation to the standards and by making the ratings public.
3. It prepares and publicly circulates reports about charitable organizations.

The principal set of these standards is the *Standards for Charitable Accountability* issued by the Better Business Bureau Wise Giving Alliance (Alliance). Included is a rule that the board of the organization should have a policy of assessing, at least every two years, the organization's "performance and effectiveness and of determining future actions required to achieve its mission." Solicitation and other information materials should be "accurate, truthful, and not misleading." There should be an annual report, including a summary of the past year's program service accomplishments, basic financial information, and a roster of directors and officers.

The organization's board of directors should provide "adequate oversight" of its operations and staff. This entails regularly scheduled appraisals of the chief executive officer and sufficient accounting procedures. There should be a board-approved budget. The charity's expenses should be "accurately" reported in its financial statements.

Audited financial statements should be obtained for organizations with annual gross income in excess of $250,000. For charities with less gross income, a review by a certified public accountant is sufficient, although where annual income is less than $100,000, an internally produced financial statement is adequate. Financial statements should include a breakdown of expenses (such as salaries, travel, and postage) that also shows the portion of the expenses allocated to program, fundraising, and administration.

A charitable organization is to "avoid accumulating funds that could be used for current program activities." Net assets available for program use should not be more than the greater of three times the size of the prior year's expenses or three times the size of the current year's budget. "Material conflicting interests" involving the board and staff are prohibited. At least 65 percent of total expenses must be for program; no more than 35 percent of contributions may be expended for fundraising. An organization that cannot comply with these percentages is permitted to demonstrate that its use of funds is nonetheless reasonable.

The organization's board of directors must be comprised of at least five voting members. There must be at least three board meeting each year, "evenly spaced," with a majority in attendance. Only one of these meetings can be by conference call.

No more than one individual on the board or 10 percent of the board, whichever is greater, can be compensated by the organization. The chair and treasurer of the entity cannot be compensated. One of the transgressions embedded in these standards is failure to respond promptly to matters brought to the attention of the alliance or local better business bureaus.

The media, funders of charitable organizations, and governmental agencies tend to embrace and rely on standards such as these. As federal and state governments evolve best practices guidelines, it may be anticipated that some of these rules will take on the force of law. As an illustration of this probability, the staff of the Senate Finance Committee in mid-2004 prepared a discussion draft of proposals for reforms in the law of tax-exempt organizations, including best practices. These proposals included rules (or guidelines) that boards of these organizations be comprised of between 3 and 15 individuals, no more than 1 board member could be compensated by the organization, the board's chair or treasurer could not be compensated, and (in the case of public charities) at least 1 board member or one-fifth of the board would have to be independent. In addition, an individual who is not permitted to serve on the board of a publicly traded company due to a law violation could not be a member of the board of a tax-exempt organization. An individual convicted of a federal or state charge of criminal fraud or comparable offense could not serve on the board or be an officer of an exempt organization for five years following the conviction. An exempt organization and its officers who knowingly permitted such an individual to be a board member would be subject to a penalty.

Q 3:10 **How will the federal tax law be affected by emerging corporate governance principles?**

As of late 2004, it appears that the corporate governance movement will be reflected in the federal tax law; it is unclear as to how this will be manifested. Congress is beginning to explore the possibility of adding forms of corporate governance principles to federal law. The Senate Finance Committee, in particular, is actively pursuing this possibility, including development of "best practices" guidelines. The IRS also is preparing guidelines of this nature. The newly revised application for recognition of exemption filed by organizations that wish classification as charitable organizations (Q 4:7) is replete with questions that attempt to push (using the technique of shaming) applicant organizations into compliance with a variety of corporate governance principles. Moreover, the annual information return (Chapter 5) is being revised, with the likelihood the questions will be added that relate to these principles.

CHAPTER 4

Acquiring Tax-Exempt Status

There is often much discussion about the substantive law of nonprofit and tax-exempt organizations—and little focus on the process by which tax-exempt status is acquired. A great myth is that the IRS grants tax-exempt status. This is not the case—and the correct concept, concerning recognition of exempt status, is frequently puzzling. The government's forms in this setting appear daunting. Various and additional rules for charitable organizations add to the perplexity. The procedure can be quite understandable, however, albeit with a little help.

Here are the questions most frequently asked about acquisition of tax-exempt status—and the answers to them.

NONPROFIT AND EXEMPT ENTITIES

Q 4:1 Are all nonprofit organizations tax-exempt organizations?

No. The concept of the *nonprofit organization* (Q 1:1) is different from that of the *tax-exempt organization.* The term *tax-exempt organization* usually is used to mean an organization that is exempt, in whole or in part, from the federal income tax (Q 1:30).

To be tax-exempt, it is not sufficient that an organization be structured as a nonprofit organization. The organization must meet specific statutory and other regulatory criteria to qualify for the tax-exempt status (Q 1:31).

Some nonprofit organizations cannot qualify as certain types of tax-exempt organizations under the federal tax law. For example, a nonprofit organization that engages in a substantial amount of lobbying cannot be a tax-exempt charitable organization (Chapter 8). Some nonprofit organizations are ineligible for any category of tax exemption. For example, an organization that provides a substantial amount of commercial-type insurance cannot be a tax-exempt charitable or social welfare organization, and may not fit within any other classification of exempt entities.

Q 4:2 Are all tax-exempt organizations nonprofit organizations?

No. In almost all cases, however, a tax-exempt organization is a nonprofit entity. An example of an exception is an instrumentality of the U.S. government, which is likely to have been created by statute rather than as a nonprofit organization.

Q 4:3 Concerning tax exemption, what taxes are involved?

The term *tax-exempt organization* usually is used to mean an organization that is exempt, in whole or in part, from the federal income tax (Q 1:28). There are other federal taxes for which there may be an exemption, such as certain excise and social security taxes (Q 1:36).

State laws have several bases enabling an organization to qualify for a tax exemption. Taxes may be levied, at the state level, on income, franchise, sales, use, tangible property, intangible property, and real property. The law varies dramatically from state to state as to the categories of exemptions that are available.

Frequently, the law providing exemption for nonprofit organizations from state income tax tracks the rules for exemption from federal income tax. Therefore, the federal rules are usually the place to start.

EXEMPTION APPLICATION BASICS

Q 4:4 How does a *nonprofit* organization become a *tax-exempt* organization?

To be tax-exempt, an organization must meet the specific statutory and other regulatory criteria for the tax-exempt status it is seeking. This is true for both federal and state tax exemptions.

The process for acquiring one or more state tax exemptions varies from state to state. Usually the procedure entails filing a form, accompanied by an explanation of the organization's programs, so the tax authorities can assess the suitability of the organization for the exemption(s) being sought. The criteria for a tax exemption, however, are basically established by a statute.

The federal income tax exemption is available to organizations that satisfy the appropriate criteria stated in applicable provisions of the Internal Revenue Code. Thus, Congress ultimately grants the federal income tax (and other federal tax) exemption. The IRS does not grant tax-exempt status; the agency grants *recognition* of tax-exempt status.

NOTE: Most tax-exempt organizations under the federal tax law are those that are described in section 501(c)(1)–(27) of the Code. Other Code provisions that provide for income tax exemption are sections 521 and 526–529. Depending on how these provisions are parsed and the breadth of the term *tax-exempt organization* used, there are at least 64 categories of tax-exempt organizations provided for in the federal income tax law.

Consequently, whether an organization is entitled to tax exemption, on either an initial or an ongoing basis, is a matter of statutory law. It is Congress that, by statute, defines the categories of organization that are eligible for tax exemption, and it is Congress that determines whether a type of tax exemption should be continued.

OBSERVATION 1: It should come as no surprise that this matter of eligibility for tax exemption has been litigated. The government, however, always wins these cases—the courts repeatedly have held that Congress has great discretion in this area. For example, in creating a category of tax exemption for cooperative hospital service organizations, Congress had the authority to exclude nonprofit laundry organizations. Likewise, Congress is able to eliminate a category of tax exemption, such as when it denied tax exemption to certain organizations that provide commercial-type insurance and to previously exempt trusts under qualified group legal services plans.

OBSERVATION 2: The Fifth Amendment guarantee of equal protection is not available here: Congress can make eligibility for tax exemption pivot on the date the entity was created. Examples: exempt insurers of financial deposits must be organized before September 1, 1957; exempt funds underlying certain pension plans must be created before June 25, 1959; and certain exempt workers' compensation reinsurance organizations must be established before June 1, 1996. Indeed, one of the exemption categories for veterans' organizations requires that the entity be formed before 1880.

Q 4:5 Is a nonprofit organization required to apply to the IRS for tax-exempt status?

There are two aspects of this answer. A very literal answer to the question is no. This is because, as noted, the IRS does not grant tax-exempt status; that is a tax feature of an organization that is available to it by operation of law (Q 4:4).

What the IRS does is grant *recognition* of tax-exempt status. This role of the IRS in recognizing the exempt status of organizations is part of its overall practice of evaluating the tax status of organizations.

Q 4:6 What does *recognition* of tax exemption mean?

Eligibility for tax-exempt status is different from *recognition* of that status (Q 4:2). When the IRS *recognizes* the exempt status of an organization, it makes a written determination that the entity constitutes a tax-exempt organization. When exercising this function, the IRS reviews, analyzes, and interprets the law, and agrees with the organization that it is exempt. The process is almost always begun by the organization's filing an application for recognition of tax-exempt status with the IRS.

Q 4:7 Is an organization required to seek recognition of exempt status from the IRS?

As a general rule, an organization desiring tax-exempt status pursuant to the federal tax law is not *required* to secure recognition of tax exemption from the IRS. Nonetheless, an organization *may*, on its own volition, seek recognition of tax-exempt status.

OBSERVATION: Organizations frequently seek rulings and like determinations from the federal government, including the IRS. There are many factors to take into account in making this judgment, including the complexity of the facts and the available time. The advantages to be gained by obtaining recognition of exempt status include the comfort of knowing that the IRS agrees that the organization qualifies, the status as a pathway to state tax exemption(s), and eligibility for various nonprofit mailing privileges.

There are, however, two categories of organizations that are required by law to seek recognition of tax-exempt status from the IRS. Most charitable organizations must seek this recognition. Likewise, certain employee benefit organizations must seek exemption recognition. Moreover, an organization that wishes to be a central organization providing tax exemption on a group basis for subordinate organizations must first obtain recognition of its own tax-exempt status (Q 4:48).

For this purpose, a *charitable organization* is an entity that is organized and operated primarily for purposes such as charitable, educational, scientific, and religious. This category also includes organizations that foster national or international amateur sports competition, prevent cruelty to children or animals, and test for public safety, as well as cooperative hospital service organizations and cooperative service organizations of operating educational organizations. These entities are collectively referenced in section 501(c)(3) of the Internal Revenue Code.

By contrast, other tax-exempt organizations include social welfare organizations, which are often advocacy organizations (section 501(c)(4)), labor organizations (section 501(c)(5)), membership associations (section 501(c)(6)), and political organizations (section 527).

Q 4:8 Are there any exemptions from the recognition requirement?

Yes. The following *charitable* organizations can be tax-exempt without having to file an application for recognition of tax exemption: (1) organizations (other than private foundations) that have gross receipts that normally are not in excess of $5,000 annually, and (2) churches (including synagogues and mosques), interchurch organizations, local units of a church, conventions and associations of churches, and integrated auxiliaries of churches.

Most other types of tax-exempt organizations are not *required* to obtain recognition of exempt status. In this category are social welfare organizations, labor organizations, trade and business associations, social clubs, fraternal groups, and veterans' organizations (Q 4:7). These entities may nonetheless seek recognition of tax-exempt status.

TIP: An organization that is not required to obtain recognition of tax-exempt status should think about doing it anyway. For the most part, the considerations are the same as those underlying the potential for any other ruling request. That is, the organization may simply want the comfort of having the IRS on record as agreeing with its qualification for tax exemption.

Q 4:9 What is the procedure for seeking recognition of tax-exempt status?

The IRS has promulgated detailed rules by which a ruling as to recognition of exemption is to be sought.

NOTE: A recognition of exemption by the IRS from an office outside Washington, DC, is termed a *determination letter*. This type of recognition from the National Office of the IRS in Washington, DC, is termed a *ruling*. In practice, both of these types of determinations are often generically referred to as *rulings*—and that will frequently be the case in this discussion.

In almost all instances, the process is begun by the filing of an application for recognition of tax-exempt status. These applications are available as IRS forms. An organization seeking recognition of exemption as a charitable organization should file Form 1023. Nearly all other applicant organizations file Form 1024, although farmers, fruit growers, and like associations file Form 1028. For a few categories of exempt organizations, there is no application form by which to seek recognition of tax exemption; in that case, the request is made by letter.

This application includes a description of the purposes and activities of the organization, its fundraising plans, the composition of its board of directors, its compensation practices, and financial information. The organization's articles of organization and bylaws and perhaps other documents must be attached.

For charitable organizations, this procedure also involves classification as charitable entities for purposes of the charitable giving rules (see Q 1:41–Q 1:44) and categorization as public charities or private foundations (see Chapter 10).

Q 4:10 Where are these applications filed?

Historically, applications for recognition of exemption were filed with the appropriate IRS key district director's office, determined in relation to the district in which the principal place of business of the organization was located. As part of the reorganization of the IRS, however, applications for recognition of exemption are filed with the IRS Service Center in Cincinnati, Ohio. Infrequently, there will be occasion to file the application with the National Office of the IRS.

Q 4:11 How long does it take the IRS to process an exemption application?

It is difficult to generalize as to the length of time required by the IRS to process an application for recognition of tax exemption. Three of the critical factors are the complexity and/or sensitivity of the case, the completeness of the application (and related documents), and the workload of the IRS representative who will be reviewing the file and preparing the ruling.

For rather straightforward filings, the organization should plan on an IRS processing period of about three to six months. The IRS is likely to have questions; this can lengthen the period. Once in a while, a case is referred to the IRS's National Office, and that development can have a bearing on the overall time period.

NOTE: It is very difficult to predict how long it will take for a ruling (a favorable one) to be issued in individual filings. An application virtually brimming with hearty exempt organization issues can sail through the process, without any IRS inquiries, and result in a ruling in a few weeks. Yet a simple case, one lacking in any issues of substance, can be worried over by an IRS exempt organizations specialist for an agonizingly long period of time.

There is a process by which the applicant organization can request the IRS to expedite the processing of the application. For this to work, the organization must convince the IRS that there is a substantive reason as to why its application should be considered out of order (such as a large gift or grant that will be lost if recognition is not quickly extended). Understandably, out of overall fairness, the IRS is reluctant to grant expedited consideration of these applications, so the case for a quick processing must be a persuasive one.

TIP: The IRS has been known to formally decline to expedite consideration of an exemption application (for the record)—and then process it speedily anyway.

Q 4:12 How long does an exemption ruling remain in effect?

These rulings are not accompanied by an expiration date. Generally, an organization whose tax-exempt status has been recognized by the IRS can rely on that determination as long as there are no substantial changes in its character, purposes, or methods of operation. Of course, a change in the law can void a ruling or cause a reevaluation of it.

> **NOTE:** Determining whether one of these changes is *substantial* is not always easy and can be a matter of considerable judgment. An applicant organization should endeavor to disclose as much information as is reasonably possible, to preclude a later contention that some material fact was omitted. Once the ruling is obtained, it is a recommended practice to periodically review the application, to see whether it reflects current programs and other practices. A ruling from the IRS is only as valid as the facts on which it is based—and a substantial change in purposes and the like could void or at least threaten the validity of the ruling.

Q 4:13 What happens if there is a substantial change in an organization's character, purposes, or methods of operation?

If there is a substantial change in an organization's character, purposes, or methods of operation, the rule of law is that the IRS is to be notified of the change or changes—obviously so that the IRS can reevaluate the organization's exempt status. This notification is supposed to take place in proximity to the change.

In practice, however, this rule is rarely followed. As the years go by, organizations can evolve into and out of varying programs and purposes, and/or change management and methods of operation, and never give a thought to what was said in the exemption application (or, for that matter, in the articles of organization or bylaws). This is not a good practice; a periodic review in this regard is recommended. There are organizations in operation today that have strayed so far from their original purposes and operations, and into nonexempt activities, that they would have their exempt status revoked were the IRS to learn the facts.

> **REMINDER:** Even if these changes are not substantial, they are to be reported to the IRS as part of the filing of the annual information return (Q 5:29).

GENERAL PROCEDURES

Q 4:14 Will the IRS issue a ruling to an organization in advance of its operations?

In general, yes. The basic rule is this: a determination letter or ruling (Q 4:9) will be issued by the IRS to an organization where its application for recognition of exemption and supporting documents establish that it meets the requirements of the category of exemption that it claimed. Tax-exempt status for an organization will be recognized by the IRS in advance of operations where the entity's proposed activities are described in sufficient detail to permit a conclusion that the organization will clearly meet the pertinent statutory requirements.

TIP: The organization should not merely restate its purposes or state only that its proposed activities will be in furtherance of the organization's purposes. This approach does not satisfy the requirements and serves only to put the IRS on notice that the application has been prepared by those who lack experience with the rules.

The applicant organization is expected to fully describe the activities in which it expects to engage, including the standards, criteria, procedures, or other means adopted or planned for carrying out the activities, the anticipated sources of receipts, and the nature of contemplated expenditures.

Where an organization cannot demonstrate, to the satisfaction of the IRS (Q 4:15), that its proposed activities will qualify it for recognition of exemption, a record of actual operations may be required before a ruling is issued.

Q 4:15 How much information must be provided to the IRS?

There is no precise standard in this regard. As noted, the IRS expects "sufficient details" and "full descriptions" (Q 4:14). Thus, an organization that took this issue to court lost in its bid to acquire recognition of exemption because it "failed to supply such information as would enable a conclusion that when operational, if ever, . . . [the organization] will conduct all of its activities in a manner which will accomplish its exempt purposes." The entity was chided by the court for offering only "vague generalizations" about its ostensibly planned activities.

Likewise, this court concluded that an organization could not be exempt, because it did not provide a "meaningful explanation" of its activities to the IRS. In another instance, a court found that an organization's failure to respond "completely or candidly" to many of the inquiries of the IRS precluded it from receiving a determination as to its tax-exempt status.

An organization is considered to have made the required "threshold showing," however, where it describes its activities in "sufficient detail" to permit a conclusion that the entity will meet the pertinent requirements, particularly where it answered all of the questions propounded by the IRS.

NOTE: The following statements by two courts summarize what this aspect of the process comes down to: the law "requires that the organization establish measurable standards and criteria for its operation as an exempt organization"; yet this standard does not necessitate "some sort of metaphysical proof of future events."

TIP: This is not the time to hold back information; it is foolish for an organization to fail to be recognized as an exempt organization on the ground that it refused to submit suitable information. The organization should be willing to tell its story fully, treating the application as a business plan (Q 4:18). This document is, after all, a public one (Q 18:9), and its proper preparation should be regarded as a first step in presenting the organization's justification for existence and tax-exempt status.

This application process is, in essence, a burden-of-proof issue—with the burden on the would-be exempt organization. Moreover, there is a negative presumption: when the representatives of an organization fail to submit the appropriate factual information to the IRS, an inference arises that the facts involved would denigrate the organization's cause.

Q 4:16 What happens if the IRS decides the application is incomplete?

If an application for recognition of tax exemption does not contain the requisite information, IRS procedures authorize it to return the application to the applicant organization without considering it on its merits.

 **NOTE:** As noted, the application will be returned to the organization—not to anyone on a power of attorney (Form 2848) (such as a lawyer or accountant), with obvious implications. A competent representative of a nonprofit organization in this regard should have no experience with this rule.

The application for recognition of tax exemption as submitted by a would-be exempt organization will not be processed by the IRS until the application is at least *substantially completed*.

Q 4:17 What is a *substantially completed* application?

An application for recognition of exemption is a substantially completed one when it

1. Is signed by an authorized individual
2. Includes an employer identification number
3. Includes information regarding any previously filed federal income tax and/or exempt organization information returns
4. Includes a statement of receipts and expenditures and a balance sheet for the current year and the three preceding years (or the years the organization has been in existence, if less than four years), although if the organization has not yet commenced operations, or has not completed one full accounting period, a proposed budget for two full accounting periods, and a current statement of assets and liabilities is acceptable
5. Includes a narrative statement of proposed activities and a narrative description of anticipated receipts and contemplated expenditures
6. Includes a copy of the document by which the organization was established, signed by a principal officer or is accompanied by a written declaration signed by an authorized individual certifying that the document is a complete and accurate copy of the original or otherwise meets the requirement that it be a conformed copy
7. If the organizing document is a set of articles of incorporation, includes evidence that it was filed with and approved by an appropriate state official

(such as a copy of the certificate of incorporation) or includes a copy of the articles of incorporation accompanied by a written declaration signed by an authorized individual that the copy is a complete and accurate copy of the original document that was filed with and approved by the state, and stating the date of filing with the state

8. If the organization has adopted bylaws, includes a current copy of that document, certified as being current by an authorized individual

9. Is accompanied by the correct user fee (Q 4:20)

The application for recognition of exemption submitted by charitable organizations requests information concerning the composition of the entity's governing body, any relationship with other organizations, the nature of its fundraising program, and a variety of other matters.

Q 4:18 Is the application for recognition of exemption an important document for an exempt organization?

Yes, this application is a significant legal document for an exempt organization, and it should be prepared and retained accordingly.

OBSERVATION: Thirty-five years of experience in this field suggests that an unduly high proportion of exempt organizations cannot locate a copy of their application for recognition of tax exemption.

The proper preparation of an application for recognition of tax exemption involves far more than merely responding to the questions on a government form. It is a process not unlike the preparation of a prospectus for a business in conformity with the securities law requirements. Every statement made in the application should be carefully considered. Some of the questions may force the applicant organization to focus on matters that solid management practices should cause it to consider, even in the absence of the application requirements. The application is a nicely constructed and factually sweeping document, and it should be approached and prepared with care and respect.

The prime objectives in this regard must be accuracy and completeness; it is essential that all material facts be correctly and fully stated (Q 4:13). Of course, the determination as to which facts are material and the marshaling of these facts requires judgment. Moreover, the manner in which the answers are phrased can be extremely significant; this exercise can be more one of art than of science.

The preparer or reviewer of the application should be able to anticipate the concerns the contents of the application may cause the IRS and to see that the application is properly prepared, while simultaneously minimizing the likelihood of conflict with the IRS. Organizations that are entitled to tax-exempt status have been denied recognition of exemption by the IRS, or have caused the process of gaining recognition to be more protracted, because of unartful phraseologies in the application that motivated the IRS to muster a case that the organization does not qualify for exemption.

Therefore, the application for recognition of tax exemption should be regarded as an important legal document and prepared accordingly. The fact that the application is available for public inspection (Q 18:9) only underscores the need for thoughtful preparation.

Q 4:19   How long does it take to prepare an application for recognition of tax exemption?

It is impossible to generalize on this point. The pertinent factors include, as noted, the complexity of the organization, the extent to which the factual information and supporting documents are readily available, and the skill and expertise of those who prepare and review the document.

Nonetheless, apparently there is a way to produce some averages of time expenditures in this regard. Thus, in conjunction with the Form 1023 (Q 4:35), it is the view of the IRS that the estimated average time required to keep records so as to be able to prepare the application (*not* including any schedules) is 89 hours and 26 minutes. If every schedule had to be prepared (Schedules A–H), another 87 hours would be required. (The complexity of the new form is illustrated by the fact that the previous one required about 55 hours of record keeping.) The agency estimates that learning about the law or the form requires 5 hours and 10 minutes, and preparation of the form entails 9 hours and 39 minutes.

NOTE: It may be conceded that, to use the hackneyed phrase, the law of tax-exempt organizations is not rocket science. Yet surely it takes a tad more than 5 hours to learn the law needed to properly prepare the application.

Q 4:20   Is there a charge for the processing of an application for recognition of exemption?

Yes, the IRS levies a user fee for processing an organization's application for recognition of exemption. This fee must be paid at the time of the filing of the application.

Under the current schedule, the fee for the processing of one of these applications is $500, where the applicant has gross receipts that annually exceed $10,000. For smaller organizations, the fee is $150. A group exemption (Q 4:47) letter fee is $500.

Q 4:21   Can an application for recognition of exemption be referred to the National Office of the IRS?

Yes. The IRS representative considering the application must refer to the National Office of the IRS an application for recognition of tax exemption that (1) presents questions the answers to which are not specifically covered by the Internal Revenue

Code, Department of Treasury regulations, an IRS revenue ruling, or court decision published in the IRS's *Internal Revenue Bulletin*, or (2) has been specifically reserved by an IRS revenue procedure and/or *Internal Revenue Manual* instructions for handling by the National Office for purposes of establishing uniformity or centralized control of designated categories of cases. In these instances, the National Office is to consider the application, issue a ruling directly to the organization, and send a copy of the ruling to the appropriate IRS office.

NOTE: One of the purposes of the recent centralization efforts by the IRS in this context (Q 4:10) is to centralize the processing of exemption applications so as to consolidate expertise and increase the efficiency of the process.

Q 4:22 Can the applicant organization seek the assistance of the National Office?

Yes. If, during the course of consideration of an application for recognition of tax exemption, an applicant organization believes that its case involves an issue as to which there is no published precedent, the organization may ask the IRS to request *technical advice* from the National Office of the IRS.

Q 4:23 Can an application for recognition of exemption be withdrawn?

Yes. An application for recognition of tax exemption filed with the IRS may be withdrawn, upon the written request of an authorized representative of the organization, at any time prior to the issuance of an initial adverse ruling. When an application is withdrawn, it and all supporting documents are retained by the IRS.

Q 4:24 If an organization is denied recognition of exemption, may it later reapply?

Absolutely—the key is correction of the problem or problems that caused the denial in the first instance.

An organization may reapply for recognition of tax exemption if it was previously denied recognition, where the facts involved are materially changed so that the organization has come into compliance with the applicable requirements. For example, a charitable organization that was refused recognition of exemption because of excessive lobbying activities, by reason of the expenditure test, may subsequently reapply for recognition of exemption for any tax year following the first tax year as to which the recognition was denied. Essentially, the reapplication form must include information demonstrating that the organization was in compliance with the law during the full tax year immediately preceding the date of reapplication and that the organization will not knowingly operate in a manner that would disqualify it from exemption.

Q 4:25 What is the effective date of these rulings?

A determination letter or ruling recognizing tax exemption usually is effective as of the date of formation of the organization, where its purposes and activities during the period prior to the date of the determination letter or ruling were consistent with the requirements for tax exemption.

If the organization is required to alter its activities or to make substantive amendments to its enabling instrument, the determination letter or ruling recognizing its tax-exempt status is effective as of the date specified in the determination letter or ruling. If a nonsubstantive amendment is made, tax exemption ordinarily is recognized as of the date the entity was formed.

Q 4:26 To what extent can the organization rely on its ruling?

In general, an organization can rely on a determination letter or ruling from the IRS recognizing its tax exemption. Reliance is not available, however, if there is a material change, inconsistent with tax exemption, in the character, purpose, or method of operation of the organization (Q 4:13).

Q 4:27 How does an organization remain tax-exempt?

The simple answer is that an organization remains tax-exempt by staying in compliance with the rules governing the particular category of tax exemption. These rules are the most pronounced for charitable organizations.

Thus, for a charitable organization to remain tax-exempt, it must meet a variety of tests on an ongoing basis, including the organizational requirements, the private inurement and private benefit limitations (Chapter 6), the lobbying restrictions (Chapter 8), the political campaign activities prohibition (Chapter 9), and avoidance of too many unrelated business activities (Chapter 14).

Q 4:28 When might an organization's tax exemption be revoked?

In general, an organization's tax exemption is revoked when the IRS determines that the organization was materially out of compliance with one or more of the requirements underlying its tax-exempt status. For example, in the case of a charitable organization, the IRS may have concluded that it engaged in a private inurement transaction or a political campaign activity.

The IRS learns of bases for revocation of tax exemption in a variety of ways. The information may come to it as the result of an audit. Someone may have provided to the IRS information involving some wrongdoing. Often the IRS obtains information leading to a revocation from the popular media (see Q 19:5).

Q 4:29 If an organization loses its tax-exempt status, can it reacquire it?

Generally, yes. An organization qualifies for tax-exempt status if it meets the statutory criteria for the particular category of exempt organization involved (Q 1:31). If it fails to satisfy the criteria, it no longer qualifies for exemption (Q 1:34). If it resumes qualification, then its tax-exempt status must be restored. These analyses are made on a year-by-year basis.

For example, if a tax-exempt social welfare organization lost its tax-exempt status for a year because it earned too much unrelated business income, it could reacquire that exempt status for subsequent years by sufficiently reducing the amount of unrelated income or by transferring the unrelated business(es) to a for-profit subsidiary (see Chapter 15).

For tax-exempt organizations that *must* seek recognition of tax-exempt status (Q 1:31), such as charitable organizations, the process is more complex. When these exempt organizations lose their tax exemption, they can reacquire it, but they must reapply for recognition of exemption.

For example, if a charitable organization lost its tax-exempt status for a year because of too much lobbying activity, it could reacquire an exempt status for subsequent years by sufficiently reducing its attempts to influence legislation or by transferring the lobbying function to a related social welfare organization (Q 4:18, Chapter 15). The organization would, however, have to formally reapply for its exempt classification.

TIP: A charitable organization in this circumstance may be able to remain tax-exempt for the years in which its revocation of exemption as a charity are in effect. The organization undoubtedly could qualify as a social welfare organization during that period, and social welfare organizations are not required to seek recognition of tax-exempt status. Classification as a social welfare organization would be replaced by classification as a charitable organization once the new determination letter took effect. But contributions to the organization would not be deductible as charitable gifts during the period it was categorized as a tax-exempt social welfare organization.

Q 4:30   Are tax-exempt organizations completely immune from taxation?

No. Despite the term, a tax-exempt organization is not completely free from the prospect of taxation. Thus, nearly all exempt organizations are subject to tax on their unrelated business taxable income (see Chapter 14). Many types of tax-exempt organizations are subject to a tax if they engage in certain types of political activities (see Q 9:18). Public charities can be taxable if they undertake a substantial amount of lobbying activities (Q 8:13, Q 8:19) or if they participate in a political campaign (Q 9:8). Private foundations must pay an excise tax on their net investment income and are susceptible to a host of other excise taxes (Q 11:6). Organizations such as social clubs, political organizations, and homeowners' organizations are taxable on their net investment income. State law also can impose taxes on entities otherwise classified as tax-exempt organizations.

Q 4:31 **In view of the massive amount of government regulation of nonprofit organizations, why don't they forfeit tax-exempt status and be treated for tax purposes the same as for-profit organizations?**

For some nonprofit organizations, this course of action could be taken, looked at purely from a tax standpoint. This is because, for most of these entities, their expenses equal or exceed their income, so that there would not be any net taxable income in any event. Nonetheless, these organizations are not legally functioning on a *for-profit* basis (Q 1:1). At the same time, an organization can be nonprofit and yet taxable.

Charitable and other organizations that are eligible to receive tax-deductible contributions would forfeit this tax feature if they were to convert to for-profit status (assuming they could as a matter of law). Gifts are not forms of income, however, so contributions would not be taxable income should a charitable entity choose to be a nonexempt organization.

CAUTION: There are special rules in this regard for membership groups. A nonexempt membership organization is not permitted simply to net all income with all expenses for tax purposes. Instead, expenses can only be deducted against income to which they functionally relate. Where expenses of a certain function exceed the income generated by that function, the excess expenses may not be offset against income from the function. This can cause taxable income where there would not be taxable income if all expenses were netted against all income.

Q 4:32 **What are the basic considerations to take into account in deciding whether an organization should be exempt as a charitable organization or a social welfare organization?**

The essential distinction between a charitable (including educational, scientific, and the like) organization and an entity qualifying as a social welfare organization is that the charitable entity is operated primarily for philanthropic and similar purposes, while the social welfare organization is likely to be an advocacy entity. Thus, the principal function of a social welfare organization may well be attempts to influence legislation or other programs designed to shape the outcome of public policy on one or more issues, such as by written materials (including propaganda), demonstrations, and boycotts. While a charitable organization may be able to engage in forms of advocacy to a certain extent, the social welfare organization usually is one that undertakes more advocacy than the federal law will tolerate for charitable organizations. Nearly every charitable organization can qualify as an exempt social welfare organization; the reverse is often not the case.

Under the federal tax laws, both types of organizations are tax-exempt. Only charitable entities, however, are eligible to receive tax-deductible charitable contributions (Q 12:1).

Q 4:33 **What are the basic considerations to take into account in deciding whether an organization should be exempt as a charitable entity or a business league?**

The essential distinction between a charitable (including educational, scientific, and the like) organization and an association qualifying as a business league is that the charitable entity is operated primarily for the benefit of the public, or a considerable segment of it, while the business league is operated principally for the advancement of its members. Thus, for example, although an organization such as a bar association or medical society may have some public benefit programs (such as community services or the maintenance of a library), in the view of the IRS its primary purpose is to improve practice conditions for lawyers or physicians. Thus, there is often a presumption that an association of members who are individuals is a business league.

In fact, however, a membership structure should not be the determining factor. An organization can be principally charitable in nature and still have a membership. This fact is evidenced by a wide variety of religious, educational, and scientific organizations (the latter including professional societies).

Under the federal tax laws, both types of organizations are tax-exempt. Only charitable entities are eligible to receive tax-deductible charitable contributions (Q 12:1).

Q 4:34 **When should a tax-exempt organization consider the establishment of a related foundation?**

In most instances, an exempt organization that establishes a related foundation is a noncharitable tax-exempt entity. It is most common for social welfare organizations and business leagues to do this, although nearly every type of exempt organization can have a related "foundation." The purpose of the foundation is to house charitable, educational, and similar functions in a separate entity, so that these functions can be supported by grants and deductible contributions. Another model is for the charitable and similar programs to be conducted in the noncharitable exempt "parent," with the foundation functioning essentially as a fundraising vehicle.

NOTE: There is no reason why a foundation of this nature should be a private foundation. These entities usually are publicly supported charities or supporting organizations (see Chapter 10).

Thus, the prime reason for use of a related foundation is to best utilize the federal tax law distinctions, but the parent organization may have other reasons for establishing the foundation. For example, a second reason may be concentration of the fundraising function in a separate entity that has its own governing board and bank account. Because the fundraising program may be better managed with this approach, many charitable organizations (such as universities and hospitals) utilize separate fundraising (or development) foundations.

A third reason for this approach may be that the foundation's public charity tax status is preferable to that of the parent organization. For example, the parent charitable organization may be ineligible to maintain a pooled income fund, while the charitable foundation has that eligibility (Q 12:26).

APPLICATION FORM

Q 4:35 What are the contents of the application?

As noted, there is more than one application form (Q 4:5). This answer pertains to the application filed by charitable organizations (Form 1023), inasmuch as it is the most extensive one.

NOTE: The reader may wish to have a copy of Form 1023 (October 2004) at hand while reviewing this portion of the chapter. The applications, part of a packet that includes general instructions as to their preparation, are available from the IRS and various commercial services and on the Internet.

This substantially revamped application, consisting of 11 parts, is designed to streamline the application process for charitable organizations, increase the amount of information provided to the IRS, and enable the agency to spot potentially abusive charities.

Q 4:36 What is required in Part I of Form 1023?

Part I of the Form 1023 requests basic information about the applicant organization and its representatives. Here the organization supplies its name, address, employer identification number, date of formation, Web site address, and accounting period. If the organization is formed under the laws of a foreign country, the country must be identified.

The name and telephone number of the applicant organization's primary contact person must be provided. If the organization is represented by an *authorized representative* (such as a lawyer or accountant), the representative's name, and the name and address of the representative's firm, must be provided. A power of attorney (Form 2848) must be included if the organization wants the IRS to communicate with the representative.

If a person—who is not a trustee, director, officer, employee, or authorized representative of the organization—is paid, or promised payment, to help plan, manage, or advise the organization about its structure, activities, or its financial and tax matters, the person's name, the name and address of the person's firm, the amounts paid or promised to be paid, and a description of the person's role must be provided.

Q 4:37   What is required in Part II of Form 1023?

Part II of the Form 1023 requests information about the applicant organization's structure. The organization must be a corporation, a limited liability company, an unincorporated association, or a trust. A copy of the organization's articles of organization (articles of incorporation, articles of organization, constitution, trust agreement, or similar document) must be attached, including any amendments. If the organization has adopted bylaws, a copy of that document must also be provided.

Q 4:38   What is required in Part III of Form 1023?

Part III of the Form 1023 is designed to ensure that the applicant organization's organizing document contains the required provisions. This portion of the form focuses on the need for a correctly framed statement of purposes and a provision that states that net assets will be distributed for charitable purposes should the organization dissolve.

Q 4:39   What is required in Part IV of Form 1023?

Part IV of the Form 1023 requires an attachment describing the applicant organization's past, present, and planned activities. The organization is invited to attach representative copies of newsletters, brochures, and similar documents for supporting details. Because the application is accessible by the public (Q 13:11–Q 13:19), the organization is reminded that this statement of activities should be "thorough and accurate."

Q 4:40   What is required in Part V of Form 1023?

Part V of the Form 1023 requires information about the compensation and other financial arrangements with the applicant organization's trustees, directors, officers, employees, and independent contractors.

The organization is required to list the names, titles, and mailing addresses of its trustees, directors, and officers. Their total annual compensation or proposed compensation for all services to the organization must be stated.

The organization must also list the names, titles, mailing addresses, and compensation amounts of each of its five highest compensated employees who receive or will receive compensation of more than $50,000 annually. Likewise, the organization must provide the names, names of businesses, mailing addresses, and compensation amounts of its five highest compensated independent contractors that receive or will receive compensation of more than $50,000 annually.

The organization must provide information as to whether any of its trustees, directors, or officers are related to each other through family or business relationships. It must describe any business relationship with any of its trustees, directors, or officers other than through their position as such. There must be an explanation if any of the trustees, directors, or officers are related to the organization's highest-compensated employees or highest-compensated independent contractors through family or business relationships.

For each of the trustees, directors, officers, highest-compensated employees, and highest-compensated independent contractors, the organization must provide their name, qualification, average hours worked, and duties. There must be an explanation if any of its trustees, directors, officers, highest-compensated employees, and highest-compensated independent contractors receive compensation from any other organization (tax-exempt or taxable) that is related to the organization through common control.

The organization is required to identify the practices it uses in establishing the compensation of its trustees, directors, officers, highest-compensated employees, and highest-compensated independent contractors. There are six recommended practices, including adherence to a conflict-of-interest policy, documentation of compensation arrangements, and/or use of compensation surveys or written offers from similarly situated organizations. If any of these practices are not followed, the organization is required to describe how it sets compensation for these persons.

The organization must explain whether it has adopted a conflict-of-interest policy. (A sample policy is provided and recommended.) If such a policy has not been adopted, the organization must explain the procedures it follows to ensure that persons who have a conflict of interest will not have influence over the organization when setting their compensation and/or regarding business deals with themselves.

The organization is required to describe any compensation arrangements involving nonfixed payments (such as bonuses and revenue-based payments) with any of its trustees, directors, officers, highest-compensated employees, or highest-compensated independent contractors. If these arrangements exist, the organization must provide information such as how the amounts are determined, who is eligible for the payments, whether a limitation is placed on total compensation, and how reasonableness of compensation is determined. Information must be provided in connection with any other employees that receive annual nonfixed payments in excess of $50,000.

Information must be provided concerning any purchases or sales of goods, services, or assets from or to any trustees, directors, officers, highest-compensated employees, or highest-compensated independent contractors. Likewise, information must be provided as to any leases, other contracts, loans, or other arrangements with these persons or with organizations in which these persons have an interest (more than 35 percent) or serve as directors or officers.

Q 4:41 What is required in Part VI of Form 1023?

Part VI of the Form 1023 requires the applicant organization to (1) describe any program involving the provision of goods, services, or funds to individuals or organizations; (2) explain whether, and if so how, any program limits the provision of goods, services, or funds to a specific individual or group of specific individuals; and (3) explain whether, and if so how, any individuals who receive goods, services, or funds through the organization's programs have a family or business relationship with any trustee, director, officer, highest-compensated employee, or highest-compensated independent contractor.

Q 4:42 **What is required in Part VII of Form 1023?**

Part VII of the Form 1023 relates to the history of the applicant organization. The organization must explain whether it has taken or will take over the activities of another organization, took over at least 25 percent of the fair market value of the net assets of another organization, or was established as the result of a conversion of an organization from for-profit to nonprofit status. The existence of any of these circumstances requires a filing of Schedule G.

If the organization is submitting the application more than 27 months after the end of the month in which it was legally formed, filing of Schedule E is required.

Q 4:43 **What is required in Part VIII of Form 1023?**

The applicant organization is required to submit information concerning many types of past, present, and planned activities, including:

- Support of or opposition to candidates in political campaigns (Chapter 9)
- Attempts to influence legislation (Chapter 8)
- Operation of bingo or other gaming activities
- Fundraising (Chapter 13), including mail solicitations; vehicle, boat, airplane, or similar contributions; foundation or government grant solicitations; and Web site donations
- Utilization of donor-advised funds (Q 10:30)
- Affiliation with a governmental unit
- Engagement in economic development
- Development of the organization's facilities
- Management of the organization's activities or facilities
- Involvement in any joint ventures (Chapter 16)
- Publishing, ownership of, or rights in intellectual property
- Acceptance of contributions of property such as real estate, conservation easements, intellectual property (Q 12:37–Q 12:40), vehicles (Q 12:41–Q 12:44), or collectibles
- Operation in one or more foreign countries
- Making of grants, loans, or other distributions to organizations, including foreign entities
- Close connection with any organization
- Operation as a school (Schedule B required)
- Operation as a hospital or other medical care facility (Schedule C required)
- Provision of housing for low-income individuals, the elderly, or the handicapped (Schedule F required)
- Provision of scholarships, fellowships, educational loans, and the like (Schedule H required)

Q 4:44 **What is required in Part IX of Form 1023?**

Part IX of the Form 1023 concerns financial data (including a statement of revenue and expenses) of the applicant organization. If the organization has been in existence for four or more years, the required information is that for the most recent four years. If the organization has been in existence for more than one year and less than four years, the information is that for each year of existence and a good-faith estimate of finances for the other years (up to three). If the organization has been in existence for less than one year, it must provide good-faith projections of its finances for the current year and the two subsequent years. A balance sheet for the most recently completed year is also required.

Q 4:45 What is required in Part X of Form 1023?

Part X of the Form 1023 pertains to the organization's public charity status (Chapter 10). The organization must identify the type of public charity status it is requesting or answer questions if it is a standard private foundation or private operating foundation. The organization, in this part, requests an advance ruling (Q 10:9) or definitive ruling (Q 10:11).

Q 4:46 What is required in Part XI of Form 1023?

Part XI of Form 1023 concern the user fee payment. (This section of the application replaced the prior user fee form, Form 8718.) If the organization's average annual gross receipts have exceeded or will exceed $10,000 annually over a four-year period, the user fee is $500. Otherwise, the fee is $150.

Q 4:47 What happens when the requested ruling as to tax-exempt status is not granted?

The IRS has developed an extensive set of procedural rules to follow, should the requested ruling be adverse to the organization. These procedures, which are somewhat outdated as a result of the reorganization and consolidation of the agency (Q 4:10), are in many ways akin to the IRS practices and procedures in any instance in which there is a tax controversy beyond the level of the initial determination.

Thus, these procedures include the right of protest and appeal, conferences, the pursuit of technical advice from the National Office of the IRS, and occasionally consideration of the case by the National Office. Beyond that, there is access to the courts; an organization can take its case to the U.S. Tax Court (without a lawyer, if it chooses) or to a U.S. District Court or the U.S. Court of Federal Claims. Appeals can be taken to the appropriate U.S. Circuit Court of Appeals; on rare occasions, an exempt organization's case will be heard by the Supreme Court. For charitable organizations only, there is a declaratory judgment procedure by which issues as to tax-exempt status, private foundation/public charity status, and/or charitable donee status may be litigated.

GROUP EXEMPTION

Q 4:48 What is the *group exemption* procedure?

The group exemption procedure was devised by the IRS to eliminate the administrative burdens that would be caused by the pursuit of rulings by identical organizations, where there are many of them (perhaps hundreds) and they are related. This procedure is designed for entities such as chapters, locals, posts, or units that are affiliated with and subject to the general supervision or control of an organization, which is usually a national, regional, or state entity.

The supervisory organization is known as the *central organization*; the organizations that are affiliated with the central organization are *subordinate organizations*.

OBSERVATION: This an unfortunate choice of terminology, in that many organizations and those who manage them do not care to be regarded as *subordinates*. A preferable term would be *affiliates*. Aside from the psychology of the terminology, there are political aspects as well: the term *central organization* to some at the affiliate level stimulates fears of too much authority and control.

Tax exemption for subordinate organizations is recognized by the IRS by reason of their relationship with the central organization. This is known as tax exemption on a group basis.

These procedures contemplate a functioning of the central organization as an agent of the IRS, requiring that the organization responsibly and independently evaluate the qualification for tax-exempt status of the subordinate organizations from the standpoint of the organizational and operational tests applicable to them.

Interestingly, the term *affiliation* is not defined in this context. Usually the requisite affiliation is found in the governance structure of the organizations involved, such as an association with chapters, a church denomination with many individual churches, or a veterans' or fraternal organization with lodges. Sometimes the affiliation is inherent in a relationship involving finances, such as dues-sharing. In general, the IRS will accept any reasonable interpretation of the word *affiliation* in this setting.

 **NOTE:** This state of affairs is understandable, in that the group exemption is saving the IRS the task of processing thousands of applications for recognition of tax exemption.

Q 4:49 How is the group exemption initially established?

First, the entity intending to be a central organization must obtain recognition from the IRS of its own tax-exempt status. Then the organization applies to the IRS for classification as a central organization.

This application (oddly, there is no IRS form for it) must establish that all of the subordinate organizations to be included in the group exemption letter are properly affiliated with the central organization (Q 4:49), are subject to its general supervision or control, have the identical tax-exempt status, are not private foundations, are not foreign organizations, have the same accounting period as the central organization if they are not to be included in group returns (Q 4:51), and, in the case of charitable entities, are formed within the 15-month period (Q 4:41) prior to the date of submission of the group exemption application.

A central organization must submit to the IRS this information on behalf of the subordinate entities:

1. Information verifying the facts evidencing the aforementioned relationships and other requirements
2. A description of the principal purposes and activities of the subordinates, including financial information
3. A sample copy of a uniform or representative governing instrument adopted by the subordinates
4. An affirmation by a principal officer of the central organization that the subordinates are operating in accordance with their stated purposes
5. A statement that each subordinate has furnished the requisite written authorization
6. A list of subordinates to which the IRS has issued a determination letter or ruling recognizing exempt status
7. If relevant, an affirmation that no subordinate organization is a private foundation
8. A list of the names, addresses, and employer identification numbers of the subordinates to be included in the group (or a satisfactory directory of them)

Certain additional information is required of a subordinate organization if it is claiming tax-exempt status as a school.

NOTE: There is only one court case involving the group exemption procedures. There, the IRS procedures were upheld, with an organization found to not be eligible for classification as a central organization because the requisite information was not provided.

Q 4:50 How is the group exemption maintained?

The group exemption is basically maintained by the central organization making an annual filing with the IRS. Certain information must be annually submitted to the IRS by the central organization (at least 90 days before the close of its annual accounting period) to sustain the group status.

This information consists of:

- Information regarding any changes in the purposes, character, or method of operation of the subordinate organization
- A list of subordinates that have changed their names or addresses during the year
- A list of subordinates that are no longer part of the group
- A list of organizations that were added to the group during the year
- The information summarized previously concerning the subordinates that joined the group during the year

Q 4:51 How are the annual information return reporting requirements satisfied?

A central organization must, as a general rule, file an annual information return (Chapter 5). So too must each subordinate organization. Many subordinate organizations are small, however, and thus may be able to take advantage of the exception for organizations with annual gross receipts that normally do not exceed $25,000 (Q 5:3).

A subordinate organization has a choice in this regard. It can file its own annual information return (assuming no basis for an exception), or it can file with the central organization as part of a group annual return.

NOTE: A central organization may exclude from its group return those subordinates the annual gross receipts of which are normally not in excess of $25,000 per year.

Q 4:52 Do the central organization and the subordinate organizations have to have the same tax-exempt status?

No. These entities can have different tax-exempt organization classifications. For example, the central organization can be exempt as a business league and the subordinates can be exempt as charitable organizations. Alternatively, the central organization can be exempt as a charitable organization and the subordinates can be exempt as social welfare organizations.

NOTE: As noted, the subordinate organizations in a group must have the same tax-exempt status. A central organization can, however, have more than one group. For example, there can be a central organization that is a charitable entity with two groups: one comprised of charitable organizations and one comprised of social welfare organizations.

Q 4:53 Can the same organization be involved in more than one group?

Yes. For example, a state organization can be a central organization with respect to a group of subordinate entities throughout the state. Simultaneously, the state organization can be one of a number of state subordinate organizations in relation to a national central organization.

Q 4:54 When can the group exemption be terminated?

There are several instances when a group exemption may be terminated. One is when the central organization dissolves or otherwise ceases to exist. Other instances in which the group status can collapse are when the central organization ceases to qualify for tax-exempt status, fails to submit the requisite information, or fails to comply with the reporting requirements.

NOTE: Loss of tax exemption by some of the subordinate organizations in a group does not adversely affect the group exemption ruling for the other members of the group.

Q 4:55 **What are the advantages of the group exemption?**

From the standpoint of the IRS, the group exemption procedure is advantageous because it relieves the agency of the processing of thousands of applications for recognition of tax exemption (Q 4:47).

The group exemption generally is favorable for clusters of nonprofit organizations that are affiliated. This approach to tax exemption obviates the need for each member entity in the group to file a separate application for recognition of exemption, and this can result in savings of time, effort, and money. It is, then, a streamlined approach to the establishment of tax-exempt status for related organizations.

Q 4:56 **Are there any disadvantages to the group exemption?**

Yes—actually, there are several. One concerns the fact that the members of the group do not individually possess determination letters as to their tax exemption. In regard to charitable organizations, this can pose difficulties for donors and grantors. That is, a contributor of a major gift may want the security of a determination letter so as to have the requisite basis for relying on the organization's representation that it is a charitable entity. A private foundation grantor may desire similar assurance to be certain that the grant constitutes a qualifying distribution (Q 11:21), is not an expenditure responsibility grant (Q 11:36), and/or is not otherwise a taxable expenditure (Q 11:32).

Another disadvantage pertains to charitable subordinate organizations. By definition, the group exemption process does not entail any IRS review of these entities' public charity status. Sophisticated donors and grantors know this and thus know that they usually cannot assume that a particular subordinate entity is a public charity—which is the assurance they need. This dilemma is compounded by the practice of the IRS to automatically accord to the subordinate entities the same public charity status as that recognized for the central organization—and to do so on the basis of definitive rulings.

A third disadvantage pertains to state tax exemptions. Often the state authorities will not recognize a state tax exemption unless the organization can produce a copy of a federal determination as to exemption under a comparable status. Obviously, with the group exemption, a subordinate organization does not have that evidence to produce, which often makes the process of securing one or more state tax exemptions more difficult.

NOTE: At some point, if these burdens become too great, the subordinate organization may have to obtain recognition of tax-exempt status from the IRS and leave the group.

Finally, if a member of a group is found liable for damages, the existence of the group exemption may be used in an effort to assert "ascending" liability on the part of the central organization.

CHAPTER 5

Annual Return Preparation

The federal tax law requires that nearly all tax-exempt organizations file an annual information return with the IRS. This document, which is generally accessible by the public, has become quite extensive in recent years. It is far more than a tax return, in that much of the information required to be submitted goes beyond financial information and involves a considerable amount of descriptive material (sentences and paragraphs). Too many organizations devote an insufficient amount of thought and care in the preparation of the return, and too often overlook or ignore the importance of this document. Congress and the IRS are of the view that this return is infrequently adequately prepared or filed late or not at all. Consequently, recent legislation has brought disclosure and dissemination requirements, and an increase in penalties.

Here are the questions most frequently asked about the basic annual information return filing rules—and the answers to them.

GENERAL REQUIREMENTS

Q 5:1 Do tax-exempt organizations have to file an annual return with the IRS?

In almost all instances, yes. The federal tax law requires the filing of an annual information return by just about every type of tax-exempt organization. This includes charitable organizations, associations and other business leagues, social welfare organizations, social clubs, fraternal organizations, labor unions, and veterans' organizations (Q 4:7). In addition, certain nonexempt charitable trusts are required to file.

NOTE: This type of trust may also have to file the tax return generally required of trusts (Form 1041). If the trust does not have any taxable income, however, Form 1041 is not required, although the annual information return still is. Even if the trust has gross receipts below $25,000 (Q 5:3), it must nonetheless file the annual return for the purpose of complying with a special requirement (Q 5:3).

There are, however, some organizations that are excused from the filing obligation (Q 5:3). Moreover, there are certain tax-exempt organizations that, although not obligated to file an annual information return of this nature, must file another information return or a tax return (Q 5:7).

The fundamental purpose of the annual information return is to provide the IRS with the required information. The return may also be used, however, to transmit elections that are required to be transmitted to the IRS, such as the election to capitalize costs.

Q 5:2 Is there any significance to use of the term *annual information return*?

Yes. The document involved is not an *annual report* (such as may be required under state law), and it is not a *tax return*. As to the latter, these documents are not publicly accessible. The document that must be filed is an *information return*, which means, among other things, it is a return that contains much more than financial information and it must be made available to the public (Q 18:1–Q 18:7).

Q 5:3 What organizations are not required to file an annual return?

Some tax-exempt organizations do not have to file because of their exemption classification. These are:

- Instrumentalities of the United States
- State institutions the gross income of which is excluded from income taxation
- Other governmental units and tax-exempt organizations that are affiliated with them
- Churches, interchurch organizations of local units of a church, conventions or associations of churches, and integrated auxiliaries of a church
- Church-affiliated organizations that are exclusively engaged in managing funds or maintaining retirement programs
- A school below college level affiliated with a church or operated by a religious order
- A mission society sponsored by or affiliated with one or more churches or church denominations, if more than one-half of the society's activities are conducted in, or directed at persons in, foreign countries
- An exclusively religious activity of a religious order

NOTE: Some organizations that are not required to file annual information returns because of a tax law exception may find they need to prepare them in satisfaction of state reporting requirements (Q 5:39).

Other tax-exempt organizations are excused from filing an annual return because of the size of their gross receipts. There are two categories in this regard: organizations normally receiving $25,000 or less in gross receipts annually and foreign organizations the annual gross receipts of which from sources within the United States are normally $25,000 or less.

> **TIP:** An organization with gross receipts that are normally not more than $25,000 should consider filing with the IRS anyway. This is done by completing the top portion of the return (name, address, and the like) and checking the box on line K. The purpose of this is to be certain that the IRS has the organization's correct address and realizes that the organization is not filing because it is not required to, rather than because it is unaware of or is ignoring the requirement. The IRS also requests that, when an organization of this type receives a Form 990 package in the mail, the top portion of the return be filed using the mailing label.

An organization that has been filing annual information returns and then becomes no longer required to file them, because of qualification under an exemption, should notify the IRS of the change in filing status. Failure to do this is likely to result in inquiries from the IRS as to why returns are not being filed; a large expenditure of time and effort may then be required in resolving the matter.

Q 5:4 What constitutes *gross receipts*?

A distinction must be made between the term *gross receipts* and the term *gross revenue*.

> **NOTE:** The reader may wish to have a copy of Form 990 at hand while reviewing the rest of this chapter. The discussion is based on the Form 990 for 2003.

On Form 990 (Q 5:7), for example, *gross revenue* means all revenue referenced in Part I, lines 1 to 12 (Q 5:16). This includes contributions, grants, exempt function revenue, investment income, and unrelated business income.

> **NOTE:** For the most part, *gross* revenue must be taken into account in determining total revenue (that is, expenses are irrelevant). However, there are four exceptions, where only net (gross less expenses) income is taken into account for this purpose: rental income (or loss) (Form 990, Part I, lines 6a to c), gain from sale of assets (or loss) (lines 8a to d), income from special events (or loss) (lines 9a to c), and gain from sales of inventory less certain items (or loss) (lines 10a to c).

>  **TIP:** Consistency is very important when reporting these numbers. In this instance, these four net revenue items must be reported again in the context of the analysis of income-producing activities (Q: 5:46) (Form 990, Part VII, lines 97 to 102).

In contrast, gross receipts are the total amount the organization received from all sources during its annual accounting period, without subtraction of any costs or expenses.

NOTE: Thus, the four exceptions noted earlier are irrelevant in computing gross receipts. Consequently, on Form 990, gross receipts are the sum of lines 1d, 2 to 5, 6a, 7, 8a (both columns), 9a, 10a, and 11. Gross receipts can also be calculated by adding back the amounts subtracted in ascertaining gross revenue.

Q 5:5   What does the term *normally* mean?

The term *normally* in this context generally means an average of the most recent three tax years of the organization (including the year relating to the return). Thus, to be entitled to this reporting exception, it is not necessary that the organization be below the $25,000 threshold each year. Specifically, an organization is considered to meet the $25,000 gross receipts test if one of these three tests apply:

1. The organization has been in existence for one year and has received, or donors have pledged to give, $37,500 or less during its first year.
2. The organization has been in existence between one and three years and averaged $30,000 or less in gross receipts during each of its first two years.
3. The organization has been in existence three or more years and averaged $25,000 or less in gross receipts for the immediately preceding three years (including the year for which the return would be filed).

Q 5:6   What happens once this $25,000 gross receipts test is exceeded?

Once it is determined that the organization's gross receipts for the measuring period (Q 5:5) are such that it has exceeded the $25,000 threshold, it has 90 days within which to file the appropriate annual return (unless another exception is available (Q 5:3)).

Q 5:7   What IRS form is this annual information return?

For most organizations, it is Form 990.

NOTE: Thus, the rest of the questions and answers in this chapter will focus exclusively on that return.

Small organizations—those with gross receipts of less than $100,000 and total assets of less than $250,000—are allowed to file a simpler (two-page) version of the return, which is Form 990-EZ.

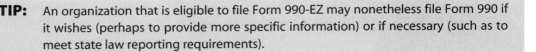

TIP: An organization that is eligible to file Form 990-EZ may nonetheless file Form 990 if it wishes (perhaps to provide more specific information) or if necessary (such as to meet state law reporting requirements).

Private foundations (Q 10:2) file Form 990-PF, and black lung benefit trusts file Form 990-BL.

There are other tax-exempt organizations that are not required to file this annual information return but are nonetheless required to file either another information return or a tax return. These are political organizations (Form 1120-POL), homeowners' associations (Form 1120-H), apostolic organizations (Form 1065), and stock bonus, pension, or profit-sharing trusts (Form 5500).

NOTE: Form 1120 is the tax return generally filed by corporations. Thus, technically, Forms 1120-POL and 1120-H are tax returns, not information returns. Form 1065 is the information return filed by partnerships; apostolic organizations are treated as partnerships for tax purposes. (Partnerships, being *pass-through entities* (Q 16:5), do not pay federal income tax.)

Charitable organizations that are not private foundations are required to also file Schedule A to accompany Form 990 (or Form 990-EZ).

Q 5:8 Is there any reason to file the simpler version of the annual information return when the organization is exempt from the filing requirement because of the amount of its gross receipts?

As noted, an organization with gross receipts that do not normally exceed $25,000 annually is excused from filing an annual information return (Q 5:3). Certain organizations with gross receipts of less than $100,000 can file a simpler version of the annual return—Form 990-EZ (Q 5:7). The question thus is whether an organization with less than $25,000 in annual gross receipts should nonetheless file Form 990-EZ.

One reason for the filing of Form 990-EZ in this situation—or at least preparing it—is so that the organization can have the benefit of understanding what its items of income, expense, assets, and liabilities are.

From a legal standpoint, however, there is a very good reason for filing Form 990-EZ even though it is not required as a matter of law. This pertains to the running of the statute of limitations on the assessment and collection of taxes. The general rule is that income taxes must be assessed within the three-year period following the filing of the return. If a return is not filed, the statute of limitations does not start to run and the tax may be assessed at any time.

As noted, the annual information return is not a tax return (Q 5:2). The original position of the IRS was that the filing of an information return did not trigger the running of the statute of limitations for purposes of assessment of the unrelated business income tax—which is to be calculated and reported on a tax return, Form

990-T. The Tax Court held, however, that the statute of limitations does begin to run in this circumstance where the information in the annual information return clearly revealed the possibilities of unrelated business income. Thereafter, the IRS relented, announcing that it would adhere to the Tax Court's approach where adequate facts as to the presence of unrelated business income are disclosed in the annual information return and it was filed in good faith.

Of course, a small organization may not have any unrelated business income, or it may have a small amount that it shielded from tax by the $1,000 specific deduction. In many instances, however, comfort can be gained by filing an annual information return despite the fact it is not required. At least the filing puts the IRS on notice that the organization exists.

Although its utility is remote, there is another reason for filing an annual information return. The statute of limitations begins to run when an organization, believing in good faith that it is a tax-exempt entity, files an annual information return and is subsequently held to be a taxable organization. This can be the outcome even where the organization has not yet been recognized as an exempt entity (Q 4:5–Q 4:7). Thus, there may be a measure of protection to be obtained in this connection.

Q 5:9 When is this annual information return due?

The annual information return is required to be filed with the IRS by the 15th day of the fifth month following the close of its accounting period. Thus, for exempt organizations using the calendar year as the accounting period, the return is due by May 15. An organization with a fiscal year ending June 30 is expected to file by November 15. An organization with a fiscal year ending October 31 must file by March 15.

If the regular due date falls on a Saturday, Sunday, or legal holiday, the due date is the next business day.

NOTE: If the organization is liquidated, dissolved, or terminated, the return should be filed by the 15th day of the fifth month after the liquidation, dissolution, or termination.

Q 5:10 Are extensions of this filing due date available?

Yes. It is common for exempt organizations to obtain an extension of the annual information return due date. The proper way to request this extension is the filing of Form 2758.

Generally, the IRS will not grant an extension of time to file the annual information return for more than 90 days, unless sufficient need for an extended period is clearly shown. The IRS will not, in any event, grant an extension of more than six months to any domestic organization.

Q 5:11 Where is the annual information return filed?

All annual information returns filed by tax-exempt organizations are required to be filed with the Internal Revenue Service Center in Ogden, Utah 84201–0027.

Q 5:12 How does an organization amend its return?

To change its return for a year, the organization must file a new return, including any required attachments. It should use the version of the annual information return applicable to the year involved. The amended return must provide all of the information called for by the return and its instructions, not just the new or corrected information. The organization should check the "Amended Return" box in the heading of the return (Q 5:17) or, if the version of the return being used lacks the box, "Amended Return" should be written at the top of the return.

The organization may file an amended return at any time to change or add to the information reported on a previously filed return for the same year. It must make the amended return available for public inspection for three years from the date the original return was due, whichever is later.

The organization must also send a copy of the amended return to any state with which it filed a copy of the return originally to meet that state's filing requirement (Q 5:39).

Q 5:13 Does the IRS provide copies of previously filed annual information returns?

Yes. A tax-exempt organization may request a copy of an annual information return it has previously filed by filing Form 4506-A with the IRS.

Q 5:14 What if the return is a final return?

In the case of a complete liquidation of a corporation or termination of a trust, the "Final Return" box in the heading of the annual information return should be checked (Q 5:17). An explanatory statement should be attached to the return.

This statement should indicate whether the assets have been distributed and the date of the distribution. A certified copy of any resolution, or plan of liquidation or termination, should be attached, along with all amendments or supplements not already filed. In addition, a schedule should be attached listing the names and addresses of all persons who received the assets distributed in liquidation or termination, the kinds of assets distributed to each one, and each asset's fair market value.

OVERVIEW OF RETURN CONTENTS

Q 5:15 How are the contents of the annual information return determined?

Some of the contents of the return are mandated by statute. These elements are very general. Most of the information required to be submitted on the return has been developed by the IRS on its own.

Q 5:16 **What are the contents of the annual information return?**

That question cannot be responded to in a single answer. The best way to survey the contents of the return is to break it down by its portions. The document consists of six pages, comprising nine parts. The accompanying Schedule A also constitutes six pages, comprising seven parts. Let us proceed part by part, beginning with the basic information required on page 1, before Part I. The IRS regards this as the *heading* of the return.

REMINDER: The reader should refer to a copy of Form 990 in tandem with the rest of the questions and answers. The discussion is based on the return and Schedule A for 2003.

Q 5:17 **What items of information are required in the heading of the return, preceding Part I?**

There are 10 items of information that are to be supplied:

1. Identification of the organization's accounting period.
2. The nature of the return: initial, final, or amended. Any change of address is to be noted.

TIP: The IRS prefers that an address change be communicated to it by the filing of Form 8822.

3. The organization's name and address.
4. The organization's employer identification number.

NOTE: Presumably, the organization has been assigned this number by the time it begins filing annual information returns. If the number has not yet been obtained, the organization acquires it by the filing of Form SS-4.

5. State registration number. The state or local jurisdiction number should be entered for each jurisdiction in which the organization files the Form 990 in lieu of a state or local form.
6. The organization is required to indicate whether it has an application for recognition of tax exemption pending.
7. The organization is to identify its tax status as an exempt organization (by completing the Internal Revenue Code citation) or a nonexempt charitable trust (see Q 5:1).

8. Information to be provided by organizations for which the tax exemption is based on a group exemption (Q 4:47–4:56), including the group exemption number.

9. The accounting method used by the organization (Q 5:26).

10. Indication that the organization is below the $25,000 threshold (see Q 5:3).

REVENUE, EXPENSES, BALANCES, ASSETS

Q 5:18   **Since the classification of government grant revenues is somewhat different for tax and accounting purposes, what issues must be considered in determining whether an item of revenue of this nature is reportable as a grant or program service revenue?**

The dilemma here is whether to report the revenue item as a grant on Part I, line 1, or as program service revenue on Part I, line 2 (Q 5:19). The latter categorization is used when the underlying document is a contract for services. Sometimes this distinction is difficult to make.

 **NOTE:**   This is not merely a reporting issue. The distinction between a grant and an item of exempt function revenue must be made in computing public support in the case of many publicly supported organizations.

One aspect of this matter is clear: the fact that the document is designated as a grant agreement or a contract for services is basically irrelevant. It is the substance of the arrangement that is controlling.

A *grant* is a payment that is akin to a gift, where the recipient of the funds is essentially free to use them as it deems appropriate. Normally, a grant is made to encourage the grantee to carry on certain programs in furtherance of its exempt purposes. There may be a grant agreement imposed by the grantor to ensure that the grantee's programs are conducted in a manner that is compatible with the grantor's programs and policies, and is beneficial to the public. The grantee may also perform a service or produce a work product that incidentally benefits the grantor.

An item of revenue is properly characterized as *exempt function revenue* (assuming the underlying activity is not an unrelated business) if a specific service, facility, or product is provided by the payee to serve the direct and immediate needs of the payor. In general, payments made primarily to enable the payor to realize or receive some economic or physical benefit as a result of the service, facility, or product obtained, are treated as items of exempt function revenue with respect to the payee.

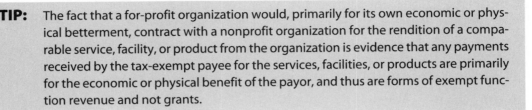

TIP: The fact that a for-profit organization would, primarily for its own economic or physical betterment, contract with a nonprofit organization for the rendition of a comparable service, facility, or product from the organization is evidence that any payments received by the tax-exempt payee for the services, facilities, or products are primarily for the economic or physical benefit of the payor, and thus are forms of exempt function revenue and not grants.

Q 5:19   What information as to revenue is required on the annual information return?

The return, in Part I, requires the reporting of all items of revenue that the organization received during the year. This requires the reporting of items of *gross* revenue; however, as indicated (Q 5:4), four items of revenue are netted, in whole or in part, in this portion of the return).

1. Line 1. On this line, the organization reports revenue that it received during the year in the form of contributions, grants, and the like.

NOTE: The return references *contributions* and *gifts*. For return reporting purposes, these words mean the same.

This can involve distinguishing between these items and exempt function revenue. For example, an organization may have to determine whether a payment was in the form of a *grant* or made pursuant to a *contract* (Q 5:18).

This financial information must be further broken down into direct and indirect public support. *Direct public support* (line 1a) means contributions to the organization from all sources: individuals, corporations, trusts, and the like; it also includes grants from private foundations. *Indirect public support* (line 1b) means a grant from a publicly supported charity; the gifts made to this grantor are deemed to be embodied in the grant, so that they are considered made indirectly to the grantee (the organization preparing the return). Government grants are also separately identified (line 1c).

This financial information is totaled (line 1d). A schedule of contributors and donors must be attached. The information on this schedule need not, however, be made accessible to the public (see Q 18:1). In addition, there must be a breakdown of these items between those made in the form of cash and those that are in noncash form. These two numbers combined should be equal to the total figure (on line 1d).

NOTE: Not all noncash items are eligible to be listed as this form of revenue. Basically, the reference to *noncash* items is to tangible personal and real property, and intangible property such as securities. Items that are *not* to be reported in this portion of the return are (1) donated services or (2) the use of materials, equipment, or facilities at no charge or at substantially less than fair rental value. These items are reported elsewhere on the return (Q 5:34).

2. Lines 2 and 3. On these lines, the organization reports its *exempt function revenue*, which essentially is revenue derived from related business activities. That is, this is revenue derived from the performance of a service (such as admission to a facility or an activity pursuant to a government grant) or the sale of one or more goods (such as publications).

   The return terms this type of income *program service revenue* (line 2). These types of revenue are detailed elsewhere on the return (see Q 5:46), and the total is inserted in this portion of the return. Another type of exempt function revenue is membership dues and assessments, which is separately reported (line 3). Membership income must also be reported elsewhere on the return (see Q 5:46).

3. Line 4. Interest on savings and temporary cash investments is reported here.

4. Line 5. Dividends and interest from securities are reported here.

5. Line 6. Gross rental income less expenses is reported here.

6. Line 7. Other investment income is reported here.

7. Line 8. Gross amounts from the sale of assets (other than inventory), including capital assets such as securities (that give rise to capital gain or loss), less their cost basis and sales expenses, are reported here. A schedule of these sales transactions must be attached.

NOTE: For organizations that engage in large numbers of securities and other sales transactions, this schedule can be sizable, amounting to several inches of paper, which can cause reproduction of the return to be expensive and time-consuming (Q 18:2).

8. Line 9. Gross income from special events, less expenses other than those for fundraising, is reported here. A *special event* is defined in the annual return instructions as an activity the sole or primary purpose of which is to raise funds (that are not contributions) to finance the organization's activities (such as dinners, dances, carnivals, and gambling activities). A schedule of these activities must be attached.

9. Line 10. Gross sales of inventory, less returns, allowances, and costs of goods sold (yielding gross profit (or loss)), is reported here. A schedule of these sales must be attached.

10. Line 11. Other revenue is reported here. This category of revenue, which includes unrelated business income, is detailed elsewhere on the return (Q 5:46).

11. Line 12. The organization's total revenue (taking into account the four instances where a form of netting is permitted) is reported here.

TIP: The information provided as to the sources of the organization's revenue should correlate, in terms of both the accuracy of the numbers and the classification of the revenue items, with the reporting of public support (Q 5:57) and the analysis of income-producing activities (Q 5:46).

Q 5:20 **What information as to expenses is required on the annual information return?**

The various categories of the organization's expenses are reported on the annual information return, in Part I. Most of this information is presented in greater detail elsewhere in the return, so this portion is a summary of the four categories of expenses. The expenses of most tax-exempt organizations are allocated across three categories: related business activities (expenditures for program), management, and fundraising.

1. Line 13. The total of the expenses associated with the organization's program activities is reported here.
2. Line 14. The total of the expenses associated with management of the organization is reported here.
3. Line 15. The total of the expenses associated with fundraising for the organization is reported here.
4. Line 16. Any payments to affiliated organizations are reported here. A schedule of these payments must be attached.

NOTE: An organization's expenses for program services, management and general, and fundraising are calculated using a method by which costs are allocated across the three functions (Q 5:3, Q 5:44).

5. Line 17. Expenses are totaled and reported here.

NOTE: There are two controversial matters as to an organization's expenses that are reflected elsewhere on the return. One is the issue of joint costs (Q 5:45). The other is the matter of compensation of key employees, independent contractors, and others, and the correlation of this with the intermediate sanctions rules (Chapter 7).

Q 5:21 **How does a public charity report a program-related investment?**

First, it is necessary to define this term. A *program-related investment* is an investment that is made primarily to accomplish an exempt purpose of the investing organization rather than to produce income. This type of investment is expressly recognized in the private foundation setting (Q 11:28).

There are three aspects of reporting program-related investments. One concerns the activity itself. A program-related investment should be reported as a program service accomplishment (Q 5:43).

The second aspect pertains to the reporting of income from the program-related investment (such as interest paid in connection with loans to victims of a disaster or rent paid in connection with a charitable lease). This income should be reported as program service revenue (Part I, line 2) (Q 5:19).

Third, the asset involved in the program-related investment (equity or debt) should be reported on the balance sheet (Part IV) (Q 5:23). It should be characterized as an "other asset" (line 58).

Q 5:22 What information as to net income or loss is required on the annual information return?

The reporting organization must calculate its net revenue (what the return terms *excess* revenue) or net loss (deficit) for the year. This is reported on line 18 of Part I of the return. This number is the organization's total revenue (Q 5:19) less total expenses (Q 5:20).

Q 5:23 What information as to net assets is required on the annual information return?

The reporting organization must calculate its *net assets or fund balances* at the beginning of the year and report this item on line 19 of Part I of the return. It must likewise calculate its net assets and fund balances at the end of the year and report this item on line 21 of the return. Any other changes in this item must be reported (on line 20), along with an explanation.

The determination as to net assets or fund balances at the beginning of the year is derived from the balance sheet that constitutes Part IV of the return. This portion of the return requires the organization to ascertain, as of the beginning of the year and the end of the year:

1. Assets
   a. Cash (non-interest bearing) (line 45).
   b. Savings and temporary cash investments (line 46).
   c. Accounts receivable, less allowance for doubtful accounts (line 47).
   d. Pledges receivable, less allowance for doubtful accounts (line 48).
   e. Grants receivable (line 49).
   f. Receivables due from trustees, directors, officers, and key employees (line 50). A schedule of end-of-the-year amounts must be attached.

NOTE: For tax-exempt organizations (other than, in some instances, private foundations), loans, advances, and the like to individuals of this nature are not prohibited (although they may be subject to special scrutiny, which is the purpose of this line). This aspect of the return verifies the point.

    g. Other notes and loans receivable, less an allowance for doubtful accounts (line 51). A schedule for end-of-the-year amounts must be attached.

    h. Inventories for sale or use (line 52).

    i. Prepaid expenses and deferred charges (line 53).

    j. Investments involving securities (line 54). A schedule for end-of-the-year amounts must be attached.

    k. Investments involving land, buildings, and equipment, less accumulated depreciation (line 55). A schedule for end-of-the-year depreciation amounts must be attached.

    l. Other investments (line 56). A schedule for end-of-the-year amounts must be attached.

    m. Land, buildings, and equipment, less accumulated depreciation (line 57). A schedule for end-of-the-year depreciation amounts must be attached.

    n. Other assets, accompanied by a description of them (line 58).

    o. Total assets (line 59).

2. Liabilities

    a. Accounts payable and accrued expenses (line 60).

    b. Grants payable (line 61).

    c. Deferred revenue (line 62).

    d. Loans from trustees, directors, officers, and key employees (line 63). A schedule for end-of-the-year amounts must be attached.

    e. Tax-exempt bond liabilities (line 64a). A schedule for end-of-the-year amounts must be attached.

    f. Mortgages and other notes payable (line 64b). A schedule for end-of-the-year amounts must be attached.

    g. Other liabilities, accompanied by a description of them (line 65).

    h. Total liabilities (line 66).

3. Net assets or fund balances for organizations that follow *Financial Statements of Not-for-Profit Organizations*, issued by the Financial Accounting Standards Board (SFAS 117).

    a. Unrestricted (line 67).

    b. Temporarily restricted (line 68).

    c. Permanently restricted (line 69).

    d. Total net assets or fund balances (line 73). This amount for the beginning of the year (column (A)) is entered on line 19 of Part I of the return. This amount for the end of the year (column (B)) is entered on line 21 of Part I of the return.

    e. Total liabilities and net assets/fund balances (line 74).

TIP: The amount on line 74 should equal the total on lines 66 (total liabilities) and 73 (total net assets or fund balances), and should be the same as the amount on line 59 (total assets). The amount entered on line 21 of the return should also be the sum of the amounts on lines 18-20.

4. Net assets or fund balances for organizations that do not follow SFAS 117.
   a. Capital stock, trust principal, or current funds (line 70).
   b. Paid-in or capital surplus, or land, building, and equipment fund (line 71).
   c. Retained earnings, endowment, accumulated income, or other funds (line 72).
   d. Total net assets or fund balances (line 73). Again, this amount for the beginning of the year (column (A)) is entered on line 19 of Part I of the return. This amount for the end of the year (column (B)) is entered on line 21 of Part I of the return.
   e. Total liabilities and net assets/fund balances (line 74).

TIP: Again, the amount on line 74 should equal the total on lines 66 (total liabilities) and 73 (total net assets or fund balances), and should be the same as the amount on line 59 (total assets). Again, the amount entered on line 21 of the return should also be the sum of the amounts on lines 18–20.

Q 5:24 Should organizations be concerned about a large amount of net assets or fund balance?

They should be somewhat concerned. There is no law that places a restriction on the amount of money or property that an exempt organization can accumulate. At the same time, a large and growing accumulation of assets can be a signal that inadequate or infrequent exempt functions are taking place.

NOTE: The IRS occasionally applies what is known as the *commensurate test*. The agency compares an organization's program activities with the extent of its financial resources to see if it is doing enough in the way of exempt functions. (So far, this test has been applied only to public charities.) A large fund balance accumulation is an element that the IRS would take into consideration in applying this test.

A factor to take into account in this context is the reason for the accumulation. The organization may denominate some or all of these assets as an endowment fund, a building fund, or some other reserve. This can go a long way in dispelling concerns about what may otherwise appear to be an unreasonable accumulation.

Some organizations avoid this dilemma by transferring some or all of their fund balance to another, controlled, entity. This organization is often generically referred to as a *foundation*; it may technically be a *supporting organization* (Q 10:15). This entity can hold the funds as an endowment fund or for a similar function. Whatever the use that is made of this type of separate entity, it causes what might otherwise appear to be an excessive accumulation of funds or property to be removed from the "bottom line" of the reporting tax-exempt organization.

Q 5:25 Under what circumstances should an amended return be filed when an organization finds that a prior-year annual information return contains an error?

Technically, an amended return should be filed whenever there is an error of substance in the original return. The annual information return applicable to the year involved should be used.

NOTE: Blank forms for prior years may be obtained from the IRS by calling 1-800-TAX-FORM (1-800-829-3676).

The "Amended Return" box in the heading of the return should be checked (Q 5:12).

Thus, if the error is insignificant or incidental, the common practice is not to bother with the filing of an amended return. In contrast, if the error is a significant one, a failure to correct it may result in penalties (Q 5:58–Q 5:60) and/or a cessation of the running of the statute of limitations (Q 5:8).

Q 5:26 What accounting method should be used in preparation of an annual information return?

A tax-exempt organization is free to select the accounting method it believes is most suitable for it. This method must be specified in the return as the cash, accrual, or other method (introduction, line F).

Q 5:27 Aren't financial statements of exempt organizations prepared on another basis of accounting?

Yes. These audited financial statements are prepared in accordance with generally accepted accounting principles, which means—among other things—that they are prepared on the accrual basis of accounting.

Q 5:28 Doesn't this use of two accounting systems require exempt organizations to maintain two sets of financial records?

Basically, yes. What the IRS has done to date in this regard is to create a segment of the annual information return, by which items on the audited financial statement are reconciled with items on the annual return. One portion of the annual return is devoted to the reconciliation of revenue items (Part IV-A) and another is used to reconcile expense items (Part IV-B).

GENERAL OPERATIONS

Q 5:29   **What happens when an organization is engaging in an activity that was not previously disclosed to the IRS?**

If a tax-exempt organization has a determination letter or ruling from the IRS recognizing its tax exemption, the organization as part of that process presumably apprised the IRS of all of its program or other activities at that time (Q 4:15).

> **NOTE:**   It is possible, of course, that an organization did not disclose all of its activities to the IRS as part of the application process. If that is the case, it could have an adverse impact on the organization's exempt status. A ruling of this nature is only as valid as the material facts on which it is based; if material facts were omitted, the IRS may have occasion to revoke the ruling, either prospectively or retroactively.

An organization may have previously reported one or more activities to the IRS on a prior annual information return or during an audit. Indeed, the law requires that an exempt organization provide the IRS with contemporaneous notice of any *material* change in the facts concerning it. This is required, of course, to accord the IRS the opportunity to review these facts, so as to determine whether the organization is no longer primarily engaged in exempt functions. It is intended to be part of the IRS's ongoing enforcement of the *operational test*.

Thus, there can be several occasions when the IRS was informed of an organization's activities. If, however, there is an activity engaged in by the organization, which it did not previously report to the IRS, the entity is required to check a "Yes" box and disclose it as part of the return (Form 990, Part VI, line 76). A detailed description of each activity of this nature must be attached to the return. Otherwise, the question is answered "No."

Q 5:30   **What happens when an organization changed its operating documents but did not previously report this to the IRS?**

Any changes made in the organizing or governing documents not reported to the IRS are to be disclosed as part of the return (Part VI, line 77). The organization is required to check a "Yes" box and a conformed copy of the amendments must be attached to the return. Otherwise, the question is answered "No."

The same problem can arise here as in respect to activities. A change in one of these documents can be a *material* change; an illustration is a substantial modification of the organization's statement of purposes. If this entailed a material change, the organization is obligated to communicate the change to the IRS contemporaneously. Again, this is required to accord the IRS the opportunity to review these facts, so as to determine whether the organization is no longer primarily engaged in exempt functions. It is intended to be part of the IRS's ongoing enforcement of the organizational test.

Q 5:31 How does the filing of the annual information return relate to the receipt of unrelated business income?

As noted, this return is an annual information return, not a tax return (Q 5:2). Thus, the details as to unrelated business income are not reported on this return, but on the unrelated business income tax return, which is Form 990-T.

Nonetheless, the annual information return requires the tax exempt organization to answer "Yes" or "No" to the question as to whether it had unrelated business gross income of $1,000 or more during the year covered by the return (Part VI, line 78a). If the answer is truthfully "No," that is the end of the matter. If the answer is "Yes," the organization must answer "Yes" or "No" to the question as to whether it filed a Form 990-T for the year (line 78b). The correct answer is "Yes," because that is the basic criterion for filing the unrelated business income tax return. If the organization is forced to respond to this question with a "No," it is best advised to quickly remedy the deficiency and/or seek professional assistance.

Q 5:32 What if the organization dissolved or substantially contracted during the year?

Dissolution or substantial contraction of an organization is a material change warranting reporting of it even if there were not a separate question on the point (Q 5:29).

The organization is required to answer the question—"Yes" or "No"—as to whether, during the year, there was a liquidation, dissolution, termination, or substantial contraction of it (Part VI, line 79). An explanatory statement must be attached when the answer is "Yes."

Q 5:33 What about relationships with other organizations?

A question on the annual information return inquires as to whether the organization is related (other than by association with a statewide or nationwide organization) through common membership, governing bodies, trustees, officers, or other means, to another organization (Part VI, line 80a). If the answer is "Yes," a box indicating that answer must be checked, and the name of the organization must be provided, along with an indication as to whether the other organization is tax-exempt (line 80b). Otherwise, the question is answered "No."

There are, however, other questions on this subject. These include ownership of taxable subsidiaries (Chapter 15) (Q 5:54), involvement in partnerships (Chapter 16) (Q 5:55), grants and loans by public charities to other organizations (Q 5:51), and transactions and relationships between public charities and other tax-exempt organizations (Q 5:56).

Q 5:34 What if the organization received a contribution of services or a gift of the use of property?

The organization must answer "Yes" or "No" to the question as to whether it received donated services or the use of materials, equipment, or facilities at no charge or at substantially less than fair rental value (Part VI, line 82a). If it did, it may indicate the value of these items on the return (line 82b).

TIP: As discussed (Q 5:19), the value of gifts of this nature cannot be included as revenue. Yet the IRS has allowed an organization to disclose this value if it can be of importance to the organization or its constituency.

Q 5:35 What about the public inspection requirements?

These are discussed elsewhere (Chapter 18). It may be noted here, however, that there is a question on the return, which must be answered "Yes" or "No," inquiring as to whether the organization complied with the public inspection requirements, in respect to both applications for recognition of exemption and annual information returns (Part VI, line 83a). Inasmuch as the law requires compliance with these requirements, the organization is well advised to answer this question in the affirmative if it possibly (and truthfully) can. The answer is "Yes" even if there were no requests for the documents. If the answer must be "No," the assistance of a lawyer is advised.

Q 5:36 What about fundraising practices?

Expenses of fundraising, in the form of professional fundraising fees, are accorded a line on the statement of expenses (Q 5:20). Other fundraising costs must be reported as well. In the case of public charities, social welfare organizations, and nonexempt charitable trusts, fundraising expenses must be derived using the functional method of accounting (Q 5:44). There is reporting in the case of joint costs incurred in connection with an educational campaign and a fundraising solicitation (Q 5:45).

One of the elements of federal fundraising regulation involves certain disclosure requirements with respect to quid pro quo contributions (Q 13:10). One of the questions on the return, which requires a "Yes" or "No" answer, is whether these disclosure requirements were complied with (Part VI, line 83b). Inasmuch as the law requires compliance with these requirements, the organization is well advised to answer this question in the affirmative if it possibly (and truthfully) can. The answer is "Yes" even if there were no quid pro quo contributions during the year. If the answer must be "No," professional assistance is advised.

Moreover, there are certain rules about the solicitation of gifts that are not tax deductible (Q 13:19). Basically, the law requires that the solicitation material contain an express statement that these contributions are not deductible. The return requires a "Yes" or "No" answer to a question as to whether any contributions of this nature were solicited (line 84a). If the answer is "No," that is the end of the matter (assuming that answer is truthful). If the answer is "Yes," the organization must answer "Yes" or "No" to the question of whether the statement as to nondeductibility was included (line 85b). Of course, the desired answer to that question is "Yes." Again, if this answer must be "No," professional assistance is advised.

If a public charity, social welfare organization, or nonexempt charitable trust performs fundraising services for a tax-exempt organization, certain information must be reported (Q 5:56).

Q 5:37 How does a tax-exempt organization change its accounting period (tax year)?

A tax-exempt organization can change its accounting period whenever it wishes, without permission from the IRS or any other government agency. When this is done, however, it must file an annual information return for the short period resulting from the change.

TIP: Write "Change of Accounting Period" at the top of this short-period return.

If an organization changes its accounting period within the 10-calendar-year period that includes the beginning of one of these short periods, and it had an annual information return filing requirement at any time during that 10-year period, it must prepare and attach an IRS form (Form 1128) to the short-period return.

NOTE: When affiliated organizations authorize their central organization to file a group return for them (Q 4:51), the accounting period of each affiliated organization and of the central organization must be the same.

Q 5:38 How does a tax-exempt organization change its accounting method?

A tax-exempt organization that wishes to change its accounting method generally must prepare and file an IRS form (Form 3115).

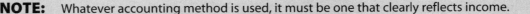

NOTE: Whatever accounting method is used, it must be one that clearly reflects income.

This form is not required, however, for tax-exempt organizations that change their methods of accounting to comply with *Accounting for Contributions Received and Contributions Made*, issued by the Financial Accounting Standards Board (SFAS 116). A change in accounting method may result in the need to make certain adjustments in the computation of income and expenses for tax purposes. An adjustment of this nature should be reported as a net asset adjustment made during the year the change is made.

NOTE: This adjustment should be identified as the effect of changing to the method provided in SFAS 116.

Q 5:39 **Don't some states require that copies of the annual return be filed with them?**

That is true. Nearly all of the states have a charitable solicitation act which, among other requirements, mandates registration and annual reporting (Chapter 13). As part of these processes, some states require the filing of a copy of this annual information return. Other states permit the filing of this return instead of all or part of separate financial information if the organization wishes to do that. The organization is required to list the states in which a copy of the annual return is filed (Part VI, line 90).

Because the IRS has developed the annual information return in conjunction with state fundraising regulation officials, it devotes a considerable amount of space in the return instructions advising about state and local filing requirements—even though the subject has no bearing whatsoever on the federal filing obligations. For example, the IRS advises organizations to consult the appropriate officials of state and local jurisdictions in which the organization does business to determine their filing requirements there. It is the view of the IRS that *doing business* in a jurisdiction may include any of the following:

1. Soliciting contributions or grants by mail or otherwise from individuals, businesses, or other charitable organizations
2. Conducting programs
3. Having employees within the jurisdiction
4. Maintaining a checking account in the jurisdiction
5. Owning or renting property in the jurisdiction

NOTE: The IRS is acting beyond the scope of its authority in proclaiming on this subject. Moreover, it is by no means clear that solicitation of gifts by mail alone constitutes doing business in a jurisdiction.

Q 5:40 **Does the annual information return require any additional information concerning general operations?**

Yes. The organization must identify who has the care of its books and records, this person's telephone number, and the location of these books and records (Part VI, line 91). In addition, a nonexempt charitable trust that is filing this return (Q 11:1) must check a box to this effect and report the amount of any tax-exempt interest that it received or accrued during the course of the year (line 92).

Q 5:41   How is the annual information return form obtained?

Most tax-exempt organizations that are required to file an annual information return receive the return each year in the mail, with the return containing a mailing label (Q 5:3). Officially, they are available at IRS offices, but, in practice, they are hard to find there. They can be obtained by telephone—call 1-800-TAX-FORM (1-800-829-3676). Many organizations rely on their accountant or lawyer for the return.

 **TIP:** The return must be printed to use it. We are not yet at the point where it can be filled out on-screen.

Tax forms, instructions, and publications are also available on CD-ROM, including prior-year forms starting with the 1991 form. For ordering information and software requirements, contact the Government Printing Office's Superintendent of Documents (202-512-1800) or Federal Bulletin Board (202-512-1387).

SPECIAL CONSIDERATIONS

Q 5:42   It was previously advised that, to be tax-exempt, an organization must primarily engage in the appropriate exempt functions. Is this rule of law reflected in the annual information return?

Very much so. One of the most important questions constituting the annual return is this: "What is the organization's primary exempt purpose?" (Form 990, Part III). An organization should be thoughtful and careful when responding to this question. This is the heart of the *operational test* as that test is applied to the organization. The answer to this question provides the general framework for most of the other questions and sets the tone for the other portions of the return. The sophisticated reader of an annual information return is likely to turn to the answer to this question first.

There is not much space on the return itself for an adequate answer, so a full response will likely have to be made on an attachment. While a general answer may suffice (such as "higher education," "trade association," or "social club"), the organization should go beyond very vague terminology (such as "charitable" or "social welfare"). Given that this is a public document (Chapter 18), the response to this question is an opportunity to tout the organization, to cast it in the most favorable light (staying within the bounds of veracity). It is an opportunity that is frequently overlooked.

> **NOTE:** The annual information return now contains much factual information other than financial data. It is no longer a document to be prepared solely by an accountant. The answers to this and most of the other questions should be conscientiously considered by the organization's management and reviewed by at least some of the volunteer leadership, the organization's lawyer, and perhaps others, such as a fundraising and/or public relations professional.

Q 5:43 What about the organization's programs? How should they be discussed?

The programs of a tax-exempt organization are the heart of the entity. The organization exists to conduct its programs. All other functions are (or should be) conducted in support of its primary activities, which are its programs. Here is one place where the annual information return should read like an annual report. The return amply provides opportunity for the organization to summarize its programs—what the return terms the organization's *program service accomplishments*.

The organization must describe its exempt purpose achievements (Part III). There is adequate room on the return to describe the four most important ones (lines a to d), although the organization should not hesitate to use one or more attachments. If more than four program service accomplishments are to be discussed, a schedule describing them should be attached (line e).

There are no bounds to creativeness here (other than accuracy). The organization should exuberantly and fully portray its programs. Specificity is in order. The return supplies some hints in this regard: the organization can state the number of clients served or publications issued. As the IRS puts it, the organization should also "discuss achievements that are not measurable."

This portion of the return involves some financial information, because one way to describe program services is by citing grants and allocations to others. This financial information is mandatory for charitable and social welfare organizations, and nonexempt charitable trusts; it is optional for all other tax-exempt organizations.

Following this descriptive and financial information, the organization's program service expenses should be totaled (line f). Of course, this number should be the same as that inserted on the face of the return for program service expenses (Q 5:20).

> **TIP 1:** Some have the attitude that the IRS should be given as little information as legally possible. Although in some settings this approach can be the correct one, this is not the place. Indeed, skimpy entries can be the basis for suspicions. Explicate!

> **TIP 2:** An organization may develop excellent descriptions of its programs and then simply reuse them over the years. This is fine as long as the summaries remain accurate and reflect contemporary priorities. There is the danger, however, that the material facts will change so that the descriptions are no longer appropriate; they may even be false or misleading. Thus, these statements should be reviewed and considered anew each year.

Q 5:44 **Surely there is more to the reporting of expenses than simply reporting program, management, and fundraising costs.**

There certainly is. As noted, these three categories of expenses must be reported on the face of the return (Q 5:20). There are some complexities to work through, however, in arriving at those three numbers.

The tax law recognizes that an expenditure may not simply be for one function. For example, payments for telephone services may all be program expenditures; or they may be part program and part management; or all management; or part program, part management, and part fundraising; or all for fundraising. Thus, an outlay can range over more than one function, and this has given rise to the concept of *functional expense reporting*.

Not all tax-exempt organizations, however, are required to report their expenses functionally. Public charities and social welfare organizations are required to do so, as are nonexempt charitable trusts. This type of reporting is optional for all other exempt entities. Every reporting exempt organization must report total expenses by category (Part II, column (A)). The return is structured to also accommodate functional reporting of expenses (columns (B) to (D)).

There are 21 categories of expenses that must be reported. They are:

CAUTION: When preparing this portion of the return, the expenses already taken into account in netting four items on the face of the return (Q 5:19) should not be reported. Moreover, payments to affiliates are separately reported (Q 5:20) and thus should not be reflected here.

1. Grants and allocations (line 22). A schedule of these items is required. Total cash items and noncash items must be reported. These items are always allocated to program services.
2. Specific assistance to individuals (line 23). A schedule is required. These items are always allocated to program services.
3. Benefits paid to or for members (line 24). A schedule is required. These items are always allocated to program services.
4. Compensation of trustees, directors, and officers (line 25).

NOTE: Additional information in this regard is required elsewhere in the return (Q 5:47).

5. Other salaries and wages (line 26).
6. Pension plan contributions (line 27).
7. Other employee benefits (line 28).
8. Payroll taxes (line 29).
9. Professional fundraising fees (line 30). This item may not be allocated to either program services or management.

10. Accounting fees (line 31).
11. Legal fees (line 32).
12. Supplies (line 33).
13. Telephone (line 34).
14. Postage and shipping (line 35).
15. Occupancy (line 36).
16. Equipment rental and maintenance (line 37).
17. Printing and publications (line 38).
18. Travel (line 39).
19. Conferences, conventions, and meetings (line 40).
20. Interest (line 41).
21. Depreciation, depletion, and the like (line 42). A schedule is required.

There is space on the return to list other expenses (line 43). An attachment may be used if necessary.

The organization's expenses are totaled (line 44). This number is carried over and inserted in the total expense line on the face of the return. If expenses are reported functionally, they are likewise carried forward and inserted in the appropriate expense line on the face of the return (Q 5:20).

Q 5:45 There has been some controversy about allocating what some regard as fundraising costs to programs. Is this reflected on the return?

Yes. The IRS refers to this situation as involving *joint costs*. Specifically, this arises where there is a combined educational campaign and a fundraising solicitation. The organization must answer, on a "Yes" or "No" basis, whether any such joint costs are being reported as part of program services expenses (Part II). If the answer is "Yes," the organization must report the aggregate amount of these joint costs, the amount allocated to program, the amount allocated to management, and the amount allocated to fundraising.

NOTE: The controversy, of course, arises when there is a perception that an organization is treating as program costs an amount of expenses that ought to be regarded as being for fundraising. This may be done to augment the size of the entity's program or reduce the amount of fundraising outlays. Critics of this type of allocation prefer a *primary purpose rule*, which would cause all of the expenses to be regarded as fundraising expenses. The principal champions of this primary purpose rule are, not surprisingly, state regulatory agencies and watchdog groups.

Q 5:46 Does the annual return require any additional information about an organization's expenses?

Yes, much more. One of the most critical portions of the return is the analysis of income-producing activities (Part VII). This segment of the return should be prepared with considerable care and understanding of the underlying points of law.

The first step is for the organization to list each of its sources of program service revenue. This information has already been gathered and reported elsewhere on the return (Q 5:20). Here is the list:

1. Program service revenue (line 93). The return provides space for the listing of six sources; an attachment may be necessary. Fees and contracts from government agencies are expressly identified (line 93g), as are membership dues and assessments (line 94).
2. Interest on savings and temporary cash investments (line 95).
3. Dividends and interest from securities (line 96).
4. Net rental income (or loss) from real estate (line 97). There must be a differentiation between revenue derived from debt-financed property and property that is not debt-financed.
5. Net rental income (or loss) from personal property (line 98).
6. Other investment income (line 99).
7. Gain (or loss) from sales of assets other than inventory (line 100).
8. Net income (or loss) from special events (line 101).
9. Gross profit (or loss) from sales of inventory (line 102).
10. Other revenue (line 103). The return provides space for the listing of five items; an attachment may be used if necessary.

Once these sources of revenue are identified, they must be classified in accordance with the unrelated business income rules (Chapter 14). Specifically, the organization must decide whether an item of income is derived from a related business or an unrelated business, or whether the income, although not from a related business, is nonetheless not taxable because it is excluded from taxation by statute.

If the organization is reporting income as being from an exempt function, that item of income, matched up with the appropriate source (as in the preceding list), is inserted in the appropriate line in column (E). Thus, all items that are considered related income are entered in column (E). Then the organization must provide a written explanation as to how each of these activities is a related one, that is, how it contributed importantly to the accomplishment of the organization's exempt purposes. Of course, these explanations should be carefully thought through; this is one place where the assistance of a tax professional may well be advisable. An attachment may be required.

NOTE: It is not sufficient that the income from an activity is used for exempt purposes. The activity must inherently be an exempt function.

If the organization is reporting income from an unrelated business, this amount or these amounts must be reported in column (B). Each unrelated business activity must be assigned a business code, which is inserted in the appropriate line in column (A). These codes are found in the Form 990-T instructions.

If the organization is reporting income that is not from a related source but is sheltered from taxation by statute, this amount or these amounts must be reported in column (D). The organization must determine which section of the Internal Revenue Code provides the exclusion, correlate that exclusion with an exclusion code, and insert that code in the appropriate line in column (C). These codes are found in the Form 990 instructions.

Then the subtotals for these three groupings of income are reported (line 104), followed by their total (line 105).

NOTE: As noted, most of these revenue items have been previously ascertained and reported. Thus, the total on line 105, plus the amount of any contributions and grants (Q 5:19), should equal the amount of total revenue reported on the face of the return (Q 5:19).

Q 5:47 What about expenses for compensation?

This is another subject of great concern to the IRS. Thus, it should not be a surprise to learn that the annual information return devotes considerable space to the reporting of compensation.

As noted, as part of the listing of its expenses, the organization is required to make a line entry for the compensation of trustees, directors, and officers, as well as for other salaries and wages. In addition to those forms of compensation, the organization must report its payments for pension plan contributions and other employee benefits (Q 5:44).

In addition, the organization must provide a list of its trustees, directors, officers, and key employees (Part V). This list is required even if any individual(s) is not compensated.

Specifically, the name and address of each of these individuals must be listed, along with his or her title, the average hours per week devoted to the position, the amount of compensation, the amount contributed to employee benefit plans, the amount of deferred compensation, and information as to expense account and other allowances.

For many tax-exempt organizations, the doctrine of *private inurement* is applicable (Chapter 6). One way to have private inurement is for the exempt organization to pay an amount of compensation that is excessive. This portion of the return is used by the IRS as part of the process of ascertaining whether there may be an unreasonable compensation package.

Sometimes a compensation package of an individual is reasonable when evaluated alone, but the total compensation of the individual may be excessive when combined with compensation from a related organization. That is why the IRS asks the question, which must be answered "Yes" or "No," as to whether any trustee, director, officer, or key employee received aggregate compensation of more than $100,000 from the organization and all related organizations, where more than $10,000 was provided by one or more related organizations (line 75). If the answer is "Yes," an explanatory schedule must be attached.

Q 5:48 **How does this matter of compensation relate to the intermediate sanctions rules?**

There is a direct connection between this matter of compensation and the intermediate sanctions rules.

To summarize (Chapter 7): if a public charity or a social welfare organization participates in an excess benefit transaction with a disqualified person, tax penalties are imposed on that person and on the organization managers who knew that the transaction gave rise to an excess benefit. Providing excessive compensation is one way to have an excess benefit transaction. Compensation arrangements involving trustees, directors, officers, and/or key employees are suspect under these rules because these individuals are almost always disqualified persons.

A public charity or a social welfare organization must answer "Yes" or "No" to a question as to whether it engaged in an excess benefit transaction during the year (Part VI, line 89b). If the answer is "Yes," it must attach a statement explaining each transaction. Moreover, the organization must report the amount of tax paid, during the year, by its organization managers or disqualified persons with respect to it (line 89c) and the amount of any of these taxes that the organization reimbursed (line 89d).

The reporting rules in this regard are more extensive for public charities. This is because these organizations are required to file Schedule A of Form 990.

This supplemental form requires much more detail as to the payment of compensation. Thus, a public charity must provide information as to the compensation of its five highest paid employees—if they were paid more than $50,000—other than trustees, directors, and officers (Schedule A, Part I). Specifically, the organization must supply the names and addresses of these employees, their titles, the average hours per week devoted to their positions, the amount of their compensation, the amount of contributions to employee benefit plans, deferred compensation, and expense accounts, and other allowances. If there are no employees of this nature, the organization should insert "None" on the first line.

A public charity must also provide information as to the highest-paid independent contractors for professional services. It is required to list the name and address of each independent contractor paid more than $50,000, the type of service provided, and the compensation paid. If there are no independent contractors of this nature, the organization should insert "None" on the first line.

A public charity is also asked whether, during the year, it, directly or indirectly, paid compensation (or paid or reimbursed expenses if more than $1,000) to any of its trustees, directors, officers, creators, key employees, or members of their families, or to any taxable organization with which any of these persons is affiliated as a trustee, director, officer, majority owner, or principal beneficiary (Schedule A, Part III, line 2d). This is a "Yes" or "No" question. If the answer is "Yes," a detailed explanation is required.

Q 5:49 **But the intermediate sanctions rules relate to much more than excessive compensation, don't they?**

Absolutely. The concept of the excess benefit transaction embraces much more than compensation arrangements. It covers the provision of excess benefits by means of sales, loans, renting, and other transactions.

There is a set of questions on the annual return that predate the intermediate sanctions rules but that are being used to ferret out possible excess benefit transactions with public charities. These questions pertain to transactions during the year, whether direct or indirect, between the public charity and any of its trustees, directors, officers, creators, key employees, or members of their families, or with any taxable organization with which any of these persons is affiliated as a trustee, director, officer, majority owner, or principal beneficiary (Schedule A, Part III).

These transactions are:

1. Sales or exchanges of property (line 2a)
2. Leasing of property (line 2a)
3. Lending of money or other extension of credit (line 2b)
4. Furnishing of goods, services, or facilities (line 2c)
5. Compensation arrangements (line 2d) (Q 12:6)
6. Transfer of any part of the organization's income or assets (line 2e)

Each of these questions must be answered "Yes" or "No." In each instance where the answer is "Yes," a detailed explanation is required.

Q 5:50 **Are there reporting requirements for public charities that make grants to individuals?**

Yes. A public charity is asked whether it makes grants for scholarships, fellowships, student loans, and the like (Form 990, Schedule A, Part III, line 3). This is a "Yes" or "No" question. If the answer is "Yes," the organization must attach a statement explaining how it determines that individuals receiving grants or loans from it, in furtherance of its charitable programs, qualify to receive the payments (line 4).

In addition, all organizations are required to report expenses that constitute grants (Q 5:44). Further, a grant, loan, or similar program is a program service, and a statement about the program(s) is likely to be required, including the amount of the grants. A grant payable should be identified on the organization's balance sheet (Q 5:23).

Q 5:51 **There must be reporting requirements for grants to organizations, as well.**

Yes, although there is not a specific "Yes" or "No" question on the point for all tax-exempt organizations. Nonetheless, if a public charity makes grants or loans to organizations, it must attach a statement explaining how it determines that the recipients of its support, in furtherance of its charitable programs, qualify to receive the payments (Form 990, Schedule A, Part III, line 4).

A public charity may also make grants or loans to other exempt organizations that are not charitable ones. If that is the case, there are other reporting requirements (Q 5:44).

Moreover, all tax-exempt organizations are required to report expenses that constitute specific assistance to individuals (Q 5:50). A scholarship, loan, or similar program is also a program service, and a statement about the program(s) is likely to be required, including the amount of the grants (Q 5:44). As noted, a grant payable should be identified on the organization's balance sheet (Q 5:23).

Q 5:52 Does the annual information return ask any questions about lobbying activities?

Yes. The IRS is very curious about lobbying activities by tax-exempt organizations (Chapter 8), and this is mirrored in the amount of space the annual information return devotes to the subject. There are essentially two sets of questions about this subject. One set pertains to public charities. The other involves membership associations, principally social welfare organizations, labor organizations, and business leagues. There are no questions about lobbying by other types of tax-exempt organizations.

NOTE: The portion of the annual return that focuses on an organization's expenses (Q 5:20) does not contain any express reference to lobbying expenditures.

A public charity is asked whether it, during the year, attempted to influence national, state, or local legislation, including any attempt to influence public opinion on a legislative matter or referendum (Form 990, Schedule A, Part III, line 1). This is a "Yes" or "No" question. If the answer is "Yes," the organization is required to report the expenses paid or incurred in this connection.

By reason of the *substantial part test*, a charitable organization is prohibited from engaging in substantial amounts of lobbying activity. An organization that is subject to this test must also complete another portion of the return that requests more specific information about the lobbying activities. If a public charity has made an election and thus is bound by the rules of the *expenditure test*, it must complete another portion of the return.

Charitable organizations that are bound by the substantial part test must answer "Yes" or "No" to eight questions pertaining to lobbying activities during the year (Schedule A, Part VI-B). These activities embrace direct lobbying, grass roots lobbying, and referenda. The questions pertain to lobbying through the use of:

1. Volunteers (line a).
2. Paid staff or management (line b).
3. Media advertisements (line c).
4. Mailings to members, legislators, or the public (line d). The amount of these expenses must be provided.

5. Publications, or published or broadcast statements (line e). The amount of these expenses must be provided.
6. Grants to other organizations for lobbying purposes (line f). The amount of these expenses must be provided.
7. Direct contact with legislators, their staffs, government officials, or a legislative body (line g). The amount of these expenses must be provided.
8. Rallies, demonstrations, seminars, conventions, speeches, lectures, or other means (line h). The amount of these expenses must be provided.

Total lobbying expenses are reported (line i). For each type of lobbying engaged in, the organization is required to attach a statement giving a detailed description of the activities.

A charitable organization that is subject to the expenditure test must indicate whether it belongs to an affiliated group (Schedule A, Part VI-A, box a) and, if so, whether the *limited control* provisions are applicable.

The focus and purpose of this portion of the return is the provision of an opportunity to make the various calculations that the expenditure test requires. Thus, the charity must report the following, for the year involved, both for the organization itself and for any affiliated group:

1. Total lobbying expenditures to influence public opinion (grass roots lobbying) (line 36).
2. Total lobbying expenditures to influence a legislative body (direct lobbying) (line 37).
3. Total lobbying expenditures (line 38, which is a total of the amounts on lines 36 and 37).
4. Other exempt purpose expenditures (line 39).
5. Total exempt purpose expenditures (line 40, which is a total of lines 38 and 39)
6. Direct lobbying nontaxable amount (line 41). The return includes a table for determining that amount.
7. Grass roots lobbying nontaxable amount (line 42). This amount is a maximum of 25 percent of the amount on line 41.
8. Grass roots lobbying taxable amount, if any (line 43, which is line 36 less line 42).
9. Direct lobbying taxable amount, if any (line 44, which is line 38 less line 41).

NOTE: If there is an amount in the eighth or ninth of these items, the organization must file Form 4720, which is used to pay the expenditure test tax on lobbying outlays.

Most organizations that are subject to the expenditure test must also report lobbying amounts for the current year and the three immediately previous years, because these calculations are made on the basis of four-year averaging. Thus, there must be reporting of the numbers for the four years, plus the total, for:

1. Direct lobbying nontaxable amount (line 45)
2. Direct lobbying ceiling amount (line 46)
3. Total direct lobbying expenditures (line 47)
4. Grass roots lobbying nontaxable amount (line 48)
5. Grass roots lobbying ceiling amount (line 49)
6. Grass roots lobbying expenditures (line 50)

In addition, a public charity must report the amount of any tax paid during the year because of lobbying expenditures (Part VI, line 89a). This involves both the tax imposed by reason of the substantial part test and the one imposed as part of the expenditure test.

As noted, a separate body of law concerns lobbying by membership associations, principally social welfare organizations, labor groups, and business leagues.

From the standpoint of tax-exempt status, these organizations are free to attempt to influence legislation without restraint. Indeed, lobbying can be their primary or even sole purpose. Amounts expended for lobbying, however, are not deductible. This rule "flows through" these membership entities and has an impact on the dues members pay; a ratio of lobbying expenses to total expenses is created, and that ratio is applied to the dues, rendering the portion of the dues attributed to lobbying nondeductible. For example, if a business association expended 25 percent of its revenue during the year for lobbying, then only 75 percent of the dues paid to it are deductible as a business expense.

This ratio must be timely communicated to the members. If this is not done, there is a penalty on the organization in the form of a *proxy tax*. The organization can voluntarily pay the proxy tax, however, thereby allowing the members to fully deduct the dues payments.

Under certain circumstances, an organization can be given, by the IRS, a waiver for the proxy tax owed for the prior year. Under certain circumstances, if an incorrect notice was sent to the membership in good faith, the organization can elect to add the taxable amount of its lobbying expenditures to its reasonable estimate of dues allocable to nondeductible lobbying expenditures for the following year.

These rules do not apply where substantially all of the dues paid to the organization by its members were not deductible in any event. Moreover, certain in-house lobbying expenditures are disregarded for this purpose if they do not exceed $2,000.

All of this is reflected on the annual information return. (This portion of the return need be completed only by social welfare organizations, labor organizations, and business leagues.) Thus, an organization must answer "Yes" or "No" to the question as to whether substantially all of the dues were nondeductible by its members (Part VI, line 85a).

NOTE: This is not an easy standard to meet. The phrase *substantially all* in this context means at least 90 percent.

The organization must also answer "Yes" or "No" to the question of whether it made only in-house lobbying expenditures of $2,000 or less (line 85b). If the answer to either question is "Yes," the organization should not complete the rest of the question unless it received a waiver for proxy tax owed for the prior year.

Assuming the organization must continue with this area of inquiry, it is required to report the amount of dues, assessments, and/or similar amounts paid by its members during the year (line 85c), as well as the amount of its lobbying expenditures (line 85d). It must report the nondeductible amount of the dues as shown on the notices (line 85e) and the taxable amount of lobbying (line 85f). The organization must answer "Yes" or "No" to the question as to whether it elected to pay the proxy tax (line 85g). The organization must also answer "Yes" or "No" to the question of whether, if dues notices were sent, the organization agrees to add the taxable amount of lobbying expenditures to its reasonable estimate of dues allocable to nondeductible lobbying expenditures for the following year (line 85h).

Q 5:53 Does the annual information return ask any questions about political activities?

Yes. The law makes a distinction between *political activities* and *political campaign activities* (Chapter 9). Political campaign activities are participations or interventions on behalf of or in opposition to candidates for public office. Political activities include political campaign activities and also embrace efforts such as support of or opposition to nominations for public office (Q 9:1)

Every tax-exempt organization that files the annual information return is required, if it, directly or indirectly, made any political expenditures during the year, to enter the amount on the return (Part VI, line 81a). The organization must also state, by a "Yes" or "No" answer, whether it filed the political organization tax return (Form 1120-POL) for the year (line 81b). This is because these political expenditures may be taxable and that is the form by which the tax is reported.

Membership associations that are caught up in the rules concerning the nondeductibility of dues because of lobbying expenditures (Q 5:52) have those rules applicable to them in the event of political expenditures.

Public charities are prohibited from engaging in political campaign activities. One tax sanction that can be applied if they do this is a tax. A public charity must report the amount of any tax paid during the year because of political campaign expenditures (Part VI, line 89a).

Q 5:54 What about the ownership by a tax-exempt organization of a taxable subsidiary?

An organization must answer "Yes" or "No" to the question as to whether, at any time during the year, the organization owned a 50 percent or greater interest in a taxable corporation (Part VI, line 88) (Chapter 15). If the answer is "Yes," another portion of the return must be completed.

This other portion of the return (Part IX) requires reporting of the name, address, and employer identification number of the corporation. The exempt organization is also required to state the percentage of its ownership interest in the corporation, as well as the nature of the corporation's business activities, total income, and end-of-year assets.

Remember, there is a question generally inquiring into the organization's relationship with another organization (Q 5:33). That question would be answered "Yes" in the instance of ownership of a taxable subsidiary, and the other information sought by that question would have to be provided.

Q 5:55 What about the involvement of a tax-exempt organization in a partnership?

An organization must answer "Yes" or "No" to the question as to whether, at any time during the year, the organization owned a 50 percent or greater interest in a partnership (Part VI, line 88) (Chapter 16). If the answer is "Yes," another portion of the return must be completed.

This other portion of the return (Part IX) requires reporting of the name, address, and employer identification number of the partnership. The exempt organization is also required to state the percentage of its ownership interest in the partnership, as well as the nature of the partnership's business activities, total income, and end-of-year assets.

Again, remember, there is a question generally inquiring into the organization's relationship with another organization (Q 5:33). That question would be answered "Yes" in the instance of involvement of the organization in a partnership, and the other information sought by that question would have to be provided.

Q 5:56 What about the organization's relationship to other tax-exempt organizations?

This has been touched on elsewhere, involving situations where the organizations are related (Q 5:33) or, in the case of public charities, are the recipients of grants or loans (Q 5:37).

Public charities are, however, additionally required to provide information regarding transfers to, and transactions and relationships with, other tax-exempt organizations that are not charities (Form 990, Schedule A, Part VII).

 **NOTE:** For this purpose, political organizations (Chapter 9) are included as tax-exempt organizations.

The public charity is required to answer "Yes" or "No" to the question as to whether it, directly or indirectly, engaged in any of the following transactions with noncharitable exempt organizations:

1. Transfers of cash (line 51a(i))
2. Transfers of other assets (line 51a(ii))
3. Sales of assets (line 51b(i))

4. Purchases of assets (line 51b(ii))
5. Rental of facilities or equipment (line 51b(iii))
6. Reimbursements (line 51b(iv))
7. Loans or loan guarantees (line 51b(v))
8. Performance of services or membership or fundraising solicitations (line 51b(vi))
9. Sharing of facilities, equipment, mailing lists, other assets, or paid employees (line 51c)

If the answer to any of these nine questions is "Yes," the organization must complete a schedule. This schedule must provide in columns, for each of the transactions being reported, the amount involved, the name of the noncharitable exempt organization, and a description of the transfers, transactions, and sharing arrangements. The *amount involved* (column (b)) can be the fair market value of the goods, other assets, or services provided by the organization. If the organization received less than fair market value in any transaction or sharing arrangement, it should reflect in the description (column (d)) the value of the goods, other assets, or services received.

TIP: For purposes of the intermediate sanctions rules (Chapter 7), a noncharitable tax-exempt organization can be a disqualified person with respect to a public charity. Thus, the information provided in this portion of the return should be evaluated from that perspective.

The organization must also answer "Yes" or "No" to a question as to whether it is, directly or indirectly, affiliated with or otherwise related to one or more noncharitable tax-exempt organizations (line 52a). If the answer is "Yes," a schedule must be completed (line 52b). This schedule must provide the name of the noncharitable entity, its tax-exempt status, and a description of the relationship.

Q 5:57 What information must be reported concerning the organization's public charity status?

A charitable organization that is a public charity (Chapter 10) is required to report information about its public charity status.

There are 11 ways for a charitable organization to constitute a public charity. These ways are enumerated in the return (Form 990, Schedule A, Part IV); the organization is required to indicate which one of the categories it is in. The categories are:

1. A church, convention of churches, or association of churches (line 5).
2. A school (line 6).

NOTE: Schools are required to complete another portion of Schedule A (Part V, the Private School Questionnaire).

3. A hospital or a cooperative service organization (line 7).
4. A federal, state, or local government or governmental unit (line 8).
5. A medical research organization operated in conjunction with a hospital (line 9). The hospital's name, city, and state must be provided.
6. An organization operated for the benefit of a college or university that is owned or operated by a governmental unit (line 10). There is a public support requirement for these organizations; a support schedule must be completed (Part IV-A).
7. An organization that is a publicly supported charity because it is the donative type (line 11a). A support schedule must be completed (Part IV-A).
8. A community trust (or community foundation) (line 11b). A support schedule must be completed (Part IV-A).
9. An organization that is a publicly supported charity because it is the service provider type (line 12). A support schedule must be completed (Part IV-A).
10. A supporting organization (line 13). The supported organization(s) must be identified by name and public charity status (the latter by selecting the appropriate line number).
11. An organization that is organized and operated to test for public safety (line 14).

SANCTIONS

Q 5:58 What can give rise to penalties on organizations concerning annual information returns?

Penalties can be imposed for failure to file the return, for a late filing, an incorrect filing, or an incomplete filing.

Q 5:59 What are these penalties?

The basic penalty is $20 per day, not to exceed the smaller of $10,000 or 5 percent of the gross receipts of the organization for the year. A penalty will not be imposed in an instance of reasonable cause for the violation.

An organization with annual gross receipts in excess of $1 million is, however, subject to a penalty of $100 for each day the failure continues. The maximum penalty per return is $50,000.

These penalties begin on the due date for filing the annual return.

 **TIP:** One way to avoid penalties is to complete all applicable line items. Each question on the return should be answered "Yes," "No," or "N/A" (not applicable). An entry should be made on all total lines (including a zero when appropriate). "None" or "N/A" should be entered if an entire part does not apply.

Q 5:60   **Are there penalties on individuals as well as organizations for nonfiling and the like?**

Yes. There is a separate penalty that may be imposed on *responsible persons*. This penalty is $20 per day, not to exceed $10,000. This penalty will not be levied in an instance of reasonable cause.

TIP: If an organization does not file a complete return or does not furnish correct information, it is the practice of the IRS to send the organization a letter that includes a fixed time to fulfill these requirements. After that period expires, the person failing to comply will be charged the penalty.

If more than one person is responsible, they are jointly and individually liable for the penalty.

There are other penalties, in the form of fines and imprisonment, for willfully not filing returns when they are required and for filing fraudulent returns and statements with the IRS.

CHAPTER 6

Private Inurement and Private Benefit

The private inurement doctrine is the most fundamental principle of law applicable to nonprofit organizations. The rule is inherent in the very definition of the word *nonprofit* organization (see Chapter 1). The doctrine exists to preclude application of a nonprofit organization's income or assets to private ends. The rule, read literally, would prevent inurement of "net earnings" (profits), but, in practice, the reach of the doctrine is far more wide-ranging. A private inurement transaction must involve a person who is an insider with respect to the organization. The private inurement doctrine is most pronounced for charitable organizations.

The rules as to private benefit are much more vague and expansive than the private inurement doctrine. A private benefit transaction can occur where an insider is not involved. Incidental private benefit will be disregarded for tax purposes, however, which is rarely the case in the realm of private inurement.

Here are the questions most frequently asked about the doctrines of private inurement and private benefit, including the emerging rules as to intermediate sanctions—and the answers to them.

Q 6:1   What is *private inurement*?

Private inurement is a term used to describe a variety of ways of transferring some or all of an organization's resources (income and/or assets) to persons in their private capacity. Private inurement is supposed to occur with for-profit organizations; in these organizations, profit (net earnings) is intended to be shifted from the entity to the private persons (usually the owners of the organization). By contrast, nonprofit organizations may not engage in forms of private inurement; that is the essence of the term *nonprofit*. Thus, the doctrine of private inurement is the fundamental dividing line between nonprofit and for-profit organizations (Q 1:1). It is a particularly critical factor for charitable organizations in acquiring and maintaining tax-exempt status.

In the nonprofit setting, the private inurement standard references transfers of *net earnings*. On its face, this phraseology suggests that private inurement transactions are akin to the payment of dividends. That is not the case, however; the law has evolved to the point where many types of transactions are considered forms of private inurement even though there is no transmission of "net earnings" in a formal accounting sense.

TIP: The IRS provided its view of the term's contemporary meaning: private inurement "is likely to arise where the beneficial benefit represents a transfer of the organization's financial resources to an individual solely by virtue of the individual's relationship with the organization, and without regard to accomplishing exempt purposes." On another occasion, the IRS was more blunt: the prohibition on inurement means that an individual "cannot pocket the organization's funds."

As the first of these quotes indicates, one of the ways the law determines the presence of private inurement is to look to the ultimate purpose of the organization. If the organization is benefiting individuals in their private capacity and not doing so in the performance of exempt functions, private inurement likely is present. If so, the organization may not qualify as a tax-exempt organization or, for that matter, a nonprofit organization.

The private inurement law does not prohibit transactions with insiders. (These transactions may well be accorded greater scrutiny by the IRS or a court, however.) Thus, a nonprofit organization—including a public charity—can pay an insider compensation, rent, interest on loans, and the like. At the same time, the amount paid must be reasonable—that is, it must be comparable to similar payments in the commercial setting.

NOTE: This aspect of private inurement differs from the self-dealing rules applicable to private foundations; in general, they have no arm's-length standard. Even transactions with insiders that are beneficial to a foundation are largely prohibited under the private foundation rules.

Private inurement focuses on types of transactions (Q 6:8–Q 6:16). It also requires the involvement of one or more *insiders* of the organization (Q 6:2). Although it is the view of the IRS that the private inurement rule is absolute, some courts have suggested that there is some form of a de minimis floor underlying it. (However, any such de minimis threshold may not be as generous as the insubstantiality test underlying the private benefit doctrine (Q 6:23).)

Q 6:2 When is a person an insider?

A person is an *insider* of a nonprofit organization when he, she, or it has a special relationship with the organization. (The federal tax law borrowed the term from the federal securities law, which prohibits, among other practices, "insider trading.") Usually the special relationship arises out of a governance arrangement; that is, an organization's insiders include its directors, trustees, and officers. Key employees can be embraced by the term if their duties and responsibilities are akin to those of an officer.

> **TIP:** The rules concerning private inurement are quite similar to those involving self-dealing in the private foundation setting (see Chapter 11). In that setting, insiders are termed *disqualified persons*. In the foundation context, the equivalent term for insiders described above is *foundation managers*.

A person can be an insider because of some other relationship with the nonprofit organization. A founder of the entity, a substantial contributor, or a vendor of services could be an insider, particularly where, because of that relationship, he or she has a significant voice in the policy making or operations of the organization.

There are attribution rules in this area. Controlled businesses and family members may also be treated as insiders.

> **TIP:** Although they are not controlling outside the private foundation context, the rules concerning disqualified persons can provide a useful analogy in defining substantial contributors, family members, and affiliated persons such as corporations, trusts, and estates.

There is no statutory definition of the term *insider*. This leaves the IRS and the courts free to apply the doctrine as circumstances warrant from their viewpoint. For example, it is the position of the IRS that all physicians on the medical staff of a hospital are insiders with respect to that hospital, irrespective of whether they are directors or officers of the hospital.

Q 6:3 What types of tax-exempt organizations are expressly subject to the private inurement rule?

Under the federal income tax law, the types of tax-exempt organizations that are bound by the private inurement rule are charitable (including educational, religious, and scientific) organizations, social welfare organizations, business leagues (including trade, business, and professional associations), social clubs (including country clubs, and golf and tennis clubs), and veterans' organizations.

Q 6:4 **What is *private benefit*?**

The term *private benefit*, unlike *private inurement*, is not part of the definition of a nonprofit organization (Q 6:1). Rather, private benefit is a term used in the context of tax-exempt organizations, principally charitable entities. It is a part of the operational test, which looks to determine whether a tax-exempt charitable organization is being operated primarily for exempt purposes. The essence of the private benefit requirement is that the entity is not supposed to be operated for private ends, other than insubstantially.

Q 6:5 **What is the difference between private inurement and private benefit?**

There are two principal differences between private inurement and private benefit:

1. A private inurement transaction must be with an insider. A private benefit transaction can involve anyone. Thus, the private benefit doctrine has a much broader sweep than does the private inurement doctrine. Any transaction or arrangement that may constitute private inurement also is a form of private benefit.
2. In the view of the IRS, the private inurement doctrine is absolute; that is, there is no de minimis threshold. (The courts have suggested that there is some threshold in this setting, albeit a rather small one (Q 6:1).) By contrast, insubstantial private benefit does not cause any violation of the private benefit limitation.

Q 6:6 **What happens when a nonprofit organization engages in either practice?**

If a form of private inurement is caused by a charitable organization or other tax-exempt organization to which the doctrine applies, the organization loses its ability to be categorized as tax-exempt under the federal income tax law. More fundamentally, the organization would violate the state law definition of a nonprofit organization and may lose its nonprofit designation under state law.

If a substantial amount (or more than an insubstantial amount) of private benefit is caused by a charitable organization, the organization loses its ability to be tax-exempt as a charity.

PRIVATE INUREMENT

Q 6:7 **What are the principal types of transactions that constitute private inurement?**

Among the many and varied types of private inurement that the IRS and the courts have identified over the years, the most predominant are unreasonable (excessive) compensation, unreasonable borrowing arrangements, and unreasonable rental arrangements. In this context, the emphasis once again is on transactions that are reasonable (Q 1:16).

Q 6:8 When is compensation private inurement?

This is one of the most often-asked questions. The answer as a matter of law is easy to articulate. An item or package of compensation is private inurement when it is paid to an insider and it is unreasonable and excessive. The process by which reasonableness is determined and the factors that must be taken into account are, however, vague. The determination depends very much on the material facts and circumstances.

The court cases in this area focus on egregious violations, and, because they are fact-specific, they offer little guidance. The IRS has offered no particular assistance in illuminating this topic. The administration of the intermediate sanctions rules, however, is clarifying the matter of the factors and to some extent is addressing the matter of the process (Q 6:14).

There are seven general factors that can be used to ascertain whether an item or package of compensation is reasonable. Before enumerating them, however, a preliminary aspect of this matter must be stated. The compensation of an individual by a nonprofit organization must take into account the complete compensation package, not just the salary component. In addition to the base salary, these elements include any bonuses or commissions, incentive compensation, fringe benefits, consulting fees, and retirement and pension plans.

The determining factors are:

1. The amount and type of compensation received by others in similar positions
2. The compensation levels paid in the particular geographic community
3. The amount of time the individual is spending in the position
4. The expertise and other pertinent background of the individual
5. The size and complexity of the organization involved
6. The need of the organization for the services of the particular individual
7. Whether the compensation package was approved by an independent board

The first two factors are based on commonality: What are others in similar positions in similar locales being paid? The geographic factor is relatively easy to isolate; the other aspects may not be. If the comparison is of association executives or foundation trustees, the exercise may be relatively mechanical. In other instances, the basis of comparison may not be so clear. For example, in ascertaining the reasonableness of the compensation of a televangelist, should the comparison be with a local member of the clergy or a television personality?

The third factor—the amount of time devoted to the position—is very important. A compensation arrangement may be quite reasonable where the individual is working full-time, but excessive where he or she is working for the organization less than full-time. Thus, the analysis must take into account whether the individual is receiving compensation from other sources and, if so, the amount of time being devoted to them (Q 2:17).

NOTE: The annual information return filed by most tax-exempt organizations (Chapter 5) requires that the details of compensation received by a director, officer, or key employee of the filing organization be disclosed when (1) more than $100,000 was paid by the organization and one or more related organizations, and (2) more than $10,000 of the compensation was provided by a related organization.

The sixth factor relates to a topic the IRS is currently addressing to a considerable extent. The IRS is generally approving, albeit reluctantly, of incentive programs. There has been a crackdown on tax-exempt hospitals that are providing inducements to physicians to attract them away from their private practice and onto the hospitals' medical staffs. The principles being laid down in this setting are spilling over into aspects of the compensation practices of other nonprofit organizations.

The seventh factor is notable for a variety of reasons. This element is giving the IRS an opportunity to have a greater say in determining who is to sit on the board of directors of a nonprofit organization. Where an independent board is in place, the founders or other principals of the organization lack control (Q 1:22–Q 1:23). Thus, this element strongly advances the thought that ostensibly "high" compensation, when derived from a controlled board, is presumptively unreasonable.

TIP: There may be some other avenues to travel with respect to this last factor. One approach is to create an independent compensation committee of the board, which would make recommendations in this area to the board. The other is to seek the opinion of a qualified firm that has expertise in ascertaining the reasonableness of individuals' compensation.

Q 6:9   Is payment of a bonus to an employee of a nonprofit organization legal?

Yes. There is no prohibition on the payment of bonuses by a nonprofit organization to its employees. The only requirement is that the bonus be reasonable. In making that analysis, all of the compensation paid to the employee will be taken into account (Q 6:8).

Q 6:10   How should a bonus compensation program for employees be defined?

There need not be any formally defined plan. That is, the management of the organization could simply decide that the merits of an individual's work warrant additional compensation.

If a bonus compensation program is defined, the management of the organization could be allowed, by the board of directors, to make additional payments of certain amounts at a specified time, such as at year-end. The board may want to set parameters for these bonuses, stated as ranges of absolute amounts or percentages of overall compensation.

If bonuses are stated as percentages, additional care should be exercised, particularly where the compensation is a function of an element other than the individual's preexisting compensation. For example, the compensation of a fundraiser could be, in whole or part, a percentage of the amount of contributions raised during a particular period. Percentages of this nature can trigger special scrutiny because the compensation arrangement may be a distribution of net earnings, which is prohibited by the doctrine of private inurement (Q 6:1). These compensatory programs are often more like commissions than bonuses.

An instance of the problems a percentage arrangement can generate was the net revenue stream sales that were recently popular in the health care community. The IRS essentially has stopped these sales. Tax-exempt hospitals would calculate the net revenue (profit) to be incurred by a particular department for a year and sell that revenue package to a partnership consisting of physicians who were on the hospital's medical staff and were practicing in that department. The arrangement's advantages to the hospitals were: it pleased the physicians, so that they stayed on the medical staff, and it enabled the hospitals to receive the net revenue from the department's operations much sooner than would have otherwise been possible. The advantages to the physicians were: they could administer the department more efficiently and generate more net revenue than originally calculated, and they were able to retain the resulting increment of earnings.

The IRS concluded that the arrangement was a form of private inurement, in that the physicians—as insiders (Q 6:2)—were obtaining a portion of the hospital's net earnings. The IRS basically forced the hospital community to discontinue this practice. Private inurement was found to be inherent in the percentage feature, termed *per se* private inurement. The IRS refused to allow this flow of revenue to be tested against a standard of reasonableness.

This type of revenue was, however, more in the nature of investment income than individual compensation. There is no absolute prohibition on the use of percentages in computing an employee's compensation, even where the employee is an insider.

TIP: If a form of percentage compensation is deemed appropriate, one feature to consider to avoid private inurement is a ceiling on the amount to be paid. This ceiling is a safeguard against a windfall. Use of this type of ceiling makes it easier to justify the compensation as being reasonable.

Q 6:11 **What role should the board of directors play in the annual review and approval of bonus awards to employees?**

The federal tax law is evolving to the point where it is being expected that the board of directors of a nonprofit organization, particularly a charitable one, will fix the parameters of all compensation programs, not just those pertaining to bonuses. Thus, as part of the exercise of its fiduciary responsibility (Q 1:19), the board should set policy for each component of the organization's compensation plan.

In instances of private inurement, it is becoming a more common practice for the IRS and the attorneys general to fault the board for its lack of involvement and to force the board to develop policies for the ongoing review of the organization's compensation practices.

Q 6:12 How is the bonus compensation program reported to the IRS and disclosed to the public?

There is no express requirement that a bonus compensation program or similar program be specifically reported to the IRS or disclosed to the public. The compensation of the five highest paid employees of a public charity (Q 10:1) must, however, be identified on the organization's annual information return filed with the IRS. Information on this return is accessible to the public. A bonus or similar amount paid to one of these employees should be reported as part of his or her total compensation.

Q 6:13 Are the seven factors mentioned above the only elements to take into account in determining the reasonableness of compensation?

No. The seven factors referenced above (Q 6:8) are the ones basically used in nearly every case. Other factors may, however, be taken into account. These include whether there is a percentage factor in the calculation of compensation (Q 6:10). The data gleaned from national compensation surveys may be important. The location of the organization is a factor, as is (in the compensation context) the existence of written offers from similar organizations competing for the services of an individual.

Q 6:14 How do the intermediate sanctions rules interrelate?

The intermediate sanctions system is an alternative to the sanction of revocation of the tax exemption of an organization that participates in a private inurement transaction.

The intermediate sanctions rules impose excise taxes, rather than loss (in most instances) of exempt status, on the participants in a private inurement transaction. These rules impose penalty excise taxes as an intermediate—or alternative—sanction in cases where an organization exempt from tax as a charitable organization (other than a private foundation) or a social welfare organization engaged in an *excess benefit transaction*. In this case, intermediate sanctions can be imposed on disqualified persons who improperly benefited from the transaction and on managers of the organization who participated in the transaction knowing that it was improper.

An excess benefit transaction includes any transaction in which an economic benefit is provided to, or for the use of, any disqualified person if the value of the economic benefit exceeds the value of consideration (including the performance of services) received by the organization for providing the benefit.

A rebuttable presumption can arise to the effect that a transaction was not an excess benefit one if the exempt organization's board had (1) delegated authority to make decisions with respect to the transaction to those board members who did not have a conflict of interest; (2) considered specific information relevant to the decision, including as much information on comparable transactions as could be collected through reasonable efforts; (3) documented the basis for its decision; and (4) approved the transaction, including a limit on the total amount that could be transferred to the controlling person in advance of its occurrence.

A disqualified person who benefited from an excess benefit transaction is subject to a first-tier penalty tax equal to 25 percent of the amount of the excess benefit (in an instance of unreasonable compensation, the amount of the compensation that is excessive). Organization managers who participated in an excess benefit transaction knowing that it was improper are subject to a first-tier penalty tax of 10 percent of the amount of the excess benefit (subject to a maximum tax of $10,000).

Additional, second-tier taxes can be imposed on a disqualified person if there was no correction of the excess benefit transaction within a specified time period. In this case, the disqualified person can be subject to a penalty tax equal to 200 percent of the amount of the excess benefit. For this purpose, the term *correction* means undoing the excess benefit to the extent possible, establishing safeguards to prevent future excess benefit, and, where a full undoing of the excess benefit is not possible, taking such additional corrective action as would be prescribed by federal tax regulations.

The intermediate sanction for excess benefit transactions can be imposed by the IRS in lieu of or in addition to revocation of the tax-exempt status of the errant organization. If more than one disqualified person or manager is liable for a penalty excise tax, then all such persons are jointly and severally liable for the tax. The IRS has the authority to abate the excise tax penalty if it is established that the violation was due to reasonable cause and not to willful neglect, and that the transaction at issue was corrected within the allowed correction period.

CAUTION: This intermediate sanctions scheme is not as benign as it may appear; one entangled in it can face heavy taxes and disgorgement obligations. Suppose an individual was compensated by a public charity in the annual amount of $200,000 and the IRS determined that $50,000 of the compensation was an excess benefit. First, the individual would be assessed a tax of $12,500 (25 percent of $50,000). Second, the individual would be required to timely correct the transaction, which is to say return the excess compensation ($50,000) to the exempt organization before the first-tier tax is assessed or a deficiency notice mailed. How is an individual making $200,000 annually going to come up with $62,500 in this relatively short time period? Third, if the transaction is not timely corrected, there would be a second-tier tax of $100,000 (200 percent of $50,000). Now the individual owes the exempt organization and the government $162,500, plus interest. Further suppose that, as is often the case, the audit is for a three-year period. The tab then becomes nearly $500,000 ($487,500, to be precise) plus interest.

Needless to say, this would be a substantial hardship where the individual acted in good faith and has already spent the salary; unable to satisfy the disgorgement and tax requirement (and related legal fees), bankruptcy (to shed nontax debt) may be the only resort. Meanwhile, one or more board members could also be taxed and the organization could have its tax exemption revoked.

Q 6:15   When is a loan private inurement?

A loan to an insider, by a nonprofit organization that is subject to the private inurement doctrine, can be private inurement. That would be the case where the terms of the loan are unreasonable.

The factors to be taken into account in assessing the reasonableness of a loan include the amount of the loan in relation to the organization's resources, whether the terms of the loan are reduced to writing (such as a note), the amount of any security, the rate of interest, the term of the note, and how the transaction is reflected on the books and records of the lender and borrower. The latter factor is significant in determining the intent of the parties, especially whether it was really expected that the loan would be repaid. (If not, the "loan" would be regarded as additional compensation.) Thus, another factor would be the zealousness of the organization in securing payments or levying against the security, should the borrower cease making timely payments.

 **TIP:** While all of these factors are important, the interest rate is particularly significant. If the rate is not reasonable (such as a point or two over the prime rate), the transaction may well be questioned. A no-interest loan to an insider would—absent the most extenuating of circumstances—be private inurement.

As with compensation, the test usually is one of commonalities (Q 6:8): What would the elements of a similar loan be if made in the commercial setting?

Q 6:16   When is a rental arrangement private inurement?

The rental of property from an insider, by a nonprofit organization that is subject to the private inurement doctrine, can be private inurement. That would be the case where the terms of the rental are unreasonable.

The factors to be taken into account in assessing the reasonableness of a rental arrangement include the amount of the rent, whether the terms of the transaction are reduced to writing (such as a lease), the term of the rental, and the need of the organization for the particular property. Regarding the latter element, the ability of the nonprofit organization to rent similar property from an unrelated party may be a factor in the analysis.

There can also be private inurement where a nonprofit organization rents property to an insider. The first of the above three factors is also relevant in this setting. Another factor to be applied would be the extent to which the organization pursued rent collection where the tenant (an insider) fell behind in rent payments.

TIP: While all of these factors are important, the amount of the rent is particularly significant. If the rental rate is not reasonable, the transaction may well be questioned. An excessive amount of rent paid to an insider would be a classic form of private inurement.

As with compensation, the test usually is one of commonalities (Q 6:8): What would be the elements of a similar rental transaction if made in the commercial setting?

Q 6:17 **Are there other forms of private inurement?**

Yes. One form of private benefit is the provision of services to insiders. Here it is essential to separate exempt functions from the possibility of private inurement. For example, an organization operated to advance the arts can be a charitable entity; if it is an art gallery that exhibits and sells its members' works, it may be engaging in private inurement. Likewise, the rendering of housing assistance for low-income families qualifies as a charitable undertaking; private inurement may be taking place where housing is provided to some of the charitable organization's key employees.

The participation by a nonprofit organization, particularly a charitable one, in a partnership or joint venture may raise issues of private inurement. The IRS is especially concerned about a situation where a public charity is considered to be running a business (such as a partnership) for the benefit of private interests. The scrutiny in this area is most intense where the charitable organization is the (or a) general partner in a limited partnership and some or all of the limited partners are insiders with respect to the organization.

The position of the IRS as to public charities in limited partnerships at this time is this: to avoid loss of tax-exempt status, the organization must be a general partner in the partnership for the purpose of advancing its charitable purposes, it must be protected against the day-to-day duties of administering the partnership, and the payments to the limited partners cannot be excessive.

The IRS is more relaxed as to the involvement of charities in general partnerships and joint ventures. There the test largely is whether the organization is furthering exempt ends. If it is, tax-exempt status is not likely to be disturbed.

TIP: One way to assess whether a transaction involves private inurement is to see whether it would constitute an act of self-dealing under the private foundation self-dealing rules (Chapter 11). If it is self-dealing, it is likely to be private inurement.

CAUTION: The foregoing tip is a generalization. In one instance serving as an exception to this guideline, a mortgage loan to a key employee was ruled by the IRS to be self-dealing when extended by a museum classified as a private foundation, but was held to not be private inurement when the museum became a public charity because the value of the loan was included in an overall reasonable compensation package. (Special rules in the foundation setting prevented treatment of the loan as an item of compensation.)

PRIVATE BENEFIT

Q 6:18 How is private benefit determined in actual practice?

The law on this point is particularly vague. The range of transactions embraced by the private benefit doctrine is not as precise as that captured by the private inurement doctrine. As noted, however, every instance of private inurement is also a form of private benefit (Q 6:5).

Because there is no requirement of the presence of an insider to bring the private benefit doctrine into play, the doctrine can become applicable with respect to any type of circumstance and any type of person. It is a fallback, catchall concept that is used to prevent the resources of a charitable organization from being misapplied—that is, applied for noncharitable ends.

There is some authority for the proposition that two types of private benefit exist: primary private benefit and secondary private benefit.

Q 6:19 What is *primary private benefit*?

The concepts of primary and secondary private benefit have been illustrated by a case involving a nonprofit school. The purpose of the school was to train individuals to be political campaign managers and consultants. The court was troubled by the fact that the graduates of the school ended up working for candidates of the same political party. Although the school's programs did not constitute political campaign activities (Chapter 9), nor violate any other then-existing rule barring tax exemption, the court nonetheless wanted to deny tax-exempt status to the school.

The court achieved this objective by conjuring up the idea of these two levels of private benefit. The first level of private beneficiaries—those enjoying *primary private benefit*—were the students of the school. This type of private benefit, however, could not be employed to deny tax-exempt status because it was also an exempt educational function. To prevent the school from acquiring tax exemption, the court turned to secondary private benefit.

Q 6:20 What is *secondary private benefit*?

Secondary private benefit is private benefit that flows to one or more persons as the consequence of the provision of private benefit to the primary beneficiaries. It is not clear whether secondary private benefit is taken into account if primary private benefit is of a nature that would cause denial or revocation of exemption.

The court in the above-described case (Q 6:19) ruled that, although the primary private benefit did not prevent tax exemption, the secondary private benefit did. The secondary private beneficiaries were the political candidates who received the services of the school's graduates. This type of private benefit was held to be more than incidental.

NOTE: The concept of secondary private benefit has not been applied before or since this opinion was issued. It is a troublesome rule of law because of its reach. Taken literally, every school has secondary private beneficiaries: those who employ its graduates and thus acquire the benefits of the knowledge and skills the school taught. For example, the partners of a law firm who utilize the training of newly graduated associates are secondary private beneficiaries to a far greater economic and other extent than the political candidates who hire trained campaign managers and consultants.

Q 6:21 What is the current status of the private benefit doctrine?

The courts and the IRS have recently applied the private benefit doctrine in ways that range far beyond situations involving inappropriate benefits accorded to individuals. The private benefit doctrine can also be invoked in circumstances where benefit is impermissibly provided to for-profit corporations. This is the case, for example, in instances involving whole-entity joint ventures (Q 16:27–Q 16:29) and ancillary joint ventures (Q 16:30). Indeed, it now appears that private benefit can be extended by charitable organizations to other tax-exempt organizations. As an illustration of this, the IRS has taken the position that foundations that provide scholarships to participants in beauty pageants, conducted by exempt social welfare organizations, cannot be tax-exempt because of private benefit conferred on the social welfare organization involved. As another example, a court would not allow an educational foundation affiliated with an exempt association (business league) to be exempt by reason of private benefit conferred on the association.

COMMENT: These two examples are extreme (and probably incorrect). It may be noted that the federal tax law permits a charitable organization to qualify as a supporting organization where the supported organization is a social welfare organization or a business league (Q 10:22). It is anomalous to think that this tax exemption can be created by statute, only to be taken away by the private benefit doctrine.

Q 6:22 Is it possible for a donor, when making a gift to a nonprofit organization, to realize a private benefit from the gift?

No private benefit is inherent in this type of a transaction, even where the donor is an insider. The benefits that flow from forms of donor recognition are not private benefit that would adversely affect tax-exempt status. For example, a gift transaction where a building or a scholarship fund is named after the contributor does not involve an extent of private benefit that would threaten the donee's tax exemption. It either is not considered this type of private benefit at all or is regarded as so incidental and tenuous as to be ignored for tax purposes.

It is quite possible, however, for a donor to receive a private benefit in exchange for a contribution, in the form of a good or service. For example, an individual could give to a charity a contribution to be used in constructing a building that would house the charity's offices. If the contributor was provided free office space in the building in exchange for the gift, that would be private benefit. The private benefit, if more than incidental (Q 6:23), could cause the charity to lose its tax exemption. (The donor would usually have to reduce the charitable contribution deduction by the value of the good or service received.)

Q 6:23 How is incidental private benefit measured?

There is no precise, mechanical test for assessing private benefit. A facts-and-circumstances test must be applied in each case. The private benefit doctrine is a very subjective legal concept. It enables the IRS or a court to assert private benefit in nearly every instance in which misdirection of the resources of a charitable, and perhaps other nonprofit, organization is occurring.

CHAPTER 7

Intermediate Sanctions

The federal tax law includes the long-awaited and much-heralded concept of *intermediate sanctions*—an emphasis on the taxation of those persons who engaged in impermissible private transactions with tax-exempt public charities and social welfare organizations, rather than revocation of the tax exemption of these entities. With this approach, tax sanctions—structured as penalty excise taxes—may be imposed on the disqualified persons who improperly benefited from a transaction and on organization managers who participated in the transaction knowing that it was improper. This body of law represents the most dramatic and important package of rules concerning exempt charitable organizations since Congress enacted the basic statutory scheme in this field in 1969. Intermediate sanctions hold the promise of transforming the private inurement and private benefit doctrines and are likely to impact the composition and functioning of many boards of directors.

Here are the questions most frequently asked about the intermediate sanctions rules—and the answers to them.

Q 7:1 What does the term *intermediate sanctions* mean?

Before the intermediate sanctions rules were enacted, the IRS had only two formal options when it found a substantial violation of the law of tax-exempt organizations by a public charity or a social welfare organization: do nothing or revoke the organization's tax exemption. These rules, however, provide the IRS with a third alternative—one that is certainly more potent than doing nothing (including, perhaps, issuing some informal warning) and less draconian than revocation of tax exemption. It is, thus, an *intermediate* sanction.

In the instance of a transaction covered by these rules (Q 7:8), tax sanctions are to be imposed on the disqualified persons (Q 7:24) who improperly benefited from the transaction and perhaps on organization managers (Q 7:26) who participated in the transaction knowing that it was improper.

Q 7:2 What is the effective date of the intermediate sanctions rules?

The effective date of these rules generally is September 14, 1995. The sanctions do not apply, however, to any benefits arising from a transaction pursuant to a written contract that was binding on that date and continued in force through the time of the transaction, and the terms of which have not materially changed.

Q 7:3 When were these rules enacted?

The intermediate sanctions law came into being on enactment of the Taxpayer Bill of Rights 2 (Act). This legislation was signed into law on July 30, 1996.

Q 7:4 What is the legislative history of this legislation?

The Senate, on July 11, 1996, adopted the legislation as passed by the House of Representatives, on April 16, 1996, without change. The House vote was 425–0; the Senate voted by unanimous consent. There is no report of the Senate Finance Committee and no conference report. Thus, the report of the House Committee on Ways and Means, dated March 28, 1996 (House Report), constitutes the totality of the legislative history of the intermediate sanctions rules.

Q 7:5 Have the Treasury Department and the IRS issued guidance as to these rules?

Yes. Final regulations to accompany the intermediate sanctions rules were issued on January 21, 2002—five and a half years after the underlying statute was signed into law.

COMMENT: These regulations are not nearly as helpful as was hoped. For the most part, they merely restate what is in the statute and the legislative history or can be found in the comparable rules in the private foundations context. Most of the interesting subtleties are embedded in the examples. Some areas of this body of law where guidance would be appropriate are completely unaddressed by the regulations, such as the criteria for determining whether sales, lending, and rental transactions are reasonable (Q 7:19–7:21). Guidance as to whether compensation is reasonable is skimpy (Q 7:17). Indeed, in one instance, the regulations are in conflict with the legislative history (Q 7:25).

Q 7:6 What types of tax-exempt organizations are involved in these rules?

These sanctions apply with respect to public charities and tax-exempt social welfare organizations. These entities are termed, for this purpose, *applicable tax-exempt organizations.*

Generally, a public charity will have received a determination letter (ruling) from the IRS as to its tax-exempt status (Q 4:7). Social welfare organizations, however, are not required to obtain an IRS ruling in this regard (*id.*). Thus, a social welfare organization is an applicable tax-exempt organization if it has applied for and received recognition of exemption from the IRS (Chapter 4), filed an application for recognition of exemption with the IRS, filed an information return (Chapter 5) as a social welfare organization with the IRS, or otherwise held itself out as a social welfare organization.

These entities include any organization described in either of these two categories of exempt organizations at any time during the five-year period ending on the date of the transaction.

CAUTION 1: This is one aspect of the intermediate sanctions law that should be closely monitored. There is discussion about broadening the concept of applicable tax-exempt organization. The most likely candidates for inclusion are tax-exempt labor organizations and/or business, professional, and trade associations and other business leagues (Q 4:7).

CAUTION 2: Just because an organization is not an *applicable tax-exempt organization* does not mean that it is not caught up in these rules. This is because an exempt organization can be a disqualified person (Q 7:29).

Q 7:7 Are there any exceptions to these rules?

No. That is, all public charities and social welfare organizations are applicable tax-exempt organizations. Private foundations (Chapter 11) are not included in this tax regime because a somewhat similar system—that involving self-dealing rules (Q 11:13–11:18)—is applicable to them. Also, a foreign organization that receives substantially all of its support from sources outside the United States is not an applicable tax-exempt organization.

Q 7:8 To what types of transactions do these rules apply?

This tax scheme has as its heart the *excess benefit transaction*. The definition of an *excess benefit transaction* is based on the contract law concept of *consideration*. It generally is any transaction in which an economic benefit is provided by an applicable tax-exempt organization (Q 7:6) directly or indirectly to or for the use of any disqualified person (Q 7:24), if the value of the economic benefit provided by the exempt organization exceeds the value of the consideration (including the performance of services) received for providing the benefit. This type of benefit is known as an *excess benefit*.

Q 7:9 How is *value* measured?

The standard is that of *fair market value*. The fair market value of property, including the right to use property, is the price at which property or the right to use it would change hands between a willing buyer and a willing seller, neither being under any compulsion to buy, sell, or transfer property or the right to use it, and both having reasonable knowledge of relevant facts.

Q 7:10 Can an economic benefit be treated as part of the recipient's compensation?

Yes, but with some qualifications. An economic benefit may not be treated as consideration for the performance of services unless the organization clearly intended and made the payments as compensation for services. Items of this nature include the payment of personal expenses, transfers to or for the benefit of disqualified persons, and non–fair-market-value transactions benefiting these persons.

In determining whether payments or transactions of this nature are in fact forms of compensation, the relevant factors include whether (1) the appropriate decision-making body approved the transfer as compensation in accordance with established procedures (such as an approved written employment contract executed on or before the date of the transfer) and (2) the organization and the recipient reported the transfer (other than in the case of nontaxable fringe benefits) as compensation on relevant returns or other forms. These returns or forms include the organization's annual information return filed with the IRS (Chapter 5), the information return provided by the organization to the recipient (Form W-2 or Form 1099), and the individual's income tax return (Form 1040).

With the exception of nontaxable fringe benefits and certain other types of nontaxable transfers (such as employer-provided health benefits and contributions to qualified pension plans), an organization is not permitted to demonstrate at the time of an IRS audit that it intended to treat economic benefits provided to a disqualified person as compensation for services merely by claiming that the benefits may be viewed as part of the disqualified person's total compensation package. Rather, the organization is required to provide substantiation that is contemporaneous with the transfer of the economic benefits at issue.

Q 7:11 What happens if an economic benefit cannot be regarded as part of the recipient's compensation?

If this happens, there basically is no other way to justify the provision of the benefit as something other than an excess benefit transaction—even if the amount involved is reasonable. This outcome is termed an *automatic excess benefit transaction*. This is a huge trap for disqualified persons of applicable tax-exempt organizations. The parties involved should be certain that these benefits are either covered by an exception or properly treated as compensation. Otherwise, the excise tax (Q 7:30) and correction requirement (Q 7:31) will be applicable.

Q 7:12 What does the phrase *directly or indirectly* mean?

The phrase *directly or indirectly* means the provision of an economic benefit directly by the organization or indirectly by means of a controlled entity. Thus, an applicable tax-exempt organization cannot avoid involvement in an excess benefit transaction by causing a controlled entity to engage in the transaction.

Q 7:13   What does the phrase *for the use of* mean?

A benefit can be provided to a disqualified person even though the transaction is with a nondisqualified person. A benefit of this nature might be enhancement of reputation, augmentation of goodwill, or some form of marketing advantage.

Q 7:14   Is there any other definition of the term *excess benefit transaction*?

Yes. The term *excess benefit transaction* includes any transaction in which the amount of any economic benefit provided to or for the use of a disqualified person is determined in whole or in part by the revenues of one or more activities of the organization, but only if the transaction results in impermissible private inurement. In this context, the excess benefit is the amount of impermissible private inurement. This category of arrangement is known as a *revenue-sharing arrangement*.

A revenue-sharing arrangement may constitute an excess benefit transaction regardless of whether the economic benefit provided to the disqualified person exceeds the fair market value of the consideration provided in return if, at any point, it permits a disqualified person to receive additional compensation without providing proportional benefits that contribute to the organization's accomplishment of its exempt purpose. If the economic benefit is provided as compensation for services, relevant facts and circumstances include the relationship between the size of the benefit provided and the quality and quantity of the services provided, as well as the ability of the party receiving the compensation to control the activities generating the revenues on which the compensation is based.

> **NOTE:**   Under preexisting law, certain revenue-sharing arrangements were determined by the IRS to not constitute private inurement. It continues to be the case that not all revenue-sharing arrangements are improper private inurement. The Department of the Treasury and the IRS are not bound, however, by any particular prior rulings in this area.

Q 7:15   Are any economic benefits disregarded for these purposes?

Yes. One set of disregarded benefits is the payment of reasonable expenses for members of the governing body of an applicable tax-exempt organization to attend meetings of the governing body of the organization. This exclusion does not encompass luxury travel or spousal travel.

An economic benefit provided to a disqualified person that the person receives solely as a member of or volunteer for an organization is disregarded for these purposes, if the benefit is provided to members of the public in exchange for a membership fee of no more than $75 annually. For example, if a disqualified person is also a member of the organization and receives membership benefits such as advance ticket purchases and a discount at the organization's gift shop that would normally be provided in exchange for a membership fee of $75 or less per year, the membership benefit is disregarded.

An economic benefit provided to a disqualified person that the disqualified person receives solely as a member of a charitable class that the applicable tax-exempt organization intends to benefit as part of the accomplishment of the organization's exempt purposes is generally disregarded for these purposes.

Q 7:16   In the context of compensation, how does one determine whether it is excessive?

Existing tax law standards (including those standards established under the law concerning ordinary and necessary business expenses) apply in determining reasonableness of compensation and fair market value. This concept is essentially the same as that in the private inurement context (Q: 6:8).

TIP: In this regard, an individual need not necessarily accept reduced compensation merely because he or she renders services to a tax-exempt, as opposed to a taxable, organization.

Compensation that is excessive is a form of excess benefit transaction; the portion that is considered excessive is an excess benefit.

Q 7:17   What are the tax law standards used in determining the reasonableness of compensation?

The criteria that have been fashioned in determining the reasonableness of compensation are:

1. Compensation levels paid by similarly situated organizations, both tax-exempt and taxable, for functionally comparable positions
2. The location of the organization, including the availability of similar specialties in the geographic area
3. Written offers from similar institutions competing for the services of the individual involved
4. The background (including experience and education) of the individual involved
5. The need of the organization for the services of a particular individual
6. The amount of time an individual devotes to the position

An additional criterion that intermediate sanctions have brought to this area of the law is whether the compensation was approved by an independent board.

COMMENT: The intermediate sanctions regulations merely extend this guidance: "Compensation for the performance of services is reasonable if it is only such amount as would ordinarily be paid for like services by like enterprises under like circumstances." Given the immense focus on compensation in relation to the excess benefit transaction standard, this meager offering in the regulations is nothing short of irresponsible.

The regulations offer some interesting rules as to what *circumstances* are to be taken into account, particularly in terms of moments in time. The general rule is that the circumstances to be taken into consideration are those existing at the date when the contract for services was made. Where reasonableness of compensation cannot be determined under those circumstances, however, the determination is to be made based on all facts and circumstances, up to and including circumstances as of the date of payment. Here is the best rule of all in this regard: in no event shall circumstances existing at the date when the contract is questioned be considered in making a determination of the reasonableness of compensation.

NOTE: There are court opinions holding that reasonableness can be ascertained taking into account developments that occurred after the transaction was consummated. A court found that an event that occurred two years after the transaction in question could be taken into account in determining reasonableness.

Q 7:18 What items are included in determining the value of compensation?

Compensation for these purposes means all items of compensation provided by an applicable tax-exempt organization in exchange for the performance of services. These items include (1) all forms of cash and noncash compensation, such as salary, fees, bonuses, and severance payments; (2) all forms of deferred compensation that is earned and vested, whether or not funded, and whether or not paid under a deferred compensation plan that is a qualified plan, but if deferred compensation for services performed in multiple prior years vests in a later year, that compensation is attributed to the years in which the services were performed; (3) the amount of premiums paid for liability or other insurance coverage, as well as any payment or reimbursement by the organization of charges, expenses, fees, or taxes not covered ultimately by the insurance coverage; (4) all other benefits, whether or not included in income for tax purposes, including payments to welfare benefit plans on behalf of the persons being compensated, such as plans providing medical, dental, life insurance, severance pay, and disability benefits, and both taxable and nontaxable fringe benefits (other than certain working condition fringe benefits and de minimis fringe benefits), including expense allowances or reimbursements or forgone interest on loans that the recipient must report as income; and (5) any economic benefit provided by an applicable tax-exempt organization, whether provided directly or through another entity owned, controlled by or affiliated with the organization, whether the other entity is taxable or tax-exempt.

Q 7:19 Do these rules apply to rental transactions?

Where an applicable tax-exempt organization rents property to a disqualified person, it is crucial that the amount of the rent, and the other terms and conditions of the transaction, be reasonable. There should be a lease, a reasonable term, probably a security deposit, and other terms and conditions that are customary with respect to the type of rental arrangement involved.

NOTE: The regulations are silent on this point, other than to define the term *value* in the context of the right to use property (Q 7:9).

Q 7:20 Do these rules apply to lending transactions?

Where an applicable tax-exempt organization lends money to a disqualified person, it is crucial that the amount lent, and the other terms and conditions of the transaction, be reasonable. There should be a note, a reasonable term, a reasonable rate of interest, probably some form of security, and other terms and conditions that are customary with respect to the type of lending arrangement involved.

Terms and conditions must also be reasonable where an applicable tax-exempt organization is borrowing money from a disqualified person.

NOTE: The regulations are silent on this point.

Q 7:21 Do these rules apply to sales transactions?

Where an applicable tax-exempt organization sells property to a disqualified person, it is crucial that the amount received (Q 7:9), and the other terms and conditions of the transaction, be reasonable. The consideration received by the organization need not be only money; it is permissible for property to be exchanged and for the consideration to be represented by one or more notes.

NOTE: The regulations are silent on this point, other than to define the term *fair market value* (Q 7:9).

Q 7:22 Who has the burden of proof in a dispute with the IRS as to whether a transaction involves an excess benefit?

In an administrative proceeding with the IRS, generally the burden of proof is on the disqualified person who participated in the transaction. There is, however, a rebuttable presumption of reasonableness, with respect to a compensation arrangement with a disqualified person.

> **NOTE:** This rebuttable presumption is not a matter of statute (that is, it is not in the Act); it is provided in the House Report. Also, it is reflected in the regulations.

This presumption arises where the arrangement was approved by a board of directors or trustees (or a committee of the board) that

1. Was composed entirely of individuals who do not have a conflict of interest (Q 7:23) with respect to the arrangement,

> **NOTE:** This committee may be composed of any individuals permitted under state law to so serve and may act on behalf of the board to the extent permitted by state law. As will be noted, however, committee members who are not board members are likely to be organization managers (Q 7:26).

2. Obtained and relied on appropriate data as to comparability prior to making its determination, and
3. Adequately documented the basis for its determination.

As to the first of these criteria, which essentially requires an *independent* board (as opposed to a *captive* board), a reciprocal approval arrangement does not satisfy the independence requirement. This arrangement occurs where an individual approves compensation of a disqualified person and the disqualified person, in turn, approves the individual's compensation (Q 7:23).

As to the second of these criteria, appropriate data includes compensation levels paid by similarly situated organizations, both tax-exempt and taxable, for functionally comparable positions; the location of the organization, including the availability of similar specialties in the geographic area; independent compensation surveys by nationally recognized independent firms; and written offers from similar institutions competing for the services of the disqualified person.

> **NOTE:** There is a safe harbor for organizations with annual gross receipts of less than $1 million when reviewing compensation arrangements. This requires data on compensation paid by three comparable organizations in the same or similar communities for similar services. A rolling average based on the three prior tax years may be used to calculate annual gross receipts.

As to the third of these criteria, adequate documentation includes an evaluation of the individual whose compensation was being established, and the basis for determining that the individual's compensation was reasonable in light of that evaluation and data. The organization's written or electronic records must note the terms of the transaction that was approved, the date of approval, the members of the governing body (or committee) who were present during debate on the transaction or arrangement that was approved and those who voted on it, the comparability data obtained and relied on by the governing body (or committee) and how the data was obtained, and the actions taken with respect to consideration of the transaction by anyone who is otherwise a member of the governing body (or committee) but who had a conflict of interest with respect to the transaction or arrangement.

The fact that a state or local legislative or agency body may have authorized or approved a particular compensation package paid to a disqualified person is not determinative of the reasonableness of the compensation paid. Likewise, this type of authorization or approval is not determinative of whether a revenue-sharing transaction violates the private inurement proscription (Q 7:14).

If these three criteria are satisfied, penalty excise taxes can be imposed only if the IRS develops sufficient contrary evidence to rebut the probative value of the evidence put forth by the parties to the transaction. For example, the IRS could establish that the compensation data relied on by the parties was not for functionally comparable positions or that the disqualified person in fact did not substantially perform the responsibilities of the position.

A similar rebuttable presumption arises with respect to the reasonableness of the valuation of property sold or otherwise transferred (or purchased) by an organization to (or from) a disqualified person if the sale or transfer (or purchase) is approved by an independent board that uses appropriate comparability data and adequately documents its determination.

Q 7:23   What does the phrase *conflict of interest* mean?

The regulations define the term by defining what is *not* a conflict of interest. Thus, a member of a governing body (or a committee of it) does not have a conflict or interest with respect to a compensation arrangement or transaction if the member

1. Is not the disqualified person and is not related to any disqualified person participating in or economically benefiting from the compensation arrangement or transaction

2. Is not in an employment relationship subject to the direction or control of any disqualified person participating in or economically benefiting from the compensation arrangement or transaction

3. Is not receiving compensation or other payments subject to approval by any disqualified person participating in or economically benefiting from the compensation arrangement or transaction

4. Has no material financial interest affected by the compensation arrangement or transaction and

5. Does not approve a transaction providing economic benefits to any disqualified person participating in the compensation arrangement or transaction,

who in turn has approved or will approve a transaction providing economic benefits to the member

Q 7:24   What does the term *disqualified person* mean?

The term *disqualified person*, in this context, means

1. Any person who was, at any time during the five-year period ending on the date of the excess benefit transaction involved, in a position to exercise substantial influence over the affairs of the applicable tax-exempt organization involved (Q 7:6) (whether by virtue of being an organization manager or otherwise),
2. A member of the family of an individual described in the preceding category, and
3. An entity in which individuals described in the preceding two categories own more than 35 percent of an interest.

Q 7:25   What is the scope of this *substantial influence* rule?

An individual is in a position to exercise substantial influence over the affairs of an organization if he or she, individually or with others, serves as the president, chief executive officer, or chief operating officer of the organization. An individual serves in one of these capacities, regardless of title, if he or she has or shares ultimate responsibility for implementing the decisions of the governing body or supervising the management, administration, or operation of the organization.

An individual also is in this position if he or she, independently or with others, serves as treasurer or chief financial officer of the organization. An individual serves in one of these capacities, regardless of title, if he or she has or shares ultimate responsibility for managing the organization's financial assets and has or shares authority to sign drafts or direct the signing of drafts, or authorize electronic transfer of funds, from the organization's bank account(s).

A person can be in a position to exercise substantial influence over a tax-exempt organization despite the fact that the person is not an employee of (and does not receive any compensation directly from) a tax-exempt organization but is formally an employee of (and is directly compensated by) a subsidiary—including a taxable subsidiary—controlled by the parent tax-exempt organization.

NOTE: There is a conflict between the legislative history of these rules (Q 7:4) and the regulations (Q 7:5). The legislative history states that an individual having the title of *trustee*, *director*, or *officer* does not automatically have status as a disqualified person. The regulations, however, provide that persons having substantial influence include any individual serving on the governing body of the organization who is entitled to vote on matters over which the governing body has authority.

TIP: Although it has been the view of the IRS that all physicians who are on the medical staff of a hospital or similar organization are insiders for purposes of the private inurement proscription, a physician is a disqualified person under the intermediate sanctions rules only where he or she is in a position to exercise substantial influence over the affairs of the organization.

There are some categories of persons who are deemed to not be in a position to exercise substantial influence. One is any other public charity. Another is an employee of an applicable tax-exempt organization who receives economic benefits of less than the amount of compensation referenced for a highly compensated employee, is not a member of the family of a disqualified person (Q 7:27), is not an individual referenced above as considered to have this influence, and is not a substantial contributor to the organization.

A person who has managerial control over a discrete segment of an organization may be in a position to exercise substantial influence over the affairs of the entire organization.

Facts and circumstances that tend to show the requisite substantial influence include the fact that the person founded the organization; is a substantial contributor to the organization; receives compensation based on revenues derived from activities of the organization that the person controls; has authority to control or determine a significant portion of the organization's capital expenditures, operating budget, or compensation for employees; has managerial authority or serves as a key advisor to a person with managerial authority; or owns a controlling interest in a corporation, partnership, or trust that is a disqualified person.

Facts and circumstances that tend to show an absence of substantial influence are where the person has taken a bona fide vow of poverty as an employee, agent, or on behalf of a religious organization; the person is an independent contractor (such as a lawyer, accountant, or investment manager or advisor), acting in that capacity, unless the person is acting in that capacity with respect to a transaction from which the person might economically benefit either directly or indirectly (aside from fees received for the professional services rendered); and any preferential treatment a person receives based on the size of that person's contribution is also offered to any other contributor making a comparable contribution as part of a solicitation intended to attract a substantial number of contributions.

Q 7:26   What does the term *organization manager* mean?

An *organization manager* is a trustee, director, or officer of an applicable tax-exempt organization, as well as an individual having powers or responsibilities similar to those of trustees, directors, or officers of the organization, regardless of title.

An individual is considered an *officer* of an organization if he or she (1) is specifically so designated under the articles of incorporation, bylaws, or other organizing documents of the organization or (2) regularly exercises general authority to make administrative or policy decisions on behalf of the organization. An individual who has authority merely to recommend particular administrative or policy decisions, but not to implement them without approval of a superior, is not an officer.

NOTE: Independent contractors, acting in a capacity as lawyers, accountants, and investment managers and advisors, are not officers.

COMMENT: Principles similar to those under the law pertaining to private foundations are followed in determining who is an organization manager (Q 11:5).

An individual who is not a trustee, director, or officer and yet serves on a committee of the governing body of an applicable tax-exempt organization that is invoking the rebuttable presumption of reasonableness (Q 7:22) based on the committee's actions is an organization manager for these purposes.

Q 7:27 What does the term *member of the family* mean?

The term *member of the family* is defined as constituting:

1. Spouses, ancestors, children, grandchildren, great-grandchildren, and the spouses of children, grandchildren, and great-grandchildren—namely, those individuals so classified under the private foundation rules, and
2. The brothers and sisters (whether by the whole or half blood) of the individual and their spouses.

NOTE: Thus, this term is defined more broadly in the public charity setting than is the case with private foundations (Q 11:5).

Q 7:28 What is the definition of a *controlled entity*?

The entities that are disqualified persons because one or more disqualified persons own more than a 35 percent interest in them are termed *35 percent controlled entities*. They are

1. Corporations in which one or more disqualified persons own more than 35 percent of the total combined voting power,
2. Partnerships in which one or more disqualified persons own more than 35 percent of the profits interest, and
3. Trusts or estates in which one or more disqualified persons own more than 35 percent of the beneficial interest.

NOTE: The term *combined voting power* includes voting power represented by holdings of voting stock, actual or constructive, but does not include voting rights held only as a director or trustee. This rule is identical to that in the private foundation context (Q 11:6–11:8).

In general, constructive ownership rules apply for purposes of determining what are 35 percent controlled entities.

Q 7:29   Can a tax-exempt organization be a disqualified person?

Yes. A tax-exempt organization, other than a public charity (Q 7:6), can be a disqualified person. All that is required is that an exempt organization be in a position to exercise substantial influence over the affairs of the applicable tax-exempt organization involved (Q 7:24–Q 7:25).

For example, in an instance of an association with a related foundation, the association can be a disqualified person with respect to the foundation. Likewise, a social welfare organization with a related educational foundation can be a disqualified person with respect to that foundation.

NOTE: Other than providing that a public charity cannot be a disqualified person, the regulations are silent as to when or whether any other type of tax-exempt organization can be a disqualified person.

Q 7:30   What are the sanctions?

The intermediate sanctions themselves are in the form of tax penalties.

A disqualified person who benefited from an excess benefit transaction is subject to and must pay an initial excise tax equal to 25 percent of the amount of the excess benefit. Again, the excess benefit is the amount by which a transaction differs from fair market value, the amount of compensation exceeding reasonable compensation, or (pursuant to tax regulations) the amount of impermissible private inurement resulting from a transaction based on the organization's gross or net income (Q 7:14).

NOTE: In addition, the matter must be rectified—corrected—by a return of the excess benefit, plus additional compensation, to the applicable tax-exempt organization (Q 7:31).

An organization manager who participated (Q 7:32) in an excess benefit transaction, knowing (Q 7:33) that it was this type of a transaction, is subject to and must pay an initial excise tax of 10 percent of the excess benefit (subject to a maximum amount of tax of $10,000), where an initial tax is imposed on a disqualified person.

The initial tax is not imposed where the participation in the transaction was not willful (Q 7:34) and was due to reasonable cause (Q 7:35).

An additional excise tax may be imposed on a disqualified person where the initial tax was imposed and if there was no correction of the excess benefit transaction within a specified time period. This time period is the *taxable period*, which means—with respect to an excess benefit transaction—the period beginning with the date on which the transaction occurred and ending on the earlier of

1. The date of mailing of a notice of deficiency with respect to the initial tax, or
2. The date on which the initial tax is assessed.

In this situation, the disqualified person would be subject to and must pay a tax equal to 200 percent of the excess benefit involved.

Q 7:31 What does the term *correction* mean?

The term *correction* means undoing the excess benefit to the extent possible and taking any additional measures necessary to place the organization in a financial position not worse than that in which it would be if the disqualified person had been dealing under the highest fiduciary standards.

Correction of the excess benefit occurs if the disqualified person repays the applicable tax-exempt organization an amount of money equal to the excess benefit, plus any additional amount needed to compensate the organization for the loss of the use of the money or other property during the period commencing on the date of the excess benefit transaction and ending on the date the excess benefit is corrected. Correction may also be accomplished, in certain circumstances, by returning property to the organization and taking any additional steps necessary to make the organization whole.

NOTE: The regulations do not state what these "certain circumstances" might be, nor do they reveal what the "additional steps" might entail.

Q 7:32 What does the term *participation* mean?

The term *participation* includes silence or inaction on the part of an organization manager where he or she is under a duty to speak or act, as well as any affirmative action by the manager. An organization manager, however, will not be considered to have participated in an excess benefit transaction where the manager has opposed the transaction in a manner consistent with the fulfillment of the manager's responsibilities to the applicable tax-exempt organization.

Q 7:33 What does the term *knowing* mean?

A person participates (Q 7:32) in a transaction, *knowing* that it is an excess benefit transaction, only if the person (1) has actual knowledge of sufficient facts so that, based solely on those facts, the transaction would be an excess benefit transaction, (2) is aware that the act under these circumstances may violate the excess benefit transactions rules, and (3) negligently fails to make reasonable attempts to ascertain whether the transaction is an excess benefit transaction, or the person is in fact aware that it is an excess benefit transaction.

Knowing does not mean having reason to know. Evidence tending to show, however, that a person has reason to know of a particular fact or particular rule is relevant in determining whether the person had actual knowledge of the fact or rule. For example, evidence tending to show that a person has reason to know of sufficient facts so that, based solely on those facts, a transaction would be an excess benefit transaction is relevant in determining whether the person has actual knowledge of the facts.

Q 7:34   What does the term *willful* mean?

Participation in a transaction by an organization manager is *willful* if it is voluntary, conscious, and intentional. No motive to avoid the restrictions of the law or the incurrence of any tax is necessary to make the participation willful. Participation by an organization manager, however, is not willful if the manager does not know (Q 7:33) that the transaction in which the manager is participating is an excess benefit transaction.

Q 7:35   What does the term *reasonable cause* mean?

An organization manager's participation is due to *reasonable cause* if the manager has exercised his or her responsibility on behalf of the organization with ordinary business care and prudence.

TIP: If a person, after full disclosure of the factual situation to a lawyer (including in-house counsel), relies on the advice of the lawyer—expressed in a reasoned written legal opinion—that a transaction is not an excess benefit transaction, the person's participation in the transaction will ordinarily not be considered knowing or willful and will ordinarily be considered due to reasonable cause, even if the transaction is subsequently held to be an excess benefit transaction. The absence of advice of legal counsel with respect to an act does not, by itself, give rise to an inference that a person participated in the act knowingly, willfully, or without reasonable cause.

CAUTION: A written legal opinion is *reasoned* so long as it addresses the facts and applicable law. An opinion is not reasoned if it does nothing more than recite the facts and state a conclusion.

Q 7:36   Can there be joint liability for these taxes?

Yes. If more than one organization manager or other disqualified person is liable for an excise tax, then all of these persons are jointly and severally liable for the tax.

Q 7:37   **If the executive of a charity or social welfare organization is receiving compensation that he or she believes to be unreasonable, should the executive voluntarily reduce the compensation or wait to see whether the IRS raises the issue?**

An executive in this position should not rely on his or her "gut feelings" about the reasonableness of the compensation. The first step an individual in this position should take is to determine whether the compensation arrangement is even subject to these rules. If the compensation is set by a pre-1995 binding unaltered contract, the excess benefit transaction rules do not apply with respect to it (Q 7:2).

CAUTION: Of course, the payment of excessive compensation in these circumstances could still amount to private inurement (Q 7:46).

If these rules do apply, the second step is to have the organization procure an independent opinion on the subject. It may turn out that the executive was wrong in his or her judgment. If it develops that the compensation is in fact excessive, however, the executive should work with the organization's board of directors in causing the salary to be lowered to the highest appropriate amount, so as to avoid future excess benefit transactions.

It is not a good idea to wait to see what the IRS may do. This is a self-reporting system (Q 7:41). A delay will involve interest and perhaps penalties should the IRS become aware of the matter. Thus, the prudent approach, having reduced the compensation, is to pay the tax and correct the past transgression(s) by correcting (Q 7:31) the situation. This would be done by returning the excess benefit, plus a suitable amount of interest (Q 7:31), for the year(s) involved to the employer organization.

CAUTION: If the board is notified of this situation by the executive and does nothing, the board members could be personally liable for taxes (Q 7:30).

Q 7:38   **If the IRS raises questions about an executive's compensation, should the executive voluntarily reduce his or her compensation in order to minimize the risk of imposition of the sanctions?**

That usually would be a bad idea. Assuming the compensation is subject to these rules (Q 7:2), a reduction in compensation in the face of an IRS inquiry would be an admission that the compensation has been too high. The better approach is to work with the board of directors of the employer organization to obtain outside advice and then proceed from there (Q 7:37).

If all else fails and the compensation is found to be excessive, the IRS may be approached to see whether there is any basis for abatement on the ground of reasonable cause (Q 7:40).

Q 7:39   **If the board of directors approves an employment contract with an executive and later determines that the compensation provided in the contract is excessive, what steps, if any, should the board take prior to expiration of the contract?**

There is a lot here for the board to do and consider. First step: see whether the contract is sheltered by the effective date rules (Q 7:2). If it is, that is the end of the matter (although it could still amount to private inurement). If it is not, then the board should seek an outside evaluation of the compensation level and determine the portion of it (if any) that is considered excessive.

A contract that is covered by the intermediate sanctions rules and embodies unreasonable compensation is nonetheless a binding contract. Thus, unless there is a provision in the agreement that allows it—an excellent idea, by the way—the board cannot unilaterally adjust the compensation level. (That would be a breach of contract.) Rather, the board should work with the individual—who, after all, will bear the brunt of the penalties (Q 7:30)—and proceed as discussed earlier (Q 7:37).

NOTE: If the excess benefit transaction consists of the payment of compensation for services under a contract that has not been completed, termination of the employment or independent contractor relationship between the organization and the disqualified person is *not* required in order to correct.

Q 7:40   **Is there any relief from this tax scheme? Any basis for being excused from these penalties?**

Yes, there are some forms of relief. One of the more fascinating aspects of the intermediate sanctions rules is the *initial contract exception*. Pursuant to this element of the law—a huge exception in relation to the general rule—the intermediate sanctions regime does not apply to a fixed payment made by an applicable tax-exempt organization (Q 7:6) to a disqualified person (Q 7:24) pursuant to an initial contract. An *initial contract* is a binding written contract between the tax-exempt organization and a person who was not a disqualified person immediately prior to entering into the contract. A *fixed payment* is an amount of money or other property specified in the contract involved, or determined by a fixed formula specified in the contract, which is to be paid or transferred in exchange for the provision of specified services or property. If the parties make a material change to an initial contract, the contract is treated as a new contract—so that the exception is no longer available—as of the date the material change is effective. Otherwise, the initial contract exception can continue, as a matter of law, without limit.

Also, the IRS has the authority to abate the intermediate sanctions excise tax in certain circumstances, principally where a taxable event was due to reasonable cause and not to willful neglect, and the transaction at issue was corrected within the specified taxable period (Q 7:31, Q 7:34, 7:35).

Q 7:41 How are these taxes reported and paid?

Under the law in existence prior to the enactment of intermediate sanctions, charitable organizations and other persons liable for certain excise taxes must file returns by which the taxes due are calculated and reported. These taxes are those imposed on public charities for excessive lobbying and for political campaign activities, and on private foundations and/or other persons for a wide range of impermissible activities. These returns are on Form 4720.

In general, returns on Form 4720 for a disqualified person or organization manager liable for an excess benefit transaction tax must be filed on or before the 15th day of the fifth month following the close of that person's tax year.

Q 7:42 Can an organization reimburse a disqualified person for these taxes?

Yes. Any reimbursements by an applicable tax-exempt organization of excise tax liability are, however, treated as an excess benefit unless they are included in the disqualified person's compensation during the year in which the reimbursement is made. (This rule is consistent with that noted earlier (Q 7:10), which is that payments of personal expenses and other benefits to or for the benefit of disqualified persons are treated as compensation only if it is clear that the organization intended and made the payments as compensation for services.) The total compensation package, including the amount of any reimbursement, is subject to the requirement of reasonableness.

Q 7:43 Can an organization purchase insurance for a disqualified person to provide coverage for these taxes?

Yes. But, again (Q 7:42), the payment by an applicable tax-exempt organization of premiums for an insurance policy providing liability insurance to a disqualified person for excess benefit taxes is an excess benefit transaction unless the premiums are treated as part of the compensation paid to the disqualified person and the total compensation (including premiums) is reasonable.

Q 7:44 Does the payment of an intermediate sanctions tax have any direct impact on a tax-exempt organization?

Yes. There are two ways in which the payment of an intermediate sanctions tax can have an impact on a tax-exempt organization. One would occur when the payment of the tax triggers a reimbursement by the organization or coverage under an insurance policy that it has purchased (Q 7:42, 7:43).

The other way an impact can occur arises from the fact that applicable tax-exempt organizations are required to disclose on their annual information returns the amount of the excise tax penalties paid with respect to excess benefit transactions, the nature of the activity, and the parties involved (Q 5:48).

Q 7:45 **Is there a limitations period, after which these taxes cannot be imposed?**

Yes. A three-year statute of limitations applies, except in the case of fraud.

Q 7:46 **Do intermediate sanctions take precedence over other sanctions used by the IRS?**

Basically, yes. Intermediate sanctions may be imposed by the IRS in lieu of or in addition to revocation of an organization's tax-exempt status. In general, these intermediate sanctions are to be the sole sanction imposed in those cases in which the excess benefit does not rise to a level where it calls into question whether, on the whole, the organization functions as a charitable or social welfare organization.

In practice, the revocation of tax-exempt status, with or without the imposition of these excise taxes, is to occur only when the organization no longer operates as a charitable or social welfare organization, as the case may be. Existing law principles apply in determining whether an organization no longer operates as an exempt organization. For example, in the case of a charitable organization, that would occur in a year, or as of a year, the entity was involved in a transaction constituting a substantial amount of private inurement.

Q 7:47 **Won't the private inurement doctrine have an impact on definitions of excess benefit transactions?**

Absolutely. The concepts of private inurement and excess benefit transaction are much the same. Thus, a great amount of existing law as to what constitutes private inurement will be applied in determining what amounts to excess benefit transactions. Although this will be the case particularly with respect to compensation issues, it will also be true in the realms of lending, borrowing, and sales arrangements, and the like. Indeed, some of this law is specifically said by the legislative history to be predicated on the private inurement doctrine, such as the rules pertaining to revenue-sharing transactions (Q 7:14).

Q 7:48 **Won't the private foundation rules as to self-dealing have a similar impact?**

No question about it. Much of what the law terms self-dealing in the foundation context will be used in ascertaining what are excess benefit transactions. The definition of self-dealing, although more specific, has generated a large amount of law (including private letter rulings and the like), which undoubtedly will be used in shaping the contours of the concept of the excess benefit transaction. Moreover, the law underlying many of the private foundation terms—such as the definition of *disqualified person* (Q 7:24), transactions for the benefit of disqualified persons (Q 7:8), meaning of *organization manager* (Q 7:26), meaning of *member of the family* (Q 7:27), and the process of correction (Q 7:31)—is being followed in the development of the law of intermediate sanctions.

Q 7:49   **Won't determinations as to what is an excess benefit shape the law of private inurement and self-dealing?**

Very much so. Just as those two terms are influencing the meaning of excess benefit transaction (Q 7:8–Q 7:15), as the coming months and years bring findings of what is an excess benefit transaction, these determinations will in turn shape the meaning of private inurement and self-dealing. Thus, each of these three terms will be constantly influencing the reach and content of the other two. To an extent, the private benefit doctrine (Q 6:4) will also be affected by this ongoing confluence of these various bodies of law.

Q 7:50   **Has any litigation concerning the intermediate sanctions rules been initiated?**

Yes, there is litigation concerning these rules in the system. Only one case has been decided, however, and that is on appeal. So far, the IRS has shown a tendency to pursue both the sanctions and revocation of exemption (Q 7:46). In the one decided case, the court found a basis for applying the sanctions but refused to allow revocation of the organization's tax exemption. In another case, a disqualified person is contending that, although economic benefits were provided to him by the exempt organization, those benefits should be offset by benefits he provided the organization, in applying the automatic excess benefit transaction rules (Q 7:11).

CHAPTER 8

Lobbying

Lobbying—principally, attempts to influence legislation—is a practice protected by the Constitution and necessary to provide information to legislatures. Yet lobbying is often considered a disreputable act and the term is frequently used in a derogatory manner. Because it is common for nonprofit organizations to operate in furtherance of one or more causes, they frequently engage in lobbying. The unseemliness of lobbying is sometimes amplified when done by nonprofit entities; there are feelings in some quarters that tax-exempt organizations—particularly public charities—should not lobby.

There are, therefore, restraints in the federal tax law on the extent to which charities and some other tax-exempt organizations can lobby. Public charities are held to a standard of insubstantiality; private foundations are not supposed to lobby at all. Trade and business associations are somewhat affected by the tax law in this regard: the portion of dues paid to them that is attributable to lobbying is not deductible as a business expense. Other exempt organizations, notably social welfare entities, can lobby without restriction. A burgeoning practice for some exempt organizations is to place their lobbying functions in a separate, but related, exempt organization.

Here are the questions most frequently asked about lobbying by nonprofit organizations, the various tax rules surrounding attempts to influence legislation (including new rules as to dues deductibility)—and the answers to them.

Q 8:1　What is *lobbying*?

The word *lobbying* derives from the caricature of someone hanging around in a lobby, waiting for the opportunity to whisper in the ear of a government official in an effort to influence the official's decision or vote. In its broadest sense, lobbying is an attempt to influence the public policy and issue-resolving functions of a regulatory, administrative, or legislative body. The term is generally used, however, to describe efforts to influence the voting of one or more members of a legislative body on one or more items of legislation. The legislative body may be a federal, state, or local one. Although lobbying is often regarded as an unsavory practice, it has a constitutional law basis: it is a form of free speech as a petitioning of a government for a redress of grievances. The U.S. Supreme Court observed that the "very idea of a government republican in form implies the right on the part of its citizens to meet peaceably for consultation in respect to public affairs and to petition for redress of grievances."

The Federal Regulation of Lobbying Act defines the term to mean an attempt by a person, who receives compensation or other consideration for the effort, to influence the passage or defeat of legislation. The federal income tax law, concerning lobbying by public charities that are under the expenditure test (Q 8:16), defines the phrase "influencing legislation" as meaning "(a) any attempt to influence any legislation through an attempt to affect the opinions of the general public or any segment thereof, and (b) any attempt to influence any legislation through communications with any member or employee of a legislative body, or with any government official or employee who may participate in the formulation of the legislation." Essentially the same definition is used in the tax regulations pertaining to lobbying by public charities that are under the substantial part test (Q 8:9) and in the federal tax statutes concerning lobbying by private foundations (Q 11:31) and lobbying for purposes of the business expense deduction (Q 8:28).

With respect to the business expense deduction rules, however, the term *lobbying* also includes efforts to influence the President of the United States, the Vice President, Cabinet members, and top White House staff. The federal law proscriptions on lobbying, however, generally do not pertain to lobbying of members of an executive branch or of independent regulatory agencies.

Q 8:2 What is *legislation*?

In general, the word *legislation* means a bill or resolution that has been introduced in a legislative body; it may or may not be considered by that body. The term is defined in the federal tax law, for purposes of the expenditure test (Q 8:16), as "action with respect to acts, bills, resolutions, or similar items by the Congress, any state legislature, any local council, or similar governing body, or the public in a referendum, initiative, constitutional amendment or similar procedure." For purposes of the substantial part test (Q 8:9), the term is similarly defined in the federal tax regulations.

Q 8:3 Is lobbying a necessary or appropriate activity for a nonprofit organization?

For many nonprofit organizations, lobbying not only is a necessary activity, it is a critical one. It is a matter of policy as to whether it is appropriate for them to engage in that activity, particularly when they are tax-exempt. There is nothing inherently illegal about lobbying by nonprofit organizations. Indeed, these organizations have the constitutional right to petition the government. The U.S. Supreme Court, however, held that it is not unconstitutional for the law to deprive charitable organizations of tax-exempt status if they engage in substantial lobbying.

There is a belief among many policy makers that it is inappropriate for charitable organizations to engage in lobbying. This view is largely based on the precept that a person should not be able to receive an income tax deduction for a gift to a charity which is used to advance that person's views on legislation; this is seen as a subsidy of one person's viewpoint by others. Consequently, public charities are constrained as to how much lobbying they can engage in without loss of tax exemption (Q 8:13, Q 8:19).

Q 8:4 What are the federal tax rules concerning lobbying that are unique to tax-exempt organizations?

The principal rule is that public charities may engage in lobbying activities only to the extent they are not substantial. A public charity that engages in substantial attempts to influence legislation is considered an *action organization* and is likely to have its tax exemption denied or revoked. Private foundations are basically constrained from any lobbying (Q 8:10). Some tax-exempt organizations can have lobbying as their principal or even their sole function; these include social welfare organizations and trade and business associations (Q 8:25–8:32). Members of an association, however, are likely to have their dues deductions reduced to the extent the organization lobbies (Q 8:28).

Q 8:5 How do charitable organizations measure substantiality?

In general, there is no precise formula for measuring whether lobbying activities are substantial. It is common practice, however, to evaluate the extent of lobbying in terms of a percentage of total funds expended in a period of time or total time expended over a particular period. These are merely informal guidelines, however; the IRS will not commit to any specific percentages. On occasion, substantiality is found as a consequence of an organization's impact on a legislative process, irrespective of outlays of funds or time. The case law makes it clear that this is a case-by-case determination. The decision that an organization has engaged in a substantial amount of lobbying is usually made in hindsight, after the particular legislative process has concluded.

In other areas of the federal tax law, precise percentages are available for defining what is substantial. For example, certain rules concerning supporting organizations define the term to mean at least 85 percent (Q 10:16). In the setting of the business expense deduction, the phrase *substantially all* means at least 90 percent (Q 8:30). Thus, a rough guide would be to define *substantial* as meaning at least 85 percent and *incidental* as meaning no more than 15 percent. The federal tax law, however, generally treats the determination of substantiality as being a facts-and-circumstances test. The exception is the expenditure test, which contains some safe harbor percentage limitations (Q 8:16).

Q 8:6 Is there more than one form of lobbying?

Generally, the law regards lobbying as being *direct* or *grass roots*.

Direct lobbying occurs when the lobbying organization communicates, for purposes of influencing legislation, with a member of a legislative body, an individual who is on the staff of such a member, or an individual who is on the staff of a committee of a legislative body. For purposes of the expenditure test (Q 8:16), there is a direct lobbying communication only where the communication refers to specific legislation and reflects a view on the legislation. In the setting of the business expense deduction, direct lobbying includes communications with certain members of the federal executive branch (Q 8:32). When the results of research are used in lobbying, the research activities themselves are automatically considered lobbying. Whether research activities in other settings constitute lobbying is a matter determined on a facts-and-circumstances basis.

Grass roots lobbying takes place when the lobbying organization communicates, for purposes of influencing legislation, with the general public, or a segment of it, in an effort to induce the persons contacted to communicate with a legislative body for the purpose of influencing legislation. Under the expenditure test (Q 8:16), a grass roots lobbying communication takes place only where the communication refers to specific legislation, reflects a view on the legislation, and encourages the recipient of the communication to take action with respect to the legislation. This latter element is known as a *call to action*.

Q 8:7   What are the various ways by which lobbying can be accomplished?

Lobbying is communication. It can be accomplished using any means of communication between human beings. Forms of direct lobbying (Q 8:6) include personal contact, correspondence, telephone calls, facsimiles, telegrams, position papers and other publications, contact via the Internet, and formal testimony. Grass roots lobbying (Q 8:6) includes these forms, along with television, radio, and print media advertisements.

Q 8:8   Are there laws concerning lobbying by nonprofit organizations, other than the federal tax rules?

Yes. The principal law outside the federal tax context is the Federal Regulation of Lobbying Act. Those who lobby for compensation as a principal portion of their activities must register with and report to the Clerk of the House of Representatives and the Secretary of the Senate. The Byrd Amendment prohibits the use of federal funds received as grants, contracts, loans, or cooperative agreements for attempts to influence an officer or employee of a governmental agency in connection with the awarding, obtaining, or making of any federal contract, grant, loan, or cooperative agreement. Regulations published by the Office of Management and Budget provide that costs associated with most forms of lobbying activities do not qualify for reimbursement by the federal government. Most states have laws regulating lobbying by nonprofit and other organizations.

CHARITIES AND THE SUBSTANTIAL PART TEST

Q 8:9 What is the substantial part test?

The federal tax law does not allow tax-exempt charitable organizations to attempt to influence legislation to the extent that the lobbying activities are a substantial part of their total activities. Public charities are permitted to lobby to the extent that the lobbying is incidental—or at least not substantial. This limitation is known as the *substantial part test*.

There is no mechanical formula for measuring what is substantial in this context (Q 8:5). Both expenditures and time can be taken into account; for example, the time of volunteers is considered under this test. The substantial part test is applicable on a year-by-year basis.

Nothing in the substantial part test specifically applies to lobbying by related organizations. For example, a public charity with chapters (separate entities) that are charitable organizations would not normally have the chapters' lobbying attributed to it. A grant by the public charity to one or more of its chapters for lobbying, however, would be a lobbying expenditure for the grantor.

Q 8:10 Can private foundations lobby to the extent of the substantial part test?

Private foundations, even though they are charitable organizations, cannot lobby to the extent of the substantial part test. Basically, private foundations are not allowed to engage in any lobbying (Q 11:31). If prohibited lobbying takes place, the foundation becomes liable for one or more federal excise taxes. There are certain exceptions to this general rule. A private foundation can (1) make available the results of nonpartisan analysis, study, or research, and (2) appear before or otherwise communicate with a legislative body with respect to a possible decision of that body that might affect the existence of the foundation, its powers and duties, its tax-exempt status, or the deductibility of contributions to the foundation. This second item is known as the *self-defense exception*.

Q 8:11 Are there exceptions to the prohibition on lobbying under the substantial part test?

Yes. A public charity will not lose its tax-exempt status because of lobbying activities where the lobbying was the result of an invitation from a legislative body or a committee of that body. Also, activities that are *educational* in nature are not considered lobbying, nor is the mere monitoring of and reporting on legislation. The statutory exceptions that are part of the expenditure test generally do not apply with respect to the substantial part test (Q 8:18).

Q 8:12 Can lobbying be considered a political campaign activity?

Generally, the federal tax rules concerning lobbying and political campaign activities (Chapter 9) are separate, discrete bodies of law. If, however, a nonprofit organization engages in lobbying, particularly grass roots lobbying, doing so in the context of a political campaign, so that the advocacy of the issue(s) involved can be tied to the political fortunes of a candidate (such as an incumbent legislator pursuing reelection), the lobbying activity can also be regarded as political campaign activity. Undertakings of this nature are known as *public policy advocacy communications*; they are said to have a *dual character*.

Q 8:13 What happens when the organization engages in substantial lobbying?

If a public charity subject to the substantial part test engages in a substantial amount of legislative activities in a tax year, it is supposed to have its tax exemption revoked. The organization is also liable for a 5 percent excise tax on the lobbying expenditures. A tax in this amount may also be imposed on the managers of the organization, who are held responsible for knowing that the expenditures would likely result in loss of the organization's tax-exempt status. These two results happen from time to time, but a charitable organization is much more likely to settle the matter with the IRS, often through an agreement to not engage in substantial lobbying activities in the future. Usually this type of agreement is evidenced by what the IRS terms a *closing agreement* (see Q 19:20).

Q 8:14 Can a charitable organization that loses its tax exemption because of excessive lobbying convert to another type of tax-exempt organization?

Yes, if it is an organization that is covered by the substantial part test. A public charity that has lost its tax-exempt status because of the extent of its lobbying activities can prospectively become a tax-exempt social welfare organization. This change of status would allow it to continue to attempt to influence legislation to a substantial extent and remain tax-exempt, although contributions to it would no longer be deductible as charitable gifts. Another approach would be to transfer the lobbying function to a related social welfare organization (Q 8:27).

Q 8:15 What planning can a charitable organization under the substantial part test engage in to avoid adverse tax consequences because of lobbying?

A public charity should evaluate its activities in this regard to ascertain whether one or more of them may not technically constitute lobbying. They may instead be educational or monitoring activities, or the organization may be able to shelter some of them by procuring an appropriate request for them (Q 8:11). The organization should have in place an adequate record-keeping system with respect to its lobbying endeavors and should follow generally accepted accounting principles in allocating joint costs (Q 8:36).

A public charity should make an effort to keep its annual outlays for lobbying to a level below 10 to 15 percent (Q 8:5). If volunteers are used for lobbying, the total amount of time expended on attempts to influence legislation in a year must be evaluated. These precautions will not, however, necessarily prevent an assertion by the IRS, successful or not, that lobbying activities were or are substantial. If a significant amount of lobbying is to be or is being undertaken, a public charity should consider electing the expenditure test rules (Q 8:16), placing its lobbying activities into a tax-exempt lobbying subsidiary (Q 8:27), or converting to a tax-exempt social welfare organization (Q 8:14).

A private foundation must avoid lobbying altogether, other than the forms of lobbying that are allowed by exceptions (Q 8:10).

CHARITIES AND THE EXPENDITURE TEST

Q 8:16 What is the *expenditure test*?

The *expenditure test* is a scheme devised by Congress to provide public charities a means to determine how much lobbying is allowable without loss of tax-exempt status, by application of precise percentages of total expenditures. The test permits a public charity to expend, for lobbying, 20 percent of its first $500,000, 15 percent of the next $500,000, 10 percent of the next $500,000, and 5 percent of the remaining expenditures. There is an annual ceiling of $1 million for lobbying outlays. Grass roots lobbying may not exceed 25 percent of total allowable lobbying. These limitations are known as the *direct lobbying allowable amount* and the *grass roots lobbying allowable amount*. These percentages are applicable to the organization's expenditures during the most recent four years.

Not all public charities may utilize this test (Q 8:17), and private foundations cannot avail themselves of it (Q 8:10). Lobbying by certain affiliated organizations is attributed to the charitable organization for purposes of the expenditure allowance. For example, an organization with chapters is likely to have this attribution rule applied to its expenditures for lobbying.

Q 8:17 How does this test become applicable to an organization?

A public charity must elect to come within the expenditure test. This is done by filing an IRS form (Form 5768). This filing can be made at any time during the organization's fiscal year; when done, it causes the expenditure test to be applicable with respect to that entire year.

Certain public charities are not permitted to elect the expenditure test. These are churches, associations of churches, conventions of churches, integrated auxiliaries of churches, and supporting organizations with respect to tax-exempt organizations other than public charities. Private foundations cannot make this election because of the general prohibition on lobbying by them (Q 8:10).

Q 8:18 Are there exceptions to the term *lobbying* under this test?

Five categories of activities are excepted from the scope of lobbying for purposes of the expenditure test:

1. Making available the results of nonpartisan analysis, study, or research.
2. Providing technical advice or assistance to a governmental body or legislative committee in response to a written request by the body or committee.
3. Appearing before, or communicating with, any legislative body with respect to a possible decision by that body that might affect the existence of the organization, its powers and duties, its tax-exempt status, or the deduction of contributions to it. This is known as the *self-defense exception.*
4. Effecting communications between the organization and its members with respect to legislation that is of direct mutual interest.
5. Communicating in a routine manner with government officials or employees.

Q 8:19 What happens when the organization engages in "too much" lobbying?

If an organization exceeds the direct lobbying allowable amount or the grass roots lobbying allowable amount (Q 8:16), it is subject to a 25 percent excise tax on the excessive portion of the outlay. If an organization exceeds either lobbying expenditure limitation by 150 percent or more, it is supposed to have its tax exemption revoked. A public charity in this circumstance is not subjected to the excise tax for engaging in substantial legislative activities (Q 8:13).

If a public charity has lost its tax-exempt status under these circumstances, it could alter its lobbying practices and reapply for recognition of tax exemption. To achieve tax exemption again, it would have to (1) reduce its lobbying expenditures for the future, to be in compliance with either the substantial part test or the expenditure test; (2) restructure its lobbying program to make effective use of one or more of the exceptions to the lobbying rules (Q 8:18); or (3) conduct some or all of its lobbying activities in a tax-exempt subsidiary (Q 8:24).

Q 8:20 Can the charitable organization convert to another type of tax-exempt organization?

As a practical matter, no. If a public charity subject to the expenditure test engages in substantial legislative activities to the extent that its tax exemption is revoked, it cannot thereafter convert to a tax-exempt social welfare organization. It could, however, convert to another type of tax-exempt entity, such as a business league, but that is usually not a suitable alternative.

Q 8:21 What types of lobbying programs are most suitable for the expenditure test?

The expenditure test is most appropriate for a public charity that is engaging, or wants to engage, in lobbying activities that are or would be *substantial*, as that term is defined under the substantial part test. The test is, therefore, often necessary for a charitable organization that would otherwise be considered an action organization (Q 8:4). (This assumes that (1) the lobbying activities are not so extensive as to be not tolerated under the expenditure test, and (2) the public charity in this circumstance is one that can make this election (Q 8:17).)

Because of the allowable lobbying amounts, the expenditure test is more beneficial to direct lobbying than to grass roots lobbying (Q 8:6, Q 8:16). That is, the limitation on grass roots lobbying (essentially, 5 percent of total expenditures, or 25 percent of 20 percent) may be too stringent for an organization that is principally or exclusively engaging in grass roots lobbying. A public charity of this nature is almost certain to find that it is preferential to be under the substantial part test, whereas the test of insubstantiality is likely to be more tolerant and does not differentiate between the two types of lobbying (Q 8:9).

Q 8:22 When should a charitable organization elect the expenditure test?

A public charity should not elect the expenditure test unless and until it is positive that the advantages of the election outweigh the disadvantages of it.

The principal advantage of the expenditure test is that it affords a public charity considerable certainty as to how much lobbying it can engage in without adverse tax consequences. The mechanical nature of the test and the warning nature of the excise tax (Q 8:16) contribute to that advantage. Other advantages include: (1) an array of activities that are specifically exempted from consideration as lobbying activities (Q 8:17), (2) exemption from the excise tax imposed on public charities in cases of excessive lobbying (Q 8:13), and (3) exclusion from the lobbying amount calculation for lobbying done by volunteers. For the latter calculation, the test applies only to expenditures; volunteer time is disregarded.

There are, however, some disadvantages to being under the expenditure test. These include: (1) the stringent limitation on allowable grass roots lobbying activities (25 percent of total allowable lobbying activities), (2) more extensive record-keeping requirements, (3) more extensive reporting requirements (Q 8:37), (4) a significant likelihood of audit exposure if the test is not elected (Q 8:23), and (5) inability to convert to a tax-exempt social welfare organization if lobbying activities become too extensive (Q 8:20).

Q 8:23 Under what circumstances would an organization elect to revoke its election to be under the expenditure test?

Having elected to come under the expenditure test, a public charity would revoke that election only where its direct lobbying or grass roots lobbying expenditures became, or were about to become, too extensive to be tolerated under the test. This could happen where the grass roots lobbying expenditures of a public charity exceeded or were about to exceed the special 25 percent limitation, even though overall lobbying expenditures remained below the 20 percent limitation. Caution should be exercised when canceling an election: it will signal to the IRS that extensive legislative activities are or will be occurring and that they are perhaps too extensive to be allowable under the substantial part test.

Q 8:24   What planning can a charitable organization under the expenditure test engage in to avoid adverse tax consequences because of lobbying?

A public charity should avoid electing the expenditure test until and unless it is certain that the test should be elected. Stated another way, a public charity should elect the test only where all of the advantages and disadvantages involved in making of the election are assessed (Q 8:22). For example, the 20 percent ceiling may initially appear attractive and then prove illusory if a significant amount of grass roots lobbying is to be undertaken. For this assessment, all applicable exceptions should be taken into account (Q 8:18). The election should not be made until sufficient record-keeping and accounting procedures are in place, so that the organization knows with some confidence precisely what its lobbying expenditures are or will be. The organization should prepare, on a test basis, the portion of the annual return required of public charities under the expenditure test. It should examine the results and determine whether it will be able to comply with these reporting requirements in subsequent years. This analysis should take into account the fact that lobbying by affiliated organizations may be attributed to the organization.

Before making the election, a public charity should consider the alternatives of placing the lobbying program in an affiliated tax-exempt social welfare organization (Q 8:27) or converting to such an organization (Q 8:14, Q 8:20).

Once the election is made, adverse consequences may result if the organization revokes it (Q 8:23). If the organization loses its tax exemption because of an inability to stay within the bounds of the expenditure test, it forgoes the opportunity to convert to an exempt social welfare organization (Q 8:20).

SOCIAL WELFARE ORGANIZATIONS

Q 8:25   Are there any restrictions on lobbying by tax-exempt social welfare organizations?

No. Tax-exempt social welfare organizations (Q 4:7) may engage in legislative activities without limitation. The only significant constraint is that their lobbying must be in advancement of exempt purposes or at least not be a deterrent to the ability of the organization to primarily engage in exempt activities. This ability of an exempt social welfare organization to extensively lobby makes it a useful repository of legislative activities as a subsidiary to a public charity (Q 8:27). The rules pertaining to the deductibility of business expenses (Q 8:28) apply with respect to social welfare organizations; however, dues paid to these entities are generally not deductible as business expenses in any event.

Q 8:26   Why don't all lobbying charities convert to social welfare organizations?

Public charities that engage in lobbying normally do not want to forgo their status as charities and become social welfare organizations. One of the principal reasons for this decision is that contributions to social welfare organizations are not tax-deductible as charitable gifts. Thus, although both charitable and social welfare organizations are tax-exempt entities, only the former can attract deductible gifts. Also, social welfare organizations, particularly those that engage in considerable lobbying, are unlikely candidates for private foundation grants. Therefore, a public charity would convert to a social welfare organization only where it would otherwise be an action organization (Q 8:4), did not or could not elect the expenditure test (Q 8:16), or did not want to use a lobbying subsidiary (Q 8:27).

Q 8:27 How can a public charity utilize a tax-exempt lobbying subsidiary?

There are several instances in the federal tax law pertaining to exempt organizations where the principle of bifurcation is usefully applied. *Bifurcation* means that the functions of what would otherwise be one organization are split, largely or exclusively for tax reasons, and placed in two entities. That is the case with respect to public charities and substantial lobbying.

A public charity that wishes to engage in substantial amounts of lobbying cannot be tax-exempt as a charitable entity. One of its options is to be a tax-exempt social welfare organization (Q 8:26). Another option is to establish a related tax-exempt organization and conduct the lobbying activities through that entity. The principal advantage of this second option is that it preserves the organization's status as a charitable organization with respect to its other programs and it retains its ability to attract tax-deductible contributions.

There are several ways in which the public charity can control its lobbying subsidiary (Q 1:3). The most common mechanism of control in this context is an interlocking (or overlapping) board of directors. With this approach, the board of directors of the social welfare organization is selected, in whole or in part (but at least a majority), by the board of directors of the charitable organization. Other control features include making the subsidiary a membership organization, with the public charity the sole member, or creating it as a stock-based nonprofit organization, with the public charity the sole shareholder (Q 1:23).

TRADE, BUSINESS, AND PROFESSIONAL ASSOCIATIONS

Q 8:28 Are there any restrictions on lobbying by tax-exempt trade and other associations?

In general, no. Tax-exempt trade, business, and professional associations may engage in legislative activities without limitation, albeit with two constraints. First, the lobbying must be in advancement of exempt purposes or at least not be a deterrent to the ability of the organization to primarily engage in exempt activities.

Second, the lobbying activities can trigger some adverse tax consequences to the association's members. Generally, the dues paid by a member to one of these associations is tax-deductible as a business expense. With minor exceptions, however, there is no business expense deduction for amounts expended in attempts to influence legislation. Where an exempt association engages in lobbying, a portion of the dues, deemed allocable to the lobbying activities by operation of a *flow-through rule*, is not deductible. For example, an exempt association that expended 30 percent of its funds for lobbying in a year and has annual dues of $100 would cause its members to have a dues deduction of only $70 for that year.

An association in this circumstance must calculate its expenditures for lobbying. In doing this calculation, it must allocate the appropriate portion of salaries paid to employees with multiple responsibilities, using one of three accounting methods. Certain *in-house expenditures* must also be taken into consideration.

Q 8:29 How does the member know how to calculate the dues deduction?

As a general rule, the association must calculate the various amounts expended for influencing legislation and then report the resulting ratio to its membership. The reporting is to be done at the time of assessment or payment of the dues. This ratio must also be reported to the IRS by means of the association's annual information return.

Q 8:30 What happens if the association makes an error in the calculation of the dues deduction ratio?

The organization may have to pay a 35 percent *proxy tax* on the difference between the amount reported to the membership and the actual lobbying amount. This can occur where the lobbying outlays are higher than anticipated or where the dues receipts are lower than projected.

There is a procedure, however, by which an association in this situation can arrange for a waiver from the IRS and adjust the figures to report the excess lobbying amounts in the subsequent year.

Q 8:31 Are there any exceptions to these rules?

There are five exceptions to these rules:

1. An association can pay the proxy tax with respect to all of the lobbying expenditures, thereby allowing the members the full amount of the dues deduction. Informal surveys are indicating that about 15 to 20 percent of associations are opting for this approach.
2. These disclosure and reporting rules do not apply where substantially all of the members of an association cannot claim the business expense deduction for dues in any event. The phrase *substantially all* in this setting means at least 90 percent. This second exception is automatically available to unions and other labor organizations. It is also available to trade, business, and professional associations that are able to demonstrate to the IRS that

substantially all of their members cannot take the dues deduction because of the 2 percent floor on miscellaneous business expenses or because the dues are paid by tax-exempt organizations. (A ruling from the IRS may be required in this instance.)

3. These rules are inapplicable with respect to charitable organizations.

4. There is a *de minimis* exception for certain in-house expenditures, where the organization's total amount of these expenditures for a year does not exceed $2,000. This exception does not apply with respect to dues payments and payments to a professional lobbyist.

5. Costs incurred for merely monitoring legislation are not considered expenses for lobbying.

Q 8:32 **Is the concept of lobbying the same as it is for public charities?**

No. The term *lobbying* is more broadly defined with respect to the rules denying the business expense deduction. In this setting, the term embraces not only lobbying of nearly all legislative bodies, but also the President of the United States, the Vice President, the members of the Cabinet and their executive staff, and the principal White House staff. The term also includes research that is undertaken and subsequently used in a lobbying effort, irrespective of the intent of the parties involved for initiating the research effort.

VETERANS' ORGANIZATIONS

Q 8:33 **Are there any restrictions on lobbying by tax-exempt veterans' organizations?**

No. Tax-exempt veterans' organizations may engage in legislative activities without limitation. The only significant constraint is that the lobbying must be in advancement of exempt purposes or at least not be a deterrent to the ability of the organization to primarily engage in exempt activities. Unlike the situation with respect to exempt social welfare organizations and trade and business associations, however, contributions to most veterans' organizations are tax-deductible as charitable gifts.

Q 8:34 **Aren't the tax rules for veterans' organizations unfair in relation to those for charitable organizations?**

In both cases, the organizations are tax-exempt and can attract deductible gifts, yet the lobbying by veterans' organizations does not affect their tax exemption or charitable donee status. The U.S. Supreme Court, in rejecting an equal protection doctrine argument on the point, held that Congress may make such distinctions in crafting the tax laws. The favoritism toward veterans' organizations in this regard was characterized as a "subsidy" created by Congress as part of the nation's long-standing policy of compensating veterans for their past contributions by providing them with numerous advantages.

REPORTING REQUIREMENTS

Q 8:35 **Are any reporting requirements imposed on tax-exempt organizations that lobby?**

A portion of the annual information return that must be filed by public charities is devoted to the reporting of their lobbying activities (Q 8:36 and Q 8:37). The information return filed by private foundations includes a provision concerning any legislative activities. The information return that must be filed by all other tax-exempt organizations inquires as to lobbying efforts. Also, certain reports must be filed pursuant to the Federal Regulation of Lobbying Act (Q 8:8). Some states' laws have similar requirements.

Q 8:36 **What are the reporting requirements under the substantial part test?**

The annual information return filed by public charities requires that those under the substantial part test include information about the use of volunteers and/or paid staff or management in attempts to influence legislation. The organization must also report the amounts it expended in furthering its lobbying efforts via media advertisements; mailings to members, legislators, or the public; publications or published or broadcast statements; grants to other organizations for lobbying purposes; direct contact with legislators, their staffs, government officials, or a legislative body; rallies, demonstrations, seminars, conventions, speeches, and lectures; and any other means of attempting to influence legislation.

Q 8:37 **What are the reporting requirements under the expenditure test?**

Public charities under the expenditure test must report total direct lobbying expenditures, total grass roots lobbying expenditures, exempt purpose expenditures, the direct lobbying nontaxable amount (the amount protected by the applicable percentages (Q 8:16)), and the grass roots lobbying nontaxable amount (not to exceed 25 percent of the foregoing amount). These figures must be separately reported for the organization and affiliated organizations.

An organization in this circumstance must also report, for each year in the four-year averaging period (Q 8:16), its direct lobbying nontaxable amount, direct lobbying ceiling amount (not to exceed 150 percent of the four years' total of the preceding amount), total direct lobbying expenditures, grass roots lobbying nontaxable amount, grass roots lobbying ceiling amount (not to exceed 150 percent of the four years' total of the preceding amount), and total grass roots lobbying expenditures.

Any taxable amounts, for either direct lobbying or grass roots lobbying, are to be reported to the IRS on a tax return.

CHAPTER 9

Political Activities

The principal body of federal tax law concerning political activities pertains to public charities. These organizations are prohibited from participating in nearly all political campaigns. Although the official position of the IRS is that this restriction is absolute, the courts tolerate at least a de minimis amount of political campaign involvement by public charities. The IRS administrative practice in this area also is one of considerable tolerance. There is a tax on political campaign activities by public charities.

Not all political activities are political campaign activities. Tax-exempt organizations that engage in noncampaign political activities may become subject to a political activities tax. Private foundations are subject to other taxes for involvement in political campaign activities.

Political organizations may be exempt, in whole or in part, from income taxation. The business expense deduction is not available for an expenditure for political campaign purposes.

Here are the questions most frequently asked about political activities by nonprofit organizations, the tax rules concerning political campaign and other efforts, and the use of political action committees—and the answers to them.

Q 9:1 What are *political activities*?

Political activities are of two categories, one subsuming the other. The broader of the two categories refers to any activity that is undertaken with a political purpose, that is, to affect the structure or other affairs of government. The narrower definition refers to an activity that is engaged in to assist or prevent an individual's election to a public office; this latter type of political activity is a *political campaign activity*. The narrower range of activities requires participation or intervention in a political campaign (Q 9:3).

For example, the presentation of testimony before the Senate Committee on the Judiciary, regarding a nominee of the President to the Supreme Court, is a political activity. This is not a political campaign activity, however, because there is no *cam-*

paign for a public office (Q 9:7). By contrast, a contribution to the campaign organization of an individual, to assist him or her in attempting to win election to the U.S. Senate, the U.S. House of Representatives, or a state legislature, is a political campaign activity.

Q 9:2 What are the rules, for tax-exempt organizations, concerning political activities?

There are several rules, but two are particularly important. One is that a charitable organization is not allowed to participate in or intervene in any political campaign on behalf of or in opposition to any candidate for a public office. This constraint pertains to political campaign activities (Q 9:1); if violated, the organization becomes classified as an *action organization* and must pay a tax and suffer revocation of its tax-exempt status.

The other rule concerns organizations that are political organizations, that is, have political activities as their exempt function (Q 9:16). These organizations frequently engage in political campaign activities; they also undertake political activities that are not political campaign activities.

The business expense deduction is not available for an expenditure for political campaign purposes. If a tax-exempt organization, such as a trade or business association or a labor union, were to make such an expenditure, the extent of deductibility of the organization's dues might be affected (Q 9:20). Because of the federal campaign laws, organizations of this nature should not engage in political campaign activities directly but can do so by means of political action committees (Q 9:22).

Q 9:3 What do *participation* and *intervention* mean?

Essentially, the words *participation* and *intervention* mean the same thing: an involvement in some way, by an individual or an organization, in a political campaign. These types of activities include the solicitation or making of political campaign contributions, the use of resources of an organization to benefit or thwart the candidacy of an individual in a political campaign, the volunteering of services for or against a candidate for a public office, and the publication or distribution of literature in support of or in opposition to a candidate for public office.

Traditionally, the IRS broadly defines these terms—sometimes finding violation of the political campaign activity constraint when some elements of the prohibited activity are not present. For example, a charitable organization was denied tax exemption because its purpose was to implement an orderly change of administration of the office of a governor in the most efficient and economical fashion possible by assisting the governor-elect during the period between his election and inauguration. In this instance, while there was to be participation and/or intervention in a government's affairs, there was no *candidate* (Q 9:6) or *campaign* (Q 9:7). The IRS ruled, however, that the organization's "predominant purpose is to effectuate changes in the government's policies and personnel which will make them correspond with the partisan political interests of both the Governor-elect and the political party he represents."

In another illustration of these rules—one that is more in conformity with the language of the prohibition—the IRS ruled that charitable organizations may not evaluate the qualifications of potential candidates in a school board election and support particular slates in a campaign. Today, however, that organization would likely qualify for tax exemption as a charitable entity if its activities were confined to the evaluative function.

In this context, the IRS has historically taken a hard-line position with respect to advocacy organizations that become entangled with political issues; where the objectives of these organizations can be achieved only through political change, they cannot—in the government's view—be charitable. In support of this position, a court held that an organization established with the dominant aim of bringing about world government as rapidly as possible cannot qualify as a tax-exempt charitable organization. This approach is difficult to rationalize under the contemporary law, however, because of the absence of any involvement in a *campaign* for or against a *candidate* for *public office* (Q 9:8).

Q 9:4 Can a charitable organization educate the public about candidates and issues in the setting of a political campaign?

Yes. The IRS, however, has been rather grudging in allowing this type of activity. In fact, there can be a fine line between participating in a political campaign and engaging in public education about that campaign. Organizations like the League of Women Voters and the Commission on Presidential Debates, which utilize the resources of organizations such as universities, have moved the law to a point where there is, today, a fuller recognition of *voter education* activities.

The contemporary view is that a charitable organization, as part of an education process, can disseminate the views, voting records, and similar information about candidates in the context of a political campaign where neutrality is, or substantially is, observed. The key factor is that the organization may not indicate partisanship on the issues. Popular practices include the compilation and dissemination of the voting records, or responses to questionnaires elicited by the organization, of members of a legislature on a variety of topics. Also in vogue is the issuance of "report cards"—a listing of votes on selected issues in which a legislator receives a "+" if his or her vote coincided with the organization's position and a "-" if it did not.

Factors the IRS takes into account are: Is there comment on an individual's overall qualifications for public office? Are there statements expressly or impliedly endorsing or rejecting an incumbent as a candidate? Has the organization observed that voters should consider matters other than voting, such as service on committees and constituent services? Is the material distributed to the organization's constituency or the general public? Is the dissemination of publications timed to coincide with an election campaign, particularly during its closing days? In one instance, the IRS position was stated this way: "[I]n the absence of any expressions of endorsement for or in opposition to candidates for public office, an organization may publish a newsletter containing voting records and its opinions on issues of interest to it provided that the voting records are not widely distributed to the general public during an election campaign or aimed, in view of all the facts and circumstances, towards affecting any particular elections."

The expansionist view as to what is participation or intervention in a political campaign is derived from a federal court of appeals opinion authored over 30 years ago. There, a religious ministry organization was denied tax-exempt status, in part because of ostensible interventions in political campaigns. The organization, by means of publications and broadcasts, attacked candidates and incumbents (the President and members of Congress) who were considered too liberal, and endorsed conservative officeholders. The court summarized the offense: "These attempts to elect or defeat certain political leaders reflected . . . the organization's objective to change the composition of the federal government." Open criticism of an elected public official, including one who is eligible for reelection, however, was held violative of this proscription, even where not done in the context of a political campaign. It is unlikely that this aspect of the opinion would be reiterated by a court today.

There is, therefore, great confusion in the federal tax law as to the reach of the prohibition on political campaign activities by public charities. That is, there is far less guidance in this area than there is in the realm of lobbying activities by public charities, where considerable detail is given in regulations, rulings, and court opinions. (See Chapter 8.) This dichotomy is aggravated by inconsistent and selective enforcement practices by the IRS, which aggressively pursues transgressions (alleged and otherwise) by the "Christian Right" (such as the activities of televangelists), yet ignores the most blatant of violations by the clergy of innumerable African American churches.

The federal and state political campaign regulation rules apply to charitable organizations, and thus can operate as an additional set of limitations on their ability to participate in political campaigns. For example, the prohibition on campaign contributions by corporations is applicable to charitable entities.

Q 9:5 Does the law differentiate between the political positions of organizations and those of individuals associated with them?

Yes. An individual does not lose his or her rights to engage in political activity solely by reason of being an employee or other representative of a public charity. The IRS, however, expects that an individual in this position will make it clear in the appropriate context that the political views expressed are his or hers, and not those of the organization. For example, in its tax guide for churches and clergy, the IRS stated that "[m]inisters and others who commonly speak or write on behalf of religious organizations should clearly indicate, at the time they do so, that public comments made by them in connection with political campaigns are strictly personal and are not intended to represent their organization." As a practical matter, this distinction is often difficult to credibly maintain.

Q 9:6   When is an individual a candidate?

For the proscription on political campaign activity to be applicable, the public charity must be a participant in the campaign of an individual who is a *candidate* for a public office. The federal tax regulations define the phrase *candidate for public office* to mean "an individual who offers himself, or is proposed by others, as a contestant for an elective public office, whether such office be national, state, or local." An individual becomes a candidate for a public office on the date he or she announces his or her candidacy for that office. But the fact that an individual is a prominent political figure does not automatically make him or her a candidate. This is the case notwithstanding speculation in the media and elsewhere as to the individual's plans or where an individual is publicly teasing about running for office. The label *candidate* is often applied with the benefit of hindsight.

The IRS refuses to commit itself to any specific rule in this regard, preferring to leave the matter to a general facts-and-circumstances test; it has been known to assert the candidacy of an individual far before any official announcement. Mere speculation in the media that an individual may campaign for an office can be the basis of an IRS insistence that the individual has become a candidate. By contrast, the federal election law defines the term *candidate* to mean an individual seeking nomination for election or election to federal office; one who has directly or indirectly received contributions or made expenditures for such a purpose in excess of $5,000 is deemed to seek nomination for election or election.

Q 9:7   When does a campaign begin?

The federal tax law lacks any definition of the term *campaign*. For the proscription on political campaign activity to be applicable, the public charity must be a participant in the *campaign* of an individual seeking a public office. This body of law is silent as to when there is a commencement of a political campaign; again, it is the practice of the IRS to apply a facts-and-circumstances test. The IRS has been known to assert the launching of a campaign far in advance of a formal announcement of candidacy.

One court opinion stated that "a campaign for public office in a public election merely and simply means running for office, or candidacy for office, as the word is used in common parlance and as it is understood by the man in the street." The federal election law likewise does not define the term *campaign*; in general, however, under that law, as to a particular individual, a campaign commences once he or she has become a candidate, which entails receiving the requisite level of contributions or making the requisite level of expenditures (Q 9:6).

Q 9:8   What is a *public office*?

For the proscription on political campaign activity to be applicable, the public charity must be a participant in the campaign of an individual seeking a *public office*. This term is specifically defined in two sets of federal tax regulations to mean a policy-making position in the executive, legislative, or judicial branch of a government; it means more than mere public employment. (These regulations relate to the definition of the phraseology in the rules concerning disqualified persons with respect to private foundations and in defining exempt functions of political organizations.)

On occasion, the IRS will openly decline to follow that definition. For example, an intraparty position, such as a precinct delegate, clearly is not a public office, yet the IRS pursued the revocation of the tax-exempt status of a public charity that influenced the selection of individuals to such delegate positions, on the ground that they are types of "public offices."

CHARITIES AND POLITICAL ACTIVITIES

Q 9:9 Is there a substantiality test for charitable organizations concerning political activities?

For the most part, no. The position of the IRS on this point is that the proscription on political activities by charitable organizations is an absolute one. The statute stating this proscription does not contain a substantiality test, as it does with respect to legislative activities (Q 9:5).

The judiciary, however, is reluctant to foreclose the possibility of a de minimis test in any setting. One court observed that "courts recognize that a nonexempt purpose, even 'somewhat beyond a de minimis level,' may be permitted without loss of exemption." Thus, for example, it is unlikely that the inadvertent application of $1.00 of the funds of a public charity to a political campaign activity would be treated as a violation of the constraint, although that would literally be a violation of the language of the statute.

Q 9:10 What happens when a public charity engages in a political campaign activity?

Actual practice is often different from what the applicable statutes mandate. A public charity's participation in a political campaign is a ground for revocation of tax-exempt status, assuming the participation is greater than a very insignificant involvement (Q 9:9). Also, it is the basis for assessment of an initial 10 percent excise tax on the organization and a 2½ percent tax on each of the organization's managers, and additional taxes of 100 percent on the organization and 50 percent on its managers. To date, however few instances have been made public where the IRS has assessed that tax. Moreover, there have been situations where the organization negotiated a closing agreement with the IRS by admitting the violation, promising to not repeat it, and making the agreement public; in these circumstances, the IRS has refrained from revoking the exemption (Q 19:20).

The IRS has two other weapons in this regard:

1. It can trigger accelerated tax assessment rules when it finds that the political campaign activities constraint on public charities is being violated. Under

these procedures, the IRS need not wait until the close of the organization's tax year to commence an audit; it can prematurely terminate the entity's year and promptly begin the audit process.

2. It has special authority to request a court injunction to stop political campaign activity by a public charity in certain circumstances.

Q 9:11   Do these rules apply to churches and other religious organizations?

As a matter of statutory law, yes. An institution of religious worship—such as a church, synagogue, or mosque—or any other type of religious organization is barred from political campaign activity. These entities are charitable ones for tax purposes, and the federal tax law prohibits charitable organizations from participating or intervening in political campaigns (Q 9:3). Moreover, churches and the like are public charities, where these rules are focused (Q 9:2).

Q 9:12   Are these rules enforced against religious organizations?

Not very often. When it is done, the enforcement is selective. There are a few court cases where these rules have been applied to religious organizations other than churches and the like. There have been, and continue to be, however, many instances where churches are directly involved in political campaigns. Candidates have campaigned in churches as part of the religious services and members of the clergy have endorsed candidates from the pulpit. These are blatant transgressions of the law—routinely engaged in by presidents, members of Congress, governors, mayors, and individuals seeking those and other positions. Even when these practices are reported in the public media or complaints are filed with the IRS, the agency rarely acts.

Q 9:13   Is the prohibition against political campaigning by religious organizations constitutional?

Yes. As long as churches and other religious organizations are treated in this regard no differently from other public charities, there is no unwarranted entanglement of church and state or impingement on the practice of religious beliefs.

The converse argument is that government should not be able to dictate what churches and similar institutions say in the context of propagation of their religious beliefs. This argument is more compelling where the church is speaking out on social issues and, only in that setting, is supporting or criticizing political candidates. It is less attractive when the church involvement is purely political, such as where a member of the clergy endorses a particular candidate from the pulpit during a church service.

In one case, a church had its tax-exempt status revoked for participation in the 1992 presidential campaign; it paid for newspaper advertisements attacking candidate Governor Clinton's positions on social issues. The courts (trial and appellate) held that the IRS had the authority to revoke exempt status. Both courts also concluded that the revocation of the tax exemption of this church was not contrary to the First and Fifth Amendments to the U.S. Constitution.

Q 9:14 What happens when a private foundation engages in a political campaign activity?

The law involving private foundations includes all of the law pertaining to public charities (Q 9:9, Q 9:10), as well as some special rules. If a private foundation engages in a political campaign activity, it may lose its tax-exempt status and also be subject to excise taxation. An expenditure of funds by a private foundation for a political campaign purpose—termed *electioneering*—is a *taxable expenditure*; the foundation would be subjected to an excise tax of 10 percent of the amount involved, plus a requirement that the expenditure be timely corrected. Foundation managers who knowingly allowed the foundation to engage in electioneering could be the recipients of a $2\frac{1}{2}$ percent tax. If there is no timely correction, the foundation could be subjected to an additional tax of 100 percent, and the managers, to an additional tax of 50 percent.

Q 9:15 Can a charitable organization utilize a political action committee without adversely affecting its tax exemption?

Yes, but only under very limited circumstances. As a general rule, the function of a political action committee is to assist one or more individuals in becoming elected to political office—a political campaign activity in which a charitable organization is forbidden to engage (Q 9:1, Q 9:16). Because the functions of a political action committee are attributed to the affiliated charitable organization for this purpose, the political activities of the committee generally would cause the charity to forfeit its tax exemption and pay the excise tax on political expenditures.

This use of a political action committee is permissible, however, where the political activities engaged in by the committee are other than political campaign activities. These activities must be exempt functions of political organizations (Q 9:16) but not political campaign activities by public charities. For example, a public charitable organization could, without loss of tax-exempt status, utilize a political action committee to work to defeat the nomination by a President of an individual to become a member of the Supreme Court. This use of a political action committee would also preclude the charity from having to pay the political organization tax on expenditures associated with that political activity (Q 9:10).

OTHER EXEMPT ORGANIZATIONS AND POLITICAL ACTIVITIES

Q 9:16 What is a *political organization*?

A *political organization* is a type of tax-exempt organization. It is a party, committee, association, fund, or other organization formed and operated primarily for the purpose of directly or indirectly accepting contributions or making expenditures

Q 9:17 | Political Activities

for an *exempt function*. The principal exempt function of a political organization is influencing or attempting to influence the selection, nomination, election, or appointment of any individual to any federal, state, or local public office or office in a political organization. An organization of this nature can also be used to effect the election of presidential or vice-presidential electors. Political organizations include political parties, political action committees, campaign funds for individual candidates, and incumbents' newsletter funds. Other activities may be engaged in, but they must not divert the organization from its principal purpose. An organization that engages wholly in legislative activities cannot qualify as a political organization.

Political organizations are taxable on all income other than exempt function income, which includes contributions, membership dues, proceeds from fundraising events, and receipts from the sale of political campaign materials. All other income, including investment income, is taxable.

The federal election laws, which do not always parallel the federal tax laws in these respects, term organizations such as political action committees *separate segregated funds*. Political organizations usually are not incorporated because of the strict limitations of the federal election law on political contributing and other political campaign activities by corporations.

Q 9:17 Aren't political action committees affiliated with other tax-exempt organizations?

They often are, but not always. The types of tax-exempt organizations that have political action committees usually are business leagues (such as trade or business associations) and labor organizations (such as labor unions) (Q 9:22). The membership of these organizations is the prospective donor base for the political entity (Q 9:23). A business enterprise can have a political action committee.

The federal election law recognizes the independent political action committee. This is a political committee that is free-standing; that is, it is not affiliated with any sponsoring organization. However, the IRS has yet to rule on the qualifications of a free-standing political action committee as a tax-exempt political organization.

Q 9:18 Is the tax imposed on political organizations confined to those organizations?

No. The tax scheme for political organizations contains a tax that can be imposed on a wide range of other tax-exempt organizations. If an exempt organization expends any amount during a tax year, either directly or through another organization, for what would be an exempt function for a political organization (Q 9:16), it must include in its taxable income for the year an amount equal to the lesser of its net investment income for the year or the aggregate amounts expended for the exempt function. This tax can be applicable where the tax-exempt organization does not keep accurate records that differentiate between soft money and hard money (Q 9:23). This rule is applicable to charitable organizations, without corresponding loss of tax exemption, where the political activities involved are exempt functions that are not political campaign activities (Q 9:15).

Q 9:19 What are the rules concerning political activities by social welfare organizations?

A tax-exempt social welfare organization is not bound by the constraints on political activities that apply to charitable organizations (Q 9:1, Q 9:3). A social welfare organization can engage in political campaign activities as long as it is not thereby prevented from the conduct of its exempt functions. There have not been any rulings or court opinions in amplification of that rule.

The political organization tax would be applicable, however, with respect to these political campaign activities (Q 9:18). Also, if the organization has a membership and the members have joined in furtherance of business purposes, the deductibility of their dues may be affected by any political campaign activities of the organization (Q 9:20). Social welfare organizations are further restricted by the federal and state political campaign regulation laws.

Q 9:20 What are the rules concerning political activities by trade and business associations?

From the standpoint of tax-exempt status, the federal tax laws are essentially silent on the matter of political campaign activities by tax-exempt associations. There is no stated limitation in this regard, other than the general one that the political activities cannot be so extensive as to preclude the association from carrying out its exempt functions. Also, tax-exempt associations are subject to the political organizations tax when they engage in political activities (Q 9:18), and they are restricted by the federal and state political campaign regulation laws. Consequently, nearly all political campaign activities of tax-exempt associations are conducted by means of political action committees.

There is another body of federal tax law, however, that must be taken into account for these purposes by a tax-exempt association. This law pertains to the deductibility, as a business expense, of the dues paid by the members of the association; as a general rule, these dues are fully deductible as expenditures made for business purposes. The deductibility of association dues can be circumscribed where the association engages in political campaign activities; these rules are the same as those pertaining to lobbying activities by business leagues (Q 8:28).

Q 9:21 Can lobbying by these organizations be considered political campaign activity?

Yes. Generally, the federal tax rules concerning lobbying (Chapter 8) and political campaign activities are separate, discrete bodies of law. There are circumstances, however, where lobbying activity by an exempt organization can be regarded as political campaign activity (Q 8:12). Again, activities of this nature are known as *public policy advocacy communications*; they are said to have a *dual character*.

Q 9:22 To what extent can exempt organizations other than charities utilize political action committees?

Nearly all types of tax-exempt organizations can utilize political action committees. In fact, this is often done to avoid the political organization tax (Q 9:18).

If a tax-exempt organization establishes a political organization and operates the political activities through it, rather than through the sponsoring organization, the political exempt functions (Q 9:16) are in the political organization and not the parent entity. As exempt functions of the political organization, they are not taxed. Inasmuch as the political activities are not in the parent exempt organization, there is no political activities tax at that level either.

Q 9:23 What do the terms *hard money* and *soft money* signify?

The distinction between *hard money* and *soft money* is critical to avoidance of the political organizations tax; that is, the principal way to avoid this tax is to confine all political activities to the affiliated political organization (Q 9:22). All hard money expenditures are to be made only by the political organization; the affiliated (parent) exempt organization may make soft money expenditures.

Hard money is money that is used for political campaign contributions and similar purposes. Soft money is money that is used to establish and administer a political organization. For example, a business association may have a political action committee. The funds used by the association to create and operate the political action committee are soft funds; the amounts expended by the political action committee to support political candidates are hard funds. To continue with this example, the association would want to avoid making hard money expenditures, so as to not be subject to the political organizations tax (Q 9:18) and not violate the federal campaign laws. This dichotomy in turn requires the parent tax-exempt organization (the association, in this example) to keep adequate records to differentiate between the two types of expenditures. In one instance, the IRS imposed the political organizations tax on an exempt organization because its records were inadequate to enable it to distinguish its soft money expenditures from its hard money outlays.

Q 9:24 How do the federal election laws interrelate with the federal tax laws?

Not particularly well. Both bodies of law pertain to many of the same subjects; the federal election law defines some pertinent terms where the tax laws do not. But the IRS does not follow the interpretations of the Federal Election Commission. For example, the IRS does not follow the Commission's rules as to definition of the term *candidate* (Q 9:6).

Q 9:25 How did passage of the Bipartisan Campaign Reform Act affect this interrelationship?

Matters in this regard certainly have gotten more complicated following the significant amendment, in 2002, of the Federal Election Campaign Act (FECA) by the Bipartisan Campaign Reform Act. The FECA now contains an intricate array of limitations and prohibitions on political campaign contributions, expenditures, and other activities. After the Supreme Court, in 2003, concluded that nearly all of these amendments are constitutional, the Federal Election Commission began consideration of potentially sweeping rules.

Some of these rules reflect the fact that some organizations are operating outside the boundaries of the FECA by raising and spending soft money for use in political campaigns. (A principal purpose of the amended FECA is to narrow the scope of unregulated political campaign financing, which is to say expand the applicability of the FECA's restrictions and prohibitions to at least some of these organizations.) The Commission has developed rules that could subject several categories of tax-exempt organizations to its jurisdiction (requiring reporting to it) by classifying them as *political committees*.

REPORTING REQUIREMENTS

Q 9:26 What are the reporting requirements for charitable organizations?

A public charity (see Chapter 10) must file an annual information return (Chapter 5) with the IRS. One of the questions on this form is whether the organization made any political expenditures. Another question is whether the organization filed the income tax return required of political organizations.

The annual information return that private foundations must file requests information about any expenditures the foundation may have made for political activities during the year.

Q 9:27 What are the reporting requirements for other tax-exempt organizations?

The first reporting requirement stated for charitable organizations (Q 9:25) is applicable to all tax-exempt organizations required to file an annual information return.

Tax-exempt social welfare organizations, business leagues (including trade, business, and professional associations), and labor organizations must also report political expenditures that pertain to the rules concerning the nondeductibility of dues (Q 8:28).

CHAPTER 10

Public Charity Status

The federal tax law separates charitable organizations into two categories: public and private. The latter are termed *private foundations* (Chapter 11). Although the law presumes that all charitable organizations are private foundations, nearly all charities are public charities. There are three basic classifications of public charities, but there are many types within each classification. Because the body of federal tax law concerning private foundations is so onerous, it is important for a charitable organization to achieve public charity status if it can.

Here are the questions most frequently asked about the difference between public charities and private foundations, how to acquire and maintain public charity status, the oft-misunderstood supporting organization—and the answers to them.

Q 10:1 What is a *public charity*?

A tax-exempt charitable organization is either a *public charity* or a *private foundation*. Every exempt charitable organization, domestic or foreign, is presumed to be a private foundation; this presumption can be rebutted by demonstrating to the IRS that the organization is a public charity. There are three basic classifications of public charities, but there are many types of them (Q 10:3).

Q 10:2 What is a *private foundation*?

There is no true definition of a *private foundation*; there is only a "virtually real" definition of that term. This definition describes charitable organizations that are not private foundations.

A generic private foundation has three characteristics: (1) it is a charitable organization that was initially funded by one source (usually an individual, a family, or a business), (2) its ongoing revenue income comes from investments (in the nature of an endowment fund), and (3) it makes grants to other charitable organizations rather than operate its own program. The nature of its funding and, sometimes, the nature of its governance (such as a closed, family-oriented board of trustees (Q 2:6)), are the characteristics that make this type of charitable organization *private*.

TIP: The federal tax rules applicable to private foundations are onerous and, because of various penalty excise taxes, can be costly. One of the most important services a lawyer for a charitable organization can offer is advice on the organization's basis for avoidance of the private foundation rules.

Q 10:3 What are the categories of public charities?

Basically, there are three categories of public charities: (1) institutions, (2) publicly supported organizations, and (3) supporting organizations.

Institutions are charitable organizations that are clearly not private foundations, simply by virtue of their programs and structure. These entities are churches, associations and conventions of churches, integrated auxiliaries of churches, colleges, universities, schools, hospitals, certain other health care providers, medical research organizations, certain supporting foundations for governmental colleges and universities, and a variety of governmental units.

Because they have a broad base of contributions from the general public, publicly supported charities generally are the antithesis of private foundations. Publicly supported organizations and supporting organizations are discussed below (Q 10:7–Q 10:29).

Q 10:4 How does an organization acquire public charity status?

Most commonly, an organization acquires public charity status at the same time it acquires recognition of tax-exempt status as a charitable organization. As part of the organization's filing of an application for recognition of exemption, it selects the category of public charity that it wants. If the IRS agrees that the organization qualifies as a type of public charity, it includes that classification on the determination letter or ruling that it issues. (This is the process by which a charitable organization rebuts the presumption that it is a private foundation (Q 10:1).) Depending on the category of public charity, the organization will receive either an advance ruling (Q 10:9) or a definitive ruling (Q 10:11).

Q 10:5 How does an organization maintain its public charity status?

The manner in which an organization maintains its public charity status depends in large part on the type of public charity that it is. If it is an institution (Q 10:3) or a supporting organization (Q 10:15–Q 10:29), it remains a public charity as long as it continues to satisfy the programmatic or structural criteria that originally gave rise to the classification. If it is a publicly supported organization (Q 10:7–Q 10:14), it must provide its public support information to the IRS each year. This is done as part of the annual information return; there is a schedule by which both donative publicly supported charitable organizations and service provider publicly supported organizations display support information for a four-year measuring period. An organization must only demonstrate that it qualifies under one of the categories each year, irrespective of the category that is reflected on its ruling.

Q 10:6 Why is it so important to be classified as a public charity and avoid private foundation status?

There are *no disadvantages* to public charity status; all of the disadvantages lie in classification as a private foundation. The disadvantages vary according to the nature of the organization; for some organizations, all of the disadvantages are important.

One of the principal disadvantages to private foundation status is the fact that, as a practical matter, private foundations will not make grants to other private foundations. A private foundation grantor must exercise *expenditure responsibility* as part of this type of grant, and most private foundations do not have the resources to undertake, and do not want the risk of, expenditure responsibility grants. Also, in some instances, this type of grant will not qualify for the mandatory payout. Any charitable organization that is structured as a private foundation has basically denied itself access to funding by private foundation grants.

Another disadvantage to private foundation status is that contributions to private foundations may be less deductible than those to public charities. For example, in a single tax year, an individual may make deductible gifts of money to public charities in amounts up to 50 percent of his or her adjusted gross income, whereas gifts of money to private foundations are subject to a 30 percent limitation. Similarly, gifts of appreciated property to public charities are deductible up to a 30 percent limitation, but the limitation generally is 20 percent in the case of private foundations. (See Q 12:2–Q 12:3.)

Other disadvantages to private foundation status include (1) compliance with the federal tax rules regulating the conduct of private foundations, (2) payment of a 2 percent tax on investment income, including capital gain, (3) the requirement of filing a more complex annual information return, and (4) the need to publish a newspaper advertisement as to the availability of the annual return.

CAUTION: On occasion, a charitable organization—not understanding the rules in this area—will indicate on the application for recognition of exemption (Q 10:4) that it is a private foundation, when in fact it will clearly be qualifying as a publicly supported charity. The IRS is unnecessarily harsh on the point, rarely permitting the organization to amend the application and instead forcing it to formally terminate its private foundation status, including "starting over" with an advance ruling (Q 10:9). This can cause enormous funding problems in the early years when reliance is placed on private foundation grants (Q 10:6). Thus, a charitable organization should be certain, when selecting foundation status, that that is the correct classification.

PUBLICLY SUPPORTED CHARITIES

Q 10:7   What is a *donative publicly supported charitable organization*?

A *donative publicly supported charitable organization* is an organization that receives a substantial amount of its support in the form of gifts and grants from the general public or from the U.S. government, a state, or a political subdivision. In this setting, *substantial* generally means at least one-third. The denominator of this support ratio includes investment income; fee-for-service revenue is not included in either the numerator or denominator. These calculations are made on the basis of a four-year moving average. (Generally, the source of the balance of the support is irrelevant.)

Support from any one source is public support to the extent that the amount does not exceed an amount equal to 2 percent of the support fraction denominator. For example, if an organization received $400,000 over its most recent four years, its public support would be the contributed amounts that did not exceed $8,000 per source (.02 × $400,000). If the organization is able to show that at least $167,000 of the $400,000 came from public support, it can be considered a donative publicly supported organization for the two years immediately succeeding the four measuring years. Unusual grants are excluded from the computation.

TIP: If an organization receives a substantial part of its support in the form of fee-for-service revenue, it cannot qualify as a donative publicly supported organization, even if it meets the support test for the small amount of contributions it receives.

Some additional rules apply to the computation of support for donative publicly supported organizations: (1) amounts from other donative publicly supported organizations constitute public support in full (that is, they are not limited by the 2 percent rule), (2) gifts and grants that exceed the 2 percent limitation constitute public support to the extent of the 2 percent limitation amount, and (3) there are attribution rules in determining sources of support (for example, gifts from a husband and wife are considered as coming from one source). To illustrate the second additional rule, if the organization in the above example received a $10,000 contribution from one source, $8,000 of it would be public support.

Two other categories of publicly supported organizations can be realized (1) by virtue of the *facts-and-circumstances test* or (2) because an organization is a community foundation. Organizations in the former category have at least 10 percent of public support and have characteristics that demonstrate public involvement with the organization (such as public use of facilities, public involvement in the programs, or a board of directors reflective of the community). A community foundation is a charitable organization that receives funding from and makes grants within a discrete community.

Q 10:8 What is a *service provider publicly supported charitable organization*?

A *service provider publicly supported organization* is the other basic type of publicly supported charity. This type of an organization normally receives at least one-third of its support in the form of gifts, grants, and exempt function revenue from the general public. The ratio calculation is made on the basis of a four-year moving average. The denominator of the ratio consists of the various forms of public support, net unrelated business income, investment income, tax revenues levied for the benefit of the organization, and the value of certain services or facilities furnished by a governmental unit. Gift and grant support from any one source is public support to the extent that the amount derived did not come from a *disqualified person*. Unusual grants are excluded from the computation.

The term *disqualified persons* includes an organization's directors, trustees, officers, key employees having responsibilities similar to those of officers, substantial contributors, family members of these individuals, and certain entities related to or affiliated with these persons. A *substantial contributor* is a person who contributed or granted more than $5,000 to the charitable organization, where that amount was more than 2 percent of the gifts and grants to the organization during the period of its existence. In almost all cases, once a person is classified as a substantial contributor, that classification remains irrespective of the growth of the charity.

Public support can include *exempt function revenue*. This is revenue in the form of gross receipts from admissions, sales of merchandise, performance of services, or furnishing of facilities, in an activity that is not an unrelated business. Revenue of this nature is not public support, however, to the extent that the receipts from any person or from any bureau or similar agency of a governmental unit in any tax year exceed the greater of $5,000 or 1 percent of the organization's support in that year. Also, this type of support from disqualified persons is not public support.

Using the figures of the above example, an organization attempting to qualify as a service provider publicly supported charity would also have to receive at least $167,000 in public support during the four-year measuring period. This support could be in the form of gifts, grants, and/or exempt function revenue. However, none of this support could be from substantial contributors, board members, or other disqualified persons.

A service provider publicly supported organization cannot normally receive more than one-third of its support from gross investment income.

NOTE: A service provider publicly supported organization that utilizes a supporting organization must be cautious: funds transferred from the supporting organization may, in whole or in part, retain their character as investment income.

Q 10:9 What is an *advance ruling*?

An *advance ruling* is a ruling issued by the IRS to a new charitable organization that is expecting to qualify as a publicly supported organization (in either category, donative or service provider). This ruling is part of the basic ruling recognizing tax-exempt status and charitable donee status. Being new, the organization does not have a financial history on which to base a determination as to whether it is publicly supported. Consequently, the IRS makes this initial determination of the organization's publicly supported charity status on the basis of a budget provided by the organization; where that information appears credible, the IRS will rule that the organization is reasonably expected to constitute a publicly supported organization. The term *advance* is used because the ruling is issued before actual development of the necessary financial data that will indicate whether the organization is in fact publicly supported. In this sense, the ruling is a probationary or tentative ruling as to publicly supported charity status.

NOTE: The concept of an advance ruling does not apply to recognition of tax exemption or charitable donee status. Advance rulings are issued to both putative donative publicly supported organizations and service provider publicly supported organizations.

If a new charitable organization wishes to be regarded by the IRS as a publicly supported charity, it must receive an advance ruling where it is in existence for only one year. (That "year" must be less than eight months.) Where the organization has a financial history that is longer, it is entitled to, but need not pursue, a definitive ruling (Q 10:11).

TIP: This area of the law can be confusing, because of the source of it. The IRS does not follow the existing regulations on the subject. Instead, it uses different rules that can be found only in the instructions accompanying the application for recognition of tax exemption.

The period of time the advance ruling is in effect is the *advance ruling period*—the organization's first five years.

NOTE: The use of the term *year* can be tricky. For purposes of being able to gain a definitive ruling with only one year of existence, the "year" must be a period of at least eight months (Q 10:11). When *measuring* an entity's advance ruling period, however, the first year can be a period of any length—months, weeks, or some number of days. This may mitigate against forming, late in a year, a charitable entity that is intended to be publicly supported.

Once the advance ruling period has expired (at the close of the appropriate year) and if the organization has satisfied one of the public support tests, the advance ruling will ripen into a definitive ruling. The organization is expected to apply for a definitive ruling within 90 days after the close of the advance ruling period. The requisite financial information should be provided on an IRS form.

Q 10:10 **At the end of the advance ruling period, will the IRS automatically request more information regarding the organization's public support, or does the organization need to initiate contact with the IRS?**

The responsibility to apply to the IRS for a definitive ruling within 90 days following the close of the advance ruling period lies with the organization. The IRS will not initiate contact with the charitable organization on this point at this time, beyond sometimes sending a copy of the requisite form (Q 10:9). Although it is not specifically required, the IRS prefers that the necessary information be tendered on that form.

Once the information is submitted, it is very rare for the IRS to request additional information; that is, the IRS will normally accept the public support information on its face. If the information reflects sufficient public support, the IRS will issue a definitive ruling. If the information shows that the organization did not receive adequate public support during the advance ruling period, the IRS—without inquiry—will classify the organization as a private foundation.

It is important for an organization in this position to accompany the form with a cover letter explaining why the organization meets the public support test (assuming it does) and to include the precise public support ratio. On occasion, if an organization has not met a public support test during the advance ruling period but seems clearly on the way to doing so in the succeeding year, the IRS will issue a favorable definitive ruling.

Q 10:11 **What is a *definitive ruling*?**

A *definitive ruling* is a ruling issued by the IRS to a charitable organization that qualifies as a publicly supported organization. This ruling is part of the basic declaration that recognizes tax-exempt status and charitable donee status. Definitive rulings are issued to both donative publicly supported organizations and service provider publicly supported organizations.

An eligible charitable organization is entitled to a definitive ruling if it has completed at least one tax year (consisting of at least eight months) and meets the requirements for one of the categories of publicly supported organization. A charitable organization that has been in existence for a period of that duration and has not yet achieved the necessary level of public support to qualify as a publicly supported organization, yet expects to qualify as a publicly supported organization, can obtain an advance ruling that it is reasonably expected to be a publicly supported organization.

Q 10:12 **Does it matter which category of publicly supported charity an organization uses?**

Once a charitable organization meets the criteria of either type of publicly supported organization (donative or service provider), the IRS does not care which category the organization is in at any point in time. For example, an organization may receive an advance ruling that it is a donative publicly supported organization and subsequently be able to qualify only as a service provider publicly supported organization. Or, once a definitive ruling as to one of the classifications is received, the organization may annually shift from one category of publicly supported charity to the other.

In general, it is preferable, if possible, for a charitable organization to be classified as a donative publicly supported organization. Policy makers and regulators tend to look more favorably on charitable organizations that are supported primarily by gifts and grants. Charitable organizations that receive significant amounts of fee-for-service revenue are far more susceptible to allegations that they are operating in a commercial manner.

Whatever its actual category, a charitable organization may prefer to be regarded as a donative publicly supported organization rather than a service provider publicly supported organization. (There is no advantage to classification as a service provider publicly supported organization instead of a donative publicly supported organization.) Only a donative publicly supported organization is eligible to maintain a pooled income fund. This eligibility extends, however, to organizations *described in* the rules pertaining to donative publicly supported organizations. If a charitable organization has received a definitive ruling that it is a service provider publicly supported organization, but it meets the support requirements for a donative publicly supported organization, it may maintain a pooled income fund (see Chapter 12).

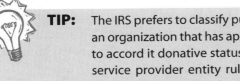

TIP: The IRS prefers to classify publicly supported organizations as donative. On occasion, an organization that has applied for service provider status will find that the IRS wants to accord it donative status. Unless it is clear that the organization will not meet the service provider entity rules or there is a specific reason for wanting the service provider category, it is best to go along with the IRS on this point.

Q 10:13 What happens when an organization ceases to be a publicly supported charity?

If a charitable organization ceases to qualify as a publicly supported entity, the technical rule is that it automatically becomes a private foundation. This can happen in one of two ways: (1) the organization may reach the end of its advance ruling period (Q 10:9) and not have the requisite public support or (2) the organization may have a definitive ruling that it has publicly supported charity status (Q 10:11) but, at a point in time, fail to continue to qualify under either category of publicly supported charity.

In either circumstance, the organization will become a private foundation unless some other category of public charity status is available. One possibility is that the organization can (temporarily or otherwise) qualify as a publicly supported organization by reason of the facts-and-circumstances test (Q 2:5, Q 10:7). Another is that the organization can be restructured as a supporting organization (Q 10:15–Q 10:29). Still another is that the organization can become one of the institutions (such as an educational organization structured as a school) (Q 10:3).

If a charitable organization in this circumstance cannot avoid private foundation status, it is hardly the "end of the world" for the entity. It may be possible for the organization to become a hybrid entity (a blend of public charity and private foundation), usually a private operating foundation or an exempt operating foundation. A charitable organization that is classified as a private foundation can at any time demonstrate compliance with one of the bases for public charity status, terminate its private foundation status, and proceed on a definitive ruling or advance ruling basis.

Q 10:14 What should an organization do when it realizes, during the course of its advance ruling period, that it will not qualify as a publicly supported organization as of the close of that period?

There is no law on this point. In practice, a charitable organization that has an advance ruling, and realizes along the course of its advance ruling period that it cannot qualify as a publicly supported organization, can convert to a supporting organization (Q 10:15–Q 10:28) or, as a less likely choice, an institution, such as a school (Q 10:3). If the organization qualifies for the alternative status, the IRS will issue a ruling to that effect and will not attempt to assess tax on the organization's investment income (Q 10:6) for the early years. The fact that the organization did not meet a public support test during the initial months of the advance ruling period is ignored.

One aspect of this matter is clear: the organization should not simply allow the advance ruling period to expire without taking action. Occasionally, where the organization meets a public support test by taking into account the year following the advance ruling period but has not timely filed the support information (Q 10:9), the IRS will still issue a definitive ruling. But this action is wholly within the discretion of the IRS personnel, and that outcome should not be assumed.

TIP: A charitable organization that expects to meet a public support test as of the close of its advance ruling period, but then does not, is likely to not have the requisite private foundation provisions in its articles of organization. Unless this matter is remedied by state law, the organization will lose its tax-exempt status. It is imperative to place the private foundation provisions in the governing instrument as a "fallback" position where the state does not impose the rules as a matter of law. On occasion, the IRS will elongate the advance ruling period where the test is met using the support in the year following the advance ruling period, but that type of administrative relief cannot be assumed.

SUPPORTING ORGANIZATIONS

Q 10:15 What is a *supporting organization*?

A *supporting organization* is a charitable organization that would be a private foundation but for its structural or operational relationship with one or more charitable organizations that are either public institutions (Q 10:3) or publicly supported organizations (Q 10:7, Q 10:8). This type of organization must be organized, and at all times thereafter operated, exclusively for the benefit of, to perform the functions of, or to carry out the purposes of at least one of these public charities, which are *supported organizations*. Also, it must be operated, supervised, or controlled by or in connection with one or more supported organizations. A supporting organization may not be controlled directly or indirectly by one or more disqualified persons (Q 10:23), other than foundation managers and one or more supported organizations.

The supporting organization must meet an *organizational test*, which basically requires that its articles of organization must limit its purposes to those of a supporting entity and not empower the organization to support or benefit any other organizations. The supported organization(s) must be specified in the articles, although the manner of the specification depends on the nature of the relationship with the supported organization(s) (Q 10:16). Also, the supporting organization must adhere to an *operational test*: it must engage solely in activities that support or benefit one or more supported organizations (Q 10:17).

Q 10:16   **What are the requisite relationships between a supporting organization and a supported organization?**

There are three of these relationships, defined as (1) *operated, supervised, or controlled by*, (2) *supervised or controlled in connection with*, or (3) *operated in connection with*. Irrespective of the relationship, the supporting organization must always be responsive to the needs or demands of one or more supported organizations and constitute an integral part of or maintain a significant involvement in the operations of one or more supported organizations.

The relationship encompassed by the phrase *operated, supervised, or controlled by* contemplates the presence of a substantial degree of direction by one or more supported organizations over the policies, programs, and activities of the supporting organization. This relationship, which is basically that of parent and subsidiary, is normally established by causing at least a majority of the directors or officers of the supporting organization to be composed of representatives of the supported organization or to be appointed or elected by the governing body, officers, or membership of the supported organization.

 **TIP:** This is the most common relationship of the three. It is the easiest and most direct control relationship to construct, and it assures the supported organization that the benefits it expects from the supporting entity will be received.

The relationship manifested by the phrase *supervised or controlled in connection with* contemplates the presence of common supervision or control by persons supervising or controlling both entities to ensure that the supporting organization will be responsive to the needs and requirements of the supported organization(s). This relationship—one of "brother and sister" entities—requires that the control or management of the supporting organization be vested in the same persons who control or manage the supported organization(s).

The relationship envisioned by the phrase *operated in connection with* contemplates that the supporting organization is responsive to and significantly involved in the operations of the supported organization(s). Generally, the supporting organization must meet both a *responsiveness test* and an *integral part test*.

The responsiveness test is satisfied where the supporting organization is responsive to the needs or demands of one or more supported organizations. The test can be satisfied where the supporting organization and the supported organization(s) are in close operational conjunction. There are several ways to show this. They include (1) having one or more of the officers or directors of the supporting organization elected or appointed by the officers or directors of the supported organization(s) or (2) demonstrating that the officers or directors of the supporting organization maintain a close and continuous working relationship with the officers and directors of the supported organization(s). The officers and directors of the supported organization(s) must have a significant voice in (1) the investment policies of the supporting organization; (2) the timing of and manner of making grants, and the selection of grant recipients by the supporting organization; and (3) the direction of the use of the income or assets of the supporting organization.

The responsiveness test may also be met where (1) the supporting organization is a charitable trust under state law, (2) each specified supported organization is a named beneficiary under the trust's governing instrument, and (3) each supported organization has the power, under state law, to enforce the trust and compel an accounting.

A supporting organization satisfies the integral part test where it maintains a significant involvement in the operations of one or more supported organizations and the beneficiary organization(s) are dependent on the supporting organization for the type of support it provides. This test is met where the activities engaged in by the supporting organization for or on behalf of the supported organization(s) are activities to perform the functions of, or to carry out the purposes of, the supported organization(s) and, but for the involvement of the supporting organization, would normally be engaged in by the supported organization(s).

There is a second way to meet the integral part test.

TIP: Although these requirements are considerably complex, these rules represent the farthest reaches under which a charitable organization can avoid private foundation status.

Under this approach, the supporting organization makes payments of substantially all of its income to or for the use of one or more supported organizations, and the amount of support received by one or more of the supported organizations is sufficient to ensure the attentiveness of the organization(s) to the operations of the supporting organization. The phrase *substantially all* means at least 85 percent. A substantial amount of the total support from the supporting organization must go to those supported organizations that meet an attentiveness requirement with respect to the supporting organization.

In general, the amount of support received by a supported organization must represent a sufficient part of its total support so as to ensure the requisite attentiveness. If the supporting organization makes payments to or for the use of a department or school of a university, hospital, or church, the total support of the department or school is the measuring base, rather than the total support of the beneficiary institution.

Even where the amount of support received by a supported organization does not represent a sufficient part of its total support, the amount of support from a supporting organization may be sufficient to meet the requirements of the integral part test if it can be demonstrated that, in order to avoid the interruption of the conduct of a particular function or activity, the beneficiary organization will be sufficiently attentive to the operations of the supporting organization. This may be the case where either the supporting organization or the beneficiary organization earmarks the support received from the supporting organization for a particular program or activity, even if the program or activity is not the beneficiary organization's primary program or activity, so long as the program or activity is a substantial one.

All pertinent factors—including the number of the supporting organizations (Q 10:19), the length and nature of the relationship between the beneficiary organization and the supporting organization, and the purpose to which the funds are put (Q 10:17)—are considered in determining whether the amount of support received by a beneficiary organization is sufficient to ensure its attentiveness to the operations of the supporting organization. Inasmuch as, in the view of the IRS, the attentiveness of a supported organization is motivated by reason of the amount of funds received from the supporting organization, the more substantial the amount involved (in terms of a percentage of the total support of the supported organization), the greater the likelihood that the required degree of attentiveness will be present. However, other evidence of actual attentiveness by the supported organization is of almost equal importance. The mere making of reports to each of the supported organizations does not alone satisfy the attentiveness requirement of the integral part test.

Where none of the supported organizations is dependent on the supporting organization for a sufficient amount of the beneficiary organization's support, the integral part test cannot be satisfied, even though the supported organizations have enforceable rights against the supporting organization under state law.

Q 10:17 What are the functions of a supporting organization?

With the emphasis on *support*, the most common function of a supporting organization is as a funding mechanism for the supported organization(s). In some instances, the supporting organization is the endowment fund for one or more beneficiary organizations. Endowments can be established by a public charity's transfer of some or all of its investment assets to a newly created supporting entity.

> **TIP:** There seems to be a widespread belief that a public charity cannot spawn a supporting organization. This is not the case. For example, in the endowment fund setting, there may be considerable merit in having the fund in a separate entity (1) for liability purposes and (2) to place the assets in the hands of trustees who are more concerned with long-term operations than immediate budgetary pressures. Health care providers and other public charities use the supporting organization vehicle to establish "holding companies" for more effective management.

The law in this area speaks also of providing a *benefit* to a supported organization (Q 10:15). Aside from providing the supported organization with money, an organization can support or benefit another organization by carrying on its own programs or activities to support or benefit a supported organization. For example, a supporting organization supported a medical school at a university by operating teaching, research, and services programs as a faculty practice plan. As another illustration, as part of its relationship with a public charity that provided residential placement services for mentally and physically handicapped adults, a supporting organization established and operated an employment facility for the handicapped and an information center about various handicapping conditions.

A supporting organization may engage in fundraising activities, such as charitable gift solicitations, special events (such as dinners and theater outings), and unrelated business activities, and give the funds for the supported organization(s) or to other permissible beneficiaries.

Q 10:18   Does the supported organization have to be identified in the organizational document of the supporting organization?

Usually, but not always. Generally, it is expected that the articles of organization of the supporting organization will designate the (or each of the) supported organization(s) by name. The manner of the specification depends on the nature of the relationship between the supported and supporting organizations (Q 6:16).

If the relationship is one of *operated, supervised, or controlled by* or *supervised or controlled in connection with*, designation of a supported organization by name is not required as long as two rules are followed:

1. The articles of organization of the supporting organization must require that it be operated to support or benefit one or more supported organizations that are designated by class or purpose.
2. The class or purpose must include one or more supported organizations to which one of the two relationships pertains, or organizations that are closely related in purpose or function to the supported organizations to which one of the relationships pertains.

If the relationship is one of *operated in connection with*, generally the supporting organization's articles must designate the specified supported organization by name.

TIP: Irrespective of the relationship, it is usually preferable—from the standpoint of all organizations involved—for the supported organization(s) to be designated by name in the supporting organization's articles.

Where the relationship between the organizations is other than *operated in connection with*, the articles of organization of a supporting organization may (1) permit the substitution of an eligible organization within a class for another organization either in the same class or in a different class designated in the articles, (2) permit the supporting organization to operate for the benefit of new or additional organizations in the same class or in a different class designated in the articles, or (3) permit the supporting organization to vary the amount of its support among different eligible organizations within the class or classes of organizations designated by the articles.

An organization that is *operated in connection with* one or more supported organizations can satisfy this specification requirement even if its articles permit an organization that is designated by class or purpose to be substituted for an organization designated in its articles, but only where the substitution is "conditioned upon the occurrence of an event which is beyond the control of the supporting organization." Such an event would be: loss of tax exemption, substantial failure or abandonment of operations, or dissolution of the supported organization(s) designated in the articles. In one instance, a charitable entity failed to qualify as a supporting organization because its articles permitted substitution too freely: whenever, in the discretion of its trustee, the charitable undertakings of the supported organizations become "unnecessary, undesirable, impracticable, impossible or no longer adapted to the needs of the public," substitution was permitted.

Q 10:19 How many supported organizations can a supporting organization support?

The law does not place any specific limitation on the number of supported organizations that can be served by a supporting organization. Whatever the number, there must be a requisite relationship between the supporting organization and each of the supported organizations (Q 10:16). As a practical matter, this relationship requirement serves as somewhat of a limitation on the number of supported organizations that can be clustered around a supporting organization. Yet there is a supporting organization that serves over 300 public charitable entities.

Q 10:20 Can a supporting organization support or benefit a charitable organization or other person, in addition to one or more specified supported organizations?

Yes, although the opportunities for doing this are limited. The constraint comes from the fact that the law requires that a supporting organization be operated *exclusively* to support or benefit one or more qualified public entities (Q 10:15). The limitation also stems from the requirement of the requisite relationship and the specification rules (Q 10:16, Q 10:18). In general, a supporting organization must engage *solely* in activities that support or benefit one or more supported organizations.

A supporting organization may make payments to or for the use of, or provide services or facilities for, individual members of the charitable class that is benefited by a specified supported organization. Also, a supporting organization may make a payment through another, unrelated organization to a member of a charitable class benefited by a specified supported organization, but only where the payment constitutes a grant to an individual rather than a grant to an organization. At the same time, a supporting organization can support or benefit a charitable organization (other than a private foundation) if it is operated, supervised, or controlled directly by or in connection with a supported organization. A supporting organization will lose its status as such, however, if it pursues a purpose other than supporting or benefiting one or more supported organizations.

A supporting organization can carry on an independent activity as part of its support function (Q 10:17). This type of support must be limited to permissible beneficiaries, as described above.

In practice, however, it is quite common for supporting organizations to make payments to noncharitable entities as part of their support activities. For example, a supporting organization can procure and pay for services that are rendered to or for the benefit of a supported organization. The supporting organization can also engage in fundraising activities, such as special events, for the benefit of a supported organization. In that capacity, the supporting organization can contract with and pay for services such as advertising, catering, decorating, and entertainment.

Q 10:21   Can a supporting organization support another supporting organization?

Although the law is not clear on the point, the answer is, for the most part, no. The law generally requires that a supporting organization operate for the benefit of, to perform the functions of, or to carry out the purposes of one or more public institutions or publicly supported organizations. A superficial reading of this law leads one to the conclusion that a supporting organization may not be supported in this manner because it is not a public institution or publicly supported organization. Nonetheless, the statute requires only that the supported organization be *described in* one of the institutions or publicly supported organizations categories. Therefore, it appears permissible that a supporting organization may support another supporting organization *if*— and only if—the supported entity also meets the test of classification as an institution (such as a church or school) or publicly supported charity (perhaps the service provider type). The IRS seems to be of the view, however, that this law was not intended to allow one supporting organization to support another—under any circumstances. Thus, it would not be advisable to structure such an arrangement in this manner without first obtaining a ruling from the IRS.

NOTE: To date, the IRS has not issued a ruling on the point. This is either because the IRS has not received a ruling request or because any such request was withdrawn in the face of an adverse position by the IRS.

Q 10:22 Can a charitable organization be a supporting organization with respect to a tax-exempt organization that is not a charitable one?

Yes. A charitable organization can support or benefit an exempt organization other than a charitable entity where the supported organization is a tax-exempt social welfare organization, a tax-exempt labor organization, or a tax-exempt association that is a business league. For this arrangement to be successful, however, the supported organization must meet the public support test applied to service provider publicly supported charitable organizations (Q 10:8). This rule is largely designed to establish nonprivate foundation status for "foundations" and other funds that are affiliated with and operated for the benefit of these eligible noncharitable exempt organizations.

Q 10:23 Are any limitations placed on the composition of the board of directors of a supporting organization?

Yes. The general concept is that a supporting organization will be controlled, through a structural or programmatic relationship, by one or more eligible public organizations. Thus, a supporting organization may not be controlled, directly or indirectly, by one or more disqualified persons (Q 10:15)—other than, of course, foundation managers and one or more supported organizations. A supporting organization is controlled by one or more disqualified persons if, by aggregating their votes or positions of authority, they may require the organization to perform any act that significantly affects its operations or may prevent the supporting organization from performing the act. Generally, a supporting organization is considered to be controlled in this manner if the voting power of disqualified persons is 50 percent or more of the total voting power of the organization's governing board or if one or more disqualified persons have the right to exercise veto power over the actions of the organization. All pertinent facts and circumstances are taken into consideration in determining whether a disqualified person indirectly controls an organization.

An individual who is a disqualified person with respect to a supporting organization (such as being a substantial contributor (Q 10:8)) does not lose that status because a supported organization appointed or otherwise designated him or her a foundation manager of the supporting organization as the representative of the supported organization.

In one instance, the IRS concluded that the board of directors of a supporting organization was indirectly controlled by a disqualified person. The organization's board of directors was composed of a substantial contributor to it, two employees of a business corporation of which more than 35 percent of the voting power was owned by the substantial contributor (making the corporation itself a disqualified person (Q 10:8)), and one individual selected by the supported organization. None of the directors had any veto power over the organization's actions. While conceding that the supporting organization was not directly controlled by the disqualified person, the IRS said that "one circumstance to be considered is whether a disqualified person is in a position to influence the decisions of members of the organization's governing body who are not themselves disqualified persons." The IRS concluded that the two individuals who were employees of the disqualified person corporation should be considered disqualified persons for purposes of applying the 50 percent control rule. This led to a ruling that the organization was indirectly controlled by disqualified persons and therefore could not qualify as a supporting organization.

TIP: This matter of indirect control by disqualified persons is very much a facts-and-circumstances test. The IRS is particularly sensitive to the possibility that creative structuring is being used to mask control of a supporting organization by one or more disqualified persons. The IRS tends to be rather strict on this point.

This control element can be the difference between the qualification of an organization as a supporting organization or as a common fund private foundation. The right of the donors to designate the recipients of the organization's grants can constitute control of the organization by them; supporting organization classification is precluded where this control element rests with substantial contributors.

Q 10:24 Should a supporting organization be separately incorporated?

The law does not require that a supporting organization be incorporated. In most instances, however, supporting organizations *are* incorporated, for the same reasons most nonprofit corporations use the corporate form (Q 2:41). One context in which the trust form may be advisable is where it may be needed as a way to satisfy the responsiveness test (Q 10:16).

Q 10:25 Should a supporting organization have bylaws?

The answer depends on the type of organization that the supporting organization is. If it is a corporation (Q 10:24) or an unincorporated association, it should have bylaws. Charitable trusts do not usually have bylaws, although when the trust form is used for a supporting organization, a set of bylaws or a document akin to bylaws is advisable.

NOTE: There is a specific organizational test in this setting (Q 10:15). However, the requisite language must be contained in the articles of organization; inclusion only in the bylaws is inadequate.

Q 10:26 **Who elects or appoints the directors of a supporting organization?**

Selection of directors depends on the type of supporting organization, that is, on the nature of the relationship between the supporting entity and the supported organization(s) (Q 10:16). If the relationship is that of *operated, supervised, or controlled by*, at least a majority of the board of the supporting organization would be elected or appointed by the supported organization. The entirety of the supporting organization's board can be selected in this manner, or the minority members can be selected by the majority members.

If the relationship is that of *supervised or controlled in connection with*, the boards of directors of the two organizations will be the same. Thus, the organizational documents of the supporting organization would state that its governing board is the same group that comprises the board of the supported entity.

Where the relationship is embraced by the phrase *operated in connection with*, the board of directors of the supporting organization can possibly be wholly independent of the supported organization from the standpoint of its governance. Thus, the board can be structured in any way that is deemed appropriate by the parties involved.

NOTE: The board of directors of the supporting organization cannot be controlled by disqualified persons with respect to it (Q 10:23).

It may be necessary to have one or more of the directors of the supporting organization elected or appointed by the directors of the supported organization, to facilitate compliance with the responsiveness test (Q 10:16).

Q 10:27 **Can a supporting organization maintain its own financial affairs (such as by means of a separate bank account and separate investments)?**

The supporting organization not only can maintain its own financial affairs but it should. This type of entity is a separate organization, and its legal status (including tax exemption) is predicated on that fact. Thus, separate financial resources are (or should be) always the case. This is particularly true with respect to supporting organizations that support or benefit noncharitable entities (Q 10:22).

One of the overarching requirements often is that the supported organization have a significant involvement in the operations of the supporting organization (Q 10:16). This is likely to mean that the board of the supported organization has direction over the investment policies of the supporting organization. For example, for purposes of meeting the responsiveness test, the officers and directors of the supported organization(s) may have to have a significant voice in the investment policies of the supporting organization, the timing of grants, the manner of making them, and the selection of recipients by the supporting organization, and in otherwise directing the use of the income or assets of the supporting organization (Q 10:16).

Q 10:28   What financial reports and disclosure should a supporting organization make to the supported organization?

The law on this point is next to nonexistent. For the most part, this is a management matter rather than a legal one. State law may apply, particularly if the supporting entity is a charitable trust.

To the extent the federal rules address the point, it is a function of the relationship between the supported organization and the supporting organization. In general, the supporting organization must be responsive to the demands of the supported organization (Q 10:16). Thus, the law generally requires that the supporting organization provide whatever financial information about itself that the board of the supported organization "demands." Where the relationship is one of *operated, supervised, or controlled by* or *supervised or controlled in connection with*, the board of the supported organization is in the position of receiving any information about the supporting organization—financial or otherwise—that it wants.

Financial disclosure to the supported organization becomes most problematic when the relationship is evidenced by the phrase *operated in connection with*. In this situation, the board composition of the supporting organization may be such that financial information is not readily available to the board of the supported organization. A problem may arise in the context of meeting the attentiveness requirement of the integral part test. The mere making of reports to a supported organization, however, does not alone enable the supporting organization to meet this requirement (Q 10:16). Thus, where the *operated in connection with* relationship is involved, the sharing of financial information may be largely political, that is, whatever the parties can work out.

Q 10:29   What oversight should the supported organization perform?

No oversight requirement is imposed by law on the supported organization (other than the supervision that may flow out of fiduciary responsibility duties (Q 1:19)). The relationship responsibilities all fall on the supporting organization, as part of its justification for nonprivate foundation status. The supporting organization must always be responsive to the needs or demands of one or more supported organizations and must constitute an integral part of or maintain a significant involvement in the operations of one or more supported organizations (Q 10:16).

Good management practice would dictate that the supported organization be concerned with, and do what it can to conserve, the state and nature of the resources held by the supporting organization. Where the relationship is one of *operated, supervised, or controlled by* or *supervised or controlled in connection with*, any management oversight duties that the supported organization may wish to undertake are readily available (Q 10:28).

Q 10:30 **How do donor-advised funds pertain to the uses of public charities and private foundations?**

First, let's define the term *donor-advised fund*. It is a segregated fund (or account) maintained by a public charity (Q 10:1) for contributions received from a donor (or donors) as to which there is an agreement that the donor (or the donor's designee) may *advise* the charity hosting the fund regarding the distribution of amounts held in the fund for charitable purposes. The fund usually bears the name of the donor (or donors). Thus, a donor-advised fund may be used rather than a private foundation (Q 10:2) where the purpose of the entity is purely grant-making. In some circumstances, the donor-advised fund can serve as a substitute for a supporting organization (Q 10:15).

As of the close of 2004, however, it appears that Congress may enact legislation concerning the operations of donor-advised funds. If that happens, the use of these funds may be less attractive than is presently the case.

CHAPTER 11

Private Foundation Rules

One of the most complex bodies of statutory law in the tax-exempt organizations setting is the battery of rules applicable to private foundations. Created over 30 years ago, the private foundation rules are the subject of hundreds of IRS private determinations (and a few court opinions), and this process continues unabated. New issues continually arise. This body of law is onerous and, because of the myriad penalty excise taxes, can be costly.

If a charitable organization can avoid being a private foundation, it is well advised to do so. If, however, private foundation status is unavoidable, these rules must be faced. Life as a private foundation is by no means impossible, but the organization's management and its advisors should proceed with caution.

Here are the questions most frequently asked about the private foundation rules—and the answers to them.

DISQUALIFIED PERSONS

Q 11:1 What is a *disqualified person*?

A basic concept of the tax laws relating to private foundations is that of the *disqualified person*. Essentially, a disqualified person is a person (including an individual, corporation, partnership, trust, or estate) that has a particular, usually intimate, relationship with respect to a private foundation.

Thus, disqualified persons are commonly trustees, directors, officers, substantial contributors, members of their families, and controlling and controlled entities. The first three of these persons are collectively known as *foundation managers*. A controlling person is a *20 percent owner*, and controlled entities are corporations, partnerships, trusts, and estates.

In the public charity context, this definition generally is inapplicable. (It is used, however, in connection with the computation of public support in the case of service provider publicly supported entities (Q 10:8).) The term *disqualified person*, however, is used as part of the intermediate sanctions rules. In that context, the term is broader in scope than that in the private foundation setting, in that the concept of *member of the family* there includes siblings (Q 7:27).

Also, in the public charity context, the *private inurement* doctrine applies. There the equivalent to the disqualified person is the *insider*. There is considerable controversy as to the sweep of this term. Clearly, the idea of the *insider* embraces trustees, directors, officers, and key employees. The controversy, however, is whether and to what extent it extends to vendors of goods and services, such as fundraising companies.

Q 11:2   What is a *substantial contributor*?

One category of disqualified person is a *substantial contributor* to a private foundation. A substantial contributor generally is any person who contributes or bequeaths an aggregate amount of more than $5,000 to the private foundation involved, where the amount is more than 2 percent of the total contributions and bequests received by the foundation before the close of its year in which the contribution or bequest is received by the foundation from that person. In making this computation, all contributions and bequests to the private foundation, made since its establishment, are taken into account.

In the case of a trust, the term *substantial contributor* also means the creator of the trust. The term *person* also includes tax-exempt organizations (except as noted in a following paragraph) but does not include governmental units. The term *person* also includes a decedent, even at the point in time preceding the transfer of any property from the estate to the private foundation.

With one exception, once a person becomes a substantial contributor to a private foundation, it can never escape that status, even though it might not be so classified if the determination were first made at a later date. This exception enables a person's status as a substantial contributor to terminate in certain circumstances after 10 years with no connection with the private foundation. For this lapse in status to occur, during the 10-year period, (1) the person (and any related persons) must not have made any contributions to the foundation, (2) the person (and any related persons) was not a foundation manager of the foundation, and (3) the aggregate contributions made by the person (and any related persons) must be determined by the IRS to be insignificant, taking into account appreciation on contributions while held by the private foundation. The term *related person* means related disqualified persons and, in the case of a corporate donor, includes the directors and officers of the corporation.

For certain purposes, the term *substantial contributor* does not include most organizations that are not private foundations or an organization wholly owned by a public charity. Moreover, for purposes of the self-dealing rules (Q 11:13), the term does not include any charitable organization—because to require inclusion of charities for this purpose would preclude private foundations from making large grants to or otherwise interacting with other private foundations.

In determining whether a contributor is a substantial one, the total of the amounts received from the contributor and the total contributions and bequests received by the private foundation must be ascertained as of the last day of each tax year. Each contribution and bequest is valued at its fair market value on the date received; an individual is treated as making all contributions and bequests made by his or her spouse.

Q 11:3 What is a *foundation manager*?

Another category of disqualified person is the *foundation manager*. A foundation manager is an officer, director, or trustee of a private foundation, or an individual having powers or responsibilities similar to one or more of these three positions. An individual is considered an *officer* of a private foundation if he or she is specifically designated as such under the documents by which the foundation was formed or if he or she regularly exercises general authority to make administrative or policy decisions on behalf of the foundation. Independent contractors acting in that capacity—such as lawyers, accountants, and investment managers and advisers—are not officers.

An organization can be a foundation manager, such as a bank, a similar financial institution, or an investment adviser.

Q 11:4 What is a *20 percent owner*?

An owner of more than 20 percent of the total *combined voting power* of a corporation, the *profits interest* of a partnership, or the *beneficial interest* of a trust or unincorporated enterprise, any of which is (during the ownership) a substantial contributor to a private foundation (Q 11:2), is a disqualified person with respect to that foundation.

Combined voting power includes voting power represented by holdings of voting stock, actual or constructive, but does not include voting rights held only as a director or trustee. Voting power includes outstanding voting power but does not include voting power obtainable but not obtained, such as voting power obtainable by converting securities or nonvoting stock into voting stock, or by exercising warrants or options to obtain voting stock. Voting power also includes the power that will vest in preferred stockholders only if and when the corporation has failed to pay preferred dividends for a specified period or has otherwise failed to meet specified requirements.

The profits interest of a partner is that equal to his, her, or its distributive share of income of the partnership as determined under special federal tax rules. The term includes any interest that is outstanding but not any interest that is obtainable but has not been obtained.

The beneficial interest in an unincorporated enterprise (other than a trust or estate) includes any right to receive a portion of distributions from profits of the enterprise or, in the absence of a profitsharing agreement, any right to receive a portion of the assets (if any) upon liquidation of the enterprise, except as a creditor or employee. A right to receive distribution of profits includes a right to receive any amounts from the profits other than as a creditor or employee, whether as a sum certain or as a portion of profits realized by the enterprise. Where there is no agreement fixing the rights of the participants in an enterprise, the fraction of the respective interest of each participant is determined by dividing the amount of all investments or contributions to the capital of the enterprise, made or obligated to be made by the participant, by the amount of all investments or contributions to capital made or obligated to be made by all of the participants.

A person's beneficial interest in a trust is determined in proportion to the actuarial interest of the person in the trust. The term *beneficial interest* includes any interest that is outstanding but not any interest that is obtainable but has not been obtained.

Q 11:5 What is a *member of the family*?

Another category of disqualified person is a member of the family of an individual who is a substantial contributor (Q 11:2), a foundation manager (Q 11:3), or a 20 percent owner (Q 11:4). The term *member of the family* is defined to include an individual's spouse, ancestors, children, grandchildren, great-grandchildren, and the spouses of children, grandchildren, and great-grandchildren. Thus, these family members are themselves disqualified persons.

A legally adopted child of an individual is treated for these purposes as a child of the individual by blood. A brother or sister of an individual is not, for these purposes, a member of the family. However, for example, the spouse of a grandchild of an individual is a member of his or her family for these purposes.

Q 11:6 When is a controlled corporation a disqualified person?

A corporation is a disqualified person if more than 35 percent of the total combined voting power in the corporation (including constructive holdings) is owned by substantial contributors (Q 11:2), foundation managers (Q 11:3), 20 percent owners (Q 11:4), or members of the family of any of these persons (Q 11:5).

Q 11:7 When is a controlled partnership a disqualified person?

A partnership is a disqualified person if more than 35 percent of the profits interest in the partnership (including constructive holdings) is owned by substantial contributors (Q 11:2), foundation managers (Q 11:3), 20 percent owners (Q 11:4), or members of the family of any of these persons (Q 11:5).

Q 11:8 When is a trust or estate a disqualified person?

A trust or estate is a disqualified person if more than 35 percent of the beneficial interest in the trust (including constructive holdings) is owned by substantial contributors (Q 11:2), foundation managers (Q 11:3), 20 percent owners (Q 11:4), or members of the family of any of these persons (Q 11:5).

Q 11:9 Can a private foundation be a disqualified person?

Yes, to a limited extent. A private foundation may be a disqualified person with respect to another private foundation—but only for purposes of the excess business holdings rules (Q 11:23). The disqualified person private foundation must be effectively controlled, directly or indirectly, by the same person or persons (other than a bank, trust company, or similar organization acting only as a foundation manager) who control the private foundation in question, or must be the recipient of contributions substantially all of which were made, directly or indirectly, by substantial contributors (Q 11:2), foundation managers (Q 11:3), 20 percent owners (Q 11:4), or members of their families (Q 11:5) who made, directly or indirectly, substantially all of the contributions to the private foundation in question. One or more persons are considered to have made *substantially all* of the contributions to a private foundation for these purposes if the persons have contributed or bequeathed at least 85 percent of the total contributions and bequests that have been received by the private foundation during its entire existence, where each person has contributed or bequeathed at least 2 percent of the total.

Q 11:10 Can a government official be a disqualified person?

Yes, but again only to a limited extent. A government official can be a disqualified person with respect to a private foundation—but only for purposes of the self-dealing rules (Q 11:13).

The term *government official* means (1) an elected public official in the U.S. Congress or executive branch, (2) presidential appointees to the U.S. executive or judicial branches, (3) certain higher compensated or ranking employees in one of these three branches, (4) House of Representatives or Senate employees earning at least $15,000 annually, (5) elected or appointed public officials in the U.S. or District of Columbia governments (including governments of U.S. possessions or political subdivisions or areas of the United States) earning at least $20,000 annually, or (6) the personal and executive assistant or secretary to any of the foregoing.

In defining the term *public office* for purposes of the fifth category of governmental officials, this term must be distinguished from mere employment. Although holding a public office is a form of public employment, not every position in the employ of a state or other governmental subdivision constitutes a public office. A determination as to whether a public employee holds a public office depends on the facts and circumstances of the case; the essential element is whether a significant part of the activities of a public employee is the independent performance of policy-making functions. Several factors may be considered as indications that a position in the executive, legislative, or judicial branch of the government of a state, possession of the United States, or political subdivision or other area of any of the foregoing, or of the District of Columbia, constitutes a public office. Among these factors—in addition to the element of policy-making authority—are that the office is created by Congress, a state constitution, or a state legislature, or by a municipality or other governmental body pursuant to authority conferred by Congress, a state constitution, or a state legislature, and that the powers conferred on the office and the duties to be discharged by the official are defined either directly or indirectly by Congress, a state constitution, or a state legislature, or through legislative authority.

> **NOTE:** In one instance, a lawyer in private practice, who had been a director of a private foundation for more than 10 years and compensated in that capacity, was appointed by the President of the United States to be chair of a government entity. Reviewing this individual's status, the IRS concluded that the individual was not a government official, in that the individual was a special government employee because the employment would not be for more than 30 days over any 365-day period.

PRIVATE FOUNDATION RULES

Q 11:11 Just what are the *private foundation rules*?

The federal tax law governing the operations of private foundations is a composite of rules pertaining to self-dealing, mandatory payout requirements, business holdings, investment practices, various types of expenditures, and more.

Q 11:12 What are the sanctions for violation of these rules?

The sanctions for violation of these rules are five sets of excise taxes, with each set entailing three tiers of taxation. The three tiers are known as the *initial tax*, the *additional tax*, and the *involuntary termination tax*.

In general, when there is a violation, the initial tax must be paid; the additional tax is levied only when the initial tax is not timely paid and the matter not timely corrected; the termination tax is levied when the other two taxes have been imposed and there continues to be willful, flagrant, or repeated acts or failures to act giving rise to one or more of the initial or additional taxes.

The IRS generally has the authority to abate these initial taxes, where the taxable event was due to reasonable cause and not to willful neglect, and the event was timely corrected. This abatement authority does not, however, extend to the initial taxes imposed in the context of self-dealing. Where a taxable event is timely corrected, any additional taxes that may have been assessed or paid are abated.

Because of the stringency of these rules, the sanctions are far more than merely taxes, being rather a system of absolute prohibitions.

Q 11:13 What are the rules concerning *self-dealing*?

In general, the federal tax law prohibits acts of self-dealing between a private foundation and a disqualified person. An act of self-dealing may be direct or indirect. The latter generally is a self-dealing transaction between a disqualified person and an organization controlled by a private foundation.

The sale or exchange of property between a private foundation and a disqualified person generally constitutes an act of self-dealing. The transfer of real or personal property by a disqualified person to a private foundation is treated as a sale or exchange if the property is subject to a mortgage or similar lien that the foundation assumes, or if it is subject to a mortgage or similar lien that a disqualified person placed on the property within the 10-year period ending on the date of transfer.

The following generally constitute acts of self-dealing: the leasing of property between a private foundation and a disqualified person, the lending of money or other extension of credit between a private foundation and a disqualified person, the furnishing of goods, services, or facilities between a private foundation and a disqualified person, and the payment of compensation (or payment or reimbursement of expenses) by a private foundation to a disqualified person.

The transfer to, or use by or for the benefit of, a disqualified person of the income or assets of a private foundation generally constitutes self-dealing. Unlike the other sets of rules describing specific categories of acts of self-dealing, this one is a catchall provision designed to sweep into the ambit of self-dealing a variety of transactions that might otherwise technically escape the discrete transactions defined to be those of self-dealing. Benefits to a disqualified person can occur when the foundation's assets are used by one or more parties that are not disqualified persons. There is no requirement that a disqualified person is intended to be benefited.

TIP 1: This is the most dangerous aspect of the self-dealing rules, in that self-dealing can occur without the parties realizing it. Part of the problem is that the *benefit* involved can be intangible, such as increased goodwill, enhanced reputation, and the provision of marketing advantages—all with respect to nondisqualified persons.

TIP 2: This phraseology is also in the definition of *excess benefit transaction* (Q 7:8). As is the case with respect to much of the law defining self-dealing, developments in the private foundation arena can be used to interpret the intermediate sanctions rules.

An agreement by a private foundation to make a payment of money or other property to a government official generally constitutes self-dealing, unless the agreement is to employ the individual for a period after termination of his or her government service if the individual is terminating service within a 90-day period.

Q 11:14   Are there any exceptions to the self-dealing rules?

There are many exceptions to the self-dealing rules. For example, in relation to the general prohibition on leasing transactions (Q 11:13), the leasing of property by a disqualified person to a private foundation without charge is not an act of self-dealing. Likewise, in respect to the general prohibition on extensions of credit (Q 11:13), this rule does not apply to an extension of credit by a disqualified person to a private foundation if the transaction is without interest or other charge and the proceeds of the loan are used exclusively for charitable purposes.

Concerning the general ban on furnishing of goods, services, or facilities (Q 11:13), the furnishing of goods, services, or facilities by a disqualified person to a private foundation is not an act of self-dealing if they are furnished without charge and used exclusively for charitable purposes. Moreover, the furnishing of goods, services, or facilities by a private foundation to a disqualified person is not self-dealing if the furnishing is made on a basis no more favorable than that on which the goods, services, or facilities are made available to the general public.

As to the rules in respect to compensation (Q 11:13), except in the case of a governmental official (Q 11:10), the payment of compensation (or payment or reimbursement of expenses) by a private foundation to a disqualified person for the performance of personal services that are reasonable and necessary to carrying out the charitable purpose of the foundation is not self-dealing if the compensation (or payment or reimbursement) is not excessive.

CAUTION: This exception is not necessarily as attractive as it might look. A court has held that the term *personal services* is confined to services that are "essentially professional and managerial in nature." In that case, the services involved were found not to qualify for the exception, being general maintenance, janitorial, and custodial services.

As to the catchall provision (Q 11:13), the fact that a disqualified person receives an incidental or tenuous benefit from a private foundation's use of its income or assets will not, by itself, make the use an act of self-dealing. In the case of a government official, the self-dealing rules do not apply to the receipt of certain prizes and awards, scholarship and fellowship grants, annuities, gifts, and traveling expenses.

By reason of another exception, a transaction between a private foundation and a corporation that is a disqualified person with respect to the foundation is not an act of self-dealing if the transaction is engaged in pursuant to a liquidation, merger, redemption, recapitalization, or other corporate adjustment, organization, or reorganization. For this exception to apply, all the securities of the same class as those held by the foundation prior to the transfer must be subject to the same terms and these terms must provide for receipt by the foundation of no less than fair market value.

Q 11:15 When does an act of self-dealing *occur*?

An act of self-dealing *occurs* on the date on which all of the terms and conditions of the transaction and the liabilities of the parties have been fixed.

Q 11:16 What is the *amount involved*?

The *amount involved* generally is the greater of the amount of money and the fair market value of the other property given or the amount of money and the fair market value of the other property received.

Q 11:17   What does *correction* mean?

Correction of an act of self-dealing means undoing the transaction that constituted the act to the extent possible, but in no case may the resulting financial position of the private foundation be worse than would be the case if the disqualified person was dealing under the highest fiduciary standards. This means return to the private foundation of the amount involved (Q 1:9), plus another element (usually the payment of a suitable amount of interest), so as to place the parties in the position they were in before the transaction occurred.

NOTE: For example, in the case of excessive compensation (Q 1:6, Q 6:13), correction of the act of self-dealing includes return to the foundation of the excess portion of the compensation paid.

There are special rules in this regard in the context of the other additional taxes (Q 11:12):

- In the case of the additional tax imposed in connection with the mandatory distribution rules (Q 11:19), the term *correct* means reducing the amount of undistributed income to zero.
- In the case of the additional tax imposed in connection with the excess business holdings rules (Q 11:23), the term means reducing the amount of the excess business holdings to zero.
- In the case of the additional tax imposed in connection with the jeopardizing investments rules (Q 11:27), the term means removing the investment from jeopardy.

Q 11:18   What are the self-dealing tax penalties?

An initial tax is imposed on each act of self-dealing between a disqualified person and a private foundation. The tax is imposed on the self-dealer at a rate of 5 percent of the amount involved with respect to the act for each year in the taxable period or part of a period. Where this initial tax is imposed, a tax of 2½ percent of the amount involved is imposed on the participation of any foundation manager in the act of self-dealing, where the manager knowingly participated in the act. This tax is not imposed, however, where such participation is not willful and is due to reasonable cause. This tax, which must be paid by the foundation manager, may not exceed $10,000.

CAUTION: The aspect of the self-dealing penalties rules represented by the words *for each year* requires emphasis. Each year with a set of self-dealing facts extant brings a new round of penalties. In one instance involving a loan to a disqualified person—remember, an extension of credit to a disqualified person can be self-dealing (Q 11:13)—the matter concerned a 40-year mortgage. The IRS observed that there was a potential in these facts for 40 separate acts of self-dealing.

Where an initial tax is imposed and the self-dealing act is not timely corrected, an additional tax is imposed in an amount equal to 200 percent of the amount involved; this tax must be paid by the disqualified person (other than a foundation manager) who participated in the act of self-dealing. An additional tax equal to 50 percent of the amount involved, up to $10,000, is imposed on a foundation manager (where the additional tax is imposed on the self-dealer) who refuses to agree to all or part of the correction.

In a case where more than one person is liable for any initial or additional tax with respect to any one act of self-dealing, all of the persons are jointly and severally liable for the tax or taxes.

Willful repeated violations of these rules will result in involuntary termination of the private foundation's status and the imposition of additional taxes. The termination tax thus serves as a third-tier tax.

Q 11:19 What are the mandatory distribution rules?

A private foundation is required to distribute, for each year, at least a minimum amount of money and/or property for charitable purposes. The amount that must annually be distributed by a private foundation is the *distributable amount*. That amount must be in the form of *qualifying distributions*, which essentially are grants, outlays for administration, and payments made to acquire charitable assets.

Generally, the distributable amount for a private foundation is an amount equal to 5 percent of the value of the noncharitable assets of the foundation; this is the *minimum investment return*. The distributable amount also includes amounts equal to repayments to a foundation of items previously treated as qualifying distributions (such as scholarship loans), amounts received on disposition of assets previously treated as qualifying distributions, and amounts previously set aside for a charitable project but not so used.

Q 11:20 What are the *charitable assets* of a private foundation?

The *charitable assets* of a private foundation are those actually used by the foundation in carrying out its charitable objectives, or assets owned by the foundation where it has convinced the IRS that their immediate use for exempt purposes is not practical and that definite plans exist to commence a related use within a reasonable period of time.

Thus, the assets that are in the minimum investment return base are those held for the production of income or for investment (such as stocks, bonds, interest-bearing notes, endowment funds, and leased real estate). Where property is used for both exempt and other purposes, it is considered to be used exclusively for tax-exempt purposes where the exempt use represents at least 95 percent of the total use; otherwise, a reasonable allocation between the two uses is required.

Q 11:21 Are there any exceptions to the mandatory distribution rules?

No, not as such. There is, however, an exception to the *timing* of distributions by a private foundation for mandatory payout purposes. This is the *set-aside*, whereby funds are credited for a charitable purpose, rather than immediately granted; where the requirements are met, the set-aside is regarded as a qualifying distribution.

One type of set-aside is that referenced in the *suitability test*; this requires a specific project, a payment period not to exceed 60 months, and a ruling from the IRS. The other type of set-aside is the subject of the *cash distribution test*; this test entails set percentages of distributions over a multiyear period and does not require an IRS ruling.

Q 11:22   What are the mandatory payout tax penalties?

An initial tax of 15 percent is imposed on the undistributed income of a private foundation that for any year has not been distributed on a timely basis in the form of qualifying distributions. In a case in which an initial tax is imposed on the undistributed income of a private foundation for a year, an additional tax is imposed on any portion of the income remaining undistributed at the close of the taxable period. This tax is equal to 100 percent of the amount remaining undistributed at the close of the period.

Payment of these taxes is required in addition to, rather than in lieu of, making the required distributions.

The termination taxes serve as third-tier taxes.

Q 11:23   What are the excess business holdings rules?

Private foundations are limited as to the extent to which they can own interests in commercial business enterprises. A private foundation and all disqualified persons with respect to it generally are permitted to hold no more than 20 percent of a corporation's voting stock or other interest in a business enterprise; these are *permitted holdings*. If effective control of the business can be shown to be elsewhere, a 35 percent limit may be substituted for the 20 percent limit. A private foundation must hold, directly or indirectly, more than 2 percent of the value of a business enterprise before these limitations become applicable.

Q 11:24   Are there any exceptions to the excess business holdings rules?

There are three principal exceptions to these rules. The rules do not apply in the case of a business of which at least 95 percent of the gross income is derived from passive sources. These sources generally include dividends, interest, annuities, royalties, and capital gain.

The second exception is for holdings in a *functionally related business*. This is a business that is substantially related to the achievement of the foundation's exempt purposes (other than merely providing funds for the foundation's programs); in which substantially all the work is performed for the private foundation without compensation; carried on by a private foundation primarily for the convenience of its employees; that consists of the selling of merchandise, substantially all of which was received by the foundation as contributions; or carried on within a larger aggregate of similar activities or within a larger complex of other endeavors that is related to the exempt purposes of the foundation.

The third exception is for program-related investments (Q 11:28).

Q 11:25 These excess business holdings rules seem strict; are there any relief provisions?

If a private foundation obtains holdings in a business enterprise, in a transaction that is not a purchase by the foundation or by disqualified persons with respect to it, and the additional holdings would result in the foundation's having an excess business holding, the foundation has five years to reduce the holdings to a permissible level without penalty.

Moreover, the IRS has the authority to allow an additional five-year period for the disposition of excess business holdings in the case of an unusually large gift or bequest of diverse business holdings or holdings with complex corporate structures. This latter rule entails several requirements, including a showing that diligent efforts were made to dispose of the holdings within the initial five-year period and that disposition within that five-year period was not possible (except at a price substantially below fair market value) by reason of the size and complexity or diversity of the holdings.

Q 11:26 What are the excess business holdings rules tax penalties?

An initial excise tax is imposed on the excess business holdings of a private foundation in a business enterprise for each tax year that ends during the taxable period. The amount of this tax is 5 percent of the total value of all of the private foundation's excess business holdings in each of its business enterprises.

If the excess business holdings are not disposed of during the period, an additional tax is imposed on the private foundation; the amount of this tax is 200 percent of the value of the excess business holdings.

The termination taxes serve as third-tier taxes.

Q 11:27 What are the jeopardizing investments rules?

There are rules governing the type of investments that a private foundation is allowed to make. In general, a private foundation cannot invest any amount—income or principal—in a manner that would jeopardize the carrying out of any of its tax-exempt purposes. An investment is considered to jeopardize the carrying out of the exempt purposes of a private foundation if it is determined that the foundation managers, in making the investment, failed to exercise ordinary business care and prudence, under the facts and circumstances prevailing at the time of the investment, in providing for the long-term and short-term financial needs of the foundation in carrying out its charitable activities.

A determination as to whether the making of a particular investment jeopardizes the exempt purposes of a private foundation is made on an investment-by-investment basis, in each case taking into account the private foundation's portfolio as a whole. Although the IRS will not rule as to an investment procedure governing investments to be made in the future, it will rule as to a currently proposed investment.

No category of investments is treated as a per se violation of these rules. The types or methods of investment that are closely scrutinized to determine whether the foundation managers have met the requisite standard of care and prudence include trading in securities on margin, trading in commodity futures, investments in oil and gas syndications, the purchase of puts and calls (and straddles), the purchase of warrants, and selling short.

Q 11:28   Are there any exceptions to these rules?

A *program-related investment* is not a jeopardizing investment. This is an investment the primary purpose of which is to accomplish one or more charitable purposes, and no significant purpose of which is the production of income or the appreciation of property. No purpose of the investment may be the furthering of substantial legislative or political campaign activities.

Q 11:29   What are the jeopardizing investments tax penalties?

If a private foundation invests an amount in a manner as to jeopardize the carrying out of any of its charitable purposes, an initial tax is imposed on the foundation on the making of the investment, at the rate of 5 percent of the amount so invested for each year or part of a year in the taxable period.

In any case in which this initial tax is imposed, a tax is imposed on the participation of any foundation manager in the making of the investment, knowing that it is jeopardizing the carrying out of any of the foundation's exempt purposes, equal to 5 percent of the amount so invested for each year of the foundation (or part of the year) in the period. With respect to any one investment, the maximum amount of this tax is $5,000. This tax, which must be paid by any participating foundation manager, is not imposed where the participation was not willful and was due to reasonable cause.

An additional tax is imposed in any case in which this initial tax is imposed and the investment is not removed from jeopardy within the period; this tax, which is to be paid by the private foundation, is at the rate of 25 percent of the amount of the investment. In any case in which this additional tax is imposed and a foundation manager has refused to agree to all or part of the removal of the investment from jeopardy, a tax is imposed at the rate of 5 percent of the amount of the investment. With respect to any one investment, the maximum amount of this tax is $10,000.

Where more than one foundation manager is liable for an initial tax or an additional tax with respect to a jeopardizing investment, all of the managers are jointly and severally liable for the taxes.

The termination taxes serve as third-tier taxes.

Q 11:30 **What are the taxable expenditures rules?**

The federal tax law provides restrictions, in addition to those discussed earlier, on the activities and purposes for which private foundations may expend their funds. These rules pertain to matters such as legislative activities, electioneering, grants to individuals, grants to noncharitable organizations, and grants for noncharitable purposes. Improper and, in effect, prohibited expenditures are termed *taxable expenditures*.

Q 11:31 **What are the rules concerning lobbying?**

One form of taxable expenditure is an amount paid or incurred by a private foundation to carry on propaganda or otherwise attempt to influence legislation. Thus, the general rule by which charitable organizations can engage in a certain amount of legislative activity (Chapter 8) is inapplicable to private foundations.

Attempts to influence legislation generally include certain communications with a member or employee of a legislative body or with an official or employee of an executive department of a government who may participate in formulating legislation, as well as efforts to affect the opinion of the general public or a segment of it. An expenditure is an attempt to influence legislation if it is for a *direct lobbying communication* or a *grass roots lobbying communication*.

Engaging in nonpartisan analysis, study, or research and making the results of this type of undertaking available to the general public (or a segment of it) or to governmental bodies or officials is not a prohibited form of legislative activity. Likewise, amounts paid or incurred in connection with the provision of technical advice or assistance to a governmental body or committee (or subdivision of it) in response to a written request from the entity do not constitute taxable expenditures. Another exception is that the taxable expenditures rules do not apply to any amount paid or incurred in connection with an appearance before or communication to a legislative body with respect to a possible decision of that body that might affect the existence of the private foundation, its powers and duties, its tax-exempt status, or the deductibility of contributions to the foundation.

Expenditures for examinations and discussions of broad social, economic, and similar issues are not taxable even if the problems are of the types with which government would be expected to deal ultimately.

Q 11:32 **What are the rules concerning electioneering?**

The term *taxable expenditure* encompasses an amount paid or incurred by a private foundation to influence the outcome of a specific public election or to carry on, directly or indirectly, a voter registration drive. The first of these prohibitions generally parallels the prohibition on political campaign activities by all charitable organizations (Chapter 9). A private foundation may engage in electioneering activities (including voter registration drives) without making a taxable expenditure, however, where a variety of criteria are satisfied, such as not confining the activity to one election period and carrying it on in at least five states.

Q 11:33   What are the rules concerning grants to individuals?

The term *taxable expenditure* also encompasses an amount paid or incurred by a private foundation as a grant to an individual for travel, study, or other similar purposes. This type of grant, however, is not prohibited if it is awarded on an objective and nondiscriminatory basis pursuant to a procedure approved in advance by the IRS and the IRS is satisfied that the grant is one of three types. These are (1) a scholarship or fellowship grant that is excludable from the recipient's gross income and used for study at an educational institution; (2) a prize or award that is excludable from the recipient's gross income, where the recipient is selected from the general public; and (3) a grant for which the purpose is to achieve a specific objective, produce a report or similar product, or improve or enhance a literary, artistic, musical, scientific, teaching, or other similar capacity, skill, or talent of the grantee.

The requirement as to objectivity and nondiscrimination generally necessitates that the group from which grantees are selected be chosen on the basis of criteria reasonably related to the purposes of the grant. The group must be sufficiently broad so that the making of grants to members of the group would be considered to fulfill a charitable purpose. The individual or group of individuals who select grant recipients should not be in a position to derive a private benefit as the result of the selection process.

These rules as to individual grants generally require (1) the receipt by a private foundation of an annual report from the beneficiary of a scholarship or fellowship; (2) that a foundation investigate situations indicating that all or a part of a grant is not being used in furtherance of its purposes; and (3) recovery or restoration of any diverted funds, and withholding of further payments to a grantee in an instance of improper diversion of grant funds. A private foundation must maintain certain records pertaining to grants to individuals.

Q 11:34   What are the rules concerning grants to noncharitable organizations?

A private foundation may make grants to an organization that is not a public charity; however, when it does so, it must exercise *expenditure responsibility* with respect to the grant. A private foundation is considered to be exercising expenditure responsibility in connection with a grant as long as it exerts all reasonable efforts and establishes adequate procedures to see that the grant is spent solely for the purpose for which it was made, obtains full and complete reports from the grantee on how the funds are spent, and makes full and detailed reports with respect to the expenditures to the IRS.

Q 11:35   What are the rules concerning grants for noncharitable purposes?

The term *taxable expenditure* encompasses an amount paid or incurred by a private foundation for a *noncharitable* purpose. Ordinarily, only an expenditure for an activity that, if it were a substantial part of the organization's total activities, would cause loss of tax exemption is a taxable expenditure.

Expenditures ordinarily not treated as taxable expenditures are (1) expenditures to acquire investments entered into for the purpose of obtaining income or funds to be used in furtherance of charitable purposes, (2) reasonable expenses with respect to investments, (3) payment of taxes, (4) any expenses that qualify as deductions in the computation of the unrelated business income tax, (5) any payment that constitutes a qualifying distribution (Q 11:19) or an allowable deduction pursuant to the investment income tax rules (Q 11:40), (6) reasonable expenditures to evaluate, acquire, modify, and dispose of program-related investments (Q 11:28), or (7) business expenditures by the recipient of a program-related investment.

Conversely, expenditures for unreasonable administrative expenses, including compensation, consultants' fees, and other fees for services rendered, are ordinarily taxable expenditures, unless the private foundation can demonstrate that the expenses were paid or incurred in the good faith belief that they were reasonable and that the payment or incurrence of the expenses were in amounts consistent with ordinary care and prudence.

Q 11:36 What are the taxable expenditures tax penalties?

An excise tax is imposed on each taxable expenditure of a private foundation, which is to be paid by the private foundation at the rate of 10 percent of the amount of each taxable expenditure. An excise tax is imposed on the agreement of any foundation manager to the making of a taxable expenditure by a private foundation. This latter initial tax is imposed only where the private foundation initial tax is imposed, the manager knows that the expenditure to which he or she agreed was a taxable one, and the agreement is not willful and is due to reasonable cause. This initial tax, which is at the rate of 2½ percent of each taxable expenditure, must be paid by the foundation manager.

An excise tax is imposed in any case in which an initial tax is imposed on a private foundation because of a taxable expenditure and the expenditure is not corrected within the taxable period; this additional tax is to be paid by the private foundation and is at the rate of 100 percent of the amount of each taxable expenditure. An excise tax, in any case in which an initial tax has been levied, is imposed on a foundation manager if there has been a taxable expenditure and the foundation manager has refused to agree to part or all of the correction of the expenditure; this additional tax, which is at the rate of 50 percent of the amount of the taxable expenditure, is to be paid by the foundation manager.

When more than one foundation manager is liable for an excise tax with respect to the making of a taxable expenditure, all the foundation managers are jointly and severally liable for the tax. The maximum aggregate amount collectible as an initial tax from all foundation managers with respect to any one taxable expenditure is $5,000, and the maximum aggregate amount so collectible as an additional tax is $10,000.

The second-tier excise taxes will be imposed at the end of the taxable period, which begins with the event giving rise to the expenditure tax and ends on the earlier of (1) the date a notice of deficiency with respect to the first-tier tax is mailed or (2) the date the first-tier tax is assessed if a deficiency notice is not mailed.

The termination taxes serve as third-tier taxes.

Q 11:37 Can these initial taxes be abated?

Generally, yes. Where the IRS is satisfied that (1) a *taxable event* was due to reasonable cause and not to willful neglect and (2) the event was corrected within the *correction period* for the event, then

- An initial tax imposed with respect to the event (including interest) will not be assessed.
- If the tax is assessed, the assessment will be abated.
- If the tax is collected, it will be credited or refunded as an overpayment.

As noted (Q 11:12), these taxes are often referred to as the *initial taxes*. They are also sometimes referred to as the *first-tier taxes*. In the abatement context, however, the taxes must be *qualified first-tier taxes*.

CAUTION: The word *qualified* is a part of this terminology for a special reason: the abatement authority of the IRS does not extend to the initial tax imposed in the self-dealing setting (Q 11:18).

For these purposes, a *taxable event* is an act, or a failure to act, that gives rise to liability for tax under the various private foundation rules (Q 11:18). The *correction period* is, with respect to a taxable event, the period beginning on the date the event *occurs* (Q 11:38) and ending 90 days after the date of mailing of a notice of deficiency with respect to the additional tax imposed on the event. This period may be extended by (1) a period in which a deficiency cannot be assessed and (2) any other period that the IRS determines is reasonable and necessary to bring about correction of the taxable event.

Q 11:38 When does a taxable event *occur*?

There are three rules for determining when a taxable event *occurs*. Two of these rules are unique to particular private foundation rules and one is general.

1. In the case of the mandatory distribution rules (Q 11:19), a taxable event is treated as occurring on the first day of the year for which there was a failure to distribute income.
2. In the case of the excess business holdings rules (Q 11:23), the taxable event is treated as occurring on the first day on which there are excess business holdings.
3. In all other instances, the taxable event is treated as occurring on the date the event actually occurred.

Q 11:39   Can these additional taxes be abated?

Yes, under certain circumstances. As noted (Q 11:12), these taxes often are referred to as the *additional taxes*. They also are sometimes referred to as the *second-tier taxes*.

The abatement rule in this context is this: if a taxable event (Q 11:38) is corrected (e.g., Q 11:17) during the applicable correction period (Q 11:37), then, as to any additional tax imposed with respect to the event (including interest, additions to the tax, and additional amounts):

- An additional tax imposed with respect to the event (including interest) will not be assessed.
- If the tax is assessed, the assessment will be abated.
- If the tax is collected, it will be credited or refunded as an overpayment.

If there is a determination by a court that a person is liable for an additional tax, and that determination has become final, the court has jurisdiction to conduct any necessary supplemental proceedings to determine whether the taxable event was corrected during the correction period. There are rules as to when these and other proceedings must begin and when they must be suspended.

Q 11:40   Are there other private foundation rules?

Yes, there are more. An excise tax of 2 percent is generally imposed on the net investment income of private foundations for each tax year. This tax must be estimated and paid quarterly, generally following the estimated tax rules for corporations. Under certain circumstances, this tax rate is reduced to 1 percent in a year where the foundation's payout for charitable purposes (Q 11:19) is increased by an equivalent amount.

As to certain of the private foundation rules, nonexempt charitable trusts and split-interest trusts are treated as private foundations.

A 4 percent tax is imposed on the gross investment income derived from sources within the United States by foreign organizations that constitute private foundations.

Q 11:41   Is there more than one type of private foundation?

Yes. The entity that is normally thought of when the term *private foundation* is used is the *standard* private foundation. This is the typical grant-making private foundation. The standard private foundation essentially has (Q 10:2) three characteristics.

Private Operating Foundation

There is a hybrid entity—a blend of the characteristics of a public charity (Q 10:1) and a private foundation—known as the *private operating foundation*. These are organizations that, while not qualifying as public charities, devote most of their earnings and much of their assets directly to the conduct of their own tax-exempt purposes. That is, they make qualifying distributions (Q 11:19) directly for the active conduct of charitable activities.

> **NOTE:** The basic distinction, then, between a standard and an operating foundation is this matter of distributions. The private operating foundation makes its required charitable expenditures by sponsoring and managing its own programs. The standard private foundation makes grants to other organizations.

Typically, a private operating foundation is an entity that should be a public charity but cannot qualify as such because it is not one of the institutions (Q 10:3) and has a large endowment that precludes it from being a publicly supported organization (*id.*). Classic examples are museums and libraries.

To be considered as *operating*, the foundation must focus and spend a specified annual amount on one or more projects in which it is significantly involved in a continuing and sustainable fashion. The requisite involvement is, as a general rule, found to be present where the foundation's expenditures are made directly or used by it to purchase the goods and services that advance its purposes, rather than being paid to or indirectly through an intermediary organization.

A typical private operating foundation, being significantly involved in its programs, maintains a staff (which may be or include volunteers) of program specialists, researchers, teachers, administrators, or other comparable personnel needed to supervise, direct, and carry out its programs on a continuing basis. This type of foundation usually acquires and maintains assets used in its programs, such as buildings, collections of art objects or specimens, or research facilities. Qualifying direct expenditures also include the purchase of books and publications, supplies, computer programs, and project costs (that is, food in the case of an organization feeding the poor and travel and equipment in the instance of an organization pursuing archeological studies).

To be a private operating foundation, the organization must satisfy an *income test*. Annually, it must expend directly, for the active conduct of its exempt activities, an amount equal to substantially all of the lesser of its adjusted net income or its minimum investment return. In this setting, the phrase *substantially all* means at least 85 percent. As noted, the minimum investment return is equal to 5 percent of the foundation's assets that are not used for charitable purposes (Q 11:19).

To qualify as a private operating foundation, an organization must satisfy at least one of three other tests:

1. The *assets test*: At least 65 percent of its assets must be devoted directly to the active conduct of its charitable activities.
2. The *endowment test*: The organization must normally expend its funds directly for the active conduct of its charitable activities in an amount equal to at least two-thirds of its minimum investment return ($2/3 \times 5 = 3\ 1/3$).
3. The *support test*: At least 85 percent of its support (other than investment income) must be normally received from the general public and/or at least five tax-exempt organizations (that are not disqualified persons); no more than 25 percent of its support can be derived from any one exempt organi-

zation; and no more than one-half of its support can be normally received in the form of gross investment income.

Because of these rules, a private operating foundation is not subject to the minimum payout requirement imposed on standard private foundations (Q 11:19). Contributions to a private operating foundation are deductible to the full extent permitted for gifts to public charities (Chapter 12). That is, the percentage limitations that restrict the deductibility of contributions to standard private foundations (Q 11:48) do not apply to gifts to private operating foundations.

Exempt Operating Foundation

Not content with the complexity introduced with the hybrid form of private foundation known as the private operating foundation, Congress created a hybrid of a hybrid. This entity is known as the *exempt operating foundation*.

NOTE: The word *exempt* does not mean exempt from federal income taxes (which private foundations generally are in any case).

Exempt operating foundations are presumably otherwise private operating foundations, but they enjoy two characteristics that the others do not have:

1. Grants to an exempt operating foundation are exempt from the expenditure responsibility requirements otherwise imposed on grantor foundations (Q 11:34).
2. An exempt operating foundation does not have to pay the tax imposed on other private foundations' net investment income.

NOTE: This, then, is the meaning of the word *exempt*: these operating foundations are exempt from these requirements and taxes.

To be an exempt operating foundation, an organization must (in addition to satisfying the requirements to be a private operating foundation) meet three tests:

1. It must have been publicly supported (Q 10:7, Q 10:8) for at least 10 years or have qualified as an operating foundation as of January 1, 1983.
2. It must have a board of directors that, during the year involved, consists of individuals at least 75 percent of whom are not *disqualified individuals* and was broadly representative of the general public (presumably using the facts and circumstances test (Q 10:7)).
3. It must not have an officer who is a disqualified individual at any time during the year involved.

These rules were written for the entities that are not really private foundations (the standard variety) but cannot meet the formal qualifications for public charity status—again, endowed entities such as museums. This approach is a compromise for them: they are treated as public charities in the sense that private foundation support for them does not trigger the expenditure responsibility requirements, and they do not have to pay the tax on net investment income.

COMMENT: Perhaps someday Congress will enact federal tax law provisions providing public charity status for entities such as museums, libraries, and like entities. The difficulty, of course, is the need to write these rules in sufficiently narrow fashion, if the original congressional intent in creating the private foundation rules is to be preserved.

NOTE: This area of the law, then, may be perceived as a spectrum, with standard private foundations on one end, followed by private operating foundations, followed by exempt operating foundations, followed by various forms of public charities. One of the anomalies of this law is that an organization that is able to qualify as an exempt operating foundation often is able to qualify under the facts and circumstances test (Q 10:7)—and thereby avoid all of the private foundation rules!

Q 11:42   Are private foundations subject to the unrelated business rules?

Yes. These rules do not often apply to private foundations, however, because foundations cannot actively engage in unrelated business undertakings; if they did, the activity would be an excess business holding, such as a sole proprietorship (Q 11:23).

The federal tax law imposes a tax on organizations that derive net income from activities that do not further their exempt functions. This income is called unrelated business income (UBI). Pursuant to the general rules, UBI is generated if (1) the activity constitutes a trade or business, (2) the trade or business is regularly carried on, and (3) the trade or business is not substantially related to the organization's exempt purposes (Chapter 14).

Private foundations, nonetheless, can derive unrelated business income from passive sources. Thus, the excess business holdings rules do not extend to a business where at least 95 percent of its income is passive, such as dividends, interest, annuities, royalties, and capital gains (Q 11:24).

A private foundation's primary UBI risk may well relate to the development of real property it acquired by gift. There may be several parcels of real property that should be further developed to maximize their respective values. The subdivision and development of certain parcels of real property may be viewed by the IRS as a trade or business resulting in recognition of UBI when the parcels are sold. If multiple sales and significant development occurs, the foundation may be viewed as a dealer in the real property rather than an investor. The foundation's sale of parcels that are treated as its inventory will be subject to the tax on UBI, whereas the sale of investment property would be exempt from UBI taxation by reason of the exclusion for capital gains.

There is no bright-line test to determine when the real property shifts from investment property to inventory and, therefore, becomes subject to UBI taxation. The IRS and the courts utilize a facts and circumstances test to determine whether the tax-exempt organization in this circumstance is a dealer. Such factors as (1) the purpose of the acquisition, (2) the cost of property sold, (3) frequency, continuity, and size of sales, (4) sales activities, (5) improvements made, (6) the proximity of time of sale and time of purchase, (7) purpose for acquisition, and (8) market conditions will be analyzed in this regard. Many planning opportunities exist to maximize value while minimizing the tax paid, including the use of an installment sale approach and use of a for-profit subsidiary to develop the property. A for-profit subsidiary may not be utilized by a private foundation (because of the excess business holdings rules) but would be available were there a conversion of the foundation to public charity status (Q 10:1).

Q 11:43 Are private foundations required to file annual information returns with the IRS?

Yes. Every private foundation is required to file an annual information return with the IRS (Chapter 5). This return is on Form 990-PF. Tax-exempt organizations generally have some exceptions in this area, such as for small organizations (that is, those that normally receive more than $25,000 in revenues annually). This is not the case with foundations; all foundations, including those without revenues or assets, are obligated to file.

This annual information return has several functions. It solicits the basic financial information—revenue, disbursements, assets, and liabilities—that is classified into meaningful categories to allow the IRS to statistically evaluate the scope and type of foundation activity, to measure the foundation's taxable investment income, and to tally the disbursements counted in connection with the foundation's minimum payout requirement.

The form has special parts containing questions designed to ferret out instances of noncompliance with the various federal tax law requirements, such as excessive compensation, other forms of self-dealing, inadequate payouts, excessive business holdings, jeopardizing investments, and taxable expenditures.

Q 11:44 Are private foundations subject to document disclosure and dissemination rules?

Yes. Private foundations are subject to the rules applicable to all tax-exempt organizations, by which their application for recognition of tax exemption and their three most recent annual information returns may be inspected at the foundation's office(s) during regular business hours (Chapter 18). Foundations are also subject to relatively recent document dissemination rules, pursuant to which photocopies of these documents must be provided to those who request them (*id.*).

NOTE: The document dissemination rules do not apply where the organization makes them "widely available" (that is, accessible on the Internet) or where the request is part of a "harassment campaign."

Q 11:45 Can a private foundation terminate its private foundation status?

Yes. A private foundation can voluntarily terminate its private foundation status. There are essentially two ways to accomplish this type of termination:

1. The foundation can terminate its status as an entity. This is done by a distribution of all of its net assets to one or more qualified public charities, as long as each of them has been in existence (as a public charity) for a continuous period of at least 60 calendar months.
2. The organization can convert to a public charity (Q 10:1). It must satisfy the rules of the public charity status it selected for an initial continuous period of 60 calendar months.

NOTE: These options are not available to a private foundation where there have been either willful repeated acts (or failures to act) or a willful and flagrant act (or failure to act) giving rise to liability for tax under one or more of the private foundation rules (Q 11:11).

Q 11:46 Are private foundations subject to the private inurement doctrine?

Yes, they most certainly are. All tax-exempt charitable organizations are subject to the *private inurement doctrine*. This is the rule of law that prohibits charitable organizations from inappropriately distributing their net income and/or net assets to persons in their private capacity (Chapter 6). A private foundation, being such a charitable organization, is bound by the private inurement doctrine. The sanction for violating the private inurement doctrine is revocation of tax-exempt status.

As a matter of practice, however, the IRS or a court is far more likely to impose one or more taxes for self-dealing (Q 11:18) in an instance of a private inurement transaction than adhere to the stricter dictates of the private inurement doctrine. At the same time, in an egregious set of circumstances, both the self-dealing rules and the private inurement doctrine may be invoked.

Q 11:47 Are private foundations subject to the private benefit doctrine?

Yes. There is, however, only one published instance of application of the doctrine (Chapter 6) in the private foundation setting. There, the IRS applied the *private benefit doctrine*, holding that even though a transaction did not amount to self-dealing, it would constitute an impermissible private benefit.

An organization, to be a tax-exempt charitable one, must not offer private benefit, unless it is merely incidental. A single nonexempt purpose, if substantial, can lead to loss of tax-exempt status. There is no need of the presence of an *insider* (disqualified person). In the private benefit setting, impermissible nonincidental benefits can be conferred on disinterested persons where the benefits serve private interests.

In the facts of this case, a private foundation was the owner of a collection of original documents and other materials created by or related to an individual (G), and his wife and children. This collection was only partially catalogued and organized; access to these materials was generally limited. Portions of the collection were in fragile condition, and conservation efforts had to be undertaken before any further public use of it could be considered. The foundation was planning on transferring the collection to a public charity.

Another individual (F) requested access to and copies of portions of the collection for the purpose of writing a book concerning G. F was an author who was writing a book about G. She requested access to the collection to research primary material for the book. Her book was not requested or authorized by the foundation. This book project was to be a commercial one. F was to hold the copyright on the book and all other proprietary rights. The private foundation was not to compensate for F's use of the collection.

A third individual (H) was the founder of and a substantial contributor to the foundation (and thus was a disqualified person with respect to it (Q 11:1)). F was a great-niece of H. She also was a great-granddaughter of G (who was not a substantial contributor to the foundation). F was not a trustee of the foundation, nor was she the child or grandchild of any trustees. She was the niece, sibling, or cousin of trustees. F was not the owner of more than 20 percent of the voting power, profit interest, or beneficial interest of any entity that was a substantial contributor to the foundation. Although F held positions on advisory committees of the private foundation, she did not have the power to vote on any action of the foundation.

F was not a disqualified person with respect to this private foundation. She was not a foundation manager, a substantial contributor, a 20 percent owner, or a family member. Basically, her relationship with the private foundation was too distant for her to be considered a disqualified person.

The IRS ruled that, in this case, the private foundation would confer impermissible private benefit to F by giving her preferential exclusive access to the collection. F's private interests would be served by allowing her to profit commercially in that the book about G would be enhanced by information found about G in the collection. Thus, the IRS held the foundation would be jeopardizing its tax-exempt status if it acceded to F's request.

COMMENT: With some tinkering with the facts, the outcome in this case could be different. For example, if F paid the foundation fair value for access to the collection, there would not be private benefit. Or if the book project was that of the foundation, rather than a commercial one, the outcome would be different. Far more important, however, is this fine example of how the private benefit doctrine applies in the private foundation setting. This is another of the traps to be found in the foundation context. Consider this: If a transaction is between a private foundation and a disqualified person, then, under the general rules at least, the transaction would be self-dealing. If, however, a disqualified person is not in the picture, the transaction may nonetheless amount to self-dealing. This is because a self-dealing transaction includes a transaction that creates a use or benefit for a disqualified person (Q 11:13). This ruling illustrates that the analysis should not stop even if the facts show that there is no disqualified person or benefit created for the use of a disqualified person. That is, nonetheless, there may be impermissible private benefit. This shifts the sanction away from the disqualified person (an excise tax) and on the foundation (revocation of tax exemption). Thus, in this area, all three of these levels of analysis may have to be—carefully—made.

Q 11:48   Are contributions to private foundations deductible?

Absolutely. Private foundations are charitable organizations (Q 11:46) and thus are able to attract contributions that are deductible for federal income, estate, and gift tax purposes (Chapter 12). Usually charitable deductions are also available under state law.

The difficulty in the income tax setting is the *extent* of gift deductibility. For the most part, the tax rules in this regard favor gifts to public charities (Q 10:1). The major determining factor in this context is the nature of the thing that is the subject of the gift. In the case of individuals, there are percentage limitations, annually applied to adjusted gross income, which can restrict the amount of charitable giving that is deductible in a year.

Thus, an individual can deduct an amount equal to as much as 50 percent of adjusted gross income in the case of one or more gifts of money to one or more public charities. For example, if an individual has adjusted gross income of $100,000 in a year, he or she can make deductible gifts of money to public charities in that year up to $50,000. (Any excess can be carried forward and deducted in subsequent years, up to five.) Contributions of money to private foundations, however, are subject to a 30 percent limitation. (Again, carryovers are available.)

An individual can deduct an amount equal to as much as 30 percent of adjusted gross income in the case of one or more gifts of property to one or more public charities. For example, if an individual has adjusted gross income of $100,000 in a year, he or she can make deductible gifts of property to public charities in that year up to $30,000.

NOTE: Where a special election is made, contributions of capital gain property may be subject to the 50 percent limitation rather than the 30 percent limitation.

Contributions of this type to private foundations, however, are subject to a 20 percent limitation. (Carryovers are available in both instances.)

Generally, contributions of property (including property that has appreciated in value) to public charities give rise to charitable deductions based on the fair market value of the property at the time of the gift. At the same time, however, property gifts to private foundations generally yield a charitable deduction equal to only the donor's basis in the property.

NOTE: There is a special rule, nonetheless, by which a contribution of most publicly traded securities to a private foundation gives rise to a charitable deduction based on the fair market value of the securities.

Q 11:49 Is there any advantage to classification as a private foundation?

There certainly is no advantage *from the standpoint of the law* as to private foundation status. In every way, the federal tax law favors public charities (Q 10:22).

Nonetheless, there are advantages to classification as a private foundation. The principal one is *control*. An individual, couple, family, corporation, or the like can make one or more gifts to the foundation and retain control over the investment and distribution of funds. The individual or individuals who established the foundation can serve on its board of trustees (without limitation) and enjoy the personal benefits that flow to those who are philanthropists. A private foundation can be a source of employment for those who created it and for their children and subsequent generations.

NOTE: Of course, these advantages also can be obtained where the charitable organization involved is a public charity.

Q 11:50 Is there any disadvantage to classification as a private foundation?

Yes. From the standpoint of the law, there are eight disadvantages. The importance of any of them largely depends on the circumstances of the particular charitable organization.

1. Private foundations must comply with the private foundation rules or suffer penalties (Q 11:11).
2. Private foundations are required to pay a tax on their net investment income (Q 11:40).

3. Contributions to private foundations are likely to be less deductible than gifts to other types of charities (Q 11:48).

4. The charitable deduction for a gift of appreciated property to a private foundation generally is confined to its basis rather than the full fair market value of the property (*id.*), although this disadvantage is somewhat ameliorated by the special treatment accorded *qualified appreciated securities (id.)*.

5. Private foundations have greater limitations on their ability to generate unrelated business income (Q 11:42).

6. Private foundations are required to file a more complex annual information return (Q 11:43).

7. More extensive record keeping requirements are involved.

8. The organization probably cannot be funded by private foundations because of the requirement that grants of this nature be the subject of expenditure responsibility (Q 11:34).

Q 11:51   Do developments in the law concerning intermediate sanctions have an impact on the private foundation rules?

Very much so. The intermediate sanctions rules (Chapter 7) are, in many ways, based on the private foundation rules. This is particularly the case with respect to the self-dealing rules. There are, however, other concepts that have been imported into the intermediate sanctions rules from the private foundation area. These include the principles of the tiers of taxation, the amount involved, and correction.

Thus, a development in the law in the intermediate sanctions context can have a meaningful impact on the comparable point of law in the private foundation setting.

CHAPTER 12

Charitable Giving Rules

The charitable contribution deduction rules are a critical element of the law concerning nonprofit organizations. Donors usually give with donative intent being the primary motive, but the stimulus of the charitable deduction cannot be minimized. This deduction often shapes the form and timing of gifts, and enables donors to give more generously than may otherwise be the case.

No form of charitable giving presents more mystery or generates more confusion than *planned giving*. The rules concerning this type of giving can be somewhat involved, particularly those pertaining to charitable remainder trusts. Out of complexity comes planning opportunities. Planners do not always use these opportunities in ways that are desirable for the charitable community; in other words, there can be abuse. Recently, Congress and the IRS have found it necessary to usher in new rules in the planned giving arena. These developments nicely enhance the intricacy of these rules of law.

Here are the questions most frequently asked about the basic principles of the charitable contribution deduction and the planned giving rules—and the answers to them.

Q 12:1 **Are all tax-exempt organizations eligible to receive tax-deductible contributions?**

No. The list of organizations that are eligible for exemption from the federal income tax is considerably longer than the list of organizations that are eligible to receive contributions that are deductible under the federal tax law as charitable gifts.

Five categories of nonprofit organizations are charitable donees for this purpose:

1. Charitable (including educational, religious, and scientific) organizations
2. A state, a possession of the federal government, a political subdivision of either, the federal government itself, and the District of Columbia, as long as the gift is made for a public purpose
3. An organization of war veterans, and an auxiliary unit of or foundation for a veterans' organization

4. Many fraternal societies that operate under the lodge system, as long as the gift is to be used for charitable purposes

5. Membership cemetery companies and corporations chartered for burial purposes as cemetery corporations

Generally, contributions to other types of tax-exempt organizations are not deductible.

NOTE: The range of charitable organizations for deductible charitable giving purposes is the same as the range of these organizations for income tax exemption purposes, with one minor exception. Organizations that test for public safety are charitable, but only for exemption purposes.

TIP: Although contributions to exempt organizations other than those in these five categories are not deductible, this limitation is rather easily sidestepped by the creation of a related charitable entity, often loosely termed a *foundation*. Tax-exempt organizations that effectively use related foundations for purposes of attracting charitable gifts include trade, business, and professional associations; social welfare organizations; labor unions and similar organizations; and social clubs. In some instances, an otherwise nonqualifying organization may be allowed to receive a deductible charitable gift where the gift property is used for charitable purposes.

Q 12:2   What are the rules for deductibility of contributions of money?

A charitable contribution is often made with money. Some prefer the word *cash*. While this type of gift is usually deductible, there are limitations on the extent of deductibility in any one tax year.

NOTE: For a contribution of money to be deductible by an individual under the federal income tax law, he or she must itemize deductions.

For individuals, where a charitable gift is made with money and the charitable donee is a public charity (Q 10:1) or a select type of private foundation, usually a private operating foundation (Q 11:41), the extent of the charitable deduction under the federal income tax law cannot exceed 50 percent of the donor's adjusted gross income. The limitation for other charitable gifts of money to charity (such as to most private foundations and fraternal organizations) generally is 30 percent. In either instance, the excess portion can be carried forward and deducted over a period of up to five subsequent years. Thus, for example, if an individual had adjusted gross income of $100,000 for a particular year and made gifts of money to public charities in that year totaling $40,000, the gifts would be fully deductible (unless other limitations apply) for that year. If all of these gifts were instead made to typical private foundations, the deduction for the year of the gifts would be $30,000; the excess $10,000 would be carried forward to later years.

The charitable contribution deduction for individuals is subject to the 3 percent limitation on overall itemized deductions. A gift of money may have to be substantiated (Q 13:6) and/or may be a quid pro quo contribution (see Q 13:10). A planned gift can be made in whole or in part with money (Q 12:4).

A for-profit corporation may make a charitable gift of money. That contribution may not exceed, in any tax year, 10 percent of the corporation's taxable income. Carryover rules are available.

Q 12:3 What are the rules for deductibility of contributions of property?

The rules pertaining to charitable contributions of property are more complex than those involving gifts of money (Q 12:2). This type of gift is usually deductible, but there are several limitations on the extent of deductibility in any tax year.

NOTE: For a contribution of property to be deductible by an individual under the federal income tax law, he or she must itemize deductions.

One set of these limitations states percentage maximums, applied in the same fashion as with gifts of money (Q 12:2). For individuals, where a charitable gift consists of property and the charitable donee is a public charity (see Q 10:1) or a select type of private foundation (see Q 11:41), the extent of the charitable deduction under the federal income tax law cannot exceed 30 percent of the donor's adjusted gross income. The limitation for other charitable gifts generally is 20 percent. For example, if an individual had adjusted gross income for a year in the amount of $100,000, and made gifts of property to public charities in that year totaling $25,000, the gifts would be fully deductible (unless other limitations apply) for that year. If all of these gifts were instead made to typical private foundations, the deduction for the year of the gifts would be $20,000. In either instance, the excess portion can be carried forward and deducted over a period of up to five subsequent years.

One of the appealing features of the federal income tax law in this context is that a charitable contribution of property that has appreciated in value often is deductible based on the full fair market value of the property. The capital gain inherent in the appreciated property, which would be taxable had the property instead been sold, goes untaxed.

NOTE: When this benefit is available, the property must be *capital gain property* rather than *ordinary income property*. As a generalization, the distinction is based on the tax treatment of the revenue that would result if the property were sold. That is, the revenue would either be long-term capital gain, or ordinary income or short-term capital gain. (Generally, long-term capital gain property is a capital asset held for at least 12 months). Where the property is ordinary income property, the charitable contribution deduction must be reduced by the amount of gain that would either be ordinary income or short-term capital gain; in other words, the deduction is confined to the donor's cost basis in the property.

As an illustration, an individual purchased an item of property for $20,000 and it is now worth $40,000. He or she contributes this property to a public charity and receives a charitable contribution deduction of $40,000. The capital gain of $20,000 escapes taxation. (By reason of the percentage limitation, this gift would yield, for a gift year, a charitable deduction of $30,000 and a carryforward of $10,000.)

TIP: This rule pertaining to the favorable tax treatment for gifts of appreciated property is equally applicable in the planned giving setting. In many situations (but not all), the deductible remainder interest is based on the full fair market value of the contributed property, and the appreciation element is not taxed.

If the property contributed is tangible personal property and the charitable donee uses the property for a noncharitable purpose, the contribution deduction must be reduced by the amount of the long-term capital gain inherent in the property. This deduction reduction rule also applies where the charitable donee is a private foundation (with limited exceptions).

NOTE: The most important of these exceptions concerns *qualified appreciated stock,* which essentially means publicly traded securities. This type of stock can be contributed to a private foundation, with the deduction based on the full fair market value of the stock (as long as all of the inherent gain is long-term capital gain).

A gift of property may have to be substantiated (Q 13:6), may be a quid pro quo contribution (Q 13:10), and/or may be subject to appraisal requirements (Q 13:14). A planned gift can be made in whole or in part with property (Q 12:4).

A for-profit corporation may make a charitable gift of property. That contribution may not exceed, in any tax year, 10 percent of the corporation's taxable income. The carryover rules apply. For corporations, there are special rules limiting the deductibility of gifts of inventory (somewhat enhanced when the property is to be used for the care of the ill, the needy, or infants) and gifts of scientific property for purposes of research. In most cases involving these two circumstances, the allowable charitable contribution deduction is an amount equal to as much as twice the corporation's basis in the property.

Q 12:4 What is *planned giving*?

The phrase *planned giving* addresses techniques of charitable giving where the contributions (usually of property) are large in amount and are normally integrated carefully with the donor's (or donors') financial and estate plans. For this reason, this giving is termed *planned* giving, because of the time and planning devoted to designing the gift transaction by both donor and charitable donee.

The relationship of this type of gift to a donor's financial needs is a critical factor. The donor often structures the gift so that he, she, or it receives income as the result of the transaction. Usually this benefit is technically accomplished by creating, in the donated property (or money), *income* and *remainder interests* (Q 12:5).

> **NOTE:** One of the most difficult aspects of obtaining planned gifts is persuading prospective contributors that they will be receiving income as the consequence of a charitable act. This is, to many, such a foreign and seemingly inconsistent concept that they will have great trouble grasping it. More difficulties can ensue when an income return is coupled with a sizable charitable contribution deduction. This hurdle can become more formidable when non–income-producing property is converted to income-producing property and/or the income to be received is greater or more tax-advantaged than that being generated before the contribution. The challenge to the gift planner is to overcome these obstacles. Once that is accomplished, the rewards (financial and psychic) are great for all concerned.

Planned gifts may be of two types: (1) the gift made during the donor's lifetime by means of a trust or other agreement, or (2) a planned gift made by will, so that the contribution comes out of a decedent's estate (a bequest or devise).

Contributions of property to charity are often made as outright gifts of the property in its entirety. That is, the donor transfers all of his, her, or its title to and interest in the property to the charitable donee. By contrast, the donor of a planned gift generally contributes something less than the donor's complete interest in the property. In the law, this is known as a contribution of a *partial interest*; planned giving usually is partial interest giving. These partial interests are either income interests or remainder interests.

> **NOTE:** For a charitable contribution deduction to be available, the gift must be to (or for the use of) a charitable organization. The planned gift vehicles are not themselves charities; they are conduits to charities. Nonetheless, it is common to say that a charitable deduction arises when a gift is made to, for example, a charitable remainder trust or pooled income fund. Technically, the deduction is for the remainder interest contributed to the charity; the giving vehicle is merely the intermediary that facilitates this type of gift.

Q 12:5 What are *income interests* and *remainder interests*?

These interests are legal fictions; they are concepts of ownership rights inherent in any item of property. An *income interest* in a property is a function of the income generated by the property. A person may be entitled to all of the income from a property for a period of time or to some portion of the income. This person is said to have an income interest in the property. Two or more persons (such as husband and wife) may have income interests in the same property (or share an income interest in the same property). These interests may be held concurrently or consecutively. The *remainder interest* in an item of property is reflective of the projected value of the property, or property produced by reinvestments, at some future date.

These interests are principally measured by the value of the donated property, the age of the donor(s), the period of time that the income interests will exist, and the frequency of the income payout. The actual computation is made by means of actuarial tables, most often those promulgated by the Department of the Treasury.

For the most part, a planned gift is a gift of an income interest or a remainder interest in a property. Commonly, the contribution is of the remainder interest. By creating an income interest (or, more accurately, retaining the income interest), the donor forms the basis for receiving a flow of income as the result of the contribution. This is known as *partial interest* giving (Q 12:4).

When a gift of a remainder interest in property is made to a charitable organization, the charity cannot acquire the property represented by that interest until the income interests have expired. When a gift is made during lifetime, the contributor receives the charitable deduction for the tax year in which the recipient charity's remainder interest in the property is created. A gift of an income interest in property to a charity enables the donee to receive the income at the outset and to continue to do so as long as the income interest(s) are in existence.

Q 12:6 How are these interests created?

Income and remainder interests in property are usually created by means of a trust. This is the vehicle used to conceptually divide the property into the two component interests. The law terms these trusts *split-interest trusts*; usually a qualified split-interest trust is required if a charitable contribution deduction is to be available. Split-interest trusts are charitable remainder trusts (Q 12:9), pooled income funds (Q 12:10), and charitable lead trusts (Q 12:11).

There are several exceptions to these general requirements of a split-interest trust in planned giving. The principal exception is the charitable gift annuity, which utilizes a contract rather than a trust (Q 12:12). Other approaches can also generate a charitable contribution deduction (Q 12:13 and Q 12:14).

In the planned giving setting, however, it is not enough to create a remainder interest. It is also critical to create a remainder interest, the gift of which yields a charitable contribution deduction. There are only a few ways in which a remainder interest can be the subject of a charitable contribution deduction. Absent qualification of an eligible partial interest (either a qualifying income interest or qualifying remainder interest), there is no charitable contribution deduction.

Q 12:7 What are the tax advantages for a charitable gift of a remainder interest?

For a lifetime gift of a remainder interest in property to a charitable organization, the federal income tax advantages are manifold. The donor creates an income flow as the result of the gift; this income may be preferentially taxed. The donor receives a charitable contribution deduction for the gift of the remainder interest, which will reduce or perhaps eliminate the tax on the income from the property. The property that is the subject of the gift may have appreciated in value in the hands of the donor (*appreciated property*); if that is the case, the capital gain tax that would have been paid had the property been sold is avoided. The trustee of the split-interest trust may dispose of the gift property and reinvest the proceeds in more productive property. Because the trust is generally tax-exempt, the capital gain from such a transaction is not taxed, nor is the income earned by the trust.

Moreover, the donor can become the beneficiary of professional fund management. All of these benefits can be available while, simultaneously, the donor is satisfying his or her charitable desires—and doing so at a level that, absent these tax incentives, would not be possible.

Q 12:8 It was said that the trust generally is tax-exempt. Why the qualification?

In the case of a charitable remainder trust, the trust is tax-exempt unless it has unrelated business taxable income (Chapter 14). In making this determination, the exempt purposes of the remainder interest charitable beneficiary are used to ascertain relatedness.

> **NOTE:** A charitable remainder trust with unrelated business taxable income is taxable on all of its income, not just the unrelated income. A charitable remainder trust with unrelated business income that is not taxable (such as because of offsetting deductions or the specific deduction (Q 14:22)) does not have income taxable under this rule.

A pooled income fund is not a tax-exempt organization. It receives a deduction, however, for its income distributions and for the amounts destined for charitable purposes.

Q 12:9 What is a *charitable remainder trust*?

A *charitable remainder trust* is one of the types of split-interest trusts (Q 12:6). As the name indicates, it is a trust that has been used to create a remainder interest (Q 12:5), which is destined for charity. Each charitable remainder trust is written specifically for the particular circumstances of the donor(s). The remainder interest in the gift property is designated for one or more charitable organizations. The donor (or donors) receives a charitable contribution deduction for the transfer of the remainder interest.

A qualified charitable remainder trust must provide for a specified distribution of income, at least annually, to one or more beneficiaries, at least one of which is *not* a charity. The flow of income must be for a life or lives, or for a term not to exceed 20 years. An irrevocable remainder interest must be held for the benefit of the charity or paid over to it. The noncharitable beneficiaries are the holders of the income interest, and the charitable organization has the remainder interest. Generally, nearly every type of property can be contributed to a charitable remainder trust (Q 12:17).

The income interests in a charitable remainder trust are ascertained in one of four ways: (1) sum certain, (2) fixed percentage/unitrust amount, and (3) and (4), the two makeup approaches. The approach used depends in large part on whether the trust is a *charitable remainder annuity trust* or a *charitable remainder unitrust*. In the case of the former, the income payments are in the form of a fixed amount—an annuity, or what the law terms a *sum certain*. In the case of the latter, the income payments are in the form of a *unitrust amount*, which is an amount equal to a fixed percentage of the net annual fair market value of the assets in the trust. A unitrust may also have one of two types of makeup feature (Q 12:16).

The newest of the charitable remainder unitrusts is the *flip unitrust*. The governing interest of this type of unitrust provides that the trust will convert (flip) once from one of the makeup types to a standard charitable remainder unitrust for purposes of calculating the unitrust amount. This conversion is allowed, however, only if the specific date or single event triggering the flip is outside the control of, or is not discretionary with, the trustee or any other person.

Both of these trusts must adhere to a 5 percent minimum. With an annuity trust, the annuity amount must be at least 5 percent of the initial net fair market value of all property placed in the trust. With a unitrust, the unitrust amount must be at least 5 percent of the net fair market value of the trust assets, calculated annually.

There is also a 50 percent maximum. In the case of an annuity trust, the annuity amount may not be greater than 50 percent of the initial net fair market value of all property placed in the trust. With a unitrust, the unitrust amount may not be greater than 50 percent of the value of the trust's assets determined annually.

Conventionally, once the income interest expires, the assets in a charitable remainder trust are distributed to, or for the use of, the charitable organization that is the remainder interest beneficiary. In some instances, the property comprising the remainder interest may be retained by the trust for charitable purposes.

NOTE: If the second option is selected, the trust will have to qualify on its own for tax-exempt status. It is likely to constitute a private foundation (Q 10:2) in this form.

Usually a bank or similar financial institution serves as the trustee of a charitable remainder trust. This financial institution should have the capacity to administer the trust, make appropriate investments, and timely adhere to all income distribution and reporting requirements. The charitable organization that is the remainder interest beneficiary, however, often acts as the trustee.

TIP: This is a subject of state law: in some states, a charitable organization cannot serve as a trustee. State law *must* be checked on this point before these arrangements are finalized.

A donor or related party may be the trustee. Caution must be exercised, however, to avoid triggering the *grantor trust* rules, which, among other outcomes, cause the gain from the sale of appreciated property (Q 12:7) by the trust to be taxed to the grantor/donor.

Generally, a charitable remainder trust is a tax-exempt organization (Q 12:8).

Q 12:10 What is a *pooled income fund*?

A *pooled income fund* is a type of split-interest trust (Q 12:6). It is a trust (fund) that has been used to create a remainder interest (Q 12:5) destined for charity.

A donor to a qualified pooled income fund receives a charitable deduction for contributing the remainder interest in the donated property to charity. This use of the fund creates income interests in noncharitable beneficiaries; the remainder interest in the gift property is designated for the charitable organization that maintains the fund.

The pooled income fund's basic instrument (a trust agreement or declaration of trust) is written to facilitate gifts from an unlimited number of donors, so the essential terms of the transaction must be established in advance for all participants.

NOTE: This is an important distinction in relation to the charitable remainder trust. Each remainder trust is designed for the circumstances of the particular donor(s) (Q 12:7). This ability to tailor the gift can be a factor in deciding which planned gift vehicle to use.

The pooled income fund is, literally, a pooling of gifts. It is sometimes characterized as functioning in the nature of a mutual fund for charities. Although there is some truth to this—it *is* an investment vehicle—the funding of a pooled income fund is basically motivated by charitable intents.

Each donor to a pooled income fund contributes an irrevocable remainder interest in the gift property to or for the use of an eligible charity. The donor creates an income interest for the life of one or more beneficiaries, who must be living at the time of the transfer. The properties transferred by the donors must be commingled in the fund (to create the necessary pool).

Contributions to pooled income funds are generally confined to cash and readily marketable securities. The pooled income fund, by its nature, must be kept liquid, to enable reinvestments and transfers of remainder interests to the charitable organization. A pooled income fund cannot invest in tax-exempt bonds and similar instruments.

The present value of an income interest in property transferred to a pooled income fund is computed on the basis of life contingencies prescribed in the estate tax regulations and an interest rate equal to the highest yearly rate of return of the fund for the three tax years immediately preceding the tax year in which the transfer to the fund is made. Special rules apply in the case of new pooled income funds (Q 12:28).

Each income interest beneficiary must receive income at least once each year. The pool amount is generally determined by the rate of return earned by the fund for the year. Income beneficiaries receive their proportionate share of the fund's income. The dollar amount of the income share is based on the number of units owned by the beneficiary; each unit must be based on the fair market value of the assets when transferred.

A pooled income fund must be maintained by one or more charitable organizations. The charity must exercise control over the fund; it does not have to be the trustee of the fund, but it must have the power to remove and replace the trustee.

NOTE: Whether a charitable organization can be the trustee of a pooled income fund is a matter of state law (Q 12:9).

A donor or an income beneficiary of the fund may not be a trustee of the fund. A donor may be a trustee or officer of the charitable organization that maintains the fund, however, as long as he or she does not have the general responsibilities toward the fund that are ordinarily exercised by a trustee.

Q 12:11   What is a *charitable lead trust*?

In essence, a *charitable lead trust* is the reverse of a charitable remainder trust (Q 12:9): the income interest is contributed to charity and the remainder interest goes to noncharitable beneficiaries. Thus, the charitable lead trust is a split-interest trust.

Under these arrangements, an income interest in property is contributed to a charitable organization for a term of years or for the life of one or more individuals. The remainder interest in the property is reserved to return, at the expiration of the income interest (the *lead period*), to the donor or other income beneficiary or beneficiaries. Often, the property passes from one generation (the donor's) to another.

The charitable lead trust can be used to accelerate into one year a series of charitable contributions that would otherwise be made annually. In some circumstances, a charitable deduction is available for the transfer of an income interest in property to a charitable organization. There are stringent limitations, however, on the deductible amount of charitable contributions of these income interests. Frequently, there is no charitable deduction; the donor's motive for establishing the trust is estate planning.

Q 12:12   What is a *charitable gift annuity*?

Unlike most other forms of planned giving, which are based on a type of split-interest trust (Q 12:9–Q 12:11), the *charitable gift annuity* is arranged in an agreement between the donor and donee. The donor agrees to make a payment and the donee agrees, in return, to provide the donor (and/or someone else) with an annuity.

With one payment, the donor actually is engaging in two transactions: (1) the *purchase* of an annuity and (2) the making of a charitable *gift*. The gift component gives rise to the charitable contribution deduction. One sum is transferred; the money in excess of the amount necessary to purchase the annuity is the charitable gift portion. Because of the dual nature of the transaction, the charitable gift annuity transfer constitutes a bargain sale.

The annuity resulting from the creation of a charitable gift annuity arrangement is a fixed amount paid at regular intervals. The exact amount is calculated to reflect the age of the beneficiary, which is determined at the time the contribution is made, and the annuity rate selected.

NOTE: As a matter of law, a charitable organization is free to offer whatever rate of return it wishes. Most charities, however, follow and utilize the rates periodically set by the American Council on Gift Annuities. These voluntary rates are in place to avoid unseemly philanthropic "price wars."

A portion of the annuity paid is tax-free because it is a return of capital. Where appreciated property is contributed, there will be capital gain on the appreciation that is attributable to the value of the annuity. If the donor is the annuitant, the capital gain can be reported ratably over the donor's life expectancy. The tax savings occasioned by the charitable contribution deduction, however, may shelter the capital gain (resulting from the creation of the annuity) from taxation.

Because the arrangement is by contract between the donor and donee, all of the assets of the charitable organization are subject to liability for the ongoing payment of the annuities. (With most planned giving techniques, the resources for payment of income are confined to those in a split-interest trust.) For this reason, some states impose a requirement that charitable organizations establish a reserve for the payment of gift annuities—and many charitable organizations are reluctant to embark on a gift annuity program. Organizations can eliminate much of the risk surrounding ongoing payment of annuities by reinsuring them.

TIP: In general, an obligation to pay an annuity is a debt. The charitable organization involved would have an acquisition indebtedness for purposes of the unrelated debt-financed income rules (Q 14:26), were it not for a special rule. To come within this rule, the value of the annuity must be less than 90 percent of the value of the property in the transaction, there can be no more than two income beneficiaries, there can be no guarantee as to a minimum amount of payments and no specification of a maximum amount of payments, and the annuity contract cannot provide for an adjustment of the amount of the annuity payments by reference to the income received from the transferred property or any other property.

TIP: A charitable organization that provides commercial-type insurance as a substantial activity cannot be tax-exempt; this activity, even when of a lesser magnitude, is an unrelated business. Arguably, a charitable gift annuity is not a form of commercial-type insurance. To eliminate uncertainty on the point, however, there is an exception from these rules for these annuities. To be eligible for this exception, a charitable deduction must be involved and the above exception from the unrelated debt-financed income rules must be available.

Q 12:13 What about gifts of life insurance?

Charitable contributions of life insurance policies are popular forms of giving. A gift of whole life insurance is an excellent way for an individual who has a relatively small amount of resources to make a major contribution to a charitable organization. Gifts of insurance are particularly attractive for younger donors.

If the life insurance policy is fully paid, the donor will receive a charitable deduction for the cash surrender value or the replacement value of the policy. If the premiums are still being paid, the donor receives a deduction for the premium payments made during the tax year. For the deduction to be available, however, the donee charity must be both the beneficiary and the owner of the insurance policy.

TIP: A policy of life insurance is valid (enforceable) only where the owner of the policy has an *insurable interest* in the life of the insured. In essence, this means that the owner and beneficiary of the policy (the same person) must be more economically advantaged with the insured alive. (Examples of relationships where insurable interests exist are healthy marriages and the employment of key individuals.) There is disagreement as to whether a charitable organization is better off with this type of donor dead or alive. In many instances, a charity is advantaged by having a donor of a life insurance policy alive: he or she may be an important volunteer (perhaps a trustee or officer) or a potential contributor of other, larger gifts.

Q 12:14 Are there other ways to make deductible gifts of remainder interests?

Yes. Individuals may give a remainder interest in their personal residence or farm to charity. They then receive a charitable deduction without using a trust (indeed, a trust cannot be used in this context). A trust is not required for a deductible gift of a remainder interest in real property when the gift is made in the form of a *qualified conservation contribution*. A contribution of an undivided portion of one's entire interest in property is not regarded as a contribution of a partial interest in property.

CHARITABLE REMAINDER TRUSTS

Q 12:15 **What types of charitable organizations can be remainder interest beneficiaries of remainder trusts?**

There are no limitations on the types of charitable organizations that can be beneficiaries of charitable remainder trusts. That is, these organizations can be either public charities or private foundations (see Chapter 10).

TIP: The percentage limitations on deductible charitable giving (Q 12:2 and Q 12:3) need to be taken into account. For example, a contribution of appreciated property to a public charity is subject to the 30 percent limitation, and the same gift to a private foundation is subject to a 20 percent limitation. These percentages apply when a gift is made by means of a charitable remainder trust. If the trust instrument does not expressly confine the charitable beneficiary to a public charity (or public charities), the lower private foundation limitations will be imposed.

Q 12:16 **How does the makeup feature work?**

Two types of *makeup features* can apply with respect to charitable remainder trusts. (These features are not available in the case of charitable remainder annuity trusts.)

TIP: The makeup feature is used when non–income-producing property is contributed to a remainder trust and there are no immediate prospects that it or any successor property will be income-producing (such as because the property cannot be sold in the foreseeable future). This characteristic of the property is critical because of the obligation to make income payments to one or more income interest beneficiaries.

One makeup feature allows the income payments to begin once a suitable amount of income begins to flow into the trust. That is, the income payments begin at a future point in time and are only prospective.

The other makeup feature has the attributes of the above-described makeup feature, with one significant difference: there is provision for a retroactive makeup of income, as well as prospective income payments.

NOTE: The makeup feature selected will have an impact on the charitable deduction for the gift of the remainder interest. Because the makeup feature that allows for retroactive payments will provide more income to the income beneficiary (or beneficiaries) than the other makeup feature, the income interest is greater and, correspondingly, the remainder interest is that much less. The result: a smaller charitable deduction when the retroactive income makeup provision is used.

Q 12:17 What types of property are suitable for charitable remainder trusts?

For the most part, nearly any type of personal or real property may be contributed to a charitable remainder trust. (Money may also be given.) Commonly, the properties contributed (aside from money) are securities (stocks and bonds) and real estate. Just about any property can be contributed, however, particularly if the property is income-producing or can be converted to income production.

There can be some tax difficulties when property is transferred to a remainder trust. Many of these problems arise when an item of tangible personal property is contributed to a charity by means of a charitable remainder trust. There principally are three of these conundrums (Q 12:20). Also, properties encumbered with debt pose some tax problems (Q 12:18).

Q 12:18 What happens if the donated property is encumbered with debt?

If property encumbered with debt is transferred to a charitable remainder trust, the result is likely to be unrelated debt-financed income. This is because the debt is an *acquisition indebtedness*. The receipt of unrelated debt-financed income, if it is unrelated business taxable income, will cause the trust to lose its tax-exempt status for each year in which that income is received (Q 12:5).

Q 12:19 What happens when an option is transferred to a charitable remainder trust?

The answer depends on the type of property that underlies the option. If the underlying property could be transferred directly to the trust, the transfer of the option poses only legal problems associated with the timing of the gift. (There is no charitable gift until the option is exercised.) If the property would be inappropriate for transfer directly to the trust, however, the transfer of the option would cause the trust to lose its tax-exempt status.

The law underlying charitable remainder trusts is intended to ensure that the amount a charitable organization receives following the close of the income payment period reflects the amount on which the donor's charitable deduction was based. This type of trust must function as a remainder trust in every respect from the date of its creation; that cannot happen unless each transfer to the trust qualifies for a charitable deduction. The IRS will be attuned to situations where the donor may be merely using a charitable remainder trust as a means to take advantage of the tax exemption for capital gain incurred by the trust.

Encumbered property in a charitable remainder trust can jeopardize the trust's tax-exempt status (Q 12:18). Where an option to purchase this type of property, rather than the property itself, is transferred to a charitable remainder trust, the IRS will assume that the donor is attempting to avoid the consequences attendant to a direct transfer of the property. If the option (or purported option) is used in an attempt to sidestep these tax results, the IRS will disqualify the trust as a charitable remainder trust.

Q 12:20   What happens when an item of tangible personal property is transferred to a charitable remainder trust?

The transfer of an item of tangible personal property to a charitable remainder trust does not cause any problems with respect to qualification of the trust. Three aspects of the general charitable giving laws are, however, implicated.

A charitable contribution of a future interest in tangible personal property is treated, for federal income tax purposes, as having been made only when all intervening interests in, and rights to, the actual possession or enjoyment of the property have expired or are held by persons other than the donor or those closely related to the donor. By contributing this type of property to the trust, the donor is creating and retaining an income interest in it, thus triggering the future interest rule. However, there would be an income tax charitable contribution when the trustee of the fund sold the property, because there would be an income interest in the proceeds of the sale.

Where there is a charitable contribution of tangible personal property and the donee uses the property in a manner that is unrelated to its exempt purpose, the amount of the deduction must be reduced by the amount of gain that would have been long-term capital gain if the property had been sold for its fair value. Usually gifts of this nature involve long-term capital assets, and it is contemplated that the trust will sell the interest. The sale would be an unrelated use. Therefore, the donor's charitable deduction (already confined to that for a remainder interest and in existence only after the sale) would have to be reduced to the amount of the donor's basis in the property allocable to the remainder interest.

Where there is a charitable contribution of tangible personal property by an individual and the donee is not a public charity (see Chapter 10), the charitable deduction for the gift generally must be confined to an amount equal to 20 percent of the donor's adjusted gross income. Where the recipient is a public charity, the limitation generally is 30 percent. The trust instrument must specifically provide that the donee or donees must be public charities for the higher of these two limitations to apply.

> **TIP:**   If the trust is silent on the point, the IRS will be of the view that one or more charitable beneficiaries can be a private foundation and hold that the smaller of the two limitations is applicable. This can happen, for example, where the donor reserves a lifetime power of appointment and a testamentary power to designate the charitable organization that will receive the remainder interest—and fails to confine the potential beneficiary or beneficiaries to public charities.

As noted, however, with tangible personal property, the charitable deduction does not come into being until the property is sold. The gift then is of the sales proceeds—money. In the case of charitable gifts, the percentage limitations generally are 50 percent for public charities and 30 percent for private foundations. The same considerations apply, however, in that the IRS will assume that the lower limitation is applicable unless the document confines the remainder interest beneficiaries to public charities (Q 12:2, Q 12:3)

Q 12:21   Who can be a donor to a charitable remainder trust?

Any person can be a donor to a charitable remainder trust. (Almost all such donors are individuals.) The income payment period, in the case of an individual, can be for one or more lifetimes or for a term of years (Q 12:9).

Q 12:22   How are amounts distributed to an income interest beneficiary from a charitable remainder trust taxed?

Under present law, these amounts are first taxed to the extent they are in the form of ordinary income, then capital gain, then tax-free income, and then as return of capital. Proposed regulations issued in 2004, however, will lead to revision of the ordering rules for characterizing distributions from charitable remainder trusts. The proposal reflects changes made to income tax rates, including those applicable to capital gains and certain dividends, by legislation enacted in 1997, 1998, and 2003.

Under the proposal, the trust's income is assigned, in the year it is required to be taken into account by the trust, into one of three categories: ordinary income, capital gains, or other. Within the ordinary income and capital gains categories, items are also assigned to different classes based on the federal income tax rate applicable to each type of income in the category.

A charitable remainder trust distribution is treated as being made from the categories in this order: ordinary income, capital gains, other income, and trust corpus. Within the ordinary income and capital gains categories, income is treated as distributed from the classes of income in that category beginning with the class subject to the highest federal income tax rate and ending with the class subject to the lowest federal income tax rate.

The proposed regulations also provide rules for netting different classes of capital gains and losses.

Q 12:23   Who can be a trustee of a charitable remainder trust?

Under the federal tax law, any person can be a trustee of a charitable remainder trust. This means that the trustee, or one of the trustees, can be the donor, an income interest beneficiary, the charity that will receive the remainder interest, another individual, or a financial institution or other corporate trustee.

TIP: Caution must be exercised when causing the donor to be the trustee: the grantor trust rules are not to be triggered. The principal consequence of application of these rules is that the capital gain resulting from the sale of trust assets would be taxed to the donor.

State law on this point must be examined, because of various limitations on what entities can be trustees of trusts, charitable or otherwise. For example, in some states, a charitable organization is not permitted to serve as trustee.

Q 12:24 Can a charitable remainder trust be prematurely terminated?

Yes, but only under certain circumstances. The critical concern for the IRS, when parties want to prematurely terminate a charitable remainder trust, is whether the early termination of the trust would result in a greater allocation of the trust's assets to the income beneficiaries, to the detriment of the charitable beneficiary, than a nonearly termination. That is, the agency is concerned that an early termination of a charitable remainder trust would deprive the charitable beneficiary of its full benefit—an outcome that would be inconsistent with the charitable deduction allowed the donor. Scrutiny is heightened when the charitable beneficiary is a private foundation, because of the self-dealing rules (Q 11:13).

The IRS has informally devised a procedure for these early terminations. The agency determines whether the proposed method of allocating assets between the charitable and noncharitable beneficiaries is reasonable. It will seek to be assured that the income beneficiaries lack any knowledge of a medical condition of any of them or other circumstance likely to result in a shorter life expectancy than that predicated by the actuarial tables. Usually the IRS will require a physician's affidavit on the point. It is understood that the agency is endeavoring to formalize this procedure.

Q 12:25 When should a charitable remainder trust be used rather than another planned giving technique?

Because the charitable remainder trust has the broadest range of possibilities of any of the planned giving techniques, one way to answer this question is to say that a remainder trust should be used when none of the other techniques can be. The remainder trust offers the greatest flexibility in terms of the types of property that can be transferred to it (Q 12:17). A donor desirous of an annuity and wishing to avoid the bargain sale rules can only use a charitable remainder annuity trust (inasmuch as these rules would be invoked where a charitable gift annuity is created (Q 12:12)). A donor can make additional contributions to a charitable remainder unitrust; that advantage is found only with that planned giving vehicle. A donor who wants to take advantage of a makeup feature must use a charitable remainder unitrust (Q 12:16). The prohibition with respect to pooled income funds (Q 12:27) does not apply to transfer of tax-exempt securities.

Q 12:26 What are the disadvantages of using a charitable remainder trust in relation to other planned giving techniques?

The greatest disadvantage may be the cost of preparing the trust documents. These are tailored to particular gift situations, so the legal fees involved could be in the thousands of dollars. Also, many charitable organizations have a minimum for the value of the property they will accept by means of a charitable remainder trust;

commonly, the starting level is $50,000, although some organizations will accept gifts as low as $25,000. Financial institutions have minimums for the amounts in trusts they will manage. From a legal standpoint, there is greater likelihood of becoming entangled in the *grantor trust* rules than with any other giving technique.

POOLED INCOME FUNDS

Q 12:27 What types of charities can be remainder interest beneficiaries of pooled income funds?

There are stringent limitations on the types of charitable organizations that can be beneficiaries of pooled income funds. These organizations can only be certain types of public charities; private foundations are ineligible to be beneficiaries (Chapter 10).

The charitable organizations that can be remainder interest beneficiaries of pooled income funds are churches, conventions and associations of churches, and integrated auxiliaries of churches; universities, colleges, and schools; hospitals, similar health care providers, and medical research organizations affiliated with hospitals; foundations affiliated with public (government-operated) colleges and universities; governmental units; and donative publicly supported charities (Q 10:3 and Q 10:7). This means that other types of public charities—principally, service provider publicly supported charities (Q 10:8) and supporting organizations (Q 10:15)—generally cannot be remainder interest beneficiaries of pooled income funds.

> **TIP:** The Internal Revenue Code, in defining the categories of eligible pooled income fund remainder interest beneficiaries, provides that they must be *described* in a qualifying provision. For example, a charitable organization may have a determination letter from the IRS classifying it as a service provider publicly supported charity, although it simultaneously meets the criteria for a donative publicly supported charity. That type of charitable organization could maintain a pooled income fund.

Q 12:28 What types of property are suitable for pooled income funds?

Generally, only property that is liquid in nature can be transferred to a pooled income fund as a charitable gift, because of the necessity of maintaining the requisite pool of assets (Q 12:10). Transferable property is generally money and publicly traded securities. It appears, however, that other types of property—such as real estate—may be transferable to a pooled income fund, if the trustee of the fund can readily sell the property.

Q 12:29 How is the rate of return calculated for a new pooled income fund?

For this purpose, a *new* pooled income fund is one that has been in existence for less than three years immediately prior to the tax year in which a transfer is made to the fund. A *deemed* rate of return must be used for any transfer to a new pooled income fund until it can compute its highest rate of return for the previous three tax years under the general rules (Q 12:10).

If a transfer is made to a new pooled income fund, the deemed rate of return is the interest rate (rounded to the nearest $^2/_{10}$ of 1 percent) that is 1 percent less than the highest annual average of the applicable federally determined monthly rates for the three calendar years immediately preceding the year in which the transfer to the fund was made.

Q 12:30 Who can be a donor to a pooled income fund?

Only individuals can be donors to pooled income funds. The income payment periods are confined to lifetimes; pooled income fund income interests cannot be determined by means of terms. Consequently, a corporation cannot be a donor to a pooled income fund.

Q 12:31 Who can be a trustee of a pooled income fund?

The charitable organization that maintains the pooled income fund is required to exercise control over the fund (Q 12:10). The charity does not have to be the trustee of the fund—although, as a matter of federal tax law, it can be—but it must have the power to remove and replace the trustee. A donor or an income interest beneficiary of the fund may not be a trustee.

 **NOTE:** A donor may be a trustee or officer of the charitable organization that maintains the fund, as long as he or she does not have the general responsibilities with respect to the fund that are ordinarily exercised by a trustee.

State law must be examined on this point, however, because of various limitations on what entities can be trustees of trusts, charitable or otherwise. For example, in some states, a charitable organization is not permitted to serve as trustee.

Q 12:32 What happens when a charitable organization that has a pooled income fund ceases to qualify as a type of public charity that can maintain a pooled income fund?

As of the year the charitable organization ceases to constitute a type of public charity that is eligible to maintain a pooled income fund, the fund would lose its favorable tax statuses. Among other outcomes, contributions to charity by means of the fund would no longer be tax-deductible as charitable gifts. Contributions made while the organization was qualified would not be adversely affected by the change in the fund's status.

Q 12:33 When should a pooled income fund be used rather than another planned giving technique?

The pooled income fund can be used where the donor of liquid property is not interested in receiving the income interest in the form of fixed income (that is, as an annuity). The fund also is useful when the gift property is relatively modest in size (that is, it may be too small to be transferred to a charitable remainder trust). Further, the pooled income fund gift is simple to document and does not entail much cost.

Q 12:34 What are the disadvantages of using a pooled income fund in relation to other planned giving techniques?

The principal disadvantage is that the income interest beneficiaries of a pooled income fund have no guarantees as to the amount of income they will receive. They receive their allocable shares of the fund's annual earnings—whatever that amount may be. Also, tax-exempt securities may not be contributed to a pooled income fund.

STARTING A PROGRAM

Q 12:35 How does a charitable organization start a planned giving program?

First and foremost, the members of the organization's board of directors must be involved. (This does not mean involved as donors—that part comes later.) They must be involved in the launching of the program. One of the important elements of this step is the passing of a resolution stating the creation of the program, who is principally responsible for implementing it, and which planned giving vehicles are going to be used (at least at the outset).

A brief presentation should be made at a board meeting on the basics of planned giving. It is best if this mini-seminar is offered by an outsider: a lawyer, professional development counselor, or bank trust officer, for example. The board members should be given some written material to peruse afterward.

Prototype documents should be prepared, such as prototype charitable remainder trusts and pooled income fund transfer agreements. These are likely to be of great interest to the potential donor's adviser, whether lawyer, accountant, financial planner, or similar individual, particularly if the adviser is unfamiliar with planned giving.

Registration of this fundraising program should be undertaken in the appropriate states (Chapter 13). Marketing literature should be prepared. The organization can either write and print these materials itself or purchase them commercially.

 **TIP:** Some organizations make the mistake of starting with every available planned giving technique and discussing them all in one sizable document, replete with lengthy illustrations. While impressive, few will read this material. It is best to have separate brochures on each of the techniques. They should be reasonably easy to read with examples kept as simple as possible.

The organization should then start the process of building a network or cadre of volunteers who will be planned giving advocates to the outside world. This group will ideally include many members of the board. These individuals will need some special training in planned giving. The purpose is not to make them planned giving experts overnight, but to cause them to become sufficiently familiar with the subject so they can meaningfully talk to prospective donors.

TIP: These individuals should all be contributors to the planned giving program. It is also important that the board members participate. The task of launching a planned giving program is made much more difficult when the organization's own leadership has not made a planned gift (or not even committed to one)—or, worse, will not give.

The next steps are obvious but the toughest: identify prospective planned givers, communicating with them, and obtaining the gifts ("closing the deal"). For organizations with an emerging planned giving program, the best way to proceed is to have a staff person or a volunteer meet with the prospective contributor and work out a generalized plan. Thereafter, a session with a planned giving professional can be held, where advice will be offered as to the specific giving method that is best for all parties. Thereafter, a lawyer can prepare any specific instruments that may be required.

A gift once unfolded in this way, resulting in the organization's first charitable remainder trust. An individual had been contacted about the planned giving program. Having coincidentally received a large sum of money as the result of a sale of property, he was looking for some tax relief. He had a sincere interest in the organization, so he and a staff person met and worked out these general guidelines: he needed a charitable deduction of X amount and an annual income of Y amount. The parties subsequently met with a lawyer, the numbers were run, the deduction and income amounts for each planned giving method were reviewed, and a specific arrangement (using a charitable remainder unitrust) was developed.

As the gifts come in and the various processes that lead to them are experienced, the parties involved will gain greater confidence and thus will need to rely less on outside counsel. The planned giving professional may be kept on call and used as circumstances warrant.

One of the excuses frequently given for postponing the inauguration of a planned giving program (or ignoring the idea of such a program altogether) is that it is not suitable for a new organization. There is no question that a university with decades of graduations has a much more solid donor base than a community service group incorporated yesterday. But that university's relative advantage is not an authentic reason for doing nothing. Every organization has a support base or it would not exist. It may be that, on day one, there is only one planned gift prospect, yet that is no reason for not asking that prospect. The largest planned giving program in the nation started with one gift.

Q 12:36   What does the future hold for planned giving?

Generally, it appears that the future for planned giving is bright. Charitable remainder trusts and charitable gift annuities remain popular and offer creative charitable giving opportunities. Interest in pooled income funds is on the wane, however, and unique uses of life insurance continue to be squelched by Congress and the IRS.

Regrettably, remainder trusts also provide opportunities for abuse; they occasionally show up on the IRS list of abusive tax shelters. There is interest in Congress in changing the way that charitable remainder trusts with unrelated business income are treated; the present system of loss of tax-exempt status (Q 12:8) is likely to be scrapped, to be replaced with a 100 percent excise tax on the unrelated business taxable income of these trusts.

NEW CHARITABLE GIVING LEGISLATION

Congress, late in 2004, passed legislation concerning charitable contributions of intellectual property and vehicles.

Q 12:37   What are the rules concerning contributions of intellectual property?

Certain properties have been added to the list of types of gifts that give rise to a charitable contribution deduction that is confined to the donor's basis, although in this instance there may be one or more subsequent charitable deductions.

A person who makes this type of gift—a *qualified intellectual property contribution*—is provided a charitable contribution deduction (subject to the annual percentage limitations (Q 12:2, Q 12:3)) equal to a percentage of net income that flows to the charitable donee as the consequence of the gift of the property. This income is termed *qualified donee income*.

Q 12:38   To what types of intellectual property do these rules apply?

This property consists of patents, copyrights (with exceptions), trademarks, trade names, trade secrets, know-how, software (with exceptions), or similar property, or applications or registrations of such property. Collectively, these properties are termed *qualified intellectual property* (except in instances when contributed to standard private foundations) (Q 10:2).

Q 12:39   How are any subsequent charitable deductions determined?

A portion of qualified donee income (Q 12:37) is allocated to a tax year of the donor, although this income allocation process is inapplicable to income received or accrued to the donee after 10 years from the date of the gift and the process is inapplicable to donee income received after the expiration of the legal life of the property.

The donee income that materializes into a charitable deduction is determined by the *applicable percentage*, which is a sliding-scale percentage determined by this table, which appears in the Internal Revenue Code:

Donor's Tax Year	Applicable Percentage
1st	100
2nd	100
3rd	90
4th	80
5th	70
6th	60
7th	50
8th	40
9th	30
10th	20
11th	10
12th	10

Thus, if, following a qualified intellectual property contribution, the charitable donee receives qualified donee income in the year following the gift, that amount becomes, in full, a charitable contribution deduction (subject to the general limitations). If such income is received by the charitable donee 8 years after the gift, the donor receives a charitable deduction equal to 40 percent of the qualified donee income. As this table indicates, the opportunity for a qualified intellectual property deduction arising out of a qualified intellectual property contribution terminates after 12 years from the date of the gift.

The IRS is authorized to issue antiabuse rules that may be necessary to prevent avoidance of this new body of law, including preventing (1) the circumvention of the reduction of the charitable deduction by embedding or bundling the patent or similar property as part of a charitable contribution of property that includes the patent or similar property; (2) the manipulation of the basis of the property to increase the amount of the initial charitable deduction through use of related persons, pass-through entities, or other intermediaries, or through the use of any provision of law or regulation (including the consolidated return regulations); and (3) a donor from changing the form of the patent or similar property to property of a form for which different deduction rules would apply.

Q 12:40   How will the donor know when to take a particular charitable deduction and how much it will be?

The reporting requirements rules concerning certain dispositions of contributed property have been amended to encompass qualified intellectual property contributions. A donee of such a contribution is required to make a return, with respect to each applicable tax year of the donee, showing (1) the name, address, and tax identification number of the donor; (2) a description of the intellectual property contributed; (3) the date of the contribution; and (4) the amount of net income of the donee for the tax year that is properly allocable to the qualified intellectual property. A copy of this return must be timely furnished to the donor.

Q 12:41   What are the rules concerning contributions of vehicles?

There are new substantiation rules for contributions of motor vehicles. These new rules supplant, in cases of contributions of qualified vehicles, the general gift substantiation rules (Q 13:6), where the claimed value of the gift exceeds $500.

Pursuant to these rules, a federal income tax charitable contribution deduction is not allowed unless the donor substantiates the contribution by a contemporaneous written acknowledgment of the contribution by the donee organization and includes the acknowledgment with the donor's income tax return reflecting the deduction.

The amount of the charitable deduction for a gift of a qualified vehicle depends on the nature of the use of the vehicle by the donee organization. If the charitable organization sells the vehicle without any significant intervening use or material improvement (Q 12:43) of the vehicle by the organization, the amount of the charitable deduction may not exceed the gross proceeds received from the sale.

The acknowledgment must contain the name and taxpayer identification number of the donor and the vehicle identification number or similar number. If the gift is of a qualified vehicle that was sold by the charity without such use or improvement, the acknowledgment must also contain a certification that the vehicle was sold in an arm's-length transaction between unrelated parties, a statement as to the gross proceeds from the sale, and a statement that the deductible amount may not exceed the amount of the gross proceeds. If there is such use or improvement, the acknowledgment must include a certification as to the intended use or material improvement of the vehicle and the intended duration of the use, and a certification that the vehicle will not be transferred in exchange for money, other property, or services before completion of the use or improvement.

Q 12:42   To what types of vehicles do these rules apply?

These rules apply to charitable contributions of motor vehicles, boats, and airplanes—collectively termed *qualified vehicles.*

Q 12:43   Are there any exceptions to this rule limiting the charitable contribution deduction?

Yes. A donor of a qualified vehicle is allowed a fair market value charitable contribution deduction in this setting if the charitable donee makes significant use of the vehicle or materially improves the vehicle. To meet the *significant use test*, a charitable organization must actually use the vehicle to substantially further the organization's regularly conducted activities, and the use must be significant. With respect to the *material improvement test*, a material improvement includes major repairs to a vehicle or other improvements to the vehicle that improve its condition in a manner that significantly increases the vehicle's value.

Q 12:44   What happens if these rules are violated?

There is a penalty for the furnishing of a false or fraudulent acknowledgment, or an untimely or incomplete acknowledgment, by a charitable donee to a donor of a qualified vehicle. If the vehicle is sold without any significant intervening use or material improvement (Q 12:43) by the donee, the penalty is the greater of (1) the product of the highest rate of income tax and the sales price stated in the acknowledgment or (2) the gross proceeds from the sale of the vehicle. In the case of an acknowledgment pertaining to any other qualified vehicle, the penalty is (1) the product of the highest rate of income tax and the claimed value of the vehicle or (2) $5,000.

CHAPTER 13

Fundraising Regulation

The process of raising funds for charitable purposes, despite protection under constitutional law, is heavily regulated by the federal and state governments. The states exercise this authority largely by means of statutory law, reflective of their police powers. Most of these laws are known as charitable solicitation acts. Nearly all of the states have some form of charitable solicitation act; 35 of them have extensive statutes in this area.

Federal regulation is largely through the tax system, although the postal and trade laws are of increasing importance: the IRS has several sets of regulations audit guidelines in this area. Other bodies of federal tax law that amount to fundraising regulation are contained in the charitable giving rules, the unrelated business rules, and the exemption application and annual reporting requirements.

Here are the questions most frequently asked about federal regulation of charitable fundraising (including the ever-expanding rules as to gift substantiation and quid pro quo situations) and the contents and enforcement of the many state charitable solicitation acts—and the answers to them.

Q 13:1 How does the federal government regulate fundraising for charitable purposes?

For the most part, federal regulation in this area is through the tax system, principally the income tax laws. The chief subparts of the law in this area are IRS audit guidelines, the charitable gift substantiation requirements, the quid pro quo contribution rules, the procedure for applying for recognition of tax exemption, the unrelated business rules, the annual information return requirements, the public charity rules, and the many intricacies of the law surrounding the income, gift, and estate tax charitable contribution deductions.

There is also some regulation at the hands of the U.S. Postal Service, through its monitoring of use of the special bulk third-class mailing rates, and the Federal Trade Commission, particularly as it regulates telemarketing (see Q 13:20).

Q 13:2 **How do the state governments regulate fundraising for charitable purposes?**

All but three of the states have some form of statutory law governing the solicitation of charitable gifts. (The states that lack any such law are Delaware, Montana, and Wyoming.) Thirty-five states have formal, comprehensive *charitable solicitation acts*. The elements of these laws are summarized below (Q 13:21). The attorney general of a state has inherent authority to oversee charities; this authority is derived from the *parens patriae* doctrine.

The states also have laws concerning the availability of tax exemptions, the deductibility of charitable gifts, the offering of securities, the sale of insurance programs, unfair trade practices, misleading advertising, and fraud—each of which can be applied in the realm of charitable fundraising.

Q 13:3 **Are these state laws constitutional?**

In general, yes, although the tension in this field is intense. A state, for example, has the police power and can use this authority to protect its citizens against charitable fundraising fraud and other abuse. This type of regulation, however, needs to be more than *reasonable* in scope, as determined by the state. Fundraising for charitable purposes is one of the highest forms of free speech, and thus governments can regulate it only by the narrowest of means.

Some features of state and local charitable solicitation acts have been struck down as being unconstitutional, in violation of free speech rights. The most infamous legislated features are limitations on the fundraising costs of charitable entities or on the levels of compensation paid to professional solicitors. Certain forced disclosures are also banned. Overall, however, the charitable solicitation acts themselves have been upheld, in the face of claims that they wrongfully hamper free speech or unduly burden interstate commerce.

The police power of the states (and local governments) directly clashes with the free speech rights of charities and their fundraisers. To date, this tension has been modulated by the courts, with the consensus being that the police power allows for the general application of the charitable solicitation laws, while constitutional law principles force governments to regulate in this area by the narrowest of means.

FEDERAL LAW REQUIREMENTS

Q 13:4 **What are the IRS audit practices as applied to fundraising charitable organizations?**

The IRS has specific concerns about charitable organizations that are engaged in charitable solicitation; these concerns are reflected in IRS audit guidelines promulgated for its examining agents. There is a set of guidelines with which charitable entities should be familiar.

The IRS published audit guidelines for college and university audits. Although these guidelines technically apply only in the context of higher education, they describe in considerable detail how the agent is to conduct the fundraising audit. There should be no doubt that an audit of any charitable organization, from the standpoint of its fundraising practices, would be conducted in a manner close to that summarized in these guidelines.

The IRS will want to identify each individual responsible for soliciting and accounting for charitable contributions. Copies of the appropriate job descriptions will be requested. The minutes of any committee involved in fundraising (such as a development, finance, or budget committee) will be reviewed; board minutes may be examined also, particularly if the board is involved in accepting gifts. Correspondence with donors will be reviewed, along with gift agreements; the IRS will be searching for restrictions, earmarkings, or conditions by which benefits may be provided to contributors. Any private benefit could affect the organization's tax exemption (see Chapter 6); certain benefits could affect the extent of deductibility of contributions (Q 13:7).

NOTE: These guidelines do not expressly describe this practice, but the IRS will read correspondence and agreements, looking for anticipatory assignments of income (where the income can be taxed to the donor) and step transactions (where the capital gain element in a gift of property can be taxed to the donor).

Fundraisers should be prepared to share with the IRS the organization's lists of contributors by name and category (such as individuals and corporations), lists of restricted gifts, lists of in-kind gifts, and other internal lists and reports relating to contributions.

Q 13:5   How do the charitable giving rules apply?

The charitable giving rules apply in many ways, because they govern the deductibility of charitable gifts for federal tax purposes (Chapter 12). The facets of this application include the definitions of the terms *charitable* and *gift*, the percentage limitations as to annual deductibility, the deduction reduction rules, the rules concerning gifts of partial interests, and a variety of rules pertaining to contributions of specific types of property.

There are, however, three bodies of charitable giving law that have particular relevance in the realm of fundraising regulation: (1) the charitable gift substantiation requirements, (2) the quid pro quo contribution rules, and (3) the appraisal requirements.

Q 13:6   What are the charitable gift substantiation requirements?

The essence of the substantiation requirements is that there is no federal income tax charitable contribution deduction for any charitable gift of $250 or more, unless the donor has contemporaneous written substantiation from the donee charitable organization. In cases where the charity has provided goods or services to the donor in exchange for the contribution, this contemporaneous written acknowledgment must include a good-faith estimate of the value of the goods or services.

TIP: If no goods or services are provided, the substantiation document must state that fact. Some charitable organizations, not realizing this, are providing to their donors documents that technically are not in compliance with these rules—thus jeopardizing the charitable deductions.

These rules are inapplicable to the provision of intangible religious benefits (Q 13:12).

If the contribution is of property, the acknowledgment must describe the property.

NOTE: The donee charitable organization is not required to value the property for the donor—and should not do so. Valuation of the donated property is the responsibility of the donor. The donee organization does have to place a value on the contributed property for purposes of its own financial records.

Separate gifts to a charitable organization are regarded as independent contributions and are not aggregated for purposes of measuring the $250 threshold. Donations made through payroll deductions are considered separate payments from each paycheck. The IRS is authorized to establish (although it has not done so) antiabuse rules to prevent avoidance of the substantiation requirements—for example, by writing separate smaller checks to the same charitable organization on the same date.

For the substantiation to be *contemporaneous*, it must be obtained no later than the date the donor files a tax return for the year in which the contribution was made. If the return is filed after the due date or on an extended due date, the substantiation must have been obtained by the due date or extended due date.

A charitable organization that knowingly provides false written substantiation to a donor may be subject to the penalties for aiding and abetting an understatement of tax liability.

There are separate gift substantiation rules, which supplant the foregoing rules, that apply in instances of contributions of qualified vehicles (Q 12:42) where the claimed value of the gift exceeds $500 (Q 12:41).

Q 13:7 **What does the phrase *goods or services* mean?**

On its face, this statutory requirement would seem to mean consideration provided in exchange for the contribution, most likely tangible services or property. That certainly was congressional intent; the point was to confine the charitable deduction to a net amount conveyed to a charitable organization. The courts, however, have ballooned this clause to encompass far more than tangible economic benefits, namely, expectations and understandings. For example, it has been held that payments to a charitable organization were not deductible as charitable gifts, because the substantiation requirements were not met, in that there was an undisclosed return benefit in the form of the donors' *expectation* that the gift funds would be invested in a certain manner.

COMMENT: This conclusion was an error. Another provision of the Internal Revenue Code (outlawing charitable split-dollar insurance arrangements) uses the phrase *understanding or expectation*. If Congress had meant *goods or services* to embrace *expectations*, it would have so legislated. By reason of these holdings, charities must be ever so cautious in preparing these substantiation documents, in that they must not only estimate and disclose any value of goods or services provided in exchange for a gift, but also must peer into the misty reaches of donor motivation and intent to discern what donors *expect* to be provided—and value and disclose that.

Q 13:8   Do these rules apply with respect to benefits provided to donors after the gifts were made, where there was no prior notification of the benefit, such as a recognition dinner?

Generally, no. These rules apply to payments made in consideration for some benefit provided by the donee charitable organization. The rules are applicable where a good or service is provided in *consideration* for a payment to the charity, meaning that the donor expects the good or service at the time the payment is made. Thus, this type of an after-the-fact benefit generally does not need to be taken into account in determining the amount of the charitable deduction.

NOTE: Some caution must be exercised here. If the charitable organization always provides a recognition dinner for certain donors, at some point, an "expectation" can be presumed, even when there is no express promise of it at the time of the gift. Lines of demarcation in this area will be made on the basis of facts and circumstances.

Q 13:9   How do the substantiation rules apply to gifts made by means of charitable remainder trusts, charitable lead trusts, and pooled income funds?

The rules do not apply to gifts made by means of charitable remainder trusts (Q 12:9) and charitable lead trusts (Q 12:11). This is because donors to these trusts are not required to designate a specific charitable organization as the beneficiary at the time money or property is transferred to the trust. Thus, there may not be a charitable organization available to provide the requisite written acknowledgment. Also, even where a specific charitable beneficiary is designated, the designation is often revocable. By contrast, the law requires that one or more charitable organizations must maintain a pooled income fund (12:10), so contributions made by means of these funds must be substantiated.

Q 13:10   **What are the quid pro quo contribution rules?**

A *quid pro quo contribution* is a payment made partly as a contribution and partly for goods or services provided to the donor by the charitable organization. A charitable organization must provide a written disclosure statement to donors who make a quid pro quo contribution in excess of $75. The required written disclosure must inform the donor that the amount of the contribution that is deductible for federal income tax purposes is limited to the excess of any money, or the excess of the value of any property, the donor contributed over the value of the goods or services provided by the charity. The disclosure must provide the donor with a good faith estimate of the value of the goods or services the donor received.

The charitable organization must furnish the statement in connection with either the solicitation or the receipt of the quid pro quo contribution. The disclosure must be in writing and presented in a manner that is reasonably likely to come to the attention of the donor. A disclosure in small print within a larger document may not satisfy the requirement.

A penalty is imposed on charitable organizations that do not meet these disclosure requirements. For failure to make the required disclosure in connection with a quid pro quo contribution of more than $75, there is a penalty of $10 per contribution, not to exceed $5,000 per fundraising event or mailing. An organization may be able to avoid this penalty if it can show that the failure to comply was due to reasonable cause.

NOTE: The basic principle that a charitable deduction is allowed only to the extent that the payment exceeds the fair market value of the goods or services received in return is generally applicable to all quid pro quo contributions. The $75 threshold pertains principally to the nature of the obligation to disclose (statutory rather than by IRS rule) and imposition of the penalty; it does not apply to the rules as to the extent of deductibility of the payment.

Q 13:11   **What is a good faith estimate?**

The statute does not define the phrase *good faith estimate*. The tax regulations state that a good faith estimate of the value of goods or services provided by a charitable organization is an estimate of the fair market value of the goods or services. These regulations add that an organization can use a reasonable methodology in making a good faith estimate, as long as it applies the methodology in good faith. These forms of circular reasoning are not much help.

Q 13:12   Are there any exceptions to the quid pro quo contribution rules?

There are seven exceptions. The first three apply where the only goods or services provided to a donor are those having an incidental value. The exceptions are:

1. Where the fair market value of all the benefits received is not more than 2 percent of the contributions or $50, whichever is less.

2. Where the contribution is $25 or more and the only benefits received by the donor in return during the calendar year have a cost, in the aggregate, of not more than a *low-cost article*. A low-cost article is one that does not cost more than $5 to the organization that distributes it or on whose behalf it is distributed.

3. Where, in connection with a request for a charitable contribution, the charity mails or otherwise distributes free, unordered items to patrons, and the cost of the items (in the aggregate) distributed to any single patron in a calendar year is not more than a low-cost article.

4. Where no donative element is involved in the transaction with the charitable organization. Illustrations of this are payments of tuition to a school, payments for health care services to a hospital, and the purchase of an item from a museum gift shop.

5. Where an *intangible religious benefit* is involved. For the exception to be available, the benefit must be provided by an organization exclusively for religious purposes and must be of a type that generally is not sold in a commercial transaction outside the donative context. An example of a religious benefit is admission to a religious ceremony. This exception also generally applies to de minimis tangible benefits, such as wine provided in connection with a religious ceremony. The intangible religious benefit exception does not apply to items such as payments for tuition for education leading to a recognized degree, travel services, or consumer goods.

6. Annual membership benefits offered for no more than $75 per year that consist of rights or privileges that the individual can exercise frequently during the membership period. These benefits include free admission to the organization's events, free parking, and discounts on the purchase of goods.

7. Annual membership benefits offered for no more than $75 per year that consist of admission to events during the membership period that are open only to members of the charitable organization and for which the organization reasonably projects that the cost per person (excluding any overhead) for each event is within the limits established for low-cost articles.

Q 13:13   How does a charitable organization value the involvement of a celebrity for purposes of the quid pro quo contribution rules?

If the celebrity performs at the event, using the talent for which he or she is celebrated (such as singing or stand-up comedy), the fair market value of the performance must be determined in calculating any benefit and thus any charitable deduction.

If the celebrity does something else, however, his or her presence can be disregarded. For example, in the case of a tour of a museum by an artist whose works are featured there, the value of the tour can be ignored.

Q 13:14 What are the appraisal requirements?

For most gifts of property (or collections of property) by an individual, partnership, or corporation to a charitable organization, where the value is in excess of $5,000, there are certain appraisal requirements. (Gifts of money and publicly traded securities are excepted from these appraisal rules.) Property to which the rules apply is termed *charitable deduction property*.

The donor of charitable deduction property must obtain a *qualified appraisal* of the property and attach an *appraisal summary* (Form 8283) to the tax return on which the deduction is claimed. The law details the items of information that must be in a qualified appraisal and an appraisal summary. The appraisal must be conducted by a *qualified appraiser*.

If a claimed deduction is over $500,000, the individual, partnership, or corporation must obtain a qualified appraisal of the property and attach it to the appropriate income tax return. (These rules are inapplicable, however, with respect to gifts of money, publicly traded securities, inventory, and vehicles.)

Q 13:15 What does the IRS look for with respect to new charitable organizations?

Nearly every organization that wants to be tax-exempt as a charitable entity, and be an organization eligible to receive tax-deductible gifts, must give notice to the IRS to that effect by filing an application for recognition of tax exemption. (The principal exceptions are those for churches and their integrated auxiliaries, and organizations that have gross receipts that normally are not in excess of $5,000.) The application requests certain information about the fundraising program of the organization.

For example, the organization must describe its actual and planned fundraising program, summarizing its actual use of, or plans to use, selective mailings, fundraising committees, professional fundraisers, and the like. Depending on the progress of its solicitation efforts, the organization can describe a very detailed fundraising program or it can state that it has yet to develop any specific processes for raising funds. If the organization has developed written material for the solicitation of contributions, it should attach copies.

The application—which is publicly accessible—must contain a disclosure of the organization's fundraising costs. Depending on the length of time the organization has been in existence, this information will be reflected in the financial statement that is a part of the application or in a proposed budget submitted with the application.

Q 13:16 How do the reporting rules apply?

Nearly every charitable organization must file an annual information return with the IRS (Chapter 5). (The most notable exceptions are churches and their integrated auxiliaries, and organizations whose gross receipts normally are not in excess of $25,000.) Certain information pertaining to the organization's fundraising program must be supplied.

The annual information return requires charitable (and other tax-exempt) organizations to use the *functional method of accounting* to report their expenses. This accounting method allocates expenses by function, including those for fundraising. Thus, swept into the fundraising category are not only direct fundraising costs (such as professional fundraisers' fees and telemarketing expenses) but outlays that are allocable only in part to fundraising (such as joint-purpose mailings). The organization must (or should) maintain detailed records as to its fundraising (and other) expenses.

The IRS defines the term *fundraising expenses* to mean all expenses, including allocable overhead costs, incurred in publicizing and conducting fundraising campaigns; soliciting bequests, grants from foundations or other organizations, and government grants; participating in federated fundraising campaigns; preparing and distributing fundraising manuals, instructions, and other materials; and conducting special fundraising events that generate contributions.

 **TIP:** The IRS does not differentiate, when referring to *professional fundraisers*, between fundraising counsel and solicitors (Q 13:23 and Q 13:24). Professional fundraising fees are those paid to "outside fund-raisers for solicitation campaigns they conducted, or for providing consulting services in connection with a solicitation of contributions by the organization itself."

Organizations must report their receipts from and expenses of special fundraising events and activities, separating the information for each type of event. Typically, these events include dinners, dances, carnivals, raffles, auctions, bingo games, and door-to-door sales of merchandise.

Q 13:17 Do the unrelated business income rules apply in the fundraising setting?

Yes. Several types of fundraising events or activities—sometimes known as *special events*—are technically *businesses* for federal income tax purposes (Q 14:6). Thus, were it not for certain provisions in the federal tax law pertaining to unrelated businesses, some or all of the net income from these events would be taxable.

Some of this revenue is sheltered from taxation on the rationale that the activity is not *regularly carried on* (Q 14:13). This shelter protects activities that are conducted only once each year, such as a dinner dance, a theater outing, or an auction. If the event is seasonal, however, such as the selling of holiday cards, the season (not the full year) is the measuring period.

Some revenue-raising activities are considered related businesses (Q 14:18). These include sales of various items in gift shops maintained by hospitals and museums, as well as in college and university bookstores. Other sales in these shops and stores may be nontaxable by operation of the *convenience doctrine* (Q 14:23).

Still other fundraising practices are protected against taxation by specific statutory exceptions. Some fundraising events are run entirely by volunteers; businesses that are conducted substantially by individuals who are unpaid for their services are not taxed.

TIP: It does not take much for a court to conclude, for purposes of this exception, that someone is compensated. In one case, involving a gambling operation conducted weekly by a tax-exempt organization, individuals who were otherwise volunteers were found to be paid because they received tips from patrons.

Another exception is for businesses that sell items that were contributed to the organization. This rule was created for the benefit of thrift stores operated by nonprofit organizations, but it can also be applicable to frequent auctions.

Still another aspect of the law that can protect fundraising revenue from taxation is the exception for *royalties* (Q 13:18, Q 14:24, Q 14:25). This exception can, for example, immunize income from an affinity card program and revenue from the rental of mailing lists from tax.

In these instances, the payments were for the use of the organization's name, logo, and mailing list.

Q 13:18 Are there limitations on the use of the royalty exception in the fundraising setting?

Yes, but where these limitations are is a matter of some controversy. The IRS position—and that of conventional wisdom—is that, for an item of revenue to be a tax-free royalty, it has to be passively derived, in the nature of investment income, for example. This view of the law sees active participation by the tax-exempt organization in the revenue-raising process as meaning that some form of joint venture is occurring, thereby defeating the exclusion.

The opposite view is that a royalty is a royalty; that is, the factor of passivity is not required. This rationale, which rests on a careful reading of the legislative history of the unrelated business rules, defines a royalty as payment for the use of valuable intangible property rights.

This issue has been the subject of litigation over many years. Basically, the federal court of appeals that seems to have largely resolved the dispute split the difference with the parties. The current state of the law thus is that a tax-exempt organization can participate to some degree in the process of generating the royalty income (so that the income need not be entirely passive), but if that involvement in the process is substantial the royalty exception is defeated.

NOTE: If the exempt organization's participation in the royalty-generation process appears to be substantial, there is still an opportunity to transform what is or may be a taxable unrelated activity into a nontaxable stream of income. Basically, this involves transferring the function to another party, giving that party the right to use the necessary intangible property rights previously held by the exempt organization, and crafting the appropriate royalty contract. If the transfer is done properly, the organization can enhance its revenue stream with a new source of revenue or with nontaxation of previously taxed revenue—or both.

TIPS: If the exempt organization becomes too heavily involved in the conduct of the royalty activity, there remains a line of law that would treat the relationship between the parties as a partnership, with resulting income to the exempt organization taxed as unrelated fee-for-service income. Also, the contract must be written so that the person running the operation that generates the royalty income is not deemed the agent of the exempt organization.

Q 13:19   Are there fundraising disclosure requirements for noncharitable organizations?

Yes. Fundraising disclosure rules apply to exempt organizations other than charitable ones, unless the organization has annual gross receipts that are normally no more than $100,000.

Under these rules, each fundraising solicitation by or on behalf of an organization must contain an express statement, in a conspicuous and easily recognizable format, that gifts to it are not deductible as charitable contributions for federal income tax purposes. (There is an exclusion for letters or telephone calls that are not part of a coordinated fundraising campaign soliciting more than 10 persons during a calendar year.)

TIP: Despite the clear reference in the law solely to "contributions and gifts," the IRS insists that the rule requires disclosure when any tax-exempt organization (other than a charity) seeks funds such as dues from members.

Failure to satisfy this disclosure requirement can result in a penalty of $1,000 per day (maximum of $10,000 per year), unless a reasonable cause justifies an exception. For an intentional disregard of these rules, the penalty for the day on which the offense occurred is the greater of $1,000 or 50 percent of the aggregate cost of the solicitations that took place on that day—and the $10,000 limitation does not apply.

For penalty purposes, the IRS counts the days on which the solicitation was telecast, broadcast, mailed, telephoned, or otherwise distributed.

Q 13:20 Are there any other federal law requirements as to fundraising?

There are several. Other applications of the federal income tax rules pertain to publicly supported charitable organizations that have that status by virtue of the facts-and-circumstances test (Q 2:5, Q 10:7). Among the criteria for compliance with this test is the extent to which the charitable organization is attracting public support; the IRS wants to know whether the entity can demonstrate an active and ongoing fundraising program. An organization can satisfy this aspect of the test (where public support can be as low as 10 percent) if it maintains a continuous and bona fide solicitation effort, seeking contributions from the general public, the community, or the membership group involved, or if it carries on activities designed to attract support from government agencies or publicly supported charitable organizations.

The U.S. Postal Service regulates some aspects of charitable fundraising by means of the postal laws. Qualified organizations (including charities) that have received specific authorization may mail eligible matter at reduced bulk third-class rates of postage.

TIP: In the parlance of the postal laws, charitable organizations are termed *philanthropic* entities. Other qualified nonprofit organizations include religious, educational, and scientific entities. Ineligible organizations include trade, business, and professional associations; certain citizens' and civic improvement associations; and social and hobby clubs.

Cooperative mailings involving the mailing of any matter on behalf of or produced for an organization not authorized to mail at the special rates must be paid at the applicable regular rates.

Material that advertises, promotes, offers, or, for a fee or other consideration, recommends, describes, or announces the availability of any product or service cannot qualify for mailing at the reduced bulk third-class rates unless the sale of the product or the provision of the service is substantially related to the exercise or performance by the organization of one or more of the purposes constituting the basis for the organization's authorization to mail at those rates. The determination as to whether a product or service is substantially related to an organization's purpose is made in accordance with the analogous federal tax law standards (see Chapter 14).

The Federal Trade Commission (FTC) has a role in the realm of fundraising for charitable purposes, primarily when the fundraising is in the form of telemarketing. The FTC has regulations on this subject, in amplification of the Telemarketing and Consumer Fraud and Abuse Prevention Act. These rules do not apply to telemarketing conducted for charitable organizations solely for the purpose of generating charitable gifts.

The FTC rules apply, however, to for-profit companies that raise funds or provide similar services to charitable and other tax-exempt organizations.

 **TIP:** Consequently, charitable organizations should be cautious when entering into telemarketing contracts. No charity wants to have its telemarketing program found in violation of these rules.

These rules (1) define the term *telemarketing*; (2) require clear and conspicuous disclosures of specified material information, orally or in writing, before a customer pays for goods or services offered; (3) prohibit misrepresenting, directly or by implication, specified material information relating to the goods or services that are the subject of a sales offer, as well as any other material aspects of a telemarketing transaction; (4) require express verifiable authorization before submitting for payment a check, draft, or other form of negotiable paper drawn on a person's account; (5) prohibit false or otherwise misleading statements to induce payment for goods or services; (6) prohibit any person from assisting and facilitating certain deceptive or abusive telemarketing acts or practices; (7) prohibit credit card laundering; (8) prohibit specified abusive acts or practices; (9) impose calling time restrictions; (10) require specified information to be disclosed truthfully, promptly, and in a clear and conspicuous manner, in an outbound telephone call; (11) require that specified records be kept; and (12) specify certain acts or practices that are exempt from the requirements.

NOTE: Although the rules on telemarketing practices do not always apply in the charitable fundraising setting, they serve as useful guidelines to proper telemarketing practices in that context.

STATE LAW REQUIREMENTS

Q 13:21   What are the elements of a typical state charitable solicitation act?

These laws usually open with a set of definitions. The key terms defined are *charitable, solicitation* (a term very broadly defined to capture every type of fundraising, whether or not successful), *contribution, professional fundraiser* (Q 13:23), *professional solicitor* (Q 13:24), and *charitable sales promotion* (Q 13:26). The ambit of these laws—which is far-reaching—is basically set by the scope of the words *charitable* and *solicitation*. Charitable in this setting includes religious, educational, arts promotion, and scientific purposes.

NOTE: *Charitable* in this context is given a much broader definition than in settings such as the federal tax law. Some state laws are applicable to fundraising by tax-exempt social welfare organizations, business and professional associations, and other types of nonprofit organizations. State laws can differ on the point (for example, some expressly exclude political fundraising), so it is necessary to check each one that is applicable (Q 13:32).

A key feature of these laws is *registration*. They almost always require soliciting charitable organizations to register, usually annually. There often is a registration fee. The information required by this process usually is extensive; the states have devised required registration forms. Many of the states also require the registration of professional fundraisers and/or professional solicitors. Some states mandate a bond for fundraisers and/or solicitors.

TIP: The registration process frequently requires charitable organizations to identify any fundraisers or solicitors they have hired. The states use this information to determine whether the fundraiser or solicitor has registered. Charities are often required to provide a list of other states in which they are registered. The registration form for fundraisers and solicitors usually requires them to identify the charities they are working with. The states cross-reference this information to see whether all parties are appropriately registered and bonded.

Another feature of these laws is annual *reporting*. Each year, charitable organizations are almost always required to submit extensive financial statements either as part of an annual report or by means of annual registration. (Some states mandate both.) Annual reports may also be required of professional fundraisers and professional solicitors. In a few states, the laws require solicitors to submit more frequent reports, for example, following each fundraising campaign.

Many of the state laws contain an extensive listing of *prohibited acts*. These are rules dictating certain fundraising practices by charitable organizations—usually in the form of practices in which they may not engage. Some of these prohibited acts go beyond the realm of fundraising and mandate certain actions (or nonactions) by charities and others generally. It is important for charities and those who assist them in the fundraising process to review each of the applicable sets of these prohibitions (Q 13:27, Q 13:32).

A growing practice is for these laws to mandate the contents of *contracts* between soliciting charitable organizations and their professional fundraisers and/or professional solicitors (Q 13:29).

Another burgeoning requirement is the presentation of *legends*. These are notices, required by law, that must prominently appear on fundraising literature and other appeals. The typical legend must state that information about the charity is available from the charity or the state; a registration number may be needed as part of the legend.

NOTE: This requirement of legends is becoming a problem for those making charitable solicitations by mail in several states. The differences in these legends are forcing the solicitation material to become cluttered, detracting from the purpose of the mailing.

Other components of the state laws include record-keeping requirements, disclosure rules, requirements as to financial accounts and sales of tickets, investigatory and injunctive powers by the state, and a range of civil and criminal sanctions.

Q 13:22 Do these laws apply to all charitable solicitations?

Yes, unless the solicitation is expressly exempted from the statutory requirements (Q 13:28). These laws apply where the solicitation is by means of the mail, telephone (telemarketing), facsimile, television, video, and radio, as well as in-person fundraising. The medium used to solicit is not significant; the key is whether the activity is a solicitation. The fact that interstate commerce is involved is not per se a bar to state regulation.

NOTE: Technically, the solicitation of charitable contributions on the Internet is embraced by these laws.

Q 13:23 How do these laws apply to professional fundraisers?

They apply to professional fundraisers in a variety of ways. The basic application of these laws is dependent, however, on the definition of the term *professional fundraiser*. First, not all states use that term; *professional fundraising counsel* or *paid fundraiser* may be used instead. Second, the definition of the term can vary. The most frequent definition is "a person who for compensation plans, manages, advises, consults, or prepares material for, or with respect to, the solicitation in this state of contributions for a charitable organization, but who does not solicit contributions and who does not employ, procure, or engage any compensated person to solicit contributions."

NOTE: The states give this term broad application. Those who work in collateral fields should be cautious: they may inadvertently become regarded as fundraisers and be subject to penalties for noncompliance with state law. Related fields include consulting in the areas of marketing, management, and public relations.

A bona fide salaried officer, employee, or volunteer of a charitable organization is not a professional fundraiser, nor are lawyers, investment advisers, or bankers.

It is common for a state charitable solicitation act to impose the following requirements on a professional fundraiser working for one or more charitable organizations: registration, bonding, annual reports, record keeping, and a contract with the charity.

Q 13:24 How do these laws apply to professional solicitors?

They apply to professional solicitors in a variety of ways. The basic application of these laws is, like those pertaining to professional fundraisers (Q 13:23), however, dependent on the definition of the term *professional solicitor*. First, not all states use that term; the terminology instead may be *paid solicitor* or *fundraiser*. Second, the definition of the term can vary. The most frequent definition is "a person who for compensation performs for a charitable organization any service in connection with which contributions are, or will be, solicited in this state by such compensated person or by any compensated person he employs, procures, or engages, directly or indirectly, to solicit." There usually is an exclusion from this definition for officers, employees, and volunteers of charitable organizations.

NOTE: The states give this term broad application—even broader than for the term *professional fundraiser*. Many individuals and firms that consider themselves professional fundraisers are regarded by the state as professional solicitors because of their (ostensible) direct involvement in the solicitation process. For example, a fundraiser who assists a charity in placing solicitation material into the mails may, for that reason alone, be regarded as a solicitor. Those who work in collateral fields should be cautious: they may inadvertently become regarded as solicitors and be subject to penalties for noncompliance with state law. Related fields include consulting in the areas of marketing, management, and public relations. Lawyers are usually exempted from the definition by statute.

It is common for a state charitable solicitation act to impose the following requirements on a professional solicitor working for one or more charitable organizations: registration, bonding, annual reports, postcampaign reports, the filing of solicitation notices, record keeping, and a contract with the charity.

NOTE: Because of greed and other abusive conduct in their ranks, professional solicitors do not enjoy positive reputations. They are in particular disfavor with state legislators and regulators. That is one of the reasons why fundraisers are loath to be perceived as solicitors. More important, by heaping regulatory requirements on them, the states are endeavoring to drive paid solicitors for charity out of their jurisdictions. The laws of some states are so onerous that one wonders how a solicitor can profitably function in the gift solicitation task. Anyone who can avoid classification as a professional solicitor should do so.

Q 13:25 **Do these laws place limitations on the fees paid to professional solicitors?**

Yes. From time to time, a state will enact a law placing a percentage limitation on the amount of compensation and other funds that can be paid to a professional solicitor. An example occurred in California, where the state legislature passed a statute that attempted to limit solicitors' fees to a maximum of 50 percent of the contributions collected for a charity. Laws of this type are blatantly unconstitutional; this California law was promptly voided.

In another example, the state of Kentucky enacted a law that placed a 50 percent limit on the amount of fees a charitable organization could pay a professional solicitor. This law was struck down as being unconstitutional.

Q 13:26 **What is a *charitable sales promotion* and how do the state laws apply to it?**

The phrase *charitable sales promotion* is generally defined as an "advertising or sales campaign, conducted by a commercial co-venturer, which represents that the purchase or use of goods or services offered by the commercial co-venturer will benefit, in whole or in part, a charitable organization or purpose." A business enterprise usually will state to the general public that a portion of the purchase price derived from the sale of goods or services during a particular period will be donated to a charity or charities. A commercial co-venturer is a business entity (other than a professional fundraiser or professional solicitor) that becomes involved in a charitable sales promotion.

NOTE: The term *commercial co-venturer*, though understandable as to its derivation, is unfortunate phraseology. It suggests that the charity involved is engaged in a *commercial* undertaking, which is not favorable from the charity's standpoint (Q 14:11). It further conveys the thought that the charity is in a joint venture, which also can have adverse legal consequences (Q 13:18).

For the most part, state law mandates accurate disclosure of the arrangement between the charitable organization and the commercial co-venturer. Some states' laws require a formal accounting by the commercial enterprise; two states mandate annual reporting and bonding.

This is an advantageous way for a charitable organization to receive a substantial gift (some of these promotions result in millions of dollars for charity), for a business enterprise to obtain some positive publicity, and for the public to feel that personal consumption of a product is of benefit to charitable programs. (The purchasers do not receive any charitable contribution deduction, however.)

TIP: It is common for a commercial co-venturer to place a limit on the amount of funds that will be transferred to a charity as the result of a particular promotion. In most states, disclosure of this cap is all that is required. In some activist states, however, the practice is deemed misleading, in that purchases made toward the close of the promotion may not, in actuality, cause any funds to pass from the business to charity.

Q 13:27 What is the significance of the portions of these laws concerning prohibited acts?

This aspect of these laws can be very extensive, with a delineation of over 20 *prohibited acts*. Some of these prohibitions apply specifically in the fundraising setting. For example, it can be a prohibited act to misrepresent the purpose of a charitable solicitation, solicit contributions for a purpose other than that expressed in the fundraising material, use a name or statement of another charitable organization where its use would tend to mislead a solicited person, lead anyone to believe that registration constitutes or implies an endorsement by the state, or enter into a contract with a person who is required to register under the state's law but who has failed to do so.

These prohibitions can apply, however, more broadly in the realm of charitable operations. For example, it can be a prohibited act to misrepresent the purpose of a charitable organization, expend contributions in a manner inconsistent with a stated charitable purpose, violate any of the applicable provisions of the state's consumer fraud law, or engage in other unlawful acts or practices as the attorney general of the state may determine.

TIP: These prohibited acts rules are applicable with respect to any solicitation in the state. A charitable organization or other person soliciting in more than one state can find that there are tens of prohibited acts with which to contend (Q 13:34).

Q 13:28 Are there any exceptions to these laws?

Almost always. The exceptions largely apply with respect to charitable organizations. Some states exempt certain types of charitable organizations from the entirety of these laws; others exempt them from only the registration and reporting requirements.

The most common exception—for religious organizations—rests primarily on constitutional law grounds.

NOTE: Ironically, many of the abuses in the field of charitable fundraising are committed in the name of religion.

The next most common exception is for schools, colleges, and universities. Other entities that often have some form of exemption are health care providers, membership organizations, libraries, veterans' groups, and small organizations. Some states exempt small solicitations and fundraising for a named individual.

NOTE: These exemptions are largely predicated on the reasonable premise that the organizations can be excused from the rigors of this regulation because those whom they solicit do not need the protections of the statute, due to their close relationship with and understanding of the charitable organization. At the same time, this approach leaves the remaining regulated charities unhappy with their burdens of compliance. Exemptions from state charitable solicitation acts can cause divisiveness in the world of public charities.

TIP: There are some traps in this area.

1. These exemptions are not uniform; a charitable organization can be exempt in its home state, yet not in another state where it is also soliciting gifts.
2. The membership exclusion cannot be utilized simply by making a donor a "member"; the state laws usually forbid that practice.
3. Some universities, health care providers, and similar organizations conduct their fundraising through related "foundations"; not all of the states that exempt these institutions likewise expressly exempt their affiliated foundations.
4. A "small" solicitation in one state is not necessarily small in another; the thresholds range from $1,500 to $25,000.

Some states exempt charitable organizations by name. These laws are of questionable constitutionality; they may be violations of the equal protection doctrine.

TIP: An exception may not be automatic. In some states, a charitable organization must make application for exemption. In other states, an otherwise applicable exemption is not available where a charitable organization uses a professional fundraiser or a professional solicitor.

Q 13:29   What provisions are generally required in a contract between a charitable organization and a professional fundraiser or professional solicitor?

The most common provisions that a state will require, in a contract between a charitable organization and a fundraiser or solicitor, are a statement of the respective obligations of the parties; a statement of the fees that are to be paid by the charitable organization; the projected beginning and end dates of the solicitation; a statement as to whether the fundraiser or solicitor will have custody of contributions; a statement of the percentage of gross revenue from which the fundraiser or solicitor will be compensated; the bank location and the number of the account in which all funds from the solicitation will be deposited; and any other information that the attorney general may prescribe.

Q 13:30 When does a charitable organization have to comply with one of these laws?

Assuming the charitable organization is not exempt from the requirement (Q 13:28), it must comply with a charitable solicitation act in a state when it is soliciting contributions in that state. At a minimum, the applicable law is that of the state in which the soliciting charitable organization is located. It is rare for a charity to solicit contributions only outside of the state in which it is headquartered. A soliciting charitable organization should first endeavor to be in compliance with the fundraising regulation law in the state in which it is based.

NOTE: An argument that a state's law is inapplicable because the charity is only using the U.S. mail or because the fundraising involves interstate commerce will fail. The state's police power enables it to regulate in this field as long as the forms of regulation are sufficiently narrow (Q 13:3).

Q 13:31 When does a professional fundraiser or a professional solicitor have to comply with one of these laws?

The considerations regarding compliance are much the same as those for charitable organizations (Q 13:30). A fundraiser or solicitor may not be assisting a charitable organization in the state where the fundraiser or solicitor is based. Although this would be infrequent, the state law may nonetheless apply. Each state's law must be examined to see how it treats this subtlety.

Q 13:32 When does a charitable organization have to comply with more than one of these laws?

This is a subject of some confusion and frustration. Basically, the law is that a charitable organization, unless exempted from the requirement (Q 13:28), must comply with *each* of the charitable solicitation acts in force in the states in which it is soliciting contributions. A charitable organization engaged in fundraising in all of the states and the District of Columbia may have to comply annually with over 40 of these laws (in addition to nonprofit corporation acts and other state laws that may apply in the fundraising context).

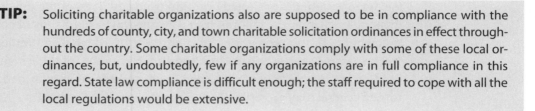

TIP: Soliciting charitable organizations also are supposed to be in compliance with the hundreds of county, city, and town charitable solicitation ordinances in effect throughout the country. Some charitable organizations comply with some of these local ordinances, but, undoubtedly, few if any organizations are in full compliance in this regard. State law compliance is difficult enough; the staff required to cope with all the local regulations would be extensive.

There is no lawful way to avoid this extent of multistate enforcement. These laws are based on the states' police power (Q 13:3) and have been generally upheld in the face of challenges as to their constitutionality. These is no legitimate authority—based on concepts of interstate commerce or other theory—for the proposition that these laws are inapplicable to charitable organizations raising funds on a multistate basis.

Q 13:33 Are solicitations of merely a few individuals subject to these state laws?

Technically, yes. Although these laws are designed to protect the *public* (Q 13:36), most of them literally apply irrespective of the number of persons solicited. An argument can be made that these laws do not apply to *private* solicitations, but there is no case law supportive of the assertion. Only a few states have addressed the subject, usually by exempting a charitable solicitation from the registration and reporting requirements where the organization does not intend to annually receive contributions from more than 10 persons. Two states exempt a solicitation where no more than 100 persons are solicited. Some states attempt to resolve this dilemma by exempting small (in terms of total funds collected) solicitations; these thresholds range from $1,500 to $25,000.

Q 13:34 When does a professional fundraiser or professional solicitor have to comply with more than one of these laws?

The considerations here are basically the same as with charitable organizations (Q 13:32). That is, a fundraiser or solicitor must be in compliance with these laws in every state in which it is working with a charitable organization to assist it in raising funds. Usually where the charitable organization is exempt from the requirements (Q 13:28), so too is the professional fundraiser and/or professional solicitor.

Q 13:35 What happens when a charitable organization, professional fundraiser, or professional solicitor violates one of these laws?

The general practice—although not reflected in any statute—is that, when a state regulatory office discovers a violation of the state's charitable solicitation act, the office will contact the offending party and request compliance. This approach is usually taken, for example, when a person is required to register in the state but has not. Where the violation is more egregious, such as the commission of a fraud, the reaction of the state authorities would likely be sterner.

If the violation is willful or ongoing, and persists despite polite requests to come into compliance, most of the state regulators have the authority to obtain an injunction and enjoin the practice that is contravening the law. For example, if a charitable organization is fundraising in a state without having first registered there, the state's attorney general could enjoin the solicitation until compliance has been achieved. Likewise, a professional solicitor could find the solicitation enjoined if the solicitor's contract with the charity is not in conformity with the state's requirements.

A host of civil and criminal law penalties can come into play as well. These sanctions are civil fines and imprisonment; both can apply.

NOTE: Despite the enforcement that exists—the intensity of which varies from state to state—many charitable organizations, professional fundraisers, and professional solicitors are not adhering to state laws or are only in partial compliance. Just as few states have the resources necessary to fully enforce these laws, most charitable organizations lack the capacity to fully comply with them. There are more outlaws in this field of the law than in any other applicable to nonprofit organizations.

Q 13:36   What is the rationale for these state laws?

The state charitable solicitation acts are intended to protect the public from fundraising in the name of charity that is fraudulent or otherwise misrepresentative as to its purpose. Some of the preambles to this type of legislation grandly resonate with this approach to consumer protection. For example, the preamble to the statute in the California law states that "there exists in the area of solicitations and sales solicitations for charitable purposes a condition which has worked fraud, deceit, and imposition upon the people of the state." The legislature in Colorado concluded that "fraudulent charitable solicitations are a widespread practice in this state which results in millions of dollars of losses to contributors and legitimate charities each year." The latter preamble adds: "Legitimate charities are harmed by such fraud because the money available for contributions continually is being siphoned off by fraudulent charities, and the goodwill and confidence of contributors continually is being undermined by the practices of unscrupulous solicitors."

Q 13:37   Are these state laws effective?

For the most part, no; the purpose of these laws is to protect people from fake charities and unscrupulous fundraisers by deterring unlawful activity and punishing the illegalities that do occur (Q 13:36). These laws keep increasing in number and complexity, but they are having little impact on abusive practices. The chief imprint these laws are placing on the charitable sector is in the form of administrative burdens (including diversions of funds from charitable programs) on legitimate charities.

The story line that describes these laws as being effective is a myth fostered by the regulatory community. On occasion, the courts will accept the rationale. In one instance a court upheld the constitutionality of a registration fee imposed on fundraising charitable organizations on the ground that it is a "user fee." The court wrote that the charitable solicitation acts enhance "donor confidence" by "eliminating illegitimate charities."

The states focus intently in this area, yet the "big picture" is often missed. Episodes such as those affecting the United Way of America and the New Era for Philanthropy Foundation unfold; state law enforcement misses them completely.

The truth is that no one knows the full extent of the ineffectiveness of these laws. More fundamentally, there are no respectable data that might reveal the magnitude of the problem these laws are supposed to rectify and prevent. It is astonishing that these laws are evolving so quickly and becoming so intricate, when there are absolutely no definitions of the reason for their existence. Research in these areas is long overdue.

Q 13:38   To be in compliance with these laws, what type of management system should a charitable organization have?

A charitable organization that is soliciting contributions in several states and wishes to be in full compliance with the law of those states needs to take several steps.

1. The organization should obtain a copy of the charitable solicitation act in effect in each of the states. It should determine, with the assistance of a lawyer if necessary, what its various obligations are, under each of these laws. At a minimum, the organization should ascertain whether any exceptions are available to it, principally with respect to registration and reporting requirements (Q 13:28). Some of these laws are amplified by rules and regulations, and the charitable organization or its lawyer should have these sets of additional law to refer to in interpreting the statutes. Some court opinions may pertain to these laws as well.

2. Once the organization has determined which of these states have registration requirements that are applicable to it (Q 13:31), it should obtain, prepare, and file the necessary registration forms. This should be done in advance of solicitation, and the organization should be certain to pay the requisite registration fee and obtain all required bonds.

3. If the organization is using the services of a professional fundraiser and/or professional solicitor, it should make a reasonable effort to see to it that each of these persons is adhering to these laws as well (Q 13:23, Q 13:24). Although, technically, the responsibility for compliance is on these persons and not the charity, the charity does not want legal difficulties to thwart a fundraising effort.

4. If the organization is subject to one or more reporting requirements, it should be certain that its financial records are properly maintained. Particular emphasis should be placed on fundraising costs, so that the organization knows precisely what its solicitation expenses are. If the entity has costs that are allocated between fundraising and program, it should obtain the services of an accountant who is knowledgeable as to those rules. The due dates for the state forms will vary. To remain in timely compliance with the filing

requirements, the organization should have a system for self-notification as the dates draw near.

5. If the charitable organization is being assisted by a professional fundraiser or professional solicitor, it should execute a written contract between itself and that person (or persons). Further, the organization should see to it that the contract (or contracts) has all of the provisions that are required by states' laws (Q 13:29). These considerations may also apply to relationships with commercial co-venturers (Q 13:26).

6. The organization should be certain that its solicitation materials contain any and all of the applicable legends (Q 13:21).

7. The organization should review the list of prohibited acts in each of these applicable laws (Q 13:27) and be certain that it is in conformity with them.

8. The organization should endeavor to be in compliance with the applicable record-keeping requirements.

There are other aspects of these laws that the charitable organization should monitor. Among them is the receipt of copies of all materials that affiliated parties file with the states, such as the solicitation notices filed by professional solicitors and reports filed by commercial co-venturers.

Q 13:39 How does state law regulation interrelate with the oversight activities of the watchdog agencies?

The standards promulgated by the "voluntary" watchdog agencies—such as the Better Business Bureau—are not law.

> **NOTE:** The word *voluntary* is in quotes because, despite what these agencies say, the charities caught up in standards enforcement are not doing so voluntarily. The motive of these charities is fear: the credibility these agencies have with funders and the media is such that levels of gifts and grants can plummet due to the adverse publicity that these agencies can quickly generate if their standards are not adhered to—to the letter.

Thus, since these standards are not rules of law, charities are not obligated to comply with them. As noted, however, compliance is coerced. One of the many flaws of these standards is that they can be inconsistent with legal requirements and contrary to good management practices. Attracted by its simplicity, the standards tend to highlight the subject of fundraising costs; this seems to be where public charities are the most vulnerable, which contributes to their obsequiousness.

Also, state regulators often look to these agencies' lists to see who is compliant and who is not. Further, state authorities have been known to alert one or more of the watchdog agencies as to charities who may be transgressing the law. Some argue that this form of regulation is preferable to that by government, but government regulation of fundraising has hardly been abated by the watchdog groups (or any other force).

Unrelated Business Activities

The taxability of income derived by a tax-exempt organization from the conduct of *unrelated business* is a key feature of the federal tax law relating to nonprofit organizations. This aspect of the law of tax-exempt organizations looms large these days as the federal government searches for ways to generate tax revenues. The concept of the unrelated business rules is crisp and clear; application of it, however, is often very difficult because the specifics of these rules can be vague and varying.

No field of the federal tax law applicable to nonprofit organizations is spawning more issues and controversies than that pertaining to unrelated business activities. This area is a high audit priority for the IRS.

Here are the questions most frequently asked about the unrelated business law (including the availability of exceptions), the tax treatment of royalties, and the impact of the "hot" issues facing hospitals, colleges, and universities—and the answers to them.

Q 14:1 **A tax-exempt organization often needs more money than it can generate through gifts, grants, and dues. Management of the organization is thinking about raising money by charging fees for some products or services, but it is concerned about taxation. Where does it begin?**

Basically, the management of the organization should not lose sight of the fundamental fact that the organization is a nonprofit, tax-exempt entity. Thus, the organization needs to be operated *primarily* for its exempt purposes. If there is to be any taxable income, it will be income that is derived from business activities that are *unrelated* to the organization's tax-exempt purpose. As long as operations are primarily for exempt purposes, the organization need not fear loss of its tax-exempt status. The income derived from the other, nonexempt activities, however, may well be subject to the federal income tax.

Q 14:2   How does an organization measure what is *primary*?

That often is not easy to do; there is no mechanical formula for measuring what is *primary*. The measurement is done on the basis of what the law likes to term the *facts and circumstances*. The IRS heartily rejects the thought of applying any particular percentage in measuring primary activities, and invokes this principle of law on a case-by-case basis. In this stance, the IRS is uniformly supported by the courts.

TIP: Percentages are used in this and comparable contexts all the time, if only as a guide. The term *primary* has been assigned percentages in other settings; for unrelated business income purposes, it can mean at least 65 percent. By comparison, *substantial* is sometimes defined as at least 85 percent; *substantially all* is sometimes set at 90 percent. *Incidental* is sometimes defined as up to 15 percent.

If these percentages have any validity—and, to a limited extent, they do for evaluation purposes—then an organization could have as much as one-third of its activities or income be unrelated. There are IRS private letter rulings upholding unrelated income in excess of 40 percent; however, in these cases, the amount of *time* actually devoted to the unrelated business was considerably less. It seems unlikely that any organization receiving over one-half of its income from unrelated business would be tax-exempt.

A prudent assessment or review would cause a tax-exempt organization to seriously evaluate its situation, if its unrelated income annually exceeds 20 or 25 percent of total revenue. The remedies may include setting up a for-profit subsidiary (Chapter 15).

The statement that there is no mechanical formula for measuring what is *primary* is not precisely accurate. In the case of tax-exempt title-holding companies, the maximum amount of unrelated business income that they can have in a year without endangering tax exemption is 10 percent. This rule does not, however, apply with respect to any other type of tax-exempt organization. For most tax-exempt organizations, 10 percent is too narrow a limitation on permissible unrelated activity.

Q 14:3   How does an exempt organization know whether an activity is a related one or an unrelated one?

This is both one of the easiest and hardest questions in the law of tax-exempt organizations.

The easy answer is that an unrelated activity is one that does not substantially advance the exempt purposes of the organization. That is, it is an activity that the organization engages in for the purpose of earning money, rather than furthering one or more programs. The fact that the money earned is used for exempt purposes does not alone make the activity itself related.

The more complex answer is that the activity must be evaluated against as many as five levels of analysis. These are:

1. Is the activity a *trade or business* (Q 14:6)?
2. Is it *regularly carried on* (Q 14:13)?
3. Is the conduct of the activity *substantially related* to the conduct of exempt functions (Q 14:18)?
4. Is the activity exempted from taxation by one or more statutory exceptions (Q 14:23)?
5. Is the income from the activity exempted from taxation by one or more statutory exceptions (Q 14:24)?

Q 14:4   What is the rationale underlying the unrelated income rules?

The basic structure of these rules was enacted in 1950. The essence of this body of law is to separate the income of a tax-exempt organization into two categories: (1) income from related business and (2) income from unrelated business. The income from unrelated business is taxed as if it was earned by a for-profit, taxable company.

The primary objective of these rules was to eliminate a source of *unfair competition* with the for-profit sector by placing the unrelated business activities of exempt organizations on the same tax basis as those conducted by nonexempt organizations, where the two are in competition. Some courts place considerable emphasis on the factor of competition when assessing whether an undertaking is an unrelated business (Q 14:10). The existence or nonexistence of competition, however, is not a statutory requirement for there to be unrelated business.

In actuality, the enactment of these rules has not quelled the cries of "unfair competition" from the business sector, particularly small business owners. More than five decades later, the issue is not so much that unrelated business by nonprofits is competitive; rather, the competition is usually derived from *related* businesses. In part, this is the result of (1) shifts in the definition of related and unrelated activities and (2) the entry of for-profits into fields of endeavor previously confined to nonprofit entities. Some small business advocates want competitive practices prohibited, as a way of "leveling the playing the field." These individuals are of the view that unrelated income taxation is not enough; they fret about the fact that some consumers are attracted to, and thus bring their business to, nonprofits just because they are nonprofit—a situation informally known as the halo effect.

Thus, the purpose of the unrelated income tax itself is to equalize the economics of a transaction, irrespective of whether the vendor of a good or service is tax-exempt or taxable. If an organization can sell a product and not pay income tax on the sales proceeds, that organization can charge a lower price for that product and have more "profit" remaining than an organization selling the same product and having to pay taxes as a cost of doing business. This ability, and occasional practices of price undercutting, is the foundation for the claim of "unfair competition."

Q 14:5   Are these claims of unfair competition leading to anything, such as law changes?

It doesn't look like it. Years ago, when the small business lobbying on this subject was at its peak, some thought that Congress would toughen the rules. There was a series of hearings before the Subcommittee on Oversight, of the House Committee on Ways and Means, in 1986–1987. The chairman of the subcommittee pushed hard for legislation but could not build a consensus for change. The nonprofit community lobbied very effectively against various proposals, the small business lobby did a particularly poor job of sustaining its efforts, and the movement for revising these laws atrophied. The individual who was the subcommittee chairman is no longer in Congress, and there is no interest, in either chamber, in law change in this area. Still, efforts to make it more difficult for nonprofits to compete are unfolding in several states.

Q 14:6   What is the *trade or business* requirement?

A statutory definition of *trade or business* is specifically applicable in the unrelated business setting. The phrase means any activity that is carried on for the production of income from the sale of goods or the performance of services. That definition is, of course, quite broad and encompasses nearly everything that a tax-exempt organization does.

In fact, the law regards a tax-exempt organization as a bundle of activities. They may be related or unrelated, but they are still *businesses*.

Q 14:7   Does this mean that the law considers the programs of exempt organizations as businesses?

Yes. Each of the organization's programs is considered a separate business. In fact, a program may embody several businesses. For example, the bookstore operated by a college is a combination of businesses. These include sales of books, cosmetics, computers, appliances, and clothing. The same is true with respect to hospital and museum gift shops and associations' sales of items to their members. In the case of charitable organizations, many of their fundraising activities are businesses.

It is very difficult to convince the IRS that a particular activity is not a business. The most likely instances where an exempt organization can prevail on this point are with respect to its investment activities and infrequent sales of assets. Occasionally a court will be more lenient, as illustrated by an opinion finding that an association's monitoring activities with respect to insurance programs for its membership, where the insurance and claims processing functions were elsewhere, did not rise to the level of a trade or business.

Moreover, an activity does not lose its identity as a trade or business if it is carried on within a larger aggregate of similar activities or within a larger complex of other endeavors that may or may not be related to the exempt purposes of the organization. This means that an activity cannot be hidden from scrutiny, as to whether it is a business, by tucking it in with other activities. The IRS has the authority to review each business of an exempt organization in isolation, in search of unrelated activity. That is, it can—figuratively speaking—fragment an organization into as many businesses as it can define. In the jargon of the field, this is known as the *fragmentation rule*.

Q 14:8 **When the federal tax law regards an exempt organization as a composite of businesses, isn't that different from how nonprofit organizations see themselves?**

No question about that. Unfortunately, the matter gets murkier. Actually, the statutory definition of *business* states that the term *trade or business* "includes" that definition of it. That word has opened the door for the courts and the IRS to add other requirements and possibilities that may cause an activity to be a business. Some courts use other criteria, such as competitive activity or commerciality, and then jump all the way to the conclusion that the activity is an unrelated business.

For example, in a completely different area of the tax law, dealing with whether a gambler gambling only for personal ends is engaged in a business for expense deduction purposes, the Supreme Court held that, for an activity to be considered a trade or business, it must be carried on with a profit motive. The Court specifically wrote that this definition of trade or business was not to be used in other tax settings. But some lower courts ignored that admonition and grafted that rule onto the definition of exempt organizations' unrelated income purposes.

Q 14:9 **Why would a tax-exempt organization object to that additional element of the definition, concerning a profit motive? Wouldn't that rule always favor exempt organizations, causing some activities to not be businesses in the first instance?**

Actually, it doesn't always work that way. In some instances, an exempt organization *wants* an activity to be considered an unrelated business. This is because income from unrelated activity and losses from other unrelated activity can be aggregated to produce a single, bottom-line item of net income or net loss.

For example, suppose an exempt organization has two unrelated activities. One produces $100,000 of net income, the other generates $70,000 of net losses. On the unrelated business income tax return, the income and losses from the two businesses are blended, and the organization pays the unrelated income tax on only $30,000. This works, however, only when both activities are in fact *businesses*.

Suppose the second of these activities consistently, year-in and year-out, yields losses. The IRS will usually take the position that, because the activity always results in an annual loss, it is not being conducted with the requisite profit motive. If that position is sustained, the activity is not considered a *business*, in which case the $70,000 of loss could not be offset against the $100,000 of gain. Then the organization would have to pay the unrelated income tax on the full $100,000.

All of this is happening even though the tax regulations state that the fact that a trade or business does not produce a net profit is not sufficient to exclude it from the definition of a trade or business.

Q 14:10 What are some of the other elements being grafted onto this definition?

Sometimes a business is found when an exempt organization is in competition with for-profit enterprises. The existence of profits may lead a court to the conclusion that an undertaking is a business (usually an unrelated business). The IRS may assert the presence of unrelated business just because a fee is charged for the product or service. Moreover—and this is becoming a growing practice—courts will jump to the conclusion that an unrelated business exists where the activity is undertaken in a *commercial* manner (Chapter 17).

Q 14:11 What is a *commercial activity*?

The commerciality doctrine has been conceived by the courts, although it is not fully articulated. There is, with one relatively minor exception, no mention of *commerciality* in the Internal Revenue Code (Q 14:12). The same is the case with respect to the tax regulations (Q 14:12).

The doctrine essentially means that a tax-exempt organization is engaged in a nonexempt activity when that activity is conducted in a manner that is considered *commercial*. An activity is a commercial one if it is undertaken in the same manner as it would be if it were being conducted by a for-profit (commercial) business. The most contemporary explication of the commerciality doctrine sets forth these criteria: (1) the tax-exempt organization sells goods or services to the public, (2) the exempt organization is in direct competition with one or more for-profit businesses, (3) the prices set by the organization are based on pricing formulas common in the comparable commercial business setting, (4) the organization utilizes advertising and other promotional materials and techniques to enhance sales, (5) the organization's hours of operation are basically the same as those of for-profit enterprises, (6) the management of the organization is trained in business operations, (7) the organization uses employees rather than volunteers, and (8) there is an absence of charitable giving to the organization.

Q 14:12 What are the statutory and regulatory references to the commerciality doctrine?

In 1986, Congress added to the federal tax law a rule stating that an organization cannot qualify as a tax-exempt charitable entity or a social welfare entity if a substantial part of its activities consists of the provision of commercial-type insurance. While that term is not statutorily defined, it generally means any insurance of a type provided by commercial insurance companies. The reach of this aspect of commerciality is being accorded broad interpretation in the courts.

As far as the regulations are concerned, there is a brief mention of commerciality in the rules pertaining to whether an activity is regularly carried on (Q 14:13). There it is stated that business activities of an exempt organization will ordinarily be deemed to be regularly carried on "if they manifest a frequency and continuity, and are pursued in a manner, generally similar to comparable commercial activities of nonexempt organizations."

Q 14:13   What are the rules as to whether a business activity is regularly carried on?

This test was derived because of the purpose of the unrelated business rules: an activity cannot be competitive with for-profit business if it is not regularly carried on.

Thus, income from an unrelated business cannot be taxed where that business is merely sporadically or infrequently conducted. The frequency and continuity of the activity, the manner in which the activity is pursued, and the continuing purpose of deriving income from the activity largely determine whether the activity is regularly carried on.

Q 14:14   How is *regularity* measured?

There is no precise means of measurement. An activity that consists of a single, one-time-only transaction or event is certainly irregular. For this reason, a sole sale of an item of property often is not taxable. A lot of fundraising events, such as annual dances and theater outings, are usually not taxed because of this rule.

Beyond that, it is a judgment call. A business occupying only a few days in a year would not be regularly carried on. For example, the tax regulations offer a quaint example of the operation of a sandwich stand by a hospital auxiliary for two weeks at a state fair. That business is said to not be regularly carried on. But it cannot be said with any certainty when too many days of activity cause the line to be crossed. The regulations add that the operation of a commercial parking lot for one day in each week of the year is a regularly carried on business. Operation on 52 days out of 365, or operation on one day each week, obviously reflects an operation that is regularly carried on.

Q 14:15   Are there any other aspects of this level of analysis?

Yes, there are three other aspects of regularity.

One is that, where a business activity is, in the commercial sector, carried on only during a particular season, the duration of this season, rather than a full year, is the measuring period for an exempt organization. For example, an organization selling Christmas trees or Christmas cards would measure regularity against the length of the Christmas season. Likewise, an operation of a horse racing track would be measured in relation to the horse racing season.

Q 14:16 **What are the other two aspects of regularity?**

One is that the IRS has adopted the view that there is more to the measurement of regularity than just the time expended for the event itself. The IRS takes into consideration the amount of time the organization spends in preparing for the event—*preparatory time*—and the time expended afterward in connection with the event—*winding-down time*. If an exempt organization were to sell a product commercially for a few days each year, in assessing regularity it is—according to the IRS view—supposed to include the preparatory time of lining up the product, creating advertising, soliciting purchasers, and the like, as well as the winding-down time spent assessing the operation and arranging for the return of unsold items.

Q 14:17 **Do some operations get converted into regular ones by using that approach?**

That can be the case. But there's more. The law in general recognizes the concept of a *principal* and an *agent*. A *principal* is a person who hires another person to act in his, her, or its stead, for the principal's benefit; the second person is an *agent*. Generally, the law considers the acts of an agent to be those of the principal. This means that the acts of an agent are attributed to the principal.

In the unrelated business setting, it is common for an exempt organization to contract with a company to perform a service. If the company is considered an agent of the organization and the company's function is in connection with an unrelated business, the IRS will take the position that the time spent by the company is attributed to the exempt organization in determining whether the unrelated activity was regularly carried on.

For example, in one case, a university contracted with a publisher to produce programs for its home football games. The contract reserved advertising space in the programs for the university, any income generated by sales of that space was retained by the university, and the university retained an advertising agency to sell its space. The IRS determined that the revenues from the sale of the advertisements constituted unrelated business income because the advertising agency was an agent of the university. Because of the agency relationship, the agency's activities were attributable to the university for purposes of determining whether the university regularly carried on the business of selling program advertising. A court, however, rejected this approach to the determination of regularity. At the same time, the IRS has openly disagreed with this holding and is adhering to its position in issuing rulings.

Q 14:18 **What about the third level of analysis, concerning the substantially related requirement?**

This is where the issue usually is: whether the business that is regularly carried on is *related* or *unrelated*. The general rule is that the income from a regularly conducted trade or business is subject to tax unless the income-producing activity is substantially related to the accomplishment of the organization's tax-exempt purpose.

To determine whether an activity is related, an examination is made of the relationship between the business activity and the accomplishment of the organization's exempt purpose. The fact that the income from the business is used for exempt programs does not make the activity a related one.

A trade or business is *related* to tax-exempt purposes only where the conduct of the business has what the tax law terms a *causal relationship* to the achievement of an exempt purpose. The business is *substantially* related only if the causal relationship is recognizably large or material. Thus, for the conduct of a trade or business from which a particular amount of gross income is derived to be substantially related to an exempt purpose, the production or distribution of the goods or the performance of the services from which the gross income is derived must contribute importantly to the accomplishment of these purposes. Where the production or distribution of goods or the performance of services does not contribute importantly to the accomplishment of the organization's exempt purposes, the income from the sale of the goods or services does not derive from the conduct of a related business.

Q 14:19 How is relatedness determined?

There is no formula in this setting. Judgments as to whether there is a causal relationship and whether there is substantiality are made in the context of the facts and circumstances involved. Unfortunately, however, there is not much "straightforwardness." This aspect of the tax law is very complex and murky.

Q 14:20 What are some examples of these judgments?

There are dozens of IRS rulings and court opinions in this area.

In one instance, a local bar association sold standard legal forms to its member lawyers for their use in the practice of law. These forms were purchased from a state bar association. The IRS ruled that the sale of the forms was an unrelated business because it did not contribute importantly to the accomplishment of the association's exempt functions. (There is a court opinion to the contrary, however. Another court held that the sale of preprinted lease forms and landlords' manuals by an exempt association of apartment owners and managers was a related business.)

This IRS ruling illustrates that, just because an association's membership uses a product in their own businesses, the sale of the product does not become a related business for the association. When an association of credit unions published and sold a consumer-oriented magazine to its members, the IRS held that to be an unrelated business because the magazine was distributed to the depositors of the members as a promotional device.

Other instances of unrelated businesses of associations include the sale of equipment to members, the operation of an employment service, the conduct of other registry programs, the selling of endorsements (including the right to use the association's name and logo), and the charging of dues to certain categories of purported associate members.

Over the years, one of the issues that has generated considerable attention for associations is whether the provision of insurance for members is an unrelated business. From the outset of the controversy, the IRS was of the position that it was. Associations prevailed at the beginning, but the tide shifted. Now the courts uniformly uphold the IRS on this subject: compensation to associations for assistance in making insurance available to their members is almost always taxable.

In one instance, the IRS examined seven activities of an exempt association and found each of them to be unrelated businesses. These activities were: (1) the sale of vehicle signs to members, (2) the sale to members of embossed tags for inventory control purposes, (3) the sale to members of supplies and forms, (4) the sale to members of kits to enable them to retain sales tax information, (5) the sale of price guides, (6) the administration of a group insurance program, and (7) the sale of commercial advertising in the association's publications.

The outcome isn't always that the business is unrelated. In one case, the IRS concluded that the sale of television time to governments and nonprofit organizations at a discount by an exempt association of television stations was a related business.

Q 14:21 Are there any other aspects of the substantially related test?

There are four other aspects of this test. One of them is the *size and extent test*.

In determining whether an activity contributes importantly to the accomplishment of an exempt purpose, the size and extent of the activity must be considered in relation to the size and extent of the exempt function it purports to serve. Thus, where income is realized by a tax-exempt organization from an activity that is in part related to the performance of its exempt functions, but that is conducted on a scale larger than is reasonably necessary for performance of the functions, the gross income attributable to that portion of the activities in excess of the needs of exempt functions constitutes gross income from the conduct of an unrelated business.

An example of this test involved an exempt association that had a membership of businesses in a particular state. One of its income-producing activities was to supply member and nonmember businesses with job injury histories on prospective employees. Rejecting the association's contention that this service contributed to accomplishment of exempt purposes, the IRS ruled that the activity was an unrelated business, in that the services went "well beyond" any mere development and promotion of efficient business practices.

As an illustration of the application of this test where the IRS concluded that the business was entirely related, the IRS considered a tax-exempt organization that provided a therapeutic program for emotionally disturbed adolescents. It operated a retail grocery store that was almost completely staffed by adolescents to help secure their emotional rehabilitation. The IRS ruled that the store operation was not an unrelated business because it was operated on a scale no larger than reasonably necessary for its training and rehabilitation program.

Another of these aspects is the *same state test*. As a general rule, the sale of a product that results from the performance of tax-exempt functions does not constitute an unrelated business where the product is sold in substantially the same state it is in upon completion of the exempt functions. This rule is significant for organizations that sell articles made by handicapped individuals as part of their rehabilitation training. By contrast, where a product resulting from an exempt function is exploited in business endeavors beyond what is reasonably appropriate or necessary for disposition in the state it is in upon completion of tax-exempt functions, the activity becomes transformed into an unrelated business. For example, an exempt organization maintaining a dairy herd for scientific purposes may sell milk and cream produced in the ordinary course of operation of the project without unrelated income taxation. If, however, the organization were to utilize the milk and cream in the further manufacture of food items, such as ice cream and pastries, the sale of these products would likely be the conduct of an unrelated business.

Another of these subtests of substantiality is the *dual use test*. This concerns an asset or facility that is necessary to the conduct of exempt functions but is also employed in an unrelated endeavor. Each source of the income must be tested to see whether the activities contribute importantly to the accomplishment of exempt purposes. For example, a museum may have a theater auditorium for the purpose of showing educational films in connection with its program of public education in the arts and sciences; use of that theater for public entertainment in the evenings would be an unrelated business. Likewise, a school may have a ski facility that is used in its physical education program; operation of the facility for the general public would be an unrelated business.

The fourth of these subtests is the *exploitation test*. In certain instances, activities carried on by an exempt organization in the performance of exempt functions generate goodwill or other intangibles that are capable of being exploited in unrelated endeavors. When this is done, the mere fact that the income depended in part on an exempt function of the organization does not make it income from a related business. This type of income will be taxed as unrelated business income, unless the underlying activities themselves contribute importantly to the accomplishment of an exempt purpose. For example, income from advertising in a publication with exempt function content generally is taxable income resulting from an exploitation of an exempt resource.

Q 14:22   How is the unrelated business income tax calculated?

In general, the tax is determined in the same manner as with for-profit entities. The unrelated income tax rates payable by most tax-exempt organizations are the corporate rates. Some organizations, such as trusts, are subject to the individual income tax rates. There is a specific deduction of $1,000.

This tax falls on *net* unrelated business income. An exempt organization is allowed to subtract its business expenses from gross unrelated income in arriving at taxable net unrelated income. The law generally states that a deductible expense must be *directly connected* with the carrying on of the business; an item of deduction must have a proximate and primary relationship to the carrying on of the business. This standard is more rigorous than the one applied to for-profit and individual taxpayers, where the law allows the deductibility of expenses that are reasonably connected with the taxable endeavor. In practice, however, exempt organizations often follow the standard of reasonableness, particularly when allocating expenses. Because of the looseness of the tax regulations, this approach has been upheld in the courts.

There is one exception to the directly connected test. This exception is for the charitable contribution deduction allowed in computing taxable unrelated income. In general, this deduction cannot exceed 10 percent of the unrelated business taxable income otherwise computed.

These taxes are paid by means of an unrelated business income tax return. Tax-exempt organizations must make quarterly estimated payments of this tax.

EXCEPTIONS

Q 14:23 **What types of activities are exempt from unrelated income taxation?**

An interesting feature of the federal tax laws is the series of *modifications* that are available in calculating taxable unrelated business income. Although these modifications largely exclude certain types of income from taxation (Q 14:24), they also exclude three types of research activities from the tax. This set of exclusions is somewhat of an oddity, in that research activities generally are exempt functions.

One exclusion is for research for the federal government, or any of its agencies or instrumentalities, or any state or political subdivision of a state. Another exclusion is for research performed for any person; however, the research institution must be a college, university, or hospital. The third exclusion is as broad as the second: the organization must be operated primarily for the purpose of carrying on fundamental research, and the results of the research must be freely available to the general public.

The modifications also eliminate from taxation revenue derived from the lending of securities by exempt organizations to brokers.

Eleven other statutory exceptions shelter types of activities from unrelated income taxation. One is for a business in which substantially all of the work in carrying on the business is performed for the tax-exempt organization without compensation. Any unrelated business can be protected from taxation by this exception, including the business of advertising. This exception can be useful in shielding fundraising functions (special events) from taxation.

 **TIP:** The concept of compensation is broadly applied. In one instance, the revenue from gambling events was held taxable because the workers, all of whom were volunteers, were frequently tipped by the patrons.

Another exception is for a business that is conducted by a tax-exempt charitable organization, or a state college or university, primarily for the convenience of its members, students, patients, officers, or employees. This broad exception—known as the *convenience doctrine*—is relied on heavily by colleges, universities, and hospitals. Much of the income from sales of items in college and university bookstores and hospital gift shops is rendered nontaxable because of this rule.

Another exception is for a business that sells merchandise, substantially all of which was contributed to the exempt organization. This exception is generally utilized by thrift shops that sell donated clothing, books, and the like to the general public.

Still other exceptions are for certain businesses of associations of employees conducted for the convenience of their members, the conduct of entertainment at fairs and expositions by a wide range of exempt organizations, the conduct of trade shows by most exempt organizations, the performance by hospitals of certain services for smaller hospitals, the conduct of certain bingo games by most tax-exempt organizations, qualified pole rentals by exempt mutual or cooperative telephone or electric companies, the distribution of low-cost articles incidental to the solicitation of charitable contributions, and the exchanging or renting of membership or donor mailing lists between tax-exempt charitable organizations.

Q 14:24 What types of income are exempt from unrelated income taxation?

The *modifications* (Q 14:23) shield a wide variety of forms of income from unrelated income taxation. These forms of income generally are annuities, capital gains, dividends, interest, rents, and royalties. For the most part, there is little controversy in this area as to the definition of these income items, inasmuch as the terms are amply defined elsewhere in the federal tax law.

There is, nonetheless, an underlying festering controversy. It is the view of the IRS that the exclusion is available only where the income is investment income or is otherwise passively received. This approach to these modifications rests on the rationale for the unrelated income rules, which is to bring parity to the economics of competitive activities involving nonprofit and for-profit organizations (Q 14:10). Passive income, by definition, is not derived from competitive activity and thus should not be taxed. But the IRS wishes to tax net income from the active conduct of commercial business activities.

This dichotomy presents itself in connection with the exclusion for rental income. Where a tax-exempt organization carries on rental activities in the nature of a commercial landlord, the exclusion is not available. The exclusion, however, is not normally voided, simply because the exempt organization provides normal maintenance services. In practice, this opportunity for taxation is obviated by the use of an independent building management and leasing company.

There can be disputes as to whether an income flow is truly rent or is a share of the profits from a joint venture; revenue in the latter form is generally taxable. A contemporary illustration of this distinction is the litigation surrounding crop-share leasing. The IRS has lost all of the cases brought to date; the courts have held that the funds received by the exempt organization were in the form of excludable rent and not from a partnership or joint venture.

The contemporary battles in this context are being waged over the scope of the exclusion for royalties. In part, this is because exempt organizations have more latitude than with any other type of income in structuring transactions to shape the resulting income. In this instance, the objective is to make the income fit the form of a royalty or at least dress it up like a royalty. For the most part, the dilemma is presented because the statute does not define the term *royalty*.

This matter has been the subject of multiyear litigation. The outcome to date is that both parties to the disputes were partially correct and partially in error. That is, the IRS position that a royalty, to be excludable, must be wholly passively received by the exempt organization was tempered to allow the organization a limited involvement in the revenue-generation process. Conversely, the view of the litigating exempt organizations that "a royalty is a royalty" so that any involvement by the organization is irrelevant was rejected; the court held that if the organization's involvement in the royalty-generating process is substantial, the royalty exception will be defeated.

Q 14:25 How can the royalty exclusion be most effectively utilized?

The key to effective utilization of the royalty exception in this context is to minimize the tax-exempt organization's involvement in the efforts that give rise to payment of the royalty. It is tempting for an organization to do just the opposite; for example, if an organization has an affinity card program, it will be inclined to engage in various practices (such as mailings, inserts in publications, and activities at the annual conference) to stimulate its members' use of the cards. While activity of this nature is permissible if it is insubstantial (Q 14:24), the more active the organization is in this regard, the greater the likelihood that the royalty exception will not be available.

An alternative approach is to bifurcate the arrangement: execute two contracts, one reflecting passive income/royalty payments and the other, payments for services rendered. The income paid pursuant to the second contract would likely be taxable. The organization would endeavor to allocate to the royalty contract as much of the income as reasonably possible. The difficulty with this approach is the form-over-substance rule: two contracts of this nature are easily collapsed and treated as one for tax purposes.

Q 14:26 Are there any exceptions to the rules stating these exclusions?

Yes, there are two exceptions. One pertains to the payment of otherwise excludable income from a controlled organization. The general rule is that payments of annuities, interest, rent, and/or royalties by a controlled corporation to a tax-exempt controlling organization are taxable as unrelated income. This is the case even though these forms of income are otherwise passive in nature. For this purpose, an organization controls another where the parent entity owns at least 50 percent of the voting power of all classes of stock entitled to vote and at least 50 percent of all other stock of the corporate subsidiary. This control element can also be manifested by stock or by an interlocking of directors, trustees, or other representatives of the two organizations.

The other exception is found in the rules concerning unrelated debt-financed property. Where income is debt-financed income, the various exclusions referred to above are unavailable.

Q 14:27 Are there any exceptions to these exceptions?

Yes. The rule concerning the taxation of income from a controlled subsidiary (Q 14:26) does not apply where the funds are dividends, because dividends are not deductible by the payor corporation. Thus, where other types of income are deductible by the controlled entity that provides the income, the exempt organization that receives the income must regard it as unrelated business income.

SPECIFIC APPLICATIONS

Q 14:28 What are the contemporary unrelated business issues for hospitals and other health care providers?

There are more unrelated business issues in the health care field than in any other involving exempt organizations. Undertakings such as gift shops, coffee shops, and parking lots usually are considered either related businesses or activities protected by the convenience doctrine (Q 14:23).

The principal areas of controversy are laboratory testing for physicians in private practice, the maintenance of medical office buildings, sales of medical equipment to the public, sales of pharmaceuticals to nonpatients, the operation of fitness centers and health clubs, and the conduct of physical rehabilitation programs.

Q 14:29 What are the contemporary unrelated business issues for colleges and universities?

The principal unrelated business issues for colleges and universities are the receipt of revenue in the form of corporate sponsorships (where the issue basically is whether the funds are contributions or payments for advertising), sales of nonexempt items in bookstores, travel tours, and rental of campus facilities to businesses.

Q 14:30 What are the contemporary unrelated business issues for museums?

The principal unrelated business issues for museums are the sales of nonexempt items in the gift shop (particularly where the items have a long-term utility, such as furniture) and sales of items by catalog.

Q 14:31 What are the contemporary unrelated business issues for trade, business, and professional associations?

The principal unrelated business issues for trade, business, and professional associations are sales, to members, of items that they utilize in their business or profession and the receipt of dues from so-called associate members. As to the latter, it is the view of the IRS that the associate members join the organization solely to obtain a service (such as insurance coverage) or access to the regular members for business promotion purposes.

Q 14:32 **How do the unrelated business rules apply in the context of charitable fundraising?**

There are instances when an activity is deemed a fundraising event, although technically it is an unrelated business. There are, however, a host of exceptions that shield the resulting income from taxation (Q 14:23 and Q 14:24). The principal exceptions are for activities that are not regularly carried on (Q 14:3), the volunteer exception, and the exception for donated goods (Q 14:23).

Another area of unrelated income taxation that entails charitable fundraising is the rental and exchange of mailing lists (those of donors and/or members). Where the parties to the transaction are eligible to receive tax-deductible contributions (chiefly, charitable and veterans' organizations), the resulting revenue is not taxed. Otherwise, the net funds from the transaction are taxable, unless the monies can be cast as royalties. Even in instances where lists are simply exchanged (that is, there is no transfer of money), it is the view of the IRS that a taxable transaction occurs (unless the exception applies), with the amount "received" being the fair market value of the list received; usually there are no offsetting deductible amounts.

Q 14:33 **How is the unrelated business income tax reported?**

The return filed by nearly all tax-exempt organizations with the IRS on an annual basis is an *information* return. This type of return is not used to report taxable income. For that purpose, a *tax* return is required. The IRS has devised a tax return for reporting unrelated business taxable income. It must be filed in addition to the annual information return.

CHAPTER **15**

Subsidiaries

As the federal laws applicable to tax-exempt organizations have become exceedingly complex, these organizations frequently must respond with more sophisticated planning techniques. Often deployed in this context is bifurcation: the use of two organizations because of legal requirements when otherwise only one entity would be utilized. One of the applications of the technique of bifurcation is the use of subsidiaries.

A tax-exempt organization uses an exempt organization subsidiary to house one or more activities that, if the parent conducted directly, would cause the parent to lose its tax exemption (or be ineligible to be exempt in the first instance). A for-profit subsidiary is used as a repository for unrelated business activities, usually where the activities are too extensive to be conducted in the parent organization without loss or denial of tax exemption.

The prospect of a subsidiary organization almost always arises in the context of solving a problem. Here are the questions most frequently asked about the creation, control, and conduct of subsidiaries (both tax-exempt and for-profit)—and the answers to them.

Q 15:1 What is a *subsidiary* in the nonprofit law context?

A *subsidiary*, in the nonprofit law context, is essentially the same as in the for-profit law context. It is a separate organization that has some special, formal, *control* relationship with another organization; the other organization is the *parent* organization. For these purposes, the parent organization always is a tax-exempt organization. The subsidiary, however, may be a tax-exempt organization or a for-profit organization.

Q 15:2 Why would a tax-exempt organization establish a subsidiary?

Part of the answer to this question depends on whether the subsidiary is a tax-exempt organization or a for-profit organization. In general, the principal reason a tax-exempt organization will establish a subsidiary is to house in another organization one or more activities that the parent organization either does not want, or cannot have, as part of its operations. Thus, a *bifurcation* occurs: what would otherwise be one entity is split into two entities. This type of bifurcation almost always is undertaken because of a requirement of law—often, the federal tax law.

Q 15:3 How does a nonprofit organization control a subsidiary?

It depends on whether the subsidiary is a nonprofit or for-profit entity.

If the subsidiary is a nonprofit, tax-exempt organization, the control is likely to be manifested by an *interlocking directorship* or, as it is more commonly called, *overlapping boards*. There are several models of this control mechanism. In one model, the board of directors of the parent organization selects at least a majority of the board of directors of the subsidiary. The *ex officio* approach is also common: the governing instrument of the subsidiary provides that individuals holding certain positions with the parent organization (such as its president or executive director) are, for that reason, the members of, or at least a majority of, the board of directors of the subsidiary. A third approach is a blend of the foregoing two methods. Whatever the method, it is important for the parent organization to have control of the subsidiary by being able to determine at least a majority of the subsidiary's board of directors. (Without that control element, there is no parent–subsidiary relationship.) It is not enough, for example, for the governing instruments of the "subsidiary" of a membership organization parent to state that the members of the subsidiary's board of directors must be members of the parent organization (unless the membership of the parent entity is exceedingly small).

Where the interlocking directorship method is used, two other features are recommended. First, the articles of organization of the subsidiary should provide that its governing instruments cannot be amended, or that any such amendment may not become effective, without the prior approval of the board of the parent organization. The purpose of this provision is to prevent a board of the subsidiary from changing the documents to eliminate the interlocking directorate. Second, the governing instruments should make it clear, where directors of the subsidiary are appointed by the parent (rather than installed through use of the *ex officio* approach), that the board of the parent organization has the right to remove these directors as well.

A tax-exempt organization can also control another tax-exempt organization by utilizing the *membership feature*. The subsidiary entity is structured as a membership organization; the parent entity is thereafter made the sole member of the subsidiary organization. Prudence dictates that the governing instruments of the subsidiary state that the prior approval of the members is required to make amendments to those documents and that the members have the right to remove directors of the subsidiary. *Ex officio* positions can also be used in combination with the membership approach.

Finally, one tax-exempt organization can control another exempt organization by means of stock. This approach is the most infrequent of the three available methods, probably because it is not widely realized that some states allow stock-based nonprofit organizations. With this approach, the subsidiary is formed as a nonprofit corporation in a state that allows this type of entity to issue stock; the parent organization then becomes the sole stockholder. Other persons are allowed to hold stock as well, but the "parent" organization must own at least 51 percent of the subsidiary's stock.

Where the subsidiary is a for-profit organization, it is almost certainly a corporation. The control mechanism will therefore be stock ownership. The *ex officio* feature can be used in conjunction with the stock approach. Other persons are allowed to hold stock as well, but the "parent" organization must own at least 51 percent of the subsidiary's stock.

Q 15:4 What body can act as the incorporator or corporate member to establish a subsidiary?

Almost always, the board of directors of a parent organization makes the decision to create and use a subsidiary. The board, usually assisted by legal counsel, also decides the form of the subsidiary and the nature of the control mechanism (Q 15:3). The board might decide that the membership feature is to be used; if so, it would make the parent entity a member—most likely, the sole member. If the corporate form is used, along with some other control feature, the board of the parent would decide which individuals would serve as incorporators of the subsidiary (Q 1:7).

Q 15:5 Is there a minimum number of board members required for a subsidiary?

There is no rule of federal law on the point. State law is likely to dictate a minimum number of board members for the subsidiary, particularly if the subsidiary is a corporation. Most states require at least three board members for a corporation (Q 2:2).

The number of board members of the subsidiary is far more likely to be determined by management or political factors. If the control mechanism is the membership feature or the issuance of stock (Q 15:3), the number of board members is irrelevant (unless there is a state-law minimum). If the control mechanism is an interlocking directorate, the parent entity will want to be able to appoint or elect at least a majority of the members of the subsidiary's board. This factor would result in an odd-numbered board of the directors of the subsidiary.

Q 15:6 What legal requirements should be followed in maintaining the parent–subsidiary relationship?

The most basic requirement is that, at all times, the parent organization must be able to show that it "owns" (or, in many instances, controls) at least 51 percent of the subsidiary—whether by stock, membership, or board positions (Q 15:3).

It is essential that all of the legal "niceties" of bona fide organizations be respected. The board of directors of the subsidiary—irrespective of the manner in which it is constituted—must have its own meetings (that is, its meetings should not be a subset or a continuation of the meetings of the parent organization) and maintain minutes of those meetings, and the subsidiary should have its own bank account(s). The law will treat this aspect of bifurcation as a sham if each organization does not have the characteristics of a bona fide separate entity. If regarded as a sham, the arrangement is ignored and the two organizations are treated as one. When this happens, the purposes for creating the subsidiary are almost always nullified: the activities of the subsidiary are attributed to the parent.

Q 15:7 What are the powers and oversight requirements of the parent organization?

The boards of directors of the two organizations—parent and subsidiary—have their own fiduciary or similar requirements (Q 1:19). In general, the oversight function is accomplished through the control mechanism (Q 15:3); whatever means is selected should afford the parent ample oversight opportunities. The law does not impose any particular standard in this context, other than the standard arising from the fact that the resources (income and assets) are indirectly resources of the parent, so that the parent should treat that bundle of resources as an asset and in accordance with the prudent person rule (Q 1:19).

The power of the parent organization with respect to the subsidiary should be complete; the parent controls and sometimes owns the subsidiary (Q 15:3). The subsidiary exists solely to do the bidding of the parent. The principal concern is that the power in the parent should not be exercised in such a way as to cause the arrangement to be perceived as a sham (Q 15:6).

Q 15:8 How is revenue from a for-profit subsidiary taxed?

In general, revenue that flows from a for-profit subsidiary to a tax-exempt parent is considered unrelated business income (Chapter 14). The basic rule is that the parent entity must include the payment as an item of gross income derived from an unrelated business to the extent the payment reduces the net unrelated income, or increases any net unrelated loss, of the controlled entity. *Control* means ownership of more than 50 percent of the stock or other interest in the subsidiary, taking into account (if necessary) constructive ownership rules. These rules apply to any interest, annuity, royalty, or rent.

For example, if the subsidiary rents property from the parent, the rental income would almost certainly be unrelated income to the parent. Likewise, if the subsidiary borrows money from the parent organization, the interest paid to the parent is likely to be unrelated business income to the parent.

There are two exceptions to this general rule. One is that income in the form of dividends from a for-profit subsidiary to an exempt parent is not unrelated income (Q 14:27).

NOTE: This is the only type of income that is accorded this exempt treatment. Dividends are not taxable to the parent because the payment of them is not deductible by the subsidiary.

Another exception pertains to exempt functions in the subsidiary. The income resulting from exempt functions is not taxable. If the income flowing to the parent from the subsidiary is partially from an exempt function and partially from nonexempt activities, only the income from the latter source is regarded as unrelated business income.

Q 15:9 What are the tax consequences of liquidation of a subsidiary into its parent organization?

The answer depends on a variety of factors. For example, have the assets in the subsidiary appreciated in value? If they have, there may be a capital gains tax when the assets of the subsidiary are transferred to the parent.

A federal tax law rule is directed at the tax consequences of liquidation of a subsidiary into a tax-exempt parent organization. Under this rule, where the assets in the subsidiary were used in an unrelated business, are transferred to the parent, and are used in a related business, the capital gains tax becomes applicable and remains applicable whenever the assets become employed in a related business, no matter how many years later. There is no tax, however, where the parent organization continues to use the assets in an unrelated business. The flaw in this ruling is that the IRS ignored the fact that the assets in a for-profit subsidiary were, after the transfer of them to the parent, used in a related business. The ruling is silent on the point, but presumably the assets were used by the subsidiary in an unrelated business—otherwise, why were they placed in a for-profit subsidiary at all?

Q 15:10 What are the federal tax reporting requirements with respect to subsidiaries?

If a subsidiary is a for-profit organization, it must file a tax return every year with the IRS. In this return, the corporation must indicate whether any entity owns, directly or indirectly, 50 percent or more of the corporation's voting stock or whether the corporation is a subsidiary in an affiliated group.

If the subsidiary is a tax-exempt organization, it (with some unlikely exceptions) must file an annual information return with the IRS.

> **NOTE:** It is possible to have a subsidiary that is a nonprofit, but not tax-exempt, organization. This type of entity would file a tax return, the same as would a for-profit organization.

The existence of the parent–subsidiary relationship must be reflected on the tax-exempt subsidiary's return. The subsidiary must identify the parent by name and state that it is a tax-exempt organization. If the tax-exempt subsidiary has unrelated business activity, it must file a tax return to report the income so derived (Q 14:33).

The parent organization, being a tax-exempt entity, files an annual information return with the IRS. If the subsidiary is owned by the parent by means of stock, that holding would be reflected on the balance sheet of the annual information return, presumably as an asset. If a director, officer, or key employee of the parent, who is compensated by the parent, is also compensated by a subsidiary, that aggregate compensation may have to be reported on the annual information return (Q 5:48). The existence of the parent–subsidiary relationship must be reflected on the parent's return. The parent must identify the subsidiary by name and state whether it is a tax-exempt or nonexempt organization.

If the subsidiary is a taxable corporation, the tax-exempt parent must complete a special part of the annual information return, stating the name, address, and employer identification number of the subsidiary, the percentage of ownership interest in the subsidiary, the nature of the business activities of the subsidiary, and the total income and end-of-year assets of the subsidiary.

If the parent organization is a tax-exempt charitable entity and the subsidiary is a tax-exempt entity other than a charitable one, the parent must prepare another special part of its annual information return, stating whether it, during the reporting year, transferred cash or other assets to the subsidiary, sold assets to or purchased them from the subsidiary, rented equipment or facilities to the subsidiary, reimbursed the subsidiary for expenses, loaned funds to the subsidiary or guaranteed a loan obligation of the subsidiary, performed any services for the subsidiary, or shared facilities, equipment, mailing lists, other assets, or paid employees with the subsidiary. The parent organization must identify the subsidiary by name, state the type of organization that the subsidiary is, and give a description of the relationship.

If the subsidiary organization is a tax-exempt charitable entity and the parent entity is a tax-exempt organization other than a charitable one, the subsidiary must prepare the special part of its annual information return as identified in the preceding paragraph.

Both organizations are subject to other federal tax reporting requirements, such as those relating to compensation of employees and to profit-sharing and pension plans.

Q 15:11 What are the state law reporting requirements with respect to subsidiaries?

As a separate entity, each organization has its own state-law reporting responsibilities. For example, if each entity is a corporation, both are likely to have to file annual reports with the secretary of state. Trusts probably must file annually with the state attorney general. If either organization engages in fundraising, there must be compliance with the state's law concerning charitable solicitations (Chapter 13).

Each state's law should be reviewed to determine specific requirements.

TAX-EXEMPT SUBSIDIARIES

Q 15:12 Why would a tax-exempt organization establish a tax-exempt subsidiary?

The principal reason a tax-exempt organization establishes a tax-exempt subsidiary is because the parent entity wants to engage in an activity (or series of activities) that its tax status precludes but that is, under the law, an exempt function for another type of tax-exempt organization. Thus, the function that is nonexempt for the parent is housed in the subsidiary.

On occasion, an activity is placed in a tax-exempt subsidiary in an attempt to shield the parent organization from liability. This reason for creating a subsidiary is also warranted because of legal considerations.

Management or similar considerations, however, may warrant the conduct of a function in a tax-exempt subsidiary even though the function could be conducted by the exempt parent without jeopardizing its tax exemption.

Q 15:13 What are some of the common uses of tax-exempt subsidiaries?

There are several of these uses, all built around the concept of bifurcation (Q 15:1). The most common combinations occasioned by the permissible-activity reason for creating an exempt subsidiary (Q 15:12) are:

1. A tax-exempt charitable organization with a tax-exempt social welfare organization subsidiary that engages in substantial lobbying activities (Q 8:24, Q 8:27).
2. A tax-exempt charitable organization subsidiary of a charitable organization in another country, where the subsidiary is fundraising in the United States.

NOTE: In general, only charitable gifts made to U.S. charities are deductible. Foreign charities seeking deductible contributions from U.S. donors need to establish a U.S.-based fundraising organization, and it cannot be merely a conduit of the funds.

3. A tax-exempt membership organization (such as a business association or labor organization) with a tax-exempt supporting organization (Q 10:22).
4. A tax-exempt organization with a subsidiary that is a political organization (Q 9:17).
5. A tax-exempt charitable organization with a tax-exempt business league subsidiary that engages in certification activities.

NOTE: It is the view of the IRS that programs of certification of organizations' memberships are not charitable activities, because of the benefits flowing to the members. Since certification is an appropriate function for a business league, a separate organization of that nature is required.

The most common combination occasioned by the liability-shield reason for creating an exempt subsidiary (Q 15:12) is the use by a tax-exempt organization of a tax-exempt title-holding organization.

The most common combinations occasioned by the management reasons for creating an exempt subsidiary (Q 15:12) are: the use by a tax-exempt, noncharitable organization of a charitable supporting organization (Q 10:22) and the use by a tax-exempt charitable organization of a separate charitable organization for fundraising purposes.

NOTE: Some public charities, such as universities and hospitals, find it more effective to solicit contributions by means of related "foundations." This approach facilitates concentration of the fundraising function in a single organization and creates a board of directors that is solely focused on charitable solicitations.

Q 15:14 **Is it necessary for a tax-exempt subsidiary to obtain separate recognition of tax-exempt status?**

It depends on the type of tax-exempt subsidiary. If the subsidiary is a charitable one, recognition of tax-exempt status must be obtained from the IRS (exceptions are unlikely). If the subsidiary is any other type of tax-exempt organization, recognition of exempt status may be acquired, but it is not mandatory.

TIP: Even where recognition of tax exemption is not required, prudence dictates that the determination should be obtained. The subsidiary then has the comfort of knowing that the IRS agrees with its exempt status, and subsequent questions as to its tax status (assuming no changes in material facts) are precluded.

State law should be reviewed to determine whether the subsidiary must or can obtain one or more tax exemptions (most likely, those with respect to income, sales, use, and/or property taxes).

Q 15:15 **Should the tax-exempt status of the subsidiary be as a charitable entity or as a supporting organization?**

This question presumes that the subsidiary is to be a tax-exempt charitable (including educational, religious, and/or scientific) organization. The question also reflects common misunderstanding of the two tax statuses. If it is appropriate to cause the subsidiary to be a supporting organization—whether in relation to a public charity (Q 10:15) or another type of tax-exempt entity (Q 10:22)—the organization must have *both* tax classifications. This is because all supporting organizations are charitable ones.

The federal tax status of an organization as a charitable entity pertains to its tax-exempt status (and its ability to receive tax-deductible contributions). The tax status of an organization as a supporting organization pertains to its ability to avoid private foundation status (Q 10:1, Q 10:15).

Q 15:16   What are the reporting requirements between the parent and subsidiary organizations?

For the most part, the law does not impose any such requirements. This communication is left largely to the realm of suitable management. Some formal reporting requirements may be appropriate for certain supporting organizations (Q 10:28).

Q 15:17   If a tax-exempt subsidiary can raise money in its own name, what disclosure requirements should it observe with respect to the parent organization?

This is largely a matter of state law. The state's charitable solicitation act—if any (Chapter 13)—will likely contain some disclosure requirement. It is common practice, however, for this type of subsidiary to reflect the existence of the parent on its stationery and fundraising literature. For example, if the subsidiary is a fundraising foundation that is supportive of a hospital, these materials should—and almost certainly will—state that fact.

As to the federal tax law, the charitable subsidiary must adhere to the charitable gift substantiation rules (Q 13:6), the quid pro quo contribution rules (Q 13:10), and the annual return reporting rules (Q 15:10). If the subsidiary is a noncharitable, tax-exempt organization, there are disclosure requirements to which it must adhere concerning the nondeductibility of gifts and the availability of information or services from the federal government.

Q 15:18   What formal action is required to transfer funds between a tax-exempt parent and a tax-exempt subsidiary?

Usually, a transfer of funds of this nature requires a formal action of the board of directors of the transferring organization—a board resolution, for example. This is particularly the case where the transfer is in the form of a contribution of capital or a loan from the parent to the subsidiary, or a rental arrangement or purchase of goods or services between the organizations. Other relationships, such as the sharing of employees, need not be the subject of formal board approval. Whatever the nature of the interorganization funding, it may have to be reported to the IRS (Q 15:10).

Q 15:19   Can a tax-exempt subsidiary raise funds for an endowment and hold these funds separate from the parent?

Yes. This type of subsidiary is likely to be a supporting organization; the maintenance of an endowment fund is a classic activity for this type of organization (Q 10:17). It is possible for the endowment function to be in a publicly supported charitable organization—most likely, a donative publicly supported entity (Q 10:7)—but as the endowment grows, the extent of investment income may cause the organization to receive an inadequate amount of public support (Q 10:14).

The supporting organization would be able to transfer income from the endowment fund to the supported organization (assuming that is the nature of the endowment structure). If the supported organization is not a charitable one, the funds transferred to the parent should be clearly restricted to charitable uses.

TIP: If the supported organization is a service provider publicly supported organization (Q 10:8), caution must be exercised. Investment income in the supporting organization will retain its character as such when transferred to the parent. This can adversely impact the ability of the parent entity to qualify as this type of public charity, because of the limitation on investment income in computing public support.

FOR-PROFIT SUBSIDIARIES

Q 15:20 Why would a tax-exempt organization establish a for-profit subsidiary?

Usually, a tax-exempt organization establishes a for-profit subsidiary because of the existence, or planned existence, of an unrelated business, or set of unrelated businesses, that is too extensive to be conducted in the parent without jeopardizing the parent's tax-exempt status (Q 14:2). Some exempt organizations incubate unrelated businesses within themselves and then transfer them *(spin them off)* to a for-profit subsidiary. Others create a subsidiary at the outset.

The approach to take may be a matter of management's judgment. If it is known at the beginning that the unrelated activity will be extensive, the for-profit subsidiary is basically dictated. If, however, the scope of the unrelated business is unknown at the outset and its prospects are dubious, the organization may want to commence with the business within itself and then spin it off when and if it becomes larger.

TIP: If the unrelated business is in the exempt organization, the only deductions that may be taken in calculating unrelated business taxable income are those that are directly related to the unrelated activity. When the unrelated business is in a for-profit subsidiary, all expenses are deductible as long as they are reasonable and necessary to the conduct of the business.

TIP: A tax-exempt organization may wish to go slowly in establishing a tax-exempt subsidiary. If the subsidiary is created and, later, it turns out that it is not needed and the parent decides to liquidate it, there may be adverse tax consequences to the parent (Q 15:9).

The decision as to whether to create a for-profit subsidiary can be a difficult one. At a minimum, it requires a determination as to whether the activity involved is related or unrelated (Q 14:3). The subsidiary may also be needed if the activity (or activities) is to be conducted in a commercial manner (Q 14:11).

Q 15:21 What are some of the common uses of for-profit subsidiaries?

The principal use of a for-profit subsidiary is to *house an unrelated business.* For example, as an offshoot of its membership services, an association may have developed an activity that appeals to the general public, such as a journal or a database. Placement of the activity in a for-profit subsidiary would enable the association to commercially develop and market the service. A research institution may have commercial testing functions or other similar functions that are best furthered by means of a for-profit subsidiary. A hospital may find it appropriate to develop and operate a medical office building in a subsidiary.

There is no limit in the law as to the type of business activity that can be operated out of a for-profit subsidiary; the tax-exempt organization can devise any type of business activity it wants as a means to generate revenue (which, however, is likely to be taxed (Q 15:8)). There is also no limit in the law as to the size of subsidiaries, either absolutely or in relation to the parent, or the number of for-profit subsidiaries a tax-exempt organization may have.

> **NOTE:** To be tax-exempt, the parent entity must function primarily in furtherance of exempt functions. The use of one or more subsidiaries should not cause the organization to deviate from that standard.

Some tax-exempt organizations will place an unrelated business in a for-profit subsidiary even where the tax laws do not require it (that is, where the business is relatively small). This is done for reasons of *politics* and *perception*, particularly where the business is competitive with commercial businesses in the community. As an illustration, a college began using its printing facilities, used primarily for its exempt functions, for occasional jobs for outside purchasers; as the business grew, some of the commercial printers in the community complained about the competition. To appease its critics, the college transferred its commercial printing operation to a for-profit subsidiary. The competition was still present, but the commercial printers were mollified when it came from a for-profit entity.

> **NOTE:** *Competition* can be synonymous with controversy and sensitivity, particularly among small businesses. When a tax-exempt organization is in competition with a commercial business, the latter sees the competition as being *unfair,* in that the exempt organization does not have to pay taxes; with taxes not a cost of doing business, the exempt organization is (at least in theory) able to underprice the commercial business. Nonetheless, despite plaintiffs' attempts, the courts have been unwilling to hold that for-profit businesses have standing to merit ruling in favor of their competitors' challenge to their tax-exempt status.

The third use of a for-profit subsidiary by a tax-exempt organization is as a *partner in a partnership*, in lieu of the exempt organization's direct participation. The exempt parent may fear the potential of liability, or participation in the partnership (usually, as a general partner) might adversely affect the parent's tax-exempt status.

 **TIP:** This is another area where it is critical that the bona fides of the subsidiary be adhered to (Q 15:6). This approach works only when the legal form of the subsidiary is respected. In one instance, the IRS ignored a tax-exempt organization's use of a for-profit subsidiary as the general partner in a partnership, and reviewed the facts as though the exempt organization was directly involved in the partnership.

If a for-profit organization that is a subsidiary of a tax-exempt organization is used in a partnership, *tax-exempt entity leasing rules* may come into play. These rules make the property involved depreciable over a longer recovery period, thereby reducing the annual depreciation deduction.

TIP: These rules can be avoided where a corporate for-profit subsidiary is used as a partner in a partnership in lieu of a tax-exempt organization, if an election is made to treat any gain on disposition of the subsidiary (and certain other accrued amounts) as unrelated business income.

Q 15:22 Are there limits on the use of tax-exempt assets to capitalize a for-profit subsidiary?

There are no specific limits. Basically, the rules are those that generally pertain to the requirement that the governing board of a tax-exempt organization act in conformity with basic fiduciary responsibilities (Q 2:4, Q 3:2).

IRS private letter rulings suggest that only very small percentages of an organization's resources ought to be transferred to subsidiaries, particularly where the parent entity is a public charity. The percentages approved by the IRS, however, are usually unduly low and, in any event, probably pertain only to cash. In some instances, a specific asset may—indeed, perhaps *must*—be best utilized in an unrelated activity, even though its value represents a meaningful portion of the organization's total resources.

Q 15:23 Are there any rules concerning accumulations of income and other assets in a for-profit subsidiary?

No, the law is essentially silent on the point. Nonetheless, in a private determination issued in late 2004, the IRS wrote that tax-exempt organizations (particularly charitable ones) "bear a very heavy burden" to demonstrate, by "contemporaneous and clear evidence," that they have plans for the use of substantial assets in a subsidiary for exempt purposes. In the case, the charitable organization invested by means of a for-profit subsidiary, which grew rapidly. "This growth presents a continuing obligation," the IRS said, on the organization to "translate this valuable asset into funds, and use these funds for the expansion" of its exempt activities. The IRS suggested that some of the subsidiary's assets be sold or a portion of the subsidiary's stock be sold, with the proceeds used to fund programs of the exempt parent.

The IRS's lawyers said that the exempt organization "cannot be allowed to focus its energies on expanding its subsidiary's commercial business and assets, and neglect to translate that financial success into specific, definite and feasible plans for the expansion of its charitable activities." The agency concluded that the "fact that the assets are being accumulated in a for-profit company under the formal legal control of [a tax-exempt organization] does not excuse [the exempt organization] from using such assets for charitable purposes." The IRS concluded: "Excess accumulations, maintained in a subsidiary entity under legal control of the exempt organization, but under the de facto control of the founder, are deemed to be for the founder's personal purposes if no exempt purpose is documented or implemented."

The IRS did not cite any authority for these sweeping pronouncements. This is not surprising, inasmuch as there isn't any.

Q 15:24   Can a supporting organization have a for-profit subsidiary?

Yes, a supporting organization (Q 10:15) can have a for-profit subsidiary. There was doubt about this for some time, inasmuch as this type of public charity is required to be operated *exclusively* to support or benefit one or more eligible public charities; in this context, *exclusively* means *solely*. There was concern, therefore, that the IRS would rule that a supporting organization cannot have a for-profit subsidiary because to do so would be a violation of the exclusivity requirement. Thus, where the reason for organizing and utilizing a subsidiary is to assist the supporting organization in benefiting a supported organization, use of the subsidiary is allowable. IRS private letter rulings state that a supporting entity's use of a for-profit subsidiary will not jeopardize its tax-exempt status or its supporting organization status, as long as it does not actively participate in the day-to-day management of the subsidiary and both entities have a legitimate business purpose (Q 15:6).

Q 15:25   Can a private foundation have a for-profit subsidiary?

In general, no. The excess business holdings rules applicable to private foundations basically limit to 20 percent the permitted holdings in a business enterprise that may be held by a private foundation and its disqualified persons. If effective control is elsewhere, the aggregate limit is 35 percent. These percentages generally preclude the extent of control required for the parent–subsidiary relationship (Q 11:23).

Nonetheless, there are some exceptions. There is no holdings limit on a business at least 95 percent of the gross income of which is derived from passive sources (such as dividends, interest, and certain rents). The limits do not apply with respect to holdings in a *functionally related business*, which usually is a business the conduct of which is substantially related to the exercise by the foundation of its charitable purposes. A functionally related business can also be (1) a business in which substantially all of the work is performed without compensation (Q 11:24), (2) a business carried on by the private foundation primarily for the convenience of its employees (Q 14:23), or (3) a business that consists of the selling of merchandise, substantially all of which has been received by the foundation as contributions (*id.*).

CHAPTER 16

Partnerships and Joint Ventures

I t is difficult to think of a contemporary issue involving tax-exempt organizations, particularly public charities, that is more controversial than their involvement in various forms of joint ventures. This issue has been at the top of the IRS list of exempt organizations' hot topics for years, fueled largely by various structures designed in the field of health care. The recent surge in activities concerning the whole-hospital joint and ancillary ventures is the latest in a long string of these developments and is not likely to be the last. Although, usually, a tax-exempt organization knows when it is in a partnership, an exempt entity can be a participant in a joint venture without realizing it.

Here are the questions most frequently asked about involvement in partnerships and joint ventures—and the answers to them.

PARTNERSHIPS BASICS

Q 16:1 What is the legal definition of a *partnership*?

A *partnership* is a form of business enterprise recognized in the law as an *entity*, as are other enterprises, such as a corporation, limited liability company, or trust. It is usually evidenced by a document, which is a partnership agreement, executed between persons who are the partners. These persons may be individuals, corporations, and/or other partnerships. Each partner owns an interest in the partnership; these interests may or may not be equal.

In the federal tax law, the term *partnership* includes a "syndicate, group, pool, joint venture, or other unincorporated organization, through or by means of which any business, financial operation, or venture is carried on, and which is not . . . a trust or estate or a corporation." A partnership must have at least two members, who are its owners.

The concept of a partnership has long been given broad interpretation. In a classic example of this, a court defined a partnership as a relationship based on a "contract of two or more persons to place their money, efforts, labor, and skill, or some or all of them, in lawful commerce or business, and to divide the profit and bear the loss in definite proportions." Thus, co-owners of income-producing real estate who operate the property (either through an agent or one or more of them) for their joint profit are operating a partnership.

An entity that does not qualify for tax purposes as a partnership will undoubtedly be regarded as an *association*, which means that it is taxed as a corporation. When that happens, certain tax attributes are lost (Q 16:5).

There are two basic types of partnerships: the *general partnership* and the *limited partnership*.

Q 16:2 What is a *general partnership*?

The difference between the two types of partnerships is delineated principally by the extent of the partners' liability for the acts of the partnership. Generally, liability for the consequences of a partnership's operations rests with the general partner or general partners. Moreover, a general partner is liable for satisfaction of the ongoing obligations of the partnership and can be called upon to make additional contributions of capital to it. Every partnership must have at least one general partner. Sometimes where there is more than one general partner, one of them is designated as the managing general partner.

Many partnerships are comprised of only general partners, who contribute cash, property, and/or services. This type of partnership is a *general partnership*. The interests of the general partners may or may not be equal. In many respects, a general partnership is akin to a *joint venture* (Q 16:6).

A general partnership is usually manifested by a partnership agreement.

Q 16:3 What is a *limited partnership*?

A *limited partnership* is one that has limited partners as participants. A limited partner is a person whose exposure to liability for the functions of the partnership is confined to the amount of that person's contribution to (investment in) the partnership.

Some partnerships need or want to attract capital from sources other than the general partner or partners. This capital can be derived from investors, who are limited partners. Their interest in the partnership is, as noted, limited in the sense that their liability is limited. The limited partners are involved to obtain a return on their investment and perhaps to procure some tax advantages.

Thus, a partnership with both general and limited partners is a limited partnership.

A limited partnership is usually manifested by a partnership agreement.

Q 16:4 Why is the partnership vehicle used?

As a general proposition, the partnership is used as a business enterprise because the parties bring unique resources to the relationship, and they want to blend these resources for the purpose of beginning and conducting a business. Another reason for the partnership form—particularly the limited partnership vehicle—is to attract financing for one or more projects. In some instances, the partnership vehicle is favored because of its tax status (Q 16:5).

Q 16:5 How are partnerships taxed?

Partnerships are not taxed. They are *pass-through entities*; this means that the entity's income, deductions, and credits are passed along to the partners.

JOINT VENTURE BASICS

Q 16:6 What is the legal definition of a *joint venture*?

A *joint venture* is a form of business enterprise recognized in the law as an *entity*, as are other enterprises, like a corporation or trust. Essentially, a general partnership (Q 16:2) and a joint venture are the same thing.

One court defined a *joint venture* as an association of two or more persons with intent to carry out a single business venture for joint profit, for which purpose they combine their efforts, property, money, skill, and knowledge, but they do so without creating a formal entity, namely, a partnership, trust, or corporation. Thus, two or more entities (including tax-exempt organizations) may operate a business enterprise as a joint venture.

The concept of a joint venture, however, is broader than that of a general partnership. One of the ways this fact can be manifested is evident when the law treats an arrangement as a joint venture for tax purpose, even though the parties involved insist that their relationship is something else (such as parties to a management agreement or a lease).

NOTE: This issue can arise in the unrelated business income context, where a tax-exempt organization is asserting that certain income it is receiving is passive in nature (and thus not taxable) and the IRS is contending that the income (most frequently rent or royalty income) is being derived from active participation in a joint venture.

The federal tax law is inconsistent in stating the criteria for ascertaining whether a joint venture is to be found as a matter of law. According to the Supreme Court, "[w]hen the existence of an alleged partnership arrangement is challenged by outsiders, the question arises whether the partners really and truly intended to join together for the purpose of carrying on business and sharing in the profits or losses or both." The Court added that the parties' "intention is a question of fact, to be determined from testimony disclosed by their 'agreement considered as a whole, and by their conduct in execution of its provisions.'" In one instance, a court examined state law and concluded that the most important element in determining whether a landlord–tenant relationship or joint venture agreement exists is the intention of the parties. This court also held that the burden of proving the existence of a joint venture is on the party who claims that that type of relationship exists (such as the IRS).

Yet another court declared that "it is well settled that neither local law nor the expressed intent of the parties is conclusive as to the existence or nonexistence of a partnership or joint venture for federal tax purposes." The court wrote that this is the test to follow: "whether, considering all the facts—the agreement, the conduct of the parties in execution of its provisions, their statements, the testimony of disinterested persons, the relationship of the parties, their respective abilities and capital contributions, the actual control of income and the purposes for which it is used, and any other facts throwing light on their true intent—the parties in good faith and acting with a business purpose intended to join together in the present conduct of the enterprise."

This latter court wrote that the "realities of the taxpayer's economic interest rather than the niceties of the conveyancer's art should determine the power to tax." The court added: "Among the critical elements involved in this determination are the existence of controls over the venture and a risk of loss in the taxpayer." Finally, the court said that it is not bound by the "nomenclature used by the parties," so that a document titled, for example, a *lease* may in law be a partnership agreement.

Q 16:7 Why is the joint venture vehicle used?

The joint venture vehicle is generally used when two or more persons share resources to advance a specific project or program. When the arrangement is formally established, it is often denominated a *general partnership* (Q 16:2). As noted, however, parties to a transaction can find themselves treated as being in a joint venture as a matter of law.

Moreover, the term *joint venture* is often broadly used. The term appears in the formal definition of a *partnership* (Q 16:1). It is often applied in other contexts, such as when the structure of a venture is based on use of a limited liability company.

Q 16:8 What is a *limited liability company*?

A *limited liability company* is a legal entity, recently recognized under state law. It is not a corporation, although it has the corporate attribute of limitation against personal liability. A limited liability company with at least two members generally is treated as a partnership for tax purposes (Q 16:10).

Q 16:9 How are joint ventures taxed?

Joint ventures are not taxed. They are *pass-through entities*; this means that the entity's income, deductions, and credits are passed along to the partners. Thus, joint ventures are treated the same as partnerships for tax purposes (Q 16:5).

There basically are two types of limited liability companies: the multiple-member limited liability company and the single-member limited liability company. In the case of the multiple-member limited liability company, the members may consist of one or more tax-exempt organizations and one or more for-profit entities (Q 16:27–Q 16:31), or the members may all be exempt organizations. The single-member limited liability company is disregarded for federal tax purposes; a tax-exempt organization can be the sole member of a limited liability company.

Q 16:10   How are limited liability companies taxed?

Limited liability companies are not taxed. They are, when they elect to do so, treated the same as partnerships for tax purposes (Q 16:5).

NOTE: Likewise, S corporations are treated as partnerships for tax purposes (Q 16:5).

TAX-EXEMPT ORGANIZATIONS AND PARTNERSHIPS

Q 16:11   Can a tax-exempt organization be involved in a general partnership?

There is no question that a tax-exempt organization can be involved in a general partnership. The principal tax law issues become, however, whether involvement in the partnership jeopardizes the entity's exempt status and/or causes it unrelated business income. To date, all of the law on the point concerns public charities in general partnerships. Inasmuch as the law in this regard is the same as that pertaining to public charities in joint ventures, it will be discussed in that context (Q 16:22–Q 16:29).

Q 16:12   Can a tax-exempt organization be involved in a limited partnership?

Again, the answer is a definite yes. And, again, the tax issues are whether tax exemption would be threatened and/or unrelated business income generated. Here, too, the law to date has focused only on public charities in limited partnerships as general partners.

Resolution of these issues depends on whether the exempt organization is in a limited partnership as a limited partner or a general partner (Q 16:13, Q 16:14).

Q 16:13   Can a tax-exempt organization be involved in a limited partnership as a limited partner?

The answer is clearly yes, although there is little law on the point. When an exempt organization is a limited partner in a limited partnership, it is in the venture as an investor. The law then is likely to focus primarily on whether the investment is a prudent one for the organization and whether its board is adhering to the requisite principles of fiduciary responsibility.

Q 16:14 **Can a tax-exempt organization be involved in a limited partnership as a general partner?**

Yes. This brings the discussion to one of the most critical aspects of this subject: the impact of involvement in a limited partnership by a public charity as a general partner on the charity's tax-exempt status. For years, the IRS has had great concerns on this point. Indeed, it was not until 1998 that the IRS formally stated that a charitable organization may form and participate in a partnership and be or remain tax-exempt.

NOTE: Nonetheless, the IRS has issued dozens of private letter rulings, technical advice memoranda, and general counsel memoranda stating that a public charity's involvement in a limited partnership will not endanger its exempt status. Indeed, on one occasion the IRS ruled that the exempt status of a charitable organization should not be revoked because of its participation as a general partner in seven limited partnerships. Moreover, the IRS has *never* issued a published private determination that involvement in a limited partnership would cause loss or denial of a charity's exempt status.

CAUTION: As to this last observation, there have been ruling requests in which the facts were altered to gain the favor of the IRS in this regard, and there have been ruling requests involving charities in limited partnerships that have been withdrawn in anticipation of an adverse ruling. Further, the IRS provided guidance indicating when an involvement in a joint venture by a charity could lead to loss of its exemption (Q 16:27).

Q 16:15 **What are IRS concerns about public charities as general partners in limited partnerships?**

Despite the fact that the debate, in and out of the IRS, over participation by public charities in limited partnerships as general partners has been openly raging for more than 20 years, the IRS and some courts are still not enamored with the idea. The primary concern the IRS has in this context is the potential of private inurement and/or private benefit accruing to the for-profit participants in the venture.

More specifically, it is the view of the IRS that substantial benefits can be provided to the for-profit participants in a limited partnership (usually the limited partners) involving a tax-exempt organization as the or a general partner. This concern has its origins in arrangements involving charitable hospitals and physicians practicing there, such as a limited partnership formed to build and manage a medical office building, with an exempt hospital as the general partner and investing physicians as limited partners.

Q 16:16 **Why has this controversy lasted so long?**

There are several reasons that this controversy about public charities in limited partnerships has spanned many years. One is the ongoing number, variation, and complexity of these arrangements. Another is the great prevalence of the use of limited partnerships in the health care setting; as the law in that sphere has ballooned, so too has the general law concerning charities in partnerships. Still another reason is that the IRS adopted a very hard-line stance in this area at the beginning.

Q 16:17   What was this original IRS hard-line position?

The original position of the IRS in this regard came to be known as the *per se rule*. Pursuant to this view, involvement by a charitable organization in a limited partnership as general partner meant *automatic* revocation or denial of tax exemption, irrespective of the structure or purpose of the partnership. The per se rule was grounded on the premise that substantial private economic benefit was being accorded the limited partners.

Here is the IRS in 1978, in first articulating this per se rule, advising a public charity: "If you entered [into] the proposed partnership, you would be a direct participant in an arrangement for sharing the net profits of an income producing venture with private individuals and organizations of a non-charitable nature. By agreeing to serve as the general partner of the proposed . . . project, you would take on an obligation to further the private financial interests of the other partners. This would create a conflict of interest that is legally incompatible with you being operated exclusively for charitable purposes."

NOTE: This was the position the IRS staked out, even though the purpose of the partnership was to advance a charitable objective (the development and operation of a low-income housing project).

There were other instances of application of the per se rule in the late 1970s and into the 1980s. Some of these cases did not involve formal partnerships (Q 16:1). For example, an IRS private letter ruling issued in 1979 concerned the issue of whether certain fees derived by tax-exempt lawyer referral services were items of unrelated business income. The IRS ruled that the fees paid by lawyers to the organizations, based on a percentage of the fees received by the lawyers for providing legal services to clients referred to them by these exempt organizations, constituted unrelated income. The reason: the subsequently established lawyer–client relationship was a commercial undertaking, and the ongoing fee arrangement with the percentage feature placed the organizations in the position of being in a joint venture in furtherance of those commercial objectives.

Q 16:18   What became of the per se rule of the IRS?

The per se rule of the IRS was rejected by a court in a very significant decision. The case concerned syndication of a play being staged at a tax-exempt theater.

OBSERVATION: Before continuing with a description of this case, it should be noted that, as a matter of fundamental litigation practice, the party advocating the rule of law being asserted (here, the IRS) endeavors to select a situation involving facts that are the most compelling from the standpoint of its position. Inexplicably, the IRS advanced its cause in a blatant violation of litigation strategy. The theater group sponsoring the play was truly struggling financially, the play was being staged at the Kennedy Center in Washington, D.C., and the production was an engaging drama in the form of a sympathetic portrayal of the Supreme Court!

Needing financial assistance, the theater group underwrote its production costs with funds provided by private investors. The IRS sought to revoke the organization's tax-exempt status for attempting to sustain the arts in this fashion but lost, both at trial and on appeal. Again, the matter involved a limited partnership that was being used to further the exempt ends of the general partner. The courts in this case placed some emphasis on the facts that the partnership had no interest in the tax-exempt organization or its other activities, the limited partners had no control over the way in which the exempt organization operated or managed its affairs, and none of the limited partners nor any officer or director of a corporate limited partner was an officer or director of the charitable organization.

NOTE: Much later, the IRS pronounced this control element a "significant" factor in this type of analysis (Q 16:27).

Shortly after this litigation, the IRS began to relax its stance in these regards. This new view was manifested in a 1983 general counsel memorandum, in which the lawyers for the IRS opined that it is possible for a charitable organization to participate as a general partner in a limited partnership without jeopardizing its tax exemption. The IRS lawyers advised that two aspects of this matter should be reviewed: whether (1) the participation may be in conflict with the goals and purposes of the charitable organization and (2) the terms of the partnership agreement contain provisions that insulate the charitable organization from certain of the obligations imposed on a general partner. In this instance, the limited partnership (another low-income housing venture) was found to further the organization's charitable purposes and several specific provisions of the partnership agreement were deemed to provide the requisite insulation for the charitable organization/general partner. Thus, the organization was permitted to serve as the partnership's general partner and simultaneously retain its tax exemption.

This development paved the way for the contemporary set of rules pertaining to public charities as general partners in limited partnerships.

OBSERVATION: The official date marking the demise of the per se rule seems to be November 21, 1991, when the IRS office of general counsel wrote that the IRS "no longer contends that participation as a general partner in a partnership is *per se* inconsistent with [tax] exemption."

Q 16:19   When can a tax-exempt organization be involved in a limited partnership as a general partner and still be tax-exempt?

The current position of the IRS as to whether a charitable organization will have its tax-exempt status revoked (or recognition denied) if it functions as a general partner in a limited partnership is the subject of a three-part test.

Under this test, the IRS first looks to determine whether the charitable organization/general partner is serving a charitable purpose by means of participation in the partnership. If involvement in the partnership is serving a charitable purpose, the IRS applies the rest of the test. Should the partnership fail to adhere to the charitability standard, however, the charitable organization/general partner will be deprived of or be denied tax-exempt status.

The first element of this test is an aspect of the fundamental *operational test* that every exempt charity must meet. This test is an evaluation of the operations of the organization. In general, for tax purposes, the activities of a partnership are often considered to be the activities of the partners. This aggregate approach is applied for purposes of the operational test. Consequently, when a charitable organization is advancing charitable ends by means of a partnership (such as the construction and operation of a medical office building on the grounds of a hospital, the purchase and operation of a CAT scanner at a hospital, or low-income housing projects), it continues to satisfy the operational test and thus be exempt.

The rest of this test is designed to ascertain whether the charity's role as general partner inhibits the advancement of its charitable purposes. Here the IRS looks to means by which the organization may, under the particular facts and circumstances, be insulated from the day-to-day responsibilities as general partner and whether the limited partners are receiving an undue economic benefit from the partnership. It is the view of the IRS that there is an inherent tension between the ability of a charitable organization to function exclusively in furtherance of its exempt functions and the obligation of a general partner to operate the partnership for the benefit of the limited partners. This tension is the same perceived phenomenon that the IRS, when it deployed the per se rule, chose to characterize as a "conflict of interest" (Q 16:17).

An application of this test is reflected in a private letter ruling made public in 1985, which involved a charitable organization that became a general partner in a real estate limited partnership that leased all of the space in the property to the organization and a related charitable organization. The IRS applied the first part of the test and found that the partnership was serving charitable ends because both of the tenants of the partnership were charitable organizations.

TIP: The IRS general counsel memorandum underlying this private letter ruling noted that if the lessee organization that was not the general partner had been an exempt organization other than a charitable one, the charity/general partner would have forfeited its tax exemption.

Upon application of the rest of the test, the IRS found that the charitable organization/general partner was adequately insulated from the day-to-day management responsibilities of the partnership and that the limited partners' economic return was reasonable.

Q 16:20 Are there any other aspects of this matter?

Yes. There seem to be other requirements that are added to the three-part test from time to time. For example, in one instance the IRS emphasized the facts that the charitable organization was "governed by an independent board of directors" composed of church and community leaders, and that it did not have any other relationship with any of the commercial companies involved in the project. The IRS added that there was not any information which indicated that the organization was controlled by or "otherwise unduly influenced" by the limited partners or any company involved in the development or management of the project.

In recent years, nearly all of the federal tax law in this setting has developed as the result of innovative financing techniques, including partnerships, by or for the benefit of hospitals and other health care organizations, institutions, and systems. Among the legitimate purposes for involvement of a health care provider in a partnership recognized by the IRS are the raising of needed capital, the bringing of new services or a new provider to a community, the sharing of a risk inherent in a new activity, and/or the pooling of diverse areas of expertise.

NOTE: In its most "official" pronouncement on these points, the IRS developed a fact situation in which a hospital became involved in a joint venture with a for-profit entity because the hospital concluded "that it could better serve its community if it obtained additional funding."

The IRS, in evaluating these situations, looks to see "what the hospital gets in return for the benefit conferred on the physician-investors." One of the curious aspects of this evolution of the rules is the apparent abandonment of the second prong of the three-part test (concerning insulation of the charity/general partner: it is skimmed over in the most important pronouncements on the point by IRS lawyers and is never mentioned in the formal summary by the IRS of this area of the law.

One other point: it has never been clear as to why the IRS formulated the per se test in the first instance, inasmuch as it has always been understood that public charities can be general partners in limited partnerships—this is in the Internal

Revenue Code, in two places. One provision speaks of "a partnership of which an [exempt] organization is a member." Another references "a partnership which has both a tax-exempt entity and a person who is not a tax-exempt entity as partners." These pronouncements from Congress would be wholly superfluous in the case of public charities if their mere participation as a general partner in a limited partnership would deprive them of their exempt status.

Q 16:21   How do the unrelated business income rules apply in the partnership context?

Normally, the unrelated business income rules become applicable to a tax-exempt organization because of a business activity conducted directly by that organization. These rules, however, can also become activated when an unrelated business is conducted in a partnership of which an exempt organization is a member.

The rule applied in this context is a *look-through rule*: if a business regularly carried on by a partnership, of which a tax-exempt organization is a member, is an unrelated business with respect to the exempt organization, in computing its unrelated business taxable income the organization must include its share (whether or not actually distributed) of the gross income of the partnership from the unrelated business. This rule applies irrespective of whether the tax-exempt organization is a general or limited partner.

TAX-EXEMPT ORGANIZATIONS AND JOINT VENTURES

Q 16:22   Can a tax-exempt organization be involved in a joint venture?

There is no question that a tax-exempt organization can be involved in a joint venture. The principal tax law issues become—just as in the case of involvement in partnerships (Q 16:11)—whether involvement in the joint venture jeopardizes the entity's exempt status and/or causes it to receive unrelated business income. To date, nearly all of the law on the point concerns public charities in joint ventures.

There are two types of these involvements. One occurs where the public charity *intends* to be in a joint venture. The other occurs where the joint venture arrangement is imposed on the parties as a matter of law.

Q 16:23   Why would a public charity want to participate in a joint venture?

The basic reason that a public charity (or other type of tax-exempt organization) wants to participate in a joint venture is to carry out a single project or program, using the efforts, money, and/or expertise of one or more other parties. It is a resource-gathering, resource-sharing operation. Often the other party or parties are not exempt organizations.

Q 16:24 **What does a public charity in a joint venture have to do to acquire or retain tax-exempt status?**

The basic rule is that a public charity (or other type of exempt organization) may enter into a joint venture with a for-profit organization (or other entity), without adversely affecting the charity's tax-exempt status, as long as doing so furthers exempt purposes and the joint venture agreement does not prevent it from acting exclusively to further those purposes. A joint venture does not present the private inurement or private benefit problems that are associated with participation by exempt organizations in limited partnerships, because there are no limited partners receiving economic benefits (Q 16:3). In contrast, an involvement in a joint venture by a tax-exempt organization would lead to loss or denial of tax exemption if the primary purpose of the exempt organization is to participate in the venture and if the function of the venture is unrelated to the exempt purposes of the tax-exempt organization.

An example of an involvement in a joint venture that does not adversely affect a public charity's exempt status is a charitable organization participating in a venture with a for-profit entity to own and operate an ambulatory surgical center. Another is a charitable organization in a venture with a for-profit entity for the purpose of organizing and operating a free-standing alcoholism/substance abuse treatment center. Still another involves a charitable hospital that participates with a for-profit organization in a venture for the purpose of providing magnetic resonance imaging services in an underserved community.

A tax-exempt organization may enter into a joint venture with another tax-exempt organization, in furtherance of the exempt purposes of both of them.

As will be discussed (Q 16:27), a joint venture of this nature may be structured by use of a limited liability company.

Q 16:25 **How can a tax-exempt organization be considered involved in joint venture against its will?**

The joint venture form is usually imposed on a relationship with one or more other parties involving a tax-exempt organization where the revenue received by the exempt organization from the relationship is to be taxed. This can happen because of the sweep of the definition of the term *joint venture* (Q 16:6).

A classic example of this comes from the practice of crop-share leasing, where the exempt organization wants the relationship to be that of landlord–tenant and the IRS wants it to be cast as a joint venture. (The IRS is not prevailing in these cases.)

This dichotomy was illustrated in a case involving a charitable organization and its tenant-farmer. The specific question before the court was whether the rent, equaling 50 percent of the crops and produce grown on the farm, constituted rent that was excludable as unrelated business income. The court looked to state law to ascertain the meaning to be given the term *rent*. It observed that the written contracts at issue contained provisions usually found in leases, the tenant furnished all of the machinery and labor in the production of crops, and the tenant generally made decisions with a farm manager as to the day-to-day operations of the farm. The court concluded that the contracts as a whole clearly reflected the intention of the parties to create a landlord–tenant relationship, rather than a joint venture.

The IRS unsuccessfully contended that the charitable organization, by furnishing the seed and one half the cost of fertilizer, weed spray, and combining, had engaged in farming as a joint venturer. The court observed that these types of arrangements were not uncommon in share-crop leases and noted that the furnishing of these items ordinarily increased the crop yield and the net return of both the landlord and tenant substantially more than the amount invested by each for the items. The court also analyzed the effect on the landlord–tenant relationship of the hiring by the charity of a farm manager for the supervision of the tenant-farmer. The farm manager advised the tenant on topics such as crops, seed, weed spray, and fertilizer; decisions were made by mutual agreement of the tenant and the manager. The court concluded that the role of the farm manager did not mitigate against the overall conclusion that the arrangement was that of landlord and tenant.

In another illustration of this point, often a tax-exempt organization is endeavoring to characterize an item of income as a royalty, which is not taxable, while the IRS is asserting that the exempt organization and other parties are actively participating in a joint venture, so that the income is taxable.

On occasion, the IRS will invoke the joint venture rationale for the purpose of revoking or denying a tax exemption. For example, it is the view of the IRS that a tax-exempt hospital endangers its tax exemption, because of private inurement, as a result of its involvement in a joint venture with members of its medical staff, where the hospital has sold to the joint venture the net revenue stream of a hospital department for a stated period of time. In this and similar situations, the application of the private inurement doctrine is triggered by the inherent structure of the joint venture (private inurement per se), irrespective of the reasonableness of the compensation.

Q 16:26 How do the unrelated business income rules apply in the joint venture context?

The unrelated business income rules apply in the joint venture context in the same way they do in the partnership setting (Q 16:21). That is, the *look-through rule* applies, so if there is unrelated business income generated by the joint venture, the exempt organization's share of it must be taken into account by the exempt organization in ascertaining its taxable income for the year.

This is why, when the IRS sees an exempt organization characterizing income as excludable income (particularly as a royalty) and simultaneously actively participating in the undertaking that gives rise to the income, the IRS elects to impose a joint venture form on the arrangement, so as to cause the income to be taxable by application of the look-through rule (Q 16:6).

Q 16:27 How do these rules apply when the joint venture uses a limited liability company?

As noted (Q 16:24), a joint venture involving an exempt organization can be structured using the vehicle of the limited liability company. Essentially, the use of a limited liability company does not change the tax outcome, inasmuch as this type of company is treated as a partnership for tax purposes (Q 16:10).

In 1998, the IRS issued a revenue ruling concerning the tax law ramifications of the whole-hospital joint venture. The ruling sketches two situations in which involvement by a hospital in one of these ventures does or does not jeopardize the hospital's tax-exempt status. The implications of this ruling extend, however, far beyond the realm of health care providers.

This ruling is so significant that it deserves to be analyzed in some depth. First, here are the two fact situations:

Fact Situation 1

The first of these situations concerns a nonprofit corporation that owns and operates an acute care charitable hospital (H1), which has concluded that it could better serve its community if it obtained additional funding. A for-profit corporation (FP1) that owns and operates a number of hospitals is interested in providing financing for the hospital if it can earn a reasonable rate of return. These two entities form a limited liability company (LLC1).

H1 contributes all of its operating assets, including the hospital, to LLC1. FP1 also contributes assets to LLC1. In return, H1 and FP1 receive ownership interests in LLC1 proportional and equal in value to their respective contributions.

LLC1's governing instruments provide that it is to be managed by a governing board consisting of three individuals selected by H1 and two individuals selected by FP1. H1 intends to appoint community leaders who have experience with hospital matters but who are not on the hospital staff and do not otherwise engage in business transactions with the hospital. These documents also provide that they may be amended only by the approval of both owners and that a majority of three board members must approve certain major decisions relating to the operation of LLC1 (such as the budget, distributions of earnings, and selection of key executives).

These governing documents further require that any LLC1-owned hospital be operated in a manner that advances charitable purposes by promoting health for a broad cross section of its community. They state that the board members' duty to adhere to this requirement overrides any obligation they may have to operate LLC1 for the financial benefit of its owners. Thus, the community benefit standard takes precedence over the consequences of maximizing profitability.

The governing documents provide that all returns of capital and distributions of earnings made to the owners of LLC1 must be proportional to their ownership interests in the venture. The terms of these instruments are legal, binding, and enforceable under state law.

LLC1 enters into an agreement with a management company (MC1) for the purpose of providing day-to-day management services to LLC1. MC1 is not related to H1 or FP1. This contract is for a five-year term and is renewable for additional five-year periods by mutual consent. MC1 will be paid a management fee based on the gross revenues of LLC1. The terms and conditions of the contract are reasonable and comparable to those that other management firms receive for comparable services for similarly situated hospitals. LLC1 may terminate this agreement for cause.

None of the directors, officers, or key employees of H1 who were involved in the decision to form LLC1 were promised employment or any other inducement by FP1 or LLC1 and their related entities if the transaction were approved. None of these individuals has any interest, directly or indirectly, in FP1 or any of its related entities.

H1 intends to use any distributions it receives from LLC1 to fund grants to support activities that promote the health of H1's community and to help the indigent obtain health care. Substantially all of H1's grant-making will be funded by distributions from LLC1. H1's projected grant-making program and its participation as an owner of LLC1 will constitute H1's only activities.

Fact Situation 2

The second of these situations concerns a nonprofit corporation that owns and operates an acute care charitable hospital (H2), which has concluded that it could better serve its community if it obtained additional funding. A for-profit corporation (FP2) that owns and operates a number of hospitals and provides management services to several other hospitals is interested in providing financing for the hospital if it can earn a reasonable rate of return. These two entities form a limited liability company (LLC2).

H2 contributes all of its operating assets, including the hospital, to LLC2. FP2 also contributes assets to LLC2. In return, H2 and FP2 receive ownership interests in LLC2 proportional and equal in value to their respective contributions.

LLC2's governing instruments provide that it is to be managed by a governing board consisting of three individuals selected by H2 and three individuals selected by FP2. H2 intends to appoint community leaders who have experience with hospital matters but who are not on the hospital staff and do not otherwise engage in business transactions with the hospital. These documents also provide that they may be amended only by the approval of both owners and that a majority of board members must approve certain major decisions relating to the operation of LLC2 (such as the budget, distributions of earnings, and selection of key executives).

These governing documents further provide that LLC's purpose is to construct, develop, own, manage, operate, and take other action in connection with operating the health care facilities it owns and to engage in other health care–related activities. The documents also provide that all returns of capital and distributions of earnings made to LLC2's owners shall be proportional to their ownership interests in LLC2.

LLC2 enters into an agreement with a management company (MC2) for the purpose of providing day-to-day management services to LLC2. MC2 is a wholly owned subsidiary of FP2. This contract is for a five-year term and is renewable for additional five-year periods at the discretion of MC2. MC2 will be paid a management fee based on the gross revenues of LLC2. The terms and conditions of the contract, other than its renewal terms, are reasonable and comparable to those that other management firms receive for comparable services for similarly situated hospitals. LLC2 may terminate this agreement only for cause.

As part of the agreement to form LLC2, H2 agrees to approve the selection of two individuals to serve as MC2's chief executive officer and chief financial officer. These individuals have previously worked for FP2 in hospital management and have business expertise. They will work with MC2 to oversee the day-to-day management of LLC2. Their compensation will be comparable to that which like executives are paid at similarly situated hospitals.

H2 intends to use any distributions it receives from LLC2 to fund grants to support activities that promote the health of H2's community and to help the indigent obtain health care. Substantially all of H2's grant-making will be funded by distributions from LLC2. H2's projected grant-making program and its participation as an owner of LLC2 will constitute H2's only activities.

Here are two rules that are central to the findings in the ruling:

1. A charitable organization may enter into a management contract with a private party, according that party authority to conduct activities on behalf of the organization and direct use of the organization's assets, as long as (1) the charity retains ultimate authority over the assets and activities being managed and (2) the terms and conditions of the contract (including compensation and the term) are reasonable.

2. If a private party is allowed to control or use the nonprofit organization's activities or assets for the benefit of the private party, and the benefit is not merely incidental, the organization will not qualify for tax exemption.

In application of these principles, H1's tax exemption was preserved. H1's exempt functions consist of the health care services it will provide through LLC1 and its grant-making activities to be funded with income distributed by LLC1. H1's capital interest in LLC1 is equal in value to the assets it contributed to the venture. The returns from LLC1 to its owners will be proportional to their investments. The governing instruments of LLC1 clearly reflect exempt functions and purposes. The appointees of H1 will control the board of LLC1. The renewal feature of the contract is favorable to H1.

Under these facts, H1 can ensure that the assets it owns, and the activities it conducts, through LLC1 are used primarily to further exempt purposes. Thus, H1 can ensure that the benefit to FP1 and other private parties, such as MC1, will be incidental to the accomplishment of charitable ends.

It was stipulated that the terms and conditions of the management contract are reasonable and that the grants by H1 are intended to support education and research and assist the indigent.

The IRS acknowledged that when H2 and FP2 form LLC2, and H2 contributes its assets to LLC2, H2 will—like H1—be engaged in activities that consist of the health care services to be provided through LLC2 and the grant-making activities it conducts using income distributed by LLC2. However, the IRS said that H2 will fail the primary purpose test because there is no binding obligation in LLC2's governing instruments for it to serve charitable purposes or otherwise benefit the community. Thus, LLC2 has the ability to deny care to segments of the community, such as the indigent.

The control element is significant in the second set of facts. H2 will share control of LLC2 with FP2. This means that H2 cannot initiate programs within LLC2 to serve new health needs within the community without the consent of at least one board member appointed by FP2. Inasmuch as FP2 is a for-profit entity, the IRS stated that it "will not necessarily give priority to the health needs of the community over the consequences for [FP2's] profits."

MC2 will have "broad discretion" over LLC2's activities and assets that may not always be under the supervision of LLC2's board. For example, MC2 can enter into all but "unusually large" contracts without board approval. Also, MC2 can unilaterally renew the management agreement.

The consequence of all of this for H2 is that FP2 will be receiving benefits resulting from the conduct of LLC2 that are private and not incidental. The operational test is failed by H2 when it participates in the formation of LLC2, contributes its operating assets to H2, and then serves as an owner of LLC2.

The fundamental flaw of the ruling lies in the starkness of the two extremes in the fact situation: a "pure" fact case and an "ugly" fact case. Exempt organizations are left, for the moment anyway, to divine what the law is as applied to the vast majority of "real-life" situations that are in the middle.

There are many factors taken into account in this ruling—and the IRS subsequently said that others may be considered. What mix of factors will permit retention of exemption and what alchemy will result in its loss? The ruling seems to make it clear that the charitable-purposes language must be in the governing instruments of the joint venture entity (here, a limited liability company). It may be essential that the charitable participant at least share control over the joint venture. But, for example, how much discretion can a management company have? (Surely not every decision must be approved by the joint venture's governing board.) Are the renewal terms in the contract between LLC2 and MC2 automatically fatal to H2's exemption? How critical is it that those who are employed by LLC2 have close ties to FP2?

The revenue ruling does not carry an effective date. Presumably, it can be applied retroactively with respect to existing arrangements.

Q 16:28   Have the courts agreed with this IRS ruling?

So far, yes. Two federal district courts and one federal court of appeals have basically accepted the agency's analysis. In one instance, a hospital lost its tax-exempt status because it, by reason of its involvement in the joint venture, ceded too much of its authority to the for-profit co-venturer. In the other case, the hospital was allowed to retain its exemption because the facts demonstrated that the institution retained the requisite control notwithstanding its participation in a venture.

Q 16:29   Does this ruling have any implications outside the health care setting?

This ruling has major implications outside the health care context. It should be noted, for example, that the term *joint venture* is not used in the revenue ruling. An exempt organization can, as noted (Q 16:6), find itself in a joint venture without realizing it; there does not have to be a formal document evidencing a joint venture or general partnership (essentially the same thing for these purposes).

What may seem, to an exempt organization, to be a management agreement or a lease may in fact—by operation of law—be the basis for a finding of a joint venture. Once that label is placed on the arrangement, the focus quickly shifts to the matter of *control*. Does the exempt organization maintain *ultimate authority* over its assets and activities? That can be the basis for an opinion letter from a lawyer. Are the terms and conditions of the arrangement *reasonable*? That can be the basis for an opinion letter from a business consultant, such as an accounting firm. An exempt organization in this position should endeavor to be certain that some private party does not have "broad discretion," and that its board retains formal control, over the organization's assets and activities.

The intermediate sanctions rules are very much a part of the analysis. With respect to a charitable organization, the for-profit venturer, the joint venture itself, and/or the management company can be *disqualified persons* (Q 7:24). The compensation arrangement for the management company, based on the gross revenues of the limited liability company, may be a *revenue-sharing arrangement* (Q 7:14).

One aspect of this revenue ruling is certain: there will be many interpretations and expansions of it for the foreseeable future.

Q 16:30 How do these rules apply when the charitable organization's involvement in a joint venture is less than the "whole-entity" approach?

It is the view of the IRS that the principles involved in the jurisprudence concerning whole-entity joint ventures (Q 16:27–Q 16:29) apply fully when an exempt organization is involved in an *ancillary joint venture*. Thus, the element of control and application of the private benefit doctrine is seen by the agency as likewise applicable in this context. A difference, however, is that, in an instance of an ancillary joint venture, an outcome may be unrelated business income taxation rather than extinguishment of tax exemption.

In one instance, reflected in a revenue ruling issued by the agency in 2004, a tax-exempt university entered into a joint venture (a limited liability company) with a for-profit company that specialized in the conduct of interactive video training programs. The sole purpose of the venture was to offer teacher-training seminars at locations off the university's campus using interactive video technology. The university and the for-profit company each held a 50 percent interest in the venture, which was proportionate to the value of their respective capital contributions. All returns of capital, allocations, and distributions were to be made in proportion to the members' respective ownership interests. The company was managed by a governing board composed of three directors selected by the university and three selected by the company. The university retained the exclusive right to approve the curriculum, training materials, and instructors, and to determine the standards for successful completion of the seminars. The company had the exclusive right to select the locations where participants could receive a video link to the seminars and to approve other personnel (such as camera operators).

Under these facts, the IRS concluded that the university retained control over the venture. This guidance is marred, however, because the agency concluded that (1) the business of the venture was related to the exercise of the university's exempt functions and (2) the activities the university conducted through the limited liability company are merely an insubstantial part of its total activities. The private benefit doctrine does not apply where the inappropriate benefit conferred is incidental (Chapter 6).

Q 16:31   Has a court agreed with this ruling?

The matter of the tax consequences of an exempt organization in an ancillary joint venture has not been considered by a court. It would be interesting to have that happen because it is not clear, despite this ruling, what the outcome is in a situation such as this, where the business of the venture is unrelated to the public charity's exempt purposes and/or its involvement is more than insubstantial. The IRS seemed to indicate that, if the public charity loses control over its resources in an ancillary joint venture, the business of the venture would be transformed from a related one to an unrelated one—a novel theory (Chapter 14). Also, even if the activities in the ancillary venture are related, if the public charity cedes authority over the resources to the for-profit venturer and the exempt organization's participation in the venture is more than incidental, it would seem that the organization's tax exemption would be jeopardized, by application of the private inurement or private benefit doctrine (Chapter 6).

INFORMATION REPORTING

Q 16:32   How does an exempt organization know what income and the like to report from a partnership?

A partnership generally must furnish to each partner a statement reflecting the information about the partnership required to be shown on the partner's tax return or information return. The statement must set forth the partner's distributive share of the partnership's income, gain, loss, deduction, or credit required to be shown on the partner's return, along with any additional information as provided by IRS forms or instructions that may be required to apply particular provisions of the federal tax law to the partner with respect to items related to the partnership.

The instructions accompanying the statement for partners (Schedule K-1, Form 1065) require the partnership to state whether the partner is a tax-exempt organization. Moreover, the partnership must attach a statement furnishing any other information needed by the partner to file its return that is not shown elsewhere on the schedule.

In the case of a partnership regularly carrying on a business, the partnership must furnish to the partners the information necessary to enable each tax-exempt partner to compute its distributive share of partnership income or gain from the business.

Partnerships of tax-exempt organizations, including those consisting wholly of exempt organizations, must annually file the federal information returns required of partnerships.

CHAPTER 17

Competition and Commerciality

One of the most troublesome aspects of the operations of nonprofit organizations today, from the standpoint of the law, is the extent to which these activities compete with, or are perceived as competing with, the undertakings of for-profit organizations. Commercial activities by nonprofit organizations are cast as forms of unfair competition with for-profit organizations. In our complex society, competition of this type is inevitable. But this practice often tarnishes the view of nonprofit organizations in the eyes of many, including those who formulate federal tax law and policy.

The concepts of competition and commerciality in the legal context are confusing. There is very little statutory law on the point; likewise, there is almost nothing about the subject in the tax regulations. What law there is—and it is growing—is mostly found in court opinions and IRS private letter rulings.

Here are the questions most frequently asked about this matter of competition and commerciality—and the answers to them.

COMPETITION

Q 17:1 Just what is this matter of nonprofit/for-profit competition all about?

Like any civil society, the United States has three basic sectors: a for-profit, commercial, business sector; a nonprofit sector; and a governmental sector. A healthy democratic society requires the presence of these three sectors, and that each of them functions to the fullest extent within suitable bounds. Personal freedoms are enhanced and maintained to the extent of the vibrancy of these sectors.

By definition and necessity, this tripartite societal structure produces friction: the sectors clash. There is ongoing struggle over what the "suitable boundaries" of the sectors are. The resulting fights are over what functions belong in which sector. A most cursory of glances at what is occurring with respect to the U.S. health care delivery system illustrates the extent to which this battle can be waged.

For the most part, these are policy determinations to be resolved by lawmakers (those in all three branches of government). That is, there is very little in the way of formal legal constraints in this setting, other than those against transgressing the bounds of federal public policy, the dictates of constitutional law principles, or perhaps state law rules. Although this is the way the system is supposed to work, these struggles generate problems for nonprofit organizations.

It is a general precept that nonprofit organizations are supposed to remain "in their place." In many respects, the U.S. economic system is still based on principles of capitalism. This means that for-profit organizations are generally treated more favorably, as to this matter of clashes between the sectors, than nonprofit organizations. That is, it is generally thought to be inappropriate for nonprofit organizations to engage in activities that are engaged in by for-profit organizations. There is a preference here: if for-profits do it, nonprofits should not do it.

Conceptually, according to this mode of thinking, nonprofit organizations are not supposed to undertake activities that are being performed by for-profit organizations. Likewise, if for-profit organizations enter a field previously unoccupied by them but traditionally the province of nonprofit organizations, the nonprofits are expected to abandon the field. In general, then, nonprofit entities—and this is particularly the case with charitable organizations—are often expected to engage only in functions conceded to them by the for-profit sector.

Q 17:2   What is the problem with nonprofit/for-profit competition?

It is basically one of economics. Almost always, the nonprofit organization is tax-exempt. This means that taxes are not a part of the entity's costs of *doing business*. Assuming all other expenses are the same as that of the for-profit counterpart, the tax-exempt nonprofit entity can engage in the competitive activity with a lower cost of operations. To acquire customers and increase market share, a nonprofit organization can pass the decreased cost of operation along to customers in the form of lower prices. What can result is a nonprofit organization and a for-profit organization performing the same activity for public consumption (sale of a good or performance of a service), with the nonprofit entity charging a lower price.

Usually the for-profit critics of competition involving nonprofit organizations charge *unfair* competition. When that word is used, the complainants are asserting that the pricing policies of nonprofit organizations are undercutting the sales of items by for-profit organizations. This use of exempt status to lower prices in competing with for-profits is at the heart of the complaints in this context about (unfair) competition.

A secondary complaint is based on the thought that a consumer, given the choice to purchase a good or service from a nonprofit entity or a for-profit entity, will select the former. This view holds that the consumer is more comfortable purchasing an item from a nonprofit organization; there seems to be a greater element of trust. This phenomenon—the grounds for assertions that nonprofit organizations ought not to be undertaking certain endeavors *at all*—is known as the *halo effect*.

Q 17:3 How common is this form of competition?

It is rather common, and the practice is growing. There are essentially two manifestations of competition between nonprofit and for-profit entities.

One arises where the very essence of what the nonprofit organization does is competitive with for-profit organizations. A clear example of this is, as noted, found in the health care field, where some hospitals and other forms of health care providers are nonprofit and some are for-profit (proprietary entities). Predictably, this is generating much debate as to whether nonprofit hospitals should remain tax-exempt at all or be exempt to a much more limited extent. Other areas in which there are counterparts in both sectors are schools, publishing entities, various types of consulting groups, and financial institutions.

NOTE: An example of this issue is the tax-exempt credit union. There is an ongoing battle as to whether such entities should remain exempt, in view of the fact that many of their operations are competitive with for-profit financial institutions. These days, Congress is being lobbied hard on the subject, with the National Credit Union Administration arguing for the exemption and the American Bankers Association contending for its repeal. This dispute was studied by the Congressional Research Service, which observed that "many believe that an economically neutral tax system requires that financial institutions engaged in similar activities should have the same tax treatment."

COMMENT: Another comparable debate has, so far, led to an opposite conclusion. This concerns tax exemption for fraternal beneficiary associations. A report from the Department of the Treasury concluded that the insurance products offered by these organizations are essentially the same as those provided by commercial insurers; it observed that the large fraternal beneficiary societies "conduct their insurance operations in a manner similar to commercial insurers." The report dismissed this commerciality, however, stating that these societies "do not use their exemption to compete unfairly with commercial insurers in terms of price or to operate inefficiently."

Most of the criticism in this area falls, however, in the realm of the other manifestation of competition. This is where the nonprofit organization is substantially engaging in tax-exempt (usually noncompetitive) activities, but is selectively engaging in one or more competitive functions. One of the most controversial contemporary illustrations of this point—which is will be discussed in another setting (Q 17:5)—is the matter of travel tours. The travel industry is incensed because of the competitive tours being packaged and sold by exempt entities, such as universities, colleges, alumni associations, and similar organizations, as educational experiences. Other examples are discussed later (Q 17:5).

Q 17:4   **Has Congress responded to these complaints about unfair competition?**

Yes. The principal response has been formulation of the unrelated business income rules (Chapter 14). Congress enacted these rules over 50 years ago. A major component of the Revenue Act of 1950, the rules were devised specifically to eliminate unfair competition between nonprofit and for-profit organizations.

This was done, or thought to be done, by placing the unrelated business activities of exempt organizations on the same tax basis as those conducted by for-profit organizations, where the two are in competition. The essence of this body of law is to separate the income of a tax-exempt organization into two categories: (1) income from related business and (2) income from unrelated business. The rationale is that by taxing the income from unrelated business, the pricing differential that can lead to unfair competition is removed. This is known as *leveling the playing field*.

COMMENT: One wag, sympathetic with the nonprofit sector in this regard, once said that the for-profits are not interested in seeing the playing field leveled. Rather, it was noted, the for-profits do not want the nonprofits to even be *on* the field.

The existence or nonexistence of competition is not, however, a statutory requirement for there to be unrelated business. Nonetheless, some courts place considerable emphasis on the factor of competition when assessing whether an undertaking is an unrelated business. This can also be the case when eligibility for tax-exempt status is under consideration.

NOTE: Some courts have rejected the thought that the unrelated business rules were enacted purely to eliminate this form of competition. Thus, one court wrote that "while the equalization of competition between taxable and tax-exempt entities was a major goal of the unrelated business income tax, it was by no means the statute's sole objective." Another court observed that "although Congress enacted the . . . unrelated business income rules to eliminate a perceived form of unfair competition, that aim existed as a corollary to the larger goals of producing revenue and achieving equity in the tax system."

There has also been some legislative activity in connection with commercial undertakings. The principal illustration of this approach was the decision by Congress in 1986 to eliminate the tax exemption for most prepaid health care plans, such as those offered by Blue Cross and Blue Shield organizations (Q 17:13). Moreover, Congress allowed the tax-exempt status of prepaid group legal plans to expire in 1992.

Q 17:5 What are some of the contemporary illustrations of issues in this area of competition?

There are many of them. Most arise in the health care delivery field. As noted (Q 17:3), there is competition between nonprofit and for-profit hospitals, as well as other health care entities such as health maintenance organizations, homes for the aged, and rehabilitation facilities. More often, however, rather than overall operations, there are specific activities of a health care provider that are regarded as competitive.

An example is the sale of pharmaceuticals. If a nonprofit hospital sells pharmaceuticals to its patients, that is considered a related (nontaxable) business, even though it may be an activity competitive with for-profit pharmacies. Yet, where a nonprofit hospital sells pharmaceuticals to private patients of physicians who have offices in a medical building owned by the hospital, or sells them to members of the general public, the activity is generally regarded as an unrelated (taxable) business. These latter types of sales are competitive with commercial pharmacies.

Another example is diagnostic laboratory testing services provided by nonprofit hospitals to physicians in their private practice. The general rule is that services of this nature constitute unrelated business activities where they are otherwise available in the community. These services are competitive with commercial laboratories that test specimens from private office patients of the hospitals' staff physicians. However, where there are unique circumstances, such as situations in which other laboratories are not available within a reasonable distance from the area served by the hospital or are inadequate to conduct tests needed by nonpatients of the hospital, the laboratory testing services are related businesses.

Another illustration of this type of competitiveness is the operation of health clubs and fitness centers by nonprofit hospitals. Of course, there are commercial entities of this nature. Where the fees for use of these facilities are sufficiently high to restrict their use to limited segments of the community, the operations are nonexempt ones or unrelated businesses, as being competitive with commercial health clubs. In contrast, if a health club or similar facility provides community-wide benefits or advances education in a substantial manner, the activity is a related business.

There are commercial enterprises that maintain physical rehabilitation programs. Thus, a nonprofit organization doing the same thing may not be tax-exempt or may be operating an unrelated business. For example, in the context of lifestyle rehabilitation programs, the IRS ruled that the operation of a miniature golf course by a nonprofit organization, the purpose of which was the advancement of the welfare of young people, was an unrelated business because the course was operated commercially, that is, in a competitive manner. Yet the IRS also ruled that a nonprofit organization, operating to improve the life of abused and otherwise disadvantaged children by means of the sport of golf, did not conduct an unrelated activity in the operation of a golf course inasmuch as the opportunity to socialize and master skills through the playing of golf was found to be "essential to the building of self-esteem and the ultimate rehabilitation of the young people" by means of the organization's programs.

The higher education setting also provides examples of competition between nonprofit and for-profit organizations. As an illustration, the commercial travel industry is, of course, a provider of tours. Yet universities, colleges, and alumni and alumnae associations also offer tours, usually as an educational experience. The IRS endeavors to differentiate between tours that are related activities and those that are unrelated (competitive) because they are primarily social, recreational, or other forms of vacation opportunities.

Schools, colleges, and universities (and other types of nonprofit organizations) frequently receive payments from corporations. These institutions wish to treat these corporate sponsorships as contributions. They also want, however, to recognize these sponsors as donors. The difficulty is that when they say something commendatory about the sponsor, particularly as to the quality or pricing of its goods or services, the purported recognition may in fact be advertising. Generally, advertising by a nonprofit, tax-exempt organization is considered an exploitation of exempt resources. The provision of advertising services is generally a commercial, competitive activity.

Other types of nonprofit organizations provide further illustrations of this point. For example, the sale of items to the public by a nonprofit museum from its gift shop is generally a related business on the grounds that the items sold generate interest in the museum's collection and promote visitation to it. However, that rationale can break down when items are sold nationally or even internationally by catalog or when the items that are sold are used in a utilitarian manner (such as furniture). Trade associations often sell items to members that they use in their trade (such as tools and manuals). These and other forms of sales activity by nonprofit organizations are often seen as enterprises that are competitive with for-profit organizations.

Q 17:6 Is the law successful in eliminating forms of this type of competition?

Sometimes, but certainly not entirely. The IRS does the best it can in enforcing the law in this area. But the agency has three basic problems in this regard. First, the law is often very vague. Second, on many occasions when the IRS makes a determination that an activity is a nonexempt function or an unrelated business, the nonprofit organizations involved are able to persuade Congress to create statutory law overriding the position of the IRS. This, in turn, leads to an expansion of the Internal Revenue Code and the need for more interpretation. Third, the IRS today lacks the funds and personnel to effectively police the competitive and commercial activities of nonprofit organizations.

An often-underappreciated phenomenon is that, in many respects, the law is changing. What may have been perceived as an unrelated activity in 1950 is considered a related activity decades later. This means that when the for-profit community alleges unfair competition, it is often related business activities, not unrelated ones, that are in dispute.

For example, universities, colleges, and schools can operate bookstores that sell many items that are also sold in commercial establishments. The same can be said for hospitals that maintain gift shops and food service operations. Some of the items are sold clearly in advancement of exempt purposes, such as the books a college sells that are required in its courses. A university bookstore or hospital gift shop, however, can sell clothing, sundry items, flowers, and the like without having those activities treated as unrelated businesses. Nonetheless, these activities are in competition with for-profit establishments, often small businesses.

Some of this sales activity is sheltered by the *convenience doctrine*.

EXPLANATION: The *convenience doctrine* is a rule of law that states that a business conducted by a charitable or educational organization for the convenience of its patients or students is not taxable as an unrelated business (Q 14:23). This doctrine is thus of great utility to schools, colleges, universities, and hospitals.

Some of these activities, however, are considered exempt functions. Thus, for example, a college can sell sports clothing, coffee cups, and toilet paper, all bearing the institution's name and logo, and not pay any tax on the net proceeds because the sale of these items is an exempt function, in that it promotes interest in the college among the student body. Likewise, a hospital can sell floral arrangements and other gift items without paying tax on the resulting net income because the sale of these items is an exempt function, in that the health of the patients is promoted by virtue of visits by friends and family bearing gifts. Yet the sale of each of these categories of goods is competitive with for-profit businesses.

COMMENT: The proprietor of a floral shop across the street from a nonprofit hospital's gift shop is not comforted by these rationales, nor is the owner of a computer sales franchise next door to a university bookstore that is selling the same hardware and software items because computer usage is mandated by the university's professors.

A frequently overlooked aspect of this matter of competition between nonprofit and for-profit entities is the conduct of businesses that are regarded as nontaxable undertakings (sometimes even as related activities) because they are done in the name of fundraising. The simple application of the term *fundraising* to an activity, however, does not convert it from a taxable to a nontaxable activity.

Special event fundraising involves many competitive functions: sports tournaments, theater outings, concerts, dances, dinners, auctions, bake sales, car washes, and more. Although these activities are by no means inherently charitable, they usually escape taxation on the ground that they are not regularly carried on.

> **⚠ CAUTION:** Often an organization is of the belief that a fundraising event is not regularly carried on because it is conducted over a few-day period. Yet the organization may spend months preparing for the event. Although the approach has been rejected in the courts to date, the IRS is of the view that *preparatory time* should be taken into account in determining regularity. When this is done, of course, a business that seemingly occupies only a short period of time can be transformed into one occupying a substantial portion of a year—and one that is taxable.

There are some statutory exceptions for fundraising events. Excluded from taxation are sales of items that were donated to the exempt organization (a special rule very helpful to nonprofit thrift shops and organizations that conduct auctions on a regular basis), businesses conducted substantially by volunteers, qualified sponsorship payments, use of premiums, qualifying entertainment activities, certain bingo games, and certain rentals of mailing lists. In some instances, revenue from fundraising activities can be protected from taxation by structuring it as royalty revenue (Q 14:23–Q 14:25).

Consequently, there are many opportunities under current law for nonprofit organizations to compete with for-profit ones, and not pay any income tax on the resulting revenue.

COMMERCIALITY

Q 17:7 How does this matter of competition relate to commerciality?

To date, rather awkwardly. One of the greatest oddities in the law of tax exempt organizations is that there is a two-track system of law operating in this area. There are the unrelated business income rules that, as noted, were fashioned largely in response to the thought that competition between nonprofit, tax-exempt and for-profit entities is unwarranted. There is also a growing body of law standing for the proposition that a nonprofit organization, particularly a charitable one, that operates in a commercial manner cannot qualify for tax-exempt status. This principle of law is known as the *commerciality doctrine*.

The subjects of competition and commerciality by no means fully overlap. The matter of competition is taken into account chiefly in ascertaining whether an activity is a related business or an unrelated business. This determination is based on statutory law. As noted (Q 17:4), it involves a question as to whether a nonprofit entity and a for-profit entity are doing the same thing. These comparisons rarely lead to a decision as to a nonprofit organization's tax exemption.

In contrast, the commerciality doctrine goes to the heart of tax exemption issues. It bypasses the issues concerning unrelated income taxation. It is not based on statutory law but was conjured up by the courts, initially almost inadvertently. The doctrine sometimes takes competition into account but, when it does, only as one of several factors. It tends to focus on the manner in which an organization is operating.

> **NOTE:** To date, the commerciality doctrine has been applied only in the context of public charities. There is no reason, however, that the doctrine could not be extended to the operations of social welfare organizations, trade and business associations, labor entities, and other types of nonprofit organizations.

Q 17:8   What is the commerciality doctrine?

The commerciality doctrine essentially is this: a nonprofit organization is engaged in a non–tax-exempt activity when that activity is engaged in a manner that is considered *commercial*. An activity is a commercial one if it is conducted in the same manner in the world of for-profit organizations.

When a court sees an activity being conducted by a for-profit business and the same activity conducted in the same fashion by a charitable organization, it is often affronted. The court is then stirred by some form of intuitive offense at the thought that a nonprofit organization is doing something that "ought to" be done only in the for-profit sector. Therefore, the court concludes that the nonprofit organization is conducting that activity in a commercial manner. This conclusion then results in a finding that the commercial activity is a nonexempt function, often leading to the decision that the nonprofit organization is not entitled to tax exemption.

> **NOTE:** The essence of the commerciality doctrine having been stated, it must also be said that, to date, it is being unevenly applied.

Q 17:9   Where did the doctrine come from?

It grew out of some loose language in early court opinions. The Supreme Court started it all back in 1924. A case before the Court concerned a tax-exempt religious order that, although operated for religious purposes, also engaged in activities that the government alleged destroyed the order's exemption: investments in securities and real estate, and sales of items such as chocolate and wine. The Court ruled that the order should remain tax-exempt. Nonetheless, it found it necessary to state the government's argument in the case, which was that the order was "operated also for business and *commercial* purposes." The Court rejected this portrayal of the order, writing that there was no "competition" and that while the "transactions yield[ed] some profit [it was] in the circumstances a negligible factor."

This articulation of the government's argument by the Court is burdened with an unnecessary redundancy: Why the use of both words *business* and *commercial?* In any event, the Supreme Court did not enunciate a commerciality doctrine. By simply employing the word *commercial*, however, the Court gave birth to the doctrine.

The doctrine was formalized by the Court in 1945. On that occasion, it was reviewing a case concerning the tax exemption of a chapter of the Better Business Bureau, which was pursuing exempt status as an educational organization. The chapter was found not to qualify for exemption, inasmuch as it was engaging in the nonexempt function of promoting a profitable business community. The Court, in the closest it has come to expressly articulating the commerciality doctrine, wrote that the organization had a "commercial hue" and that its activities were "largely animated by this commercial purpose."

The 1960s saw the commerciality doctrine flourish. This came about because of a number of cases concerning nonprofit publishing organizations. One case, decided in 1961, pertained to a publisher of religious literature that, as the court put it, generated "very substantial" profits. Rejected was the IRS contention that profits alone precluded tax exemption. But then the court added these fateful words: "If, however, defendant [the IRS] means only to suggest that it [profits] is at least some evidence indicative of a *commercial* character we are inclined to agree." In finding the organization not to be tax-exempt, the court declined to apply the unrelated income tax rules. This court obviously thought that the organization's primary activities were unrelated, inasmuch as exemption was revoked, but, inexplicably, the word *commercial*, rather than *unrelated*, was used.

In a 1962 case, another nonprofit publishing organization failed to receive tax exemption because the "totality of [its] activities [was] indicative of a business, and . . . [the organization's] purpose [was] thus a commercial purpose and nonexempt." A 1964 case involving a religious organization that conducted training projects saw rejection of application of the commerciality doctrine, with the court observing that "we regard consistent nonprofitability as evidence of the absence of commercial purposes." In a 1968 case that was overruled, a lower court determined that a publisher of religious materials could not be tax-exempt because it "was clearly engaged primarily in a business activity, and it conducted its operations, although on a small scale, in the same way as any commercial publisher of religious books for profit would have done."

Several other commerciality doctrine cases followed. In 1980 a court said this: "Profits may be realized or other nonexempt purposes may be necessarily advanced incidental to the conduct of the commercial activity, but the existence of such nonexempt purposes does not require denial of exempt status so long as the organization's dominant purpose for conducting the activity is an exempt purpose, and so long as the nonexempt activity is merely incidental to the exempt purpose." In 1981 a publisher of religious materials lost its tax exemption because it became embued with a "commercial hue" and evolved into a "highly efficient business venture." An appellate court in 1984, even while overruling a lower court's decision that a religious publishing house was no longer exempt, found the opportunity to say that if an exempt organization's "management decisions replicate those of commercial enterprises, it is a fair inference that at least one purpose is commercial."

Recent cases in which commerciality was used as a basis for denial of tax exemption include one involving an organization selling religious tapes, one operating prisoner rehabilitation programs, and one operating a number of canteen-style lunch trucks.

There are several other commerciality doctrine cases depicting its evolution, but this is how the doctrine started and grew into its contemporary framework.

Q 17:10 What factors are looked at in determining commerciality?

The commerciality doctrine is not so fully articulated as to enable a crisp response. The most expansive explanation of the commerciality doctrine was provided in an appellate court case decided in 1991. The organization involved was a nonprofit entity associated with a church that operated, in advancement of church doctrine, vegetarian restaurants and health food stores. The lower court wrote, in denying exemption as a charitable and/or religious organization, that the entity's "activity was conducted as a business and was in direct competition with other restaurants and health food stores." The court added (in what, by then, was an understatement): "Competition with commercial firms is strong evidence of a substantial nonexempt purpose."

This appellate court opinion stated the factors relied upon in its finding of commerciality. They were that (1) the organization sold goods and services to the public (thereby making the establishments "presumptively commercial"), (2) the organization was in "direct competition" with for-profit restaurants and food stores, (3) the prices set by the organization were based on pricing formulas common in the retail food business (with the "profit-making price structure looming large" in the court's analysis and the court criticizing the organization for not having "below-cost pricing"), (4) the organization utilized promotional materials and "commercial catch phrases" to enhance sales, (5) the organization advertised its services and food, (6) the organization's hours of operation were basically the same as those of for-profit enterprises, (7) the guidelines by which the organization operated required that its management have "business ability" and six months' training, (8) the organization did not utilize volunteers but paid salaries, and (9) the organization did not receive any charitable contributions.

These criteria should not be disregarded simply because they were articulated back in 1991. In 2003, a court ruled that an organization operating a conference center could not be tax-exempt as a charitable or educational entity because of a "distinctively commercial hue" associated with its operations. This court applied precisely the same criteria as was employed in the 1991 opinion.

Q 17:11 What is to be made of the commerciality doctrine?

The doctrine of commerciality certainly is here to stay and is expected to grow in importance. Thus, the focus should be on the reach and the elements of the doctrine.

On the basis of the definition of the doctrine as articulated by a court in 1991 (Q 17:10), the doctrine is obviously too encompassing. For example, many tax-exempt organizations properly sell goods or services to the public (such as in the fields of education, health care, and theater); too much emphasis was placed by the court on that factor in the decision. Yet the court was correct in emphasizing competition, motive for engaging in the activity, and pricing. Probably the factor of advertising was appropriately included, although many nonprofit organizations advertise their exempt functions (such as hospitals, colleges, symphonies, and ballets). Factors like hours of operation and payment of salaries seem nonsensical in the modern era.

In contrast, some of these factors are dismaying, if not old-fashioned and plainly silly. For example, what is to be made of the court's wish for "below-cost pricing"? How long can an entity function (in the absence of a large endowment) doing that?

COMMENT: One is reminded of the radio advertisement in which the owner of a business is excitedly announcing an upcoming spectacular sale, with prices slashed. Once he is finished, his very critical mother appears, admonishing him. She tells the public, in a heavy accent, "He's a nice boy but not too good with the math."

Equally discouraging is the reference to lack of contributions. This remains a bugaboo that should have been put to rest years ago. There is no requirement in the law that, to be charitable, an organization must be funded, primarily or at all, by gifts. Indeed, the law is clear that an organization funded entirely by exempt function income or investment income can be charitable. The absence of contributions should not be an element in evaluating the presence of commerciality. Another factor that is foolish, if not completely unrealistic today, is reliance on the lack of volunteer assistance in concluding that an organization is commercial.

COMMENT: In fact, there are many nonprofit organizations that perform activities in a commercial manner using volunteers. These include theaters, symphonies, and ballets.

One of these elements that is particularly galling is the fact that the nonprofit organization's employees have some expertise and training. This country is long overdue in improving the quality of nonprofit organization operations in the realm of, for example, management, law, and fundraising. Much impressive progress in this regard is being made. Today there are more college programs, seminars, books, and the like than ever before. In the midst of all of this, along comes a court, finding knowledgeable employees of a nonprofit entity evidence that it is operating commercially!

So, while the commerciality doctrine is playing an increasing role in determining eligibility for tax-exempt status, the law is still awaiting a comprehensive and realistic definition of the doctrine.

Q 17:12 Are there other factors that are taken into account in determining commerciality?

Yes, usually by the media. These critiques are often based on a fundamental misunderstanding of what is meant by a nonprofit, tax-exempt organization. Two examples will suffice.

The *Kansas City Star*, piqued at the decision of the National Collegiate Athletic Association (NCAA) to leave that city and move to Indianapolis, published six days in a row a series of articles about the organization. The opening article proclaimed that "for a lesson in commercialism, you can't beat" the NCAA. According to the article, over the past 23 years, the NCAA's revenues have increased 8,000 percent. It has a $1.7 billion television contract, a staff of 250 individuals, a real estate subsidiary, a marketing division, and it licenses its name and logo for use on clothing. It owns a Learjet. It is a "powerful sports cartel that is addicted to making money."

The *New York Times*, enervated by the celebration of the 50th anniversary of the Educational Testing Service (ETS), published an article about the organization. It seems that the ETS has "quietly grown into a multinational operation complete with for-profit subsidiaries, a reserve fund of $91 million, and revenue last year of $411 million." This article portrayed ETS as an entity transformed into a "highly competitive business operation that is as much multinational monopoly as nonprofit institution, one capable of charging hefty fees, laying off workers and using sharp elbows in competing against rivals."

These and other inflammatory analyses are likely to have a lot to do with the evolution and enlargement of the commerciality doctrine. Being, unfortunately, all too typical, these articles missed the point of what is meant by being a nonprofit organization. Check off the list: there is nothing in the federal tax law prohibiting an exempt organization from operating in more than one country, having one or more for-profit subsidiaries, having a reserve fund, charging fees, and entering into licensing and other contracts. The articles focus on factors that are reflective of a yearning for an earlier, simpler era when nonprofit organizations were mostly struggling charities, eking out a year-by-year existence with barely enough in the way of contributions and held together by a dedicated cadre of volunteers. Thus, commerciality is seen in the size of the organization, the fact it has a paid staff, and ownership of an airplane.

COMMENT: This view is even stretched to find commerciality in the fact that a nonprofit organization lays off workers and uses "sharp elbows" against rivals. Terminating an individual's employment can be no more than sound management practice. And anyone worried about sharp elbows in this context has not been paying any attention to hospitals, colleges, and universities lately.

These and like reports, of course, include legitimate factors to take into account in determining commerciality. These are the reasons for (but not necessarily for the extent of) expansion, increase in and use of revenues, the charging of "hefty fees," and maybe even being a monopoly.

The *New York Times* article stated that "competition with for-profit rivals is a trend that bedevils nonprofit institutions across the country." As noted at the outset, there is much truth to this statement. What is also "bedeviling" nonprofit organizations these days is the confusion about them that is fostered by muddled analyses such as these.

Q 17:13   Is Congress likely to legislate some form of the commerciality doctrine?

It appears inevitable that a version of the commerciality doctrine will find its way into the statutory law. It is basically a matter of time.

In the meantime, Congress has already gingerly entered this fray. As noted (Q 17:4), by the mid-1980s, Congress arrived at the conclusion that, irrespective of their initial novelty and worthiness, prepaid health care plans were no longer entitled to tax exemption (usually as social welfare organizations) because they were operating in a commercial manner, like for-profit insurers. Thus, in 1986, Congress adopted the following rule: a nonprofit organization cannot be tax-exempt (as a charitable organization or a social welfare organization) if a substantial part of its activities is the provision of commercial-type insurance. The term *commercial-type insurance* means any form of insurance that is available in the for-profit sector, that is, is obtainable commercially.

This is the only time that any version of a commerciality doctrine has been added to the Internal Revenue Code. It may well be a provision that Congress will expand by extending it to fields other than insurance.

COMMENT: Even in this tentative foray into the mysteries of the meaning and shaping of the commerciality doctrine, Congress went too far. For example, the term *commercial-type insurance* was not, despite its origins, confined to *health* insurance. Thus, this statutory commerciality doctrine began to be applied in circumstances where charitable organizations needed various types of insurance in furtherance of their exempt programs (such as vehicle insurance for organizations that deliver meals to the elderly or provide transportation for the disabled) yet could not obtain the coverage because it was not available or because of its cost. Realizing its overreaching, Congress in 1996 wrote a rule exempting qualified *charitable risk pools* from the ambit of the law denying tax exemption to *commercial* insurers.

NOTE: The commerciality doctrine is tucked away in a sentence in the tax regulations. There the term *commercial* is used as part of the elements for determining whether a business is *regularly carried on*. Thus, the regulations state that specific business activities of an exempt organization are ordinarily deemed to be regularly carried on if they "manifest a frequency and continuity, and are pursued in a manner, generally similar to comparable commercial activities of nonexempt organizations."

Q 17:14   What is the future of the commerciality doctrine?

For the short term, the doctrine will continue to be developed in the courts. At some point in time, as noted, Congress will be motivated to either write an expansive definition of the term or augment the existing rules that presently are confined to insurance (Q 17:13).

The nonprofit community can expect many more reports in the media such as those noted earlier (Q 17:12), as the debate over this type of competition intensifies. Nonprofit organizations are likely to lose this battle on one or more fronts, perhaps including restrictive federal and/or state statutory law changes. If this happens, the process will have been hastened and inflamed by misleading reports such as these, which reflect great ignorance of what it means to be a nonprofit organization and what such organizations are allowed to do as a matter of law.

Q 17:15 What should nonprofit organizations be doing in this regard in the interim?

A tax-exempt, nonprofit organization should examine its operations in light of the elements of the commerciality doctrine enumerated earlier (Q 17:10, Q 17:11). The organization should evaluate each program activity the way the IRS or a court might do, by asking these questions: (1) Is the program competitive with an activity in the for-profit sector? (2) Why is the program being carried on? (3) If fees are charged for the provision of a good or service, how are the prices set? (4) Are prices calculated to return income in excess of related expenses (that is, generate a profit)? (5) Are exempt functions subsidized by contributions and/or grants (fundraising) or by an endowment fund? (6) Does the organization advertise or otherwise promote its operations? and (7) Are the salaries paid to employees and fees paid to vendors and other independent contractors reasonable? The organization should formulate the best possible answers to these questions from its standpoint (as always, staying within the bounds of veracity). It should be prepared to defend itself against charges of commerciality.

Once these rationales are devised, they should be reflected in all written materials developed by the organization. This is particularly important in respect to language in the articles of organization, annual information returns (Chapter 5), annual reports, footnotes in financial statements, promotional literature, newsletters, and minutes of the board of directors. In many instances, as part of assembling a case that an organization is operating in a commercial manner, an IRS examiner or judge will select quotations from an organization's own materials, using them against the organization.

CHAPTER 18

Disclosure and Distribution Rules

The federal tax law embodies a variety of disclosure and distribution rules that are imposed on tax-exempt organizations. The most significant of these are the requirements with respect to annual information returns and applications for recognition of tax exemption. Other disclosure rules pertain to private letter rulings, the availability of certain information or services, and certain solicitations of charitable gifts.

Here are the questions most frequently asked about disclosure and distribution requirements—and the answers to them.

ANNUAL INFORMATION RETURNS

Q 18:1 It was mentioned earlier that the annual information returns are public documents. What does that mean?

There are two aspects of this matter. One is that these documents are available from the IRS. The other is that an exempt organization is required to make copies of them accessible to whoever asks to see them. Let us focus on the second of these aspects first.

Tax-exempt organizations must make their annual information returns (Chapter 5) available for public inspection. The requirement pertains to the three most recent annual information returns.

 **NOTE:** There are separate publicity requirements for private foundations.

This requirement does not cause disclosure of the names or addresses of donors.

An exempt organization is required to make a copy of each return available for inspection, during regular business hours, at its principal office, by any individual. If an exempt organization regularly maintains one or more regional or district offices having at least three employees, this distribution requirement applies with respect to each office.

It is not necessary, under these rules, that copies be provided for retention by those who request them; the documents need only be provided for review.

This body of law, however, has been largely superseded by distribution rules.

Q 18:2 What are the distribution rules?

Congress, in 1996, enacted distribution rules in this context. These rules are amplified by tax regulations, which were issued in the final form in 1999 (for tax-exempt organizations generally) and 2000 (for private foundations).

Generally, under these rules, anyone who requests a copy of one or more of the three most recent annual returns, in person or in writing, will have to be provided these copies. The individual requesting them will be able to retain these copies.

If a request for copies is made in person, the organization will have to provide them immediately. Response to a request in writing will have to be made within 30 days. The only charge that can be imposed for these copies is a reasonable fee for photocopying and mailing costs.

This annual return distribution requirement extends to all schedules and attachments filed with the IRS. For charitable organizations, this includes Schedule A. An organization is not required, however, to disclose the parts of the return that identify names and addresses of contributors to the organization. Moreover, a tax-exempt organization is not required to disclose its unrelated business income tax return (Form 990-T).

There are rules concerning the documents that must be made available by an organization that is recognized as tax-exempt under a group exemption (Q 4:47–Q 4:56).

A tax-exempt organization must make the specified documents available for public inspection at its principal, regional, and district offices. The documents generally have to be available for inspection on the day of the request during the organization's normal business hours. An office of an organization is considered a regional or district office only if it has three or more paid full-time employees (or paid employees, whether part-time or full-time, whose aggregate number of paid hours per week is at least 120).

Certain sites where the organization's employees perform solely exempt function activities are excluded from consideration as a regional or district office. The rules prescribe how an organization that does not maintain a permanent office or whose office has very limited hours during certain times of the year can comply with the public inspection requirements.

A tax-exempt organization must accept requests for copies made in person at the same place and time that the information must be available for public inspection. An organization is generally required to provide the copies on the day of the request. In unusual circumstances, an organization is permitted to provide the requested copies on the next business day.

Where a request is made in writing, an exempt organization must furnish the copies within 30 days from the date the request is received. If an organization requires advance payment of a reasonable fee for copying and mailing, it may provide the copies within 30 days from the date it receives payment (rather than from the date of the request).

There are rules that provide guidance as to what constitutes a *request*, when a request is considered *received*, and when copies are considered *provided*. Instead of requesting a copy of an entire annual return, individuals may request a specific portion of the document. A principal, regional, or district office of an organization may use an agent to process requests for copies.

The reasonable fee a tax-exempt organization is permitted to charge for copies may be no more than the fees charged by the IRS for copies of exempt organization returns and related documents. This is $1.00 for the first page and $.15 for each subsequent page. In addition, actual postage costs can be charged. An organization is permitted to collect payment in advance of providing the requested copies.

If an organization receives a written request for copies with payment not enclosed, and the organization requires payment in advance, the organization must request payment within seven days from the date it receives the request. Payment is deemed to occur on the day an organization receives the money, check (provided the check subsequently clears), or money order. An organization is required to accept payment made in the form of money or money order and, when the request is made in writing, to accept payment by personal check. An organization is permitted, though not required, to accept other forms of payment. To protect requesters from unexpected fees where an exempt organization does not require prepayment and where a requester does not enclose prepayment with a request, an organization must receive consent from a requester before providing copies for which the fee charged for copying and postage is in excess of $20.

Q 18:3 What is an individual able to do if denied a copy of the return?

The tax regulations provide guidance for an individual denied inspection, or a copy, of an annual return. Basically, the individual must provide the IRS with a statement that describes the reason that the individual believes the denial was in violation of legal requirements.

Q 18:4 Are there any exceptions to the inspection requirement?

Not really. No excuses are allowed. As noted, certain donor information need not be provided (Q 18:1). Otherwise, as long as the request is made during regular business hours, copies of the returns must be made available for inspection.

Q 18:5 Are there any exceptions to the distribution requirement?

Yes, under two circumstances an exempt organization is relieved of the obligation to provide copies of the returns. An exception is available where the organization has made the documents *widely available.* The other exception obtains where the IRS determines, following application by the organization, that the organization is subject to a *harassment campaign* and that a waiver of the disclosure obligation is in the public interest.

Q 18:6 What does the term *widely available* mean?

A tax-exempt organization is not required to comply with requests for copies of its annual returns if the organization has made them widely available. An organization can make its annual information return *widely available* by posting the document on its World Wide Web page on the Internet or by having the applicable document posted on another organization's Web page as part of a database of similar materials.

For this exception to be available, however, six criteria must be followed:

1. The entity maintaining the Web page must have procedures for ensuring the reliability and accuracy of the application or return that is posted.
2. This entity must take reasonable precautions to prevent alteration, destruction, or accidental loss of the posted document.
3. The application or return must be posted in the same format used by the IRS to post forms and publications on the Web page of the IRS.
4. The Web page that is used must clearly inform readers that the document is available and provide instructions for downloading it.
5. When downloaded and printed in hard copy, the document must be in substantially the same form as the original application or return and contain the same information as provided in the original document filed with the IRS (other than information that can be lawfully withheld).
6. A person can access and download the document without payment of a fee to the organization maintaining the Web page.

The IRS is authorized to prescribe, by revenue procedure or other guidance, other methods that an organization can use to make its annual return widely available.

An organization that makes its return widely available must inform individuals who request copies how and where to obtain the requested document.

Q 18:7 What does the term *harassment campaign* mean?

Generally, a *harassment campaign* exists where an organization receives a group of requests, and the relevant facts and circumstances show that the purpose of the group of requests is to disrupt the operations of the exempt organization rather than to collect information.

These facts and circumstances include a sudden increase in the number of requests, an extraordinary number of requests made through form letters or similarly worded correspondence, evidence of a purpose to significantly deter the organization's employees or volunteers from pursuing the organization's exempt purpose, requests that contain language hostile to the organization, direct evidence of bad faith by organizers of the purported harassment campaign, evidence that the organization has already provided the requested documents to a member of the purported harassing group, and a demonstration by the exempt organization that it routinely provides copies of its documents upon request.

The regulations contain examples that evaluate whether particular situations constitute a harassment campaign and whether an organization has a reasonable basis for believing that a request is part of this type of campaign.

TIP: Organizations may not suspend compliance with a request for copies from a representative of the news media even though the organization believes or knows that the request is part of a harassment campaign.

An organization can disregard requests in excess of two per 30-day period or four per year from the same individual or from the same address. There are procedures for requesting a determination that an organization is subject to a harassment campaign and the treatment of requests for copies while a request for a determination is pending.

NOTE: These two exceptions are exceptions only from the rules concerning *distribution* of returns. They are not exceptions from the *inspection* requirements (Q 18:1).

Q 18:8 How are these returns available from the IRS?

Copies of exempt organizations' annual information returns are available for public inspection and photocopying from the IRS, although trade secrets, and names and addresses of contributors, cannot be disclosed.

A request for inspection must be in writing, include the name and address (city and state) of the organization that filed the return, and include the type (number) of the return and the year(s) involved. The request may be sent to the IRS district director (Attention: Disclosure Officer) of the district in which the requester desires to inspect the return. If inspection at the IRS National Office is desired, the request should be sent to the Commissioner of Internal Revenue, Attention: Freedom of Information Reading Room, 1111 Constitution Avenue, N.W., Washington, DC 20224.

A copy of one or more annual information returns is available through the IRS. Form 4506-A is used for this purpose. There is a fee for photocopying.

EXEMPTION APPLICATIONS

Q 18:9 What is the disclosure requirement with respect to applications for recognition of exemption?

The inspection requirement described earlier (Q 18:1) is likewise applicable with respect to applications for recognition of exemption. Again, certain information can be withheld from public inspection, such as trade secrets and patents.

Q 18:10 Do the distribution requirements apply to applications for recognition of exemption?

Yes. All of the rules as to distribution of documents, and the exceptions to them (Q 18:2–Q 18:7) are applicable with respect to applications for recognition of exemption.

Q 18:11 Are copies of exemption applications available from the IRS?

Yes. The application for recognition of tax exemption and any supporting documents filed by most tax-exempt organizations must be made accessible to the public by the IRS where a favorable determination letter is issued to an organization.

NOTE: This disclosure rule applies only to documents filed by the exempt organization. It does not extend to documents submitted by third parties (such as members of Congress) in support of or opposition to the application.

An organization, for which application for recognition of exemption is open to public inspection, may request in writing that information relating to a trade secret, patent, process, style of work, or apparatus be withheld. The information will be withheld from public inspection if the IRS determines that its disclosure would adversely affect the organization.

An application and related materials may be inspected at the appropriate field office of the IRS. Inspection may also occur at the National Office of the IRS; a request for inspection may be directed to the Assistant to the Commissioner (Public Affairs), 1111 Constitution Avenue, N.W., Washington, DC 20224.

Once an organization's exemption application and related and supporting documents become open to public inspection, the determination letter issued by the IRS becomes publicly available as well. Also open to inspection are any technical advice memoranda issued with respect to any favorable ruling.

NOTE: A favorable ruling recognizing an organization's tax-exempt status may be issued by the IRS's National Office. These rulings and the underlying applications for recognition of tax exemption are available for inspection in the Freedom of Information Reading Room of the IRS in Washington, DC.

In 2004, a federal court of appeals ruled that IRS rulings and related documents concerning *denials* of applications for recognition of exemption and *revocations* of exemption are written determinations from the agency that also must be made public. The IRS began complying with this ruling later that year.

COMMENT: This appellate court erred in its application of the rules of statutory construction in this case. This mistake is manifested in two developments. In 2000, the staff of the Joint Committee on Taxation proposed that the law be changed to make these revocation and denial rulings open to the public. In the next year, the Senate passed legislation to do just that. If this court's reading of the law were correct, the recommendations would have been unnecessary and the legislation superfluous—an unlikely set of circumstances.

DISCLOSURE AND DISTRIBUTION SANCTIONS

Q 18:12 **What is the penalty on organizations for failure to comply with the public inspection requirements?**

The penalty is $20 per day for each day that inspection is not permitted, up to a maximum of $10,000 for each return. In the case of exemption applications, the penalty is $20 per day as long as the failure to comply continues. This penalty is inapplicable in instances of reasonable cause.

Q 18:13 **What is the penalty on individuals for failure to comply with the public inspection requirements?**

An individual who willfully fails to comply with the inspection requirements is subject to a penalty of $5,000.

Q 18:14 **What are the penalties for failure to comply with the distribution requirements?**

These penalties are the same as those imposed for violation of the public inspection requirements (Q 18:12, Q 18:13).

PROVISION OF GOODS AND SERVICES

Q 18:15 **What are the disclosure rules regarding the availability of goods and services?**

There are disclosure rules that become applicable if a tax-exempt organization offers to sell or solicits money for specific information or a routine service for an individual that could be readily obtained by the individual without charge or for a nominal charge from an agency of the federal government.

A penalty can be imposed when the tax-exempt organization, in making the offer or solicitation, fails to make an express statement—in a conspicuous and easily recognizable format—that the information or service can be so obtained. Imposition of this penalty requires an intentional disregard of these requirements.

Q 18:16 What are the parameters of this type of *solicitation*?

This requirement of disclosure applies only if the information to be provided involves the *specific individual* solicited. Thus, for example, the requirement applies with respect to obtaining the Social Security earnings record or the Social Security identification number of an individual solicited, but is inapplicable with respect to the furnishing of copies of newsletters issued by federal agencies or providing copies of or descriptive material on pending legislation. Moreover, this requirement is not applicable to the provision of professional services (such as tax return preparation, grant application preparation, or medical services), as opposed to routine information retrieval services, to an individual even if they may be available from the federal government without charge.

Q 18:17 What is the penalty for violation of this rule?

The penalty for violation of this disclosure rule is applicable for each day on which the failure occurred. This penalty is the greater of $1,000 or 50 percent of the aggregate cost of the offers and solicitations that occurred on any day on which the failure occurred and with respect to which there was this type of failure.

FUNDRAISING DISCLOSURE

Q 18:18 What are the fundraising disclosure rules for noncharitable organizations?

There are rules designed to prevent noncharitable organizations from engaging in gift-solicitation activities under circumstances in which donors will assume, or be led to assume, that the contributions are tax-deductible when, in fact, they are not.

NOTE: These rules are targeted principally at tax-exempt social welfare organizations (Chapter 10).

These rules do not, however, apply to an organization that has annual gross receipts that are normally no more than $100,000.

Under these rules, each *fundraising solicitation* by or on behalf of an exempt noncharitable organization must contain an express statement, in a "conspicuous and easily recognizable format," that gifts to it are not deductible as charitable contributions for federal income tax purposes. A fundraising solicitation is any solicitation of gifts made in written or printed form, or by television, radio, or telephone. There is an exclusion for letters or calls not part of a coordinated fundraising campaign soliciting more than 10 persons during a calendar year.

CAUTION: Despite the reference in the statute to *contributions and gifts*, the IRS interprets this rule to mandate disclosure when any noncharitable organization seeks funds, such as dues from members. Thus, for example, it applies with respect to dues solicitations by membership associations and social clubs, and contribution solicitations by political organizations (Q 4:7).

Q 18:19   What are the penalties for violation of these rules?

The penalty for failure to satisfy this disclosure requirement for noncharitable organizations is $1,000 per day (maximum of $10,000 per year), albeit with a reasonable cause exception. In an instance of "intentional disregard" of these rules, however, the penalty for the day on which the offense occurred is the greater of $1,000 or 50 percent of the aggregate cost of the solicitations that took place on that day; the $10,000 limitation is inapplicable.

Q 18:20   What are the fundraising disclosure rules for charitable organizations?

One disclosure rule is that if a charitable organization receives a quid pro quo contribution in excess of $75, the organization must, in connection with the solicitation or receipt of the solicitation, provide a written statement that

1. Informs the donor that the amount of the contribution that is deductible for federal income tax purposes is limited to the excess of the amount of any money and the value of any property other than money contributed by the donor over the value of any goods or services provided by the organization, and
2. Provides the donor with a good-faith estimate of the value of the goods or services.

A *quid pro quo contribution* is a payment "made partly as a contribution and partly in consideration for goods or services provided to the payor by the donee organization" (Q 13:10–Q 13:13).

NOTE: This term does not include a payment made to an organization, operated exclusively for religious purposes, in return for which the donor receives solely an intangible religious benefit that generally is not sold in a commercial transaction outside the donative context.

Also, charitable gift *substantiation* rules require the charitable donee to provide certain information pertaining to the gift in writing to donors, where the contribution is $250 or more in a year (Q 13:6–Q 13:9).

Also, a charitable donee that sells, exchanges, consumes, or otherwise disposes of gift property within two years after the date of the donor's contribution of the property must file an information return (Form 8282) with the IRS.

Q 18:21   What are the penalties for violation of these rules?

The penalty for violation of the rules concerning *quid pro quo contributions* is $10 per contribution, capped at $5,000 per particular fundraising event or mailing, absent reasonable cause. The penalty for transgressing the charitable gift substantiation rules is denial of the charitable contribution deduction to the donor—even though the deduction may otherwise be allowable in full.

CHAPTER 19

IRS Audits of Nonprofit Organizations

Nonprofit, tax-exempt organizations do not escape IRS audits. At the same time, an audit of an exempt organization is not likely to yield a large sum of money, and the IRS audit resources are sparse. These facts are forcing the IRS to conserve its audit abilities and focus them on entities where the revenue potential is the greatest: historically, this has been health care institutions, colleges and universities, and associations.

Other types of tax-exempt organizations are audited; a few (relatively speaking) are audited on a regular basis. Today, however, it is common for an exempt organization to go for years—perhaps decades—without experiencing an IRS audit. Still, the issues raised by these audits and the resolution of those issues contribute to the body of federal tax law applicable in the exempt organizations context in general.

Here are the questions most frequently asked about IRS audits (including why they start and how they are administered), the issues that can arise on audit, and (inevitably) the likelihood of audit—and the answers to them.

Q 19:1 How is the IRS organized from the standpoint of its audit function?

The IRS, an agency of the Department of the Treasury, is administered at the national level by its office in Washington, DC. This office is headed by a Commissioner of Internal Revenue, who generally superintends the assessment and collection of all taxes imposed by any law providing for federal (internal) revenue. An Oversight Board is responsible for overseeing the IRS in its administration, conduct, direction, and supervision of the execution and application of the internal revenue laws.

The fundamental organization of the IRS involves four operating divisions, one of which is the Tax Exempt and Governmental Entities (TE/GE) Division. Within this arrangement is the Exempt Organizations Division, which develops policy and administers the law of tax-exempt organizations. The Director of this division, who reports to the Tax Exempt Entities/Governmental Entities Commissioner, is responsible for planning, managing, and executing nationwide IRS activities in the realm of exempt organizations. The Director also supervises and is responsible for the programs of the offices of Customer Education and Outreach, Rulings and Agreements, Examinations, and Exempt Organizations Electronic Initiatives.

Another component of the IRS at the national level is the Office of the IRS Chief Counsel, which is part of the Legal Division of the Treasury Department. The Chief Counsel is the principal legal adviser on federal tax matters to the Commissioner. Among the Associate Chief Counsels is the Associate Chief Counsel (Employee Benefits and Exempt Organizations). One of the functions of this Associate Chief Counsel's office, which includes an Assistant Chief Counsel with direct responsibility in the exempt organizations area, is to develop legal policy and strategy in the field of tax-exempt organizations.

The Examinations office, based in Dallas, Texas, focuses on exempt organizations examinations programs and review projects. Its support functions include Examination Planning and Programs, Classification, Mandatory Review, Special Review, and Examinations Special Support. The TE/GE strategic plan calls for improvement of the presence of the IRS in the exempt organizations community to promote greater overall law compliance and fairness in the sector. The IRS is working to balance its workforce resources between the examination and determination functions, and to develop more effective methods of allocating and utilizing Examinations resources.

One of the agency's initiatives in this area is establishment of an Exempt Organizations Compliance Unit, to address exempt organizations customer compliance using correspondence and telephone contacts (Q 19:7). Another new component of this office is the Data Analysis Unit, which is using various databases and other information to investigate emerging compliance trends to improve the identification and selection of source work in the exempt organizations area.

Q 19:2 Where does the IRS derive its audit authority?

The IRS is empowered by statute to audit the activities and records of all persons in the United States, including tax-exempt organizations. This examination activity is designed to ensure that exempt organizations and other persons are in compliance with all pertinent requirements of the federal tax law.

Q 19:3 What issues are addressed in an exempt organization's audit?

An IRS audit of this type of organization may address matters such as continuation of tax-exempt status, private inurement and/or private benefit, ongoing non–private foundation status, legislative and/or political campaign activities, susceptibility to the tax on unrelated business income, deferred compensation and retirement programs, tax-exempt bond financing, and employment tax issues.

Q 19:4   How is an IRS audit initiated?

An IRS audit is usually initiated in the field, under the auspices of the appropriate district office. The examiners involved are specialists in tax-exempt organization matters and function under the direction of a supervisor in the district office.

NOTE: The IRS prepared material to guide national headquarters and field personnel who have responsibilities for the examination of tax-exempt organizations. This material, which is publicly available, is known as the *Exempt Organizations Examination Guidelines Handbook.*

The Exempt Organizations Division at the National Office of the IRS (Q 19:1) has the responsibility for establishing the procedures and policy for the conduct of exempt organization audit programs.

Q 19:5   Why is an IRS audit initiated?

Although the IRS, from time to time, initiates audits of particular types of tax-exempt organizations (such as health care organizations, associations, churches, colleges and universities, and private foundations) as a matter of national policy, audits are typically commenced based on the size of the entity and the length of time that has elapsed since any prior audit. Often an audit is commenced as the result of an examination of an information or tax return; one of the functions of the IRS is to ascertain the correctness of returns. Other reasons for the development of an audit include complaints filed by disgruntled (often former) employees, media or third-party reports of alleged wrongdoing by a taxpayer, selection based on a person's claim for a refund of taxes, or selection as part of an IRS program to focus on a particular problem area (often termed an *industry* by the IRS).

NOTE: Examples of audits of the latter category that are taking place at this time are examinations of consumer credit counseling agencies, downpayment assistance organizations, entities that are suspected of paying excessive amounts of compensation to their executive personnel, and exempt organizations directly involved in or accommodating abusive tax shelters.

Q 19:6   What items of a tax-exempt organization will the IRS review on audit?

The IRS is authorized to examine any books, papers, records, or other data that may be relevant or material to an inquiry. The records that must be produced during an audit of a tax-exempt organization will likely include all organizational documents (such as articles of organization, bylaws, resolutions, and minutes of meetings), documents relating to tax status (such as any application for recognition of tax exemption and IRS determinations as to exempt and private status), financial statements (including underlying books and records), recent annual information returns, and newsletters, journals, and other publications. Other items that may be requested will depend on the type of audit being conducted; the audit may or may not encompass payroll records, pension and retirement plans, returns of affiliated organizations, and the like. In some instances, an organization may find it appropriate to produce information only upon the presentation of a summons.

Q 19:7 Are there different types of IRS audits?

Yes. Some examinations are *office examinations*, where contact between the IRS and a taxpayer is by IRS office interview. A *correspondence audit* involves an IRS request for additional information from a taxpayer by letter, fax, or e-mail correspondence. Other examinations are *field examinations*, in which one or more IRS agents review the books and records of the taxpayer on the taxpayer's premises. IRS audits of tax-exempt organizations of any consequence are field examinations.

One of the problems with IRS audit practices in the past was that a typical audit focused on a single organization, ignoring subsidiaries and other affiliates and joint ventures. This deficiency (from the government's viewpoint) was remedied with the development of the *coordinated examination program* (CEP), where complex issues were addressed and managed using a team audit approach. The objectives of the CEP were to (1) perform effectively planned and managed coordinated examinations, (2) secure support for district assistance where appropriate, and (3) accumulate and disseminate novel examination techniques, issues unique to specific organizations, tax avoidance and evasion schemes, and other useful examination information.

The coordinated examination program is being phased out; its replacement is the *team examination program* (TEP). The TEP audit will be utilized in connection with a wider array of exempt organizations than was the case with the coordinated examination program. The IRS plans to identify, then examine, TEP entities entailing significant potential noncompliance. Field examinations of large, complex organizations, which require coordination among IRS functions (and perhaps other government agencies), will be conducted using team audit procedures.

NOTE: An illustration of this type of coordinated audit is the series of audits under way of consumer credit counseling agencies (Q 19:5). These examinations are being conducted jointly by the IRS and the Federal Trade Commission.

COMMENT: It is not clear what the substantive difference between CEP and TEP audits will be. Early experience indicates that the TEP approach may utilize less personnel and not last as long. With the CEP audit, agents often established offices within the exempt organization; that does not seem to be happening with TEP audits.

Another relatively contemporary IRS examination technique is the *package audit*. This type of audit arises out of the review of one or more annual information returns and/or unrelated business income tax returns. It entails ascertaining whether the exempt organization is filing or has filed all other required federal tax returns, such as the employment tax returns, other information returns, employee benefit plan returns, and the returns of related entities.

Q 19:8 How does an exempt organization cope with IRS personnel during an audit?

Carefully and courteously. The techniques for coping with IRS personnel on the occasion of an audit are easily summarized, but their deployment and success are likely to depend heavily on the personalities involved. The key staff personnel, accountants, and legal counsel of the audited organization should be involved in the process from the beginning, and it is advisable to select one individual who will serve as liaison with the IRS during the audit. The projected duration of the audit and the procedures that are to be followed by the parties involved should be ascertained at the outset, and records should be carefully maintained as information and documents are examined or copied by the revenue agents. All interviews of those associated with the audited organization should be monitored by the liaison individual, with appropriate records made of each interview. At least some of the questioning should occur only in the presence of legal counsel.

Where issues arise, one or both sides may decide to pursue the technical advice procedure.

Q 19:9 What does the IRS do after the audit has been completed?

Upon completion of an audit, the IRS will take one of three actions:

1. If the IRS determines that there are no inaccuracies with the taxpayer's return, the taxpayer will be issued a *no change letter*, which indicates that no change is being made to the taxpayer's tax liability as reported.
2. If the IRS determines that the taxpayer has overpaid tax, the IRS will issue an overadjustment entitling the taxpayer to a tax refund.
3. If the IRS determines that there is a deficiency in the amount of tax paid or reported by the taxpayer, or some other taxpayer error (such as a failure to file a required tax form), the IRS agent will present the taxpayer with findings that assert a deficiency in tax. If the taxpayer agrees with the alleged deficiency, a form can be executed and the taxpayer is sent a statement for the additional tax owed. If the taxpayer disagrees with the IRS on the point, the collections process will commence.

Q 19:10 What is the likelihood that a tax-exempt organization will be audited by the IRS?

Overall, the likelihood that an exempt organization will be audited by the IRS is remote. The IRS has limited audit resources, and the number of tax-exempt organizations is increasing. The IRS simply does not have the personnel to audit all exempt organizations on a regular basis. Consequently, the IRS audit focus is confined to the larger organizations or those within a targeted industry or field (Q 19:5).

Q 19:11 Can the IRS prevent abuse by tax-exempt organizations by means other than examination and revocation of exempt status?

Yes, but this remedy is limited. The IRS now has the authority (as of late 2003) to *suspend* the tax-exempt status of an organization that has been designated as supporting or engaging in terrorist activity or supporting terrorism. Contributions made to an organization during the period of suspension of exemption are not deductible for federal tax purposes.

Specifically, federal income tax exemption and the eligibility of an organization to apply for recognition of exemption (Chapter 4) must be suspended for a particular period if it is a terrorist organization. Contributions to such an organization are not deductible during the period, for income, estate, and gift tax purposes.

An organization is a *terrorist organization* if it is designated or otherwise individually identified (1) under provisions of the Immigration and Nationality Act as a terrorist organization or foreign terrorist organization, (2) in or pursuant to an executive order that is related to terrorism and issued under the authority of the International Emergency Economic Powers Act or the United Nations Participation Act for the purpose of imposing on such organization an economic or other sanction, or (3) in or pursuant to an executive order issued under the authority of any federal law, if the organization is designated or otherwise individually identified in or pursuant to the executive order as supporting or engaging in terrorist activity or supporting terrorism, and the executive order refers to this federal law.

The period of suspension of tax exemption begins on the date of the first publication by the IRS of a designation or identification with respect to the organization and ends on the first date that all designations and identifications with respect to the organization are rescinded pursuant to the applicable statutory law or executive order.

A person may not challenge a suspension of tax exemption, a designation or identification of an entity as a terrorist organization, the period of a suspension, or a denial of a charitable deduction in this context in an administrative or judicial proceeding. This law provides for a refund or credit of income tax (if necessary) in the case of an erroneous designation or identification of an entity as a terrorist organization.

IRS AUDITS OF HEALTH CARE ORGANIZATIONS

Q 19:12 What is the IRS audit program for hospitals and other health care organizations?

The IRS, in recent years, has been making the audit of tax-exempt hospitals and other health care entities a matter of special priority. The IRS developed audit guidelines specific to these types of tax-exempt organizations (although many of the guidelines are equally applicable to other types of exempt entities).

The guidelines emphasize nearly all aspects of qualification for tax-exempt status by hospitals, with emphasis on private inurement and private benefit situations (see Chapter 6). They also focus on joint venture arrangements (Chapter 16) and unrelated business income circumstances (Chapter 14).

Q 19:13 What is the focus of the IRS concerning the tax-exempt status of nonprofit hospitals?

The tax exemption of nonprofit hospitals today rests on the *community benefit* standard: the hospital must function to promote health in a particular community. In determining whether a hospital meets this standard, IRS agents are expected to consider five factors:

1. Is the hospital's governing board composed of "prominent civic leaders" rather than hospital administrators, physicians, and the like? (The agents are requested to review the minutes of the board meeting to determine how active the members are.)

2. Is the organization part of a multientity hospital system, and do the minutes reflect "corporate separateness"? (The minutes should show that the board members understand the purposes and activities of the various entities (Q 2:42)).

3. Is admission to the medical staff open to all qualified physicians in the area, consistent with the size and nature of the facilities?

4. Does the hospital operate a full-time emergency room open to everyone, regardless of ability to pay?

5. Does the hospital provide nonemergency care to everyone in the community who is able to pay either privately or through third parties (such as Medicare and Medicaid)?

The guidelines contain criteria for assessing whether an "open staff policy" exists at a hospital. The auditing agent is to identify qualification requirements for admission to staff (by referring to the medical staff bylaws), review application procedures and methods of staff selection, review minutes of medical staff meetings, determine whether staff admission fees are charged on a preferential basis, ascertain whether new physicians in the geographic area are admitted to the staff (the absence of new members could indicate a closed staff), consider the number of physicians in each membership category (such as active, associate, and courtesy), interview knowledgeable officials to determine whether physicians have been denied admission to the staff for other than reasonable cause, review the minutes of the credentials committee, and review the hospital's daily consensus report to determine the percentage of use of hospital facilities by various physicians (the names of the patients and the physicians providing services for these patients are listed in the consensus report).

The guidelines also contain criteria for determining whether use of an emergency room is restricted. The agent is to (1) review the manual of operations, brochures, posted signs, and the like, (2) interview ambulance drivers to determine whether they are instructed to take indigent patients to another hospital, (3) interview emergency room staff to determine admission procedures, (4) interview social workers in the community, who are familiar with delivery of emergency health care services, to determine whether the services are known to be available at the hospital, and (5) ascertain when and how determinations of financial responsibility are made and whether a deposit is required of any patient before care is rendered. Examining agents are expected to ascertain whether a hospital engages in the practice known as patient "dumping."

An examining agent is admonished to determine whether nonemergency services are available to everyone in the community who has the ability to pay. To this end, the agent is to review the hospital admission policy, determine whether the hospital admits and treats Medicare and Medicaid patients in a nondiscriminatory manner, review files on denied admissions to ascertain the reasons for denial, determine whether members of the professional staff also serve in administrative capacities and restrict admissions to only patients of staff members, review the accountants' reports for a statement of the hospital's charity care policy and expenditures, and compare the proportion of services provided to Medicaid patients to the proportion of Medicaid beneficiaries living in the area served by the hospital (the latter data are available either from the institution or from the state Medicaid agency).

The examining agent is to obtain copies of any private letter rulings issued to the hospital by the IRS, and to determine whether the hospital is involved in projects and programs that improve the health of the community (such as by reviewing newsletters, press releases, and calendars of events).

Q 19:14 What is the emphasis by the IRS in this area on private inurement and private benefit?

The guidelines contain a discussion of private inurement and private benefit, and the difference between the two doctrines (Chapter 6). The IRS recognizes two key distinctions between these two concepts. First, the IRS has reiterated its position that even a "minimal amount" of private inurement will result in loss of tax-exempt status (Q 6:1), and private benefit is tested against an "insubstantiality" threshold (Q 6:4). Second, private inurement applies only with respect to "insiders," but private benefit can accrue to anyone (Q 6:5). (The IRS considers a physician an insider in relation to a hospital in which he or she practices and/or is a member of the hospital's governing body.)

The following seven guidelines are to be followed in determining private inurement or private benefit:

1. Identify the members of the board of directors or trustees and key staff members of the administrative and medical staff. Examine any business relationships or dealings with the hospital. Note transactions where supplies or services are provided at prices exceeding competitive market prices or at preferred terms. Be alert for any loan agreement at less than prevailing interest rates. Scrutinize any business arrangements under which hospitals fi-

nance the construction of medical buildings owned by staff physicians on favorable financial terms.

2. Review contracts and leases. Scrutinize any contracts under which the hospital requires physicians to conduct private practices on hospital premises.

3. Review the minutes of the board of directors' executive committee and finance committee for indications of transactions with physicians, administrators, and board members.

4. Review the articles of incorporation, bylaws, minutes, filings with regulatory authorities, correspondence, brochures, newspaper articles, and the like to determine the existence of related parties.

5. Determine whether the hospital is engaged in commercial or industrial research or testing that would benefit private individuals or firms, rather than scientific or medical research that would benefit the general public.

6. Review third-party reports (such as accountants' audit reports, management letters, and annual reports) to determine whether the hospital's activities further an exempt purpose or serve private interests.

7. Review any conflict-of-interest statements (Q 2:30) to determine whether medical staff or board members have an economic interest in, or significant dealings with, the hospital.

These guidelines focus on the matter of unreasonable compensation and require examining agents to inquire as to recruiting incentives, incentive compensation arrangements, below-market loans, below-market leases, and hospital purchases of a physician's practice. The guidelines also contain an extensive list of "common compensation arrangements" between hospitals and physicians.

Q 19:15 What is the interest of the IRS in this area with respect to joint ventures?

The guidelines focus on joint ventures (Chapter 16), pointing out that a variety of forms may be involved, such as a cooperative agreement or the creation of a separate legal entity. Examples of the items or services involved in these joint ventures are said to include clinical diagnostic laboratory services, medical equipment leasing, durable medical equipment, and other out-patient medical or diagnostic services.

Agents are advised to carefully examine joint ventures between taxable and tax-exempt parties in search of private inurement or private benefit (Chapter 6). The facts must be reviewed to determine whether the partnership involved serves a charitable purpose, whether and how participation by the exempt entity furthers an exempt purpose, and whether the arrangement permits the exempt entity to act exclusively in furtherance of its exempt purposes. Examples of private inurement issues in this setting include participation in a venture that imposes obligations on the tax-exempt health care organization that conflict with its exempt purposes, a disproportionate allocation of profits and losses to the nonexempt partners (particularly if they are physicians), loans made by the exempt partner to the joint venture on a commercially unreasonable basis (such as a low interest rate or inadequate security), provision by the exempt partner of property or services to the joint venture at less than fair market value, and receipt by a nonexempt partner of more than reasonable compensation for the sale of property or services to the joint venture.

The auditing agent is advised to "[b]e alert for joint ventures involving the sale by a hospital of the gross or net revenue stream from an existing hospital service for a defined period of time to private interests." Alertness is also advised with respect to "arrangements with physician group practices or clinics where the hospital transfers something of value in return for an agreement to refer patients to the hospital for inpatient, surgical, or diagnostic services."

Q 19:16   What types of financial analyses is the IRS likely to make in these audits?

Sixteen types of "financial analyses" by examining agents are requested. These include:

1. Review income and expenditures of affiliated entities to determine whether nonexempt purposes, private inurement, serving of private interests, or unrelated business income may be present (Chapters 6 and 14).

2. Look for lobbying or political activities or expenditures; determine whether the hospital has elected the expenditure test as to lobbying expenditures (Chapters 8 and 9).

3. Reconcile the hospital's books with the figures on its annual information return. Reconcile the working trial balance to the general ledger, accountants' report, and the return.

4. Review the accountants' report and management letter for indications of unrelated business income.

5. Review Medicare cost reports for indications of insider (related party) transactions or unrelated activities.

6. Review the correspondence files on large gifts and grants; look for unusual transactions that may prohibit the "donor" from receiving a charitable deduction.

7. Check the value shown on the books for donated property against any appraisals in the file; if any property was sold, note the difference between the book value and the selling price.

8. Review the travel ledger accounts of the administrative department and the board of directors; be alert for personal items such as spouse's travel and ensure that there has been "proper accounting" (Q 2:21).

9. Where private individuals or outside entities operate the hospital cafeteria, gift shop, pharmacy, parking lot, and the like, determine whether the agreements with these individuals or firms provide for reasonable payments to the hospital.

10. Reconcile expenses on the tax return used to report unrelated business income. If specific cost centers are maintained, review them for possible account analysis. If specific cost centers are not maintained, request a copy of the allocation method used and determine whether it is reasonable in accordance with the federal tax requirements.

Q 19:17   What are the rules for analyzing a hospital's balance sheet?

The guidelines contain eight rules for analyzing a hospital's balance sheet:

1. Review the general ledger control account for receivables from officers, trustees, and members of the medical staff, and analyze for private benefit and additional compensation; review loan or other agreements underlying these transactions.
2. Check notes receivable for interest-free loans to insiders (for example, a mortgage loan to an administrator given as an inducement to accept or continue employment at the hospital); these arrangements are to be scrutinized for inurement, proper reporting, and the like.
3. Review property records to determine whether any assets are being used for personal purposes that should be taxable income to the user (such as vehicles and residential property held for future expansion).
4. Review trust funds to see whether the trusts should be filing separate returns.
5. Review investment portfolios and check for controlled entities.
6. Review the ledger accounts and check for notes and mortgages payable that could lead to unrelated debt-financed income (Q 14:15) issues.
7. Analyze any self-insurance trust or fund set up by the hospital to provide liability insurance.
8. Refer to the appropriate IRS guidelines when there is evidence that the hospital has purchased or sold health care facilities utilizing tax-exempt bonds.

Q 19:18   Are there any special rules for hospitals in connection with package audits?

Yes. In the context of discussing package audit items (Q 19:7), the guidelines also contain rules for determining whether physicians are employees of the hospital (rather than independent contractors). According to these guidelines, if the following factors are present, the physician is "most likely" an employee (even if the contract describes the position as an independent contractor): the physician does not have a private practice, the hospital pays wages to the physician, the hospital provides supplies and professional support staff, the hospital bills for physician services, there is a percentage division of physician fees with the hospital (or vice versa), there is hospital regulation of or a right to control the physician, the physician is on duty at the hospital during specified hours, and/or the physician's uniform bears the hospital name or insignia.

One aspect of the package audit accorded prominence in these audit guidelines is an arrangement where a tax-exempt hospital pays certain personal or business expenses of affiliated physicians and the taxable compensation is not properly reflected as wages or other form of compensation in the annual information returns, employment tax returns, or compensation information returns. The example is provided of college and university medical school faculty physicians who often have employment contracts with medical schools that limit their compensation to low levels compared to compensation obtainable in private practice. These physicians may enter into employment contracts as consultants with several hospitals or clinics unrelated to the medical schools where they teach. The written employment contract with these hospitals or clinics may be supplemented by a verbal agreement that provides for the hospital or a third party to pay associated business or personal expenses (such as lease of luxury automobiles, house improvements, and country club memberships) as part of the total annual employment contract amount. Examining agents are cautioned that the compensation information return may reflect the cash amount paid by the hospital or clinic directly to the physician but exclude amounts paid to other parties on the physician's behalf.

The other package audit issues outlined in these procedures cause the examining agent(s) to undertake the following:

1. Review contracts with hospital-based specialists, such as anesthesiologists, radiologists, and pathologists. These physicians may be employees for federal employment tax purposes, including income tax withholding. The agent is to interview these physicians "when necessary to clarify and verify contract items."

2. Review professional service contracts, which usually specify who will carry the malpractice insurance. If the hospital pays for the insurance, that may be an indication that the physician is an employee (rather than an independent contractor) or may constitute private inurement. The agent is to be alert to efforts on the part of physicians to be treated as employees for some purposes (such as deferred compensation benefits) but as independent contractors for compensation purposes.

3. Review fellowships, stipends, or other payments to interns, residents, medical students, and nursing students, to determine whether these arrangements represent taxable income subject to tax and social security withholding if paid in connection with services rendered.

4. Determine how private duty nurses are compensated if the hospital has a responsibility to file a compensation information return.

5. Determine whether the hospital contracts to purchase services that are outside the ambit of those that may be performed by cooperative hospital service organizations. Are these services purchased from one of these organizations or from unrelated tax-exempt organizations? Determine whether the nature and extent of the services purchased indicate that the exempt organization providing the services should be considered for examination.

6. Review employment contracts of medical personnel who have tax-deferred annuity contracts, to ensure that only common-law employees are receiving the benefits of these annuities. Check to determine whether reduction agreements are on file and whether the exclusion allowances are within the federal tax limits.

7. Determine what types of retirement plans, insurance plans, and nonqualified deferred compensation arrangements are in place. Obtain background information by inspecting the brochures provided to employees, interview hospital officials in regard to transactions between the hospital and the plan,

identify deferred compensation arrangements and determine the correct tax consequences, and, if the hospital has a profit-sharing plan, determine the effect on the tax-exempt status of the institution and whether an examination of the plan is necessary.

8. Prepare an information report on significant amounts of excess indemnification (patient refunds) received under medical insurance policies where the indemnification is attributable to an employer's contribution, inasmuch as these refunds are includable in the gross income of the patient.

9. Determine whether the hospital has filed or is liable for an array of IRS forms.

Q 19:19 What unrelated business income issues involving health care institutions arise on audit?

Concerning the unrelated business aspects of audits of health care institutions, IRS agents are provided a comprehensive listing of issues and authorities and are advised to be particularly inquisitive about these "[s]pecific examples common in [the] health care field": laboratory testing; pharmacy sales; cafeterias, coffee shops, and gift shops; parking facilities; medical research; laundry services; leasing of medical buildings; supply departments; and services to other hospitals (Q 14:23).

Q 19:20 How is the IRS using closing agreements in the health care context?

Increasingly, the IRS is employing the device of the closing agreement to resolve tax disputes in the tax-exempt organizations context. Although use of the closing agreement is not new, the approach is receiving a new emphasis at the IRS and is being used with increasing frequency to resolve a variety of exempt organization matters. With this technique, the organization obtains both certainty that the matter is permanently concluded and guidance as to future conduct, while the IRS resolves a compliance problem that otherwise would consume time and resources (through the revocation or assessment process) and obtains a commitment as to future compliance. By use of a closing agreement, a tax-exempt organization can avoid revocation of its tax exemption.

The closing agreement procedure is authorized by statute. It is a final agreement between the IRS and a taxpayer on a specific issue or liability. The IRS can negotiate a written closing agreement with any taxpayer to make a final resolution of any of the taxpayer's tax liabilities for any period. After the IRS approves an agreement, it is final and conclusive, and—unless there is a showing of fraud, malfeasance, or misrepresentation of one or more material facts—it cannot be reopened on the basis of the matters agreed on or modified by the IRS, nor may it (or any legal action in accordance with it) be annulled, modified, set aside, or disregarded in any lawsuit, other action, or proceeding. Simple unintentional errors are not treated as fraud, malfeasance, or misrepresentation that would allow reopening of a closing agreement.

The existence of any disqualifying elements is subject to review by a court—a review that may entail examination of an organization's books and records. The burden of proof in establishing the disqualifying factor or factors is on the party seeking to set the agreement aside.

The key determinants governing the election of closing agreements are (1) an apparent benefit in having the case permanently and conclusively closed, (2) good and sufficient reasons on the part of the taxpayer for desiring the arrangement, and (3) evidence that the fulfillment of the agreement will not be detrimental to the federal government.

> **NOTE:** There is no requirement of a showing that the resulting closing agreement will confer any advantage to the federal government.

A closing agreement can cover the entire tax liability for one or more years, be limited to a specific tax item, and/or cover future periods. This type of agreement can be made a condition to the issuance of a letter ruling. Agreements for subsequent periods are subject to changes in or modifications of the law enacted subsequent to the date of the agreement.

There is no revenue procedure specifically applicable to closing agreements concerning tax-exempt organizations. However, the general procedures for the execution of closing agreements can be adapted to exempt organization cases. These general procedures discuss formulation and drafting of agreements, format, step-by-step instructions, identification of parties and issues, and special circumstances.

A tax-exempt health care organization may negotiate and execute with the IRS a closing agreement with assurance that it will conclusively determine tax liability, tax-exempt status, and/or public charity/private foundation status.

In general, favorable occasions for the execution of closing agreements between the IRS and tax-exempt organizations would be situations in which revocation of exemption is supported by the facts but is harsh or excessive—for example, where revocation of exemption for narrow technical infractions would jeopardize a charitable organization's ability to continue its programs. From the viewpoint of the IRS, if technical flaws such as these can be eliminated definitively by means of agreed-on changes in an exempt organization's operations or procedures, it will be receptive to a closing agreement. By contrast, the IRS is not likely to be interested in the closing agreement procedure where an organization has engaged in flagrant and continuous acts compelling revocation and has not been operating in good faith.

COLLEGES AND UNIVERSITIES

Q 19:21 What is the focus of the IRS as to the tax-exempt status of colleges and universities?

The IRS has developed examination guidelines for its agents to use during the audits of colleges and universities. These guidelines provide factors to be considered in determining how a college or university is structured. Focus is also placed on its accounting methods, financial information, compensation arrangements, fringe benefit issues, joint ventures, scholarships and fellowships, unrelated business issues (see Chapter 14), and fundraising practices (see Chapter 13). While formally confined to institutions of higher education, the guidelines contain much information of use by nearly all tax-exempt organizations, and their managers and advisers.

Q 19:22 How does the IRS approach an audit of a college or university?

Recognizing that there is no typical structure of a college or university, the guidelines require the auditing agent to engage in a pre-examination analysis of the institution, to ascertain the particular structure. This is to be done by reviewing financial reports filed by the institution with other federal departments and agencies in documenting reimbursable direct costs incurred in the performance of sponsored research. These documents are expected to "provide insight into an institution's accounting system and practices and internal controls." The agent also is to review audit reports relating to private research contracts, derive information from the institution's internal auditors, determine whether the institution has adopted and operates in accordance with a racially nondiscriminatory policy as to students, and see whether there are problems related to withholding for and payments to nonresident aliens.

Only then is the agent ready to make the initial contact with the institution, by acquiring "internal items" that provide an overview of its size, structure, and activities.

Q 19:23 What internal items of a college or university will the auditing agent review?

From a large institution, the agent is to request a contact individual who can provide information about each component of the institution. The agent is to peruse bulletins and course catalogs, telephone directories, minutes of the governing board, minutes of committees (including the faculty senate or assembly), student newspapers (which may provide a "different perspective"), alumni bulletins and magazines, catalogs or lists of institution publications, a description of the institution's accounting system, requisition and purchase order files, reports of coaches disclosing outside income, sponsored-research financial reports, descriptions of computer hardware and software, and formats of files and records maintained on computer.

Q 19:24 What other information is the agent likely to evaluate?

The agent is expected to evaluate "outside documentation," which includes audited financial statements, auditors' letters to management, accreditation and reaccreditation reports, and state and local real property tax exemption documents. Also to be studied is information required by the Office of Management and Budget, including indirect cost proposal data. The instructions guide the agent in making an income analysis, expense analysis, and balance sheet analysis, as well as in examining the institution's statement of cash flows and accountants' statements as to related-party transactions.

Q 19:25   What issues are likely to be reviewed during this type of audit?

The agent is likely to examine employee (rather than independent contractor) status, compliance with the employment tax rules, cafeteria plans, fringe benefits (including tuition remission plans), retirement and pension plans, other deferred compensation arrangements, and the institution's debt structure. In addition, compliance with the bond rules is to be ascertained, where governmental bonds have been issued to state colleges and universities or where "qualified private activity bonds" (or 501(c)(3) bonds) have been issued.

Large charitable contributions are to be reviewed "to identify any conditional contributions that may have questionable terms." In this setting, the agent is to be alert for forms of private inurement or private benefit (Chapter 6). The process by which the institution values gift properties is to be explored. Where the appraisal rules apply (Q 13:14), the agent is to determine whether the institution completed its portion of the appraisal summary and whether the institution filed the information return reporting sales of gift properties within two years of the contribution (Q 18:7). Compliance with the quid pro quo contribution rules is to be looked into (Q 13:10).

If property was accepted by the institution subject to a mortgage, the agent is to consider potential unrelated debt-financed income implications. Contracts with financial institutions for fund-management services are to be looked at for possible private inurement or impermissible private benefit. The special rules pertaining to contributions that give rise to the right to purchase tickets to athletic events are to be applied. The agent is to examine the possibility of gifts that are in actuality contributions to a fraternity or sorority, with the institution as a mere conduit. Contributions of items of inventory (such as books) are to be evaluated to see whether there has been compliance with the special tax rules applicable to them.

The agent is to devote a significant portion of the audit time to the matter of sponsored research funded by industry or government. Attention is drawn to the subject of technology transfer; the guidelines caution that the "relationship between institutions and these [commercial] licensees is growing more complex." Looking for private inurement, private benefit, and/or unrelated business income (see Chapters 6 and 14), the agent is to probe research contracts, joint ventures, venture capital funds, industry liaison programs, spin-off companies, consortia, jointly owned research facilities, material transfers, commercial licenses, and consultations and clinical trial agreements. The examination is to include a determination as to whether true "research" is being undertaken, rather than testing, sampling, or certification.

The agent is to review the institution's safeguards for managing and reporting conflicts of interest (Q 2:8). Also to be scrutinized is the institution's policy regarding ownership of intellectual property, such as inventions or computer software, and the payment of royalties to faculty inventors. Patent licensing arrangements are to be looked at, as are sample closed research projects and payments to individuals as fellowships or stipends for research activities.

All scholarship and fellowship programs are to be examined for the presence of any gross income items (as opposed to excludable ones), proper withholding and reporting, and the applicability of the social security and unemployment taxes. The agent is to be alert to situations where the "grants" are really payments for services rendered. An examination is to be made of scholarship restrictions on the basis of race, from the perspective of potential violation of the public policy doctrine. The qualified tuition reductions are to be reviewed.

Q 19:26 **Do the rules pertaining to lobbying and political campaign activity get reviewed in these audits?**

Yes. The agent is to review the activities of the college or university in relation to the proscriptions on substantial legislative and any political campaign activities (see Chapters 8 and 9). Any written policies in this regard are to be examined, as are student newspapers, minutes of committee meetings, and the activities of the institution's department for "political or legislative relationships." Lobbying offices in Washington DC, and/or state capitals are to be looked into.

Q 19:27 **What unrelated business income issues involving colleges and universities arise on audit?**

The guidelines place considerable emphasis on bookstore operations, including application of the convenience exception (Q 14:23). Note is made of the fact that the convenience exception does not shelter sales to alumni. Sales of computers are discussed. Other topics are public use of facilities, operation of hotels and motels, operation of parking lots, and travel tours (Q 14:29).

Q 19:28 **What other issues can arise in these audits?**

The examining agent is to identify related tax-exempt and taxable entities (Chapter 15). Situations where an individual is being compensated by more than one entity (including the institution) are to be scrutinized in pursuit of unreasonable compensation (Q 6:8, Q 6:12). Arrangements involving shared facilities are to be examined, including the methods of allocating expenses among related entities (Q 14:22). Payments from athletic booster clubs to coaches, other staff, and athletes are to be reviewed for any reporting noncompliance. Separate endowment and similar funds, and joint ventures with charitable remainder unitrusts, research foundations, and fundraising foundations are all subject to examination.

Index

1294

ROWAN UNIVERSITY CAMPBELL LIBRARY

3 3001 00913 057 5

J

KF 1388 .Z9 H667 2005
Hopkins, Bruce R.
650 essential nonprofit law
 questions answered

DATE DUE			
GAYLORD	No. 2333		PRINTED IN U.S.A.